MEN IN
WHITE

MEN IN WHITE

THE GUTSY, AGAINST-ALL-ODDS RETURN OF PENN STATE FOOTBALL

CHRIS RAYMOND

ST. MARTIN'S
PRESS
NEW YORK

First published in the United States by St. Martin's Press,
an imprint of St. Martin's Publishing Group

MEN IN WHITE. Copyright © 2024 by Chris Raymond. All rights reserved.
Printed in the United States of America. For information, address
St. Martin's Publishing Group, 120 Broadway, New York, NY 10271.

www.stmartins.com

Designed by Steven Seighman

The Library of Congress Cataloging-in-Publication Data is available upon request.

ISBN 978-1-250-28048-0 (hardcover)
ISBN 978-1-250-28049-7 (ebook)

Our books may be purchased in bulk for promotional, educational, or business use.
Please contact your local bookseller or the Macmillan Corporate and Premium Sales
Department at 1-800-221-7945, extension 5442, or by email at
MacmillanSpecialMarkets@macmillan.com.

First Edition: 2024

10 9 8 7 6 5 4 3 2 1

For Lynne, Adam, and Will, who teach me daily about life and love and the tried-and-true values championed in this book

CONTENTS

The ultimate measure of a man is not where he stands in moments of comfort and convenience, but where he stands at times of challenge and controversy.

—Martin Luther King Jr.

INTRODUCTION

HE WAS DRIVING back to campus when the phone call arrived.

It was the strength coach, warning him to be prepared for the following morning.

Bad news was on the way.

For Michael Mauti, this was not a surprise, even in the tranquility of summer break. The world he once knew had been crumbling around him for months. It had started with the arrest of Jerry Sandusky, a former Penn State coach charged on November 5, 2011, with forty counts of child molestation, and unfolded in seismic waves that rocked the leafy campus, unseating the university president, the athletic director, and head coach Joe Paterno—devastating the football program he had erected and studiously maintained over half a century.

The horrific details of Sandusky's crime spree had shaken the American public to its core, fueling round-the-clock discussion on cable news programs, talk radio, and social media forums in every corner of the country.

When Bill O'Brien arrived from the National Football League's New England Patriots in January to replace Paterno, it was supposed to signal a fresh start. But here was Mauti, the team's star linebacker, returning to campus from a friend's home in Youngstown, Ohio—days before fall practice was to begin for the 2012 season—and the fault lines were rumbling again.

The National Collegiate Athletic Association, college football's governing body, was preparing to spring into action against the school. The organization could not pin a single infraction from its voluminous rule book on a Penn State player or coach, so it had dipped into its constitution to address the university's lapse in judgment—a failure to alert law enforcement officials—when confronted with an eyewitness account of Sandusky's criminal behavior. Penn State would be penalized for failing to uphold the "fundamental values" of civility, honesty, and responsibility.

What did that mean? No one knew for sure. The NCAA and Penn State's new president had jockeyed for weeks over a suitable explanation and punishment. A state representative would later uncover internal emails suggesting the NCAA's executives were simply hoping to bluff their way to some form of punitive action. And so, when Mauti and his teammates, who were barely in kindergarten when Sandusky had last coached at Penn State, finally gathered in the players' lounge on July 23, 2012, to hear the NCAA's ruling, they were braced for more turmoil, but they had no clue how severe things would get.

The group watched on TV as NCAA president Mark Emmert stepped to a lectern in a black suit coat, white shirt, and oddly muted tie and somberly issued his verdict. He started with a $60 million fine and added a four-year ban from postseason bowl games, a drastic reduction in scholarships, and an edict that instantly erased 111 victories from the team's all-time total (dropping Paterno from first to fifth in the NCAA's record books). And then Emmert did something no one in the program saw coming: He released the players from all obligations to the school.

On the surface, the gesture seemed noble. It allowed the players—every last one—to walk away from the scandal and the sanctions scot-free. Each could select a new team at a new school and start over, no questions asked. But in reality it created a feeding frenzy.

Within minutes, rival coaches were ringing the players' phones, vying to lure them away from the program. "It was open season," said star running back Silas Redd. "Everybody was getting hit up."

Before long, zealous recruiters were walking the streets, camped out in restaurants, knocking on apartment doors to pitch their programs.

They phoned players' parents, high school coaches, roommates, and girlfriends—anyone who might give them an in.

For the players, many less than three years removed from high school, it was a shock. When the day began, they were united as a team; now each was on his own—fighting off advances from grown men with no scruples. Many of the authority figures they had known and trusted were gone, dismissed in the wake of Paterno's departure. And, because it was midsummer, there were few school officials on hand to guide them through the madness.

"What are you guys hearing?" asked strength coach Craig Fitzgerald when Mauti reported to the training facility with his roommate Michael Zordich the following morning. Both had awakened to a flood of voicemails and text messages from recruiters.

The three men started scribbling names on yellow legal pads, working the phones to figure out what remained of the team—who was entertaining thoughts of leaving. They feared they wouldn't have enough bodies to host a practice, much less a Big Ten Conference game.

Mauti and Zordich, both sons of former Penn State players, had decided to stay at the university. Determined to prevent a mass exodus, they took the extraordinary step of issuing a players-only statement on ESPN.

They tried crafting the words on paper but elected to speak off the cuff. The message had to come from the heart. "We weren't speaking for us," said Zordich. "We were speaking for anybody who ever had anything to do with Penn State."

On July 25, 2012, trailed by more than two dozen teammates, the two seniors strode from the weight room to the practice field, inched up to a TV camera, and side by side vowed to hold the team together, calling on fellow students, alumni, lettermen, and fans to rally for the cause. "This program was not built by one man," said Mauti. "And this program sure as hell is not going to be torn down by one man."

The event lasted less than three minutes, but the sentiment behind it rippled across the next five seasons, resulting in one of the most incredible comebacks in sports history. It was a grueling journey, both physically and emotionally. The players would suffer embarrassing setbacks against Ohio and Temple and longtime rivals like Ohio State and Michigan and undergo yet another unexpected coaching change midway through their ascent. But they never lost heart.

They used hidden talents, unconventional strategies, and an abundance of grit to continue on, pressing freshmen, walk-ons, and a host of unexpected heroes into action to field a competitive team. And, late on October 22, 2016, in the waning minutes of a prime-time game televised by ABC, the bonds that held the team together paid off: Penn State defeated bitter rival Ohio State, a national title contender, on what is arguably the most memorable play in school history—a fourth-quarter field goal attempt blocked by safety Marcus Allen, a lucky bounce that gave cornerback Grant Haley the ball, and a mad dash downfield for the go-ahead touchdown.

My eleven-year-old son and I watched the drama unfold from our living room, just north of New York City, jumping for joy while stifling shouts to avoid waking the whole house. We fought to control ourselves even as 108,000 fans dressed in ivory sweatshirts and sweaters—in keeping with Penn State's White Out game tradition—erupted in glee on the TV screen.

As an alum, a Penn State–trained journalist who had covered the team for the student newspaper back in the program's mid-'80s heyday, a reporter who had seen up-close the profound impact of Paterno's Grand Experiment on the football players in my graduating class, I could not have been more pleased. The idea of losing all the coach had built to one man, a creep with no morals, was heartbreaking. I had written about that very thing for *Esquire* days after the scandal had broken and never completely shaken the pain.

In 1987, the glory days of Joe Paterno's program, the NCAA had cracked down hard on another college football powerhouse, issuing what became colloquially known as the "death penalty" to Southern Methodist University. The Mustangs were banned from play for a full season for making under-the-table payments to star recruits to lure them to the school's tiny Texas campus. To this day, the SMU program has not fully recovered.

For Penn State, the rehabilitation would take just five years, culminating weeks after that thrilling Ohio State upset in another momentous come-from-behind win versus Wisconsin for the Big Ten Championship. It's a story for the ages.

This is the tale of the players who made it happen, a band of college kids who paid a steep price for the sins of a man they had never met. Despite the backlash from the Sandusky scandal, the vitriol it invited, they risked everything—reputation, athletic careers, NFL dreams, future earning potential—to uphold the ideals that brought them to Penn State, to demonstrate that principles like those were worthy of such sacrifice. Their odyssey is packed with the real-life drama and emotional appeal found in sports classics such as *Hoosiers* and *Friday Night Lights*.

At the urging of former senator George Mitchell, who agreed to serve as an independent monitor of Penn State's program, NCAA president Mark Emmert eventually retracted nearly every one of the punishments handed down on that July afternoon in 2012. Within three years, he quietly restored scholarships, the team's bowl eligibility, and all of Joe Paterno's victories.

The legendary coach did not quite live up to the ideals he had set for the program. When the time for decisive action arrived, he had failed to follow through. In the last interview before he passed away, a victim of lung cancer at age eighty-five, Paterno acknowledged that he didn't know how to handle the situation. He handed things off to people in the administration and "backed away," relying on others to take the appropriate steps. "It didn't work out that way," he said.

But the players held fast to Paterno's exacting standards, even after he was gone and they were unfairly swept up in a scandal created by a cunning criminal who had retired from coaching football more than a decade before they set foot on campus. They quietly accepted their fate and worked to restore the program's good name—with excellence on the field and off.

This is how they pulled it off.

ONE

ALL IN

COLLEGE FOOTBALL PLAYERS *are used to change. It's part of the game. From one season to the next, you lose a dozen teammates to graduation, bid farewell to position coaches snatched up by rival schools, and make way for talented freshmen hell-bent on taking your job. But, even by those standards, the shifts that greeted Penn State's team in January of 2012 were exceptional.*

Just two months earlier, fresh off Joe Paterno's record-setting 409th career win, the Nittany Lions—named for the majestic predators that once roamed the peaks of nearby Mount Nittany—were sitting on an 8–1 record, their only misstep an early-season loss to would-be national champion Alabama. And then, out of the blue, the Jerry Sandusky scandal had erupted, stripping them of nearly every point of pride: a legendary coach, a distinguished history, and a hard-earned reputation for winning with honor.

The man chosen to replace Paterno had no ties to the school, had never worked as a head coach, and had yet to sever ties with the National Football League's New England Patriots. In fact, he would not be available to the players full-time until after Super Bowl XLVI.

In his stead, he sent an envoy plucked from the staff of Steve Spurrier at the University of South Carolina, a fiery strength and conditioning coach named Craig Fitzgerald.

BILL O'BRIEN: Fitz was the first guy I hired. I was still in New England, going to the playoffs, and he came in and started the winter workouts, laid the foundation for working out fast, being in good condition, being tough—mentally tough.

ERIC SHRIVE, OFFENSIVE LINEMAN, 2009–13: That was a huge hire. The strength coach spends more time with the players than any other person in the program. The players are with him five, six, seven days a week through the winter, spring, and summer. I mean, you probably spend triple the time with the strength staff than you do with your position coach.

Fitz came in and from day one it was a completely different way of lifting and running.

STEPHON MORRIS, DEFENSIVE BACK, 2009–12: I remember Fitz tearing up the weight room, updating things. Seeing that new weight room put fresh air in our lungs.

MICHAEL YANCICH, LINEBACKER AND SPECIAL TEAMS ACE, 2008–12: He took it from being a place of doom and gloom to a place you wanted to be. If you were having a bad day, you looked forward to working out, because he made it fun, made you want to be a better version of yourself.

MATT STANKIEWITCH, OFFENSIVE LINEMAN, 2008–12: The weight room was revamped with free weights and more of a functional-movement-type of program. That's not to say the old weightlifting program wasn't functional. It was just totally different. In the new one, one fourth of the team could work out at a time.

MICHAEL YANCICH: Everybody was there, cheering you on, throwing water on your face, and acting goofy if it got you ready for a five-hundred-pound squat.

When John Thomas was our strength coach, we wouldn't run on the day we worked out. When Craig Fitzgerald came to town, he told us you're going to run and you're going to work out and we all looked at each other like he had worms crawling out of his ears. But it's crazy how quickly he conditioned us, outside in the bitter cold at 5 a.m., running hills.

CRAIG FITZGERALD: Bill was still in Boston, prepping for the Super Bowl. You'd talk to him by phone and hear him hammering out notes for the Patriots offense. He was banging on his keyboard and getting updates from me on how the guys were doing. We'd go in my office or the athletic trainer's office on the speakerphone and hear Bill talking, dictating, typing.

BRAD "SPIDER" CALDWELL, EQUIPMENT AND FACILITIES COORDINATOR: In the spring semester, they'd let guys take later classes on Tuesdays and Thursdays to make room for labs and stuff they didn't have time to schedule in the fall. We always worked out in the morning, so they'd have time for those classes. So Coach O'Brien would fly in from Boston, because Tuesday was the Patriots' day off. He'd watch winter workouts at five in the morning, talk to the team, then fly out. Back to New England. That's how he put the whole team together.

His assistant coaches weren't allowed to use the football office right away. They were off-campus—I think at the Penn Stater Hotel and Conference Center—because they had to go through all these clearances prompted by the Sandusky investigation. The university was being super careful, doing background checks. So even the assistant coaches were working from afar.

CRAIG FITZGERALD: Tim Bream, the athletic trainer, and I were together early and just got started with the guys. You could tell they were excited. They'd been through a heck of a fall, so they were eager to get going.

Getting to know them was important, because Bill hadn't really had a chance to do that yet. He'd met with the team and some of the leaders, talked to them about their concerns, but other than that, he hadn't been there. So Tim and I tried to get a read on the vibe.

"Here are some of the things the players are doing well, some of the things they're looking for this year. The leaders came up to us and said they want to see more of this or that."

The NCAA—and I still think it's this way—had set it up where you get eight hours a week with the players, two for football-specific activities and the other six hours for general strength and conditioning. So Tim and I had seventy-five percent of the time with the guys.

And Bill, one of his great decisions was to say, "Let's take our time developing these guys. Let's not rush into spring ball." He wanted to observe the workouts, get to know the guys, before he started blowing the whistle and putting them in pads.

MATT STANKIEWITCH: The first time he came to talk to us, he wore this winter peacoat. It stretched down past his shins, almost to his feet. In Boston, they need coats like that, because it's so cold up there. He looked so professional. Of course, this was like a week or two after he'd made news by telling Tom Brady off on the sideline. We're like, wow, this guy's . . . we'd heard his nickname was Teapot, because he's ready to blow.

MICHAEL MAUTI: He walks in with this full-length peacoat. From Boston, the New England Patriots, and the room—you could hear a pin drop. Everybody was sitting up. Full attention. He looks like a freakin' rock star. And he addressed the group.

"I'm your new coach. This is the way it's going to be . . ."

MATT STANKIEWITCH: He said, "Listen, guys, I don't know what your offense was doing for the last five, ten years, but I'm used to scoring 35, 45 points a game. So, if you want to score points, be on national television, I don't know why you'd want to leave."

And we're like, "Hell yeah, we're all in."

He had a very commanding presence. A lot of guys bought in right away.

JORDAN HILL, DEFENSIVE TACKLE, 2009–12: When he opened it up for questions, guys were asking him football stuff, general stuff. I asked the first strange question. He's trying to wrap it up and I'm like, "Hey, coach, before we roll, I got a question for you. Are we allowed to have facial hair? 'Cause with Joe, we weren't."

He's like, "What the hell are you guys talking about?"

MICHAEL MAUTI: Under Coach Paterno, you couldn't have anything more than a three-day beard. It's funny to hear that now. But that's where our world was. We were in this little bubble. "Just tell us what to do, where to be, man, and we'll follow you."

JORDAN HILL: O'Brien just started laughing. He's like, "Absolutely!"

MICHAEL MAUTI: We needed a leader to come take the reins, because it was total chaos at the time, and that's the guy who did it. From day one, we had buy-in. How rare it is for any program to have that kind of transition.

MATT STANKIEWITCH: So then we go into winter workouts.

CRAIG FITZGERALD: The winter workouts were big. The first few were outside. What better way to wake you up than cold air on your face? It kind of set the tone. And, I'll never forget, Bill said, "Hey, 5:30 is when we're going to start."

At 5 a.m., the players were all out there on the field. We were setting up at about 4:30 and the players start coming out of the locker room. At 4:55, it looks pretty full. At 5 o'clock, Mike Mauti comes up to say, "We're all here." I was like, "Bill, unless you want everybody to freeze their asses off for thirty minutes, we might as well get started." He said, "Yeah, let's go." That stuck out to me. I thought *These guys are special.*

PAT ZERBE, FULLBACK, 2009–13: Classic Fitz! Winter workouts, outside, twenty-degree weather, shorts and a T-shirt. Nothing's gonna faze us.

They started using the phrase Iron Lions. That's basically what our team was in 2012 and 2013: Iron Lions. That's how we lived and worked.

JOHN URSCHEL, OFFENSIVE LINEMAN, 2009–13: Fitz and O'Brien, they were really pushing us, trying to see who could play and who could not. It was interesting. By the time we got to the summer, we were jelling as a team, really getting a sense of what these new coaches were like.

JORDAN HILL: It was the first winter workout with Fitz, early in the morning. We're in Holuba Hall. I want to say we're damn near forty-five minutes into it and you just hear O'Brien screaming. We're like, yep, he's doing what we seen on ESPN. He's screaming. *Screaming.* And he's going after the older guys.

Long story short, I was one of the older guys.

So workout's over, I shower up, and I'm walking through All-American Hall. It's only me. He's like . . . He must have been waiting. He's standing at the end of the hall.

I'm like, "Damn it, man." Walking with my head down, trying to avoid him.

He's like, "Pick your head up." Looks at me and gives me a story about Vince Wilfork, who played nose tackle for the Patriots.

I'm like, "I thought I was doing good."

He's like, "Yeah, you were doing really good. You're one of the quiet leaders, you lead by example. I had to go at you so I got respect from all the younger guys."

Right there, I understood what he was trying to do. My respect level went through the roof.

BILL O'BRIEN: We didn't recruit those guys. But they bought into what we were doing and how we wanted to do things. They led it from the meeting room to the locker room, the practice field to the game field.

MICHAEL MAUTI: Looking back, I'm sure we were an easy group to coach, because we worked our asses off. We were just fired up to not be dealing with any more garbage.

JORDAN HILL: The things we hated most about football—the morning workouts—became the things we loved. When we were there, nothing else mattered. It was getting this dominator done, this last sprint done, this last rep in the weight room done. That's all. The other stuff wasn't on our mind. The sanctions weren't on our mind.

MATT MCGLOIN, QUARTERBACK, 2008–12: Practice was fun, lifting was fun, watching film was fun. The most fun I've had playing football in my entire career. It didn't get any better than that.

You had a collection of seniors who were wise beyond their years.

Knew what they were playing for week-in and week-out. It was more than football and we accepted that.

JORDAN HILL: What was going to happen to us, we couldn't control. What we could do was wake up, make sure we were on time, make sure we were busting our asses, doing the things we had to do. Because if we did play football, we didn't want to be like, ah, man, we underprepared. We're out of shape, because of all that had happened.

Let's not let that get in our way. Let's control the controllable and go from there.

TWO

OB

FOR PEOPLE OUTSIDE *the program, it took a while longer to warm to Bill O'Brien.*

He was not Paterno—or even a Paterno guy. In fact, he had no real ties to Penn State. Born and raised in Dorchester, Massachusetts, he had graduated from Brown University—which, by chance, was Paterno's alma mater—then moved to Georgia Tech to coach under George O'Leary and later Maryland, where he worked under Ralph Friedgen, before ending up at Bill Belichick's side in New England.

"I don't envy him at all," said ex–Penn State linebacker Brandon Short. "He doesn't have the support of the vast majority of former Penn State players. And the vast majority of the student body and the faculty won't support him."

That was not true, not even remotely true, but onetime stars like LaVar Arrington and D.J. Dozier had also voiced their disappointment, mainly because the new head coach had been hired by interim athletic director Dave Joyner, who had not bothered to consult with program alums during the eight-week search for Paterno's replacement.

In short order, though, Penn State's lettermen would be rallying around Bill O'Brien, too.

CRAIG FITZGERALD: If you look at the Miracle on Ice, Herb Brooks was the perfect coach for that team. There were other good hockey coaches in that era, right? But he might be the only one who could get the players to believe they could beat the Russians.

I'm not saying this just because Bill's a friend. Bill was the perfect coach for that time at Penn State. I don't care who else you could have gotten. In those two years, Bill made the right decision every time for those players. There wasn't one bad decision.

I would sit back in the team room and watch him say, "Hey, here's what we're going to do . . ."

Now remember, he's in his first year as a head coach. Forty-two years old. How about that?

KEITH CONLIN, OFFENSIVE LINEMAN, 1991–95: Bill O'Brien was the *perfect* man to keep the ship afloat, the perfect guy to follow Joe.

ERIC SHRIVE: A lot of people would have come in and tried to do everything Joe did and I don't know if you could have handled it that way. I think Bill was the perfect hire. He had a demeanor that really pushed us in the right direction.

AUDREY SNYDER, PENN STATE BEAT WRITER, *THE ATHLETIC*: His temperament was so perfect for that team. The way those players bought into him and everything he did—I just don't see how you duplicate that. It was this perfect storm of personalities, players who were pissed off at how they'd been treated and a coach they could rally around.

JOHN URSCHEL: When Paterno coached, there were a lot of long-standing rules, a lot of tradition, a certain way things were done. When O'Brien got there, things got very different very quickly.

KYLE CARTER, TIGHT END, 2011–15: He let us be men, trusted us to handle our business on and off the field. He treated us like we were in the NFL, and we all appreciated that.

MICHAEL YANCICH: He had the same ideals as Joe. If you didn't go to class, you weren't going to play. If you weren't performing on the practice field, you weren't going to play. It didn't matter if your dad had played there, the best person for the job was going to step in and lead.

JOHN URSCHEL: He only cared about rules to the extent that they helped make us the best football team we could be.

He was very firm about going to class, but from a pure football perspective, he was much more flexible, whereas Paterno had been doing this for a long time, doing it well, and knew how he wanted things done—and that's how things were done.

When we played for Paterno, we were not allowed to have facial hair, for example, unless it was a mustache. Paterno thought it was important that we look a certain way. If you asked O'Brien about something like that, he could care less.

PAT ZERBE: We found out O'Brien had been hired, I think, through the mainstream media, ESPN or something.

ERIC SHRIVE: Nobody knew who the hell he was. The thing going around the locker room was the video of him and Tom Brady almost fist-fighting on the sidelines. It was like, *Man, this guy is our new head coach?*

PAT ZERBE: *Holy crap, this guy's cursing out one of the greatest players ever.*

MICHAEL MAUTI: We're like, *Oh, man, this dude's a maniac. Like, he could take it to* that *level.*

ERIC SHRIVE: There was a lot of excitement. I remember sitting in the team meeting room and hearing his message, his excitement to be our head coach. And then watching him try to win a Super Bowl, knowing that right after the Super Bowl, he was going to be our head coach.

I remember lineman Miles Dieffenbach busting his balls in the team meeting room after he lost the Super Bowl, telling him the Steelers were the only team with six rings. That lightened the mood.

GENO LEWIS, WIDE RECEIVER, 2012–15: He was one of Tom Brady's coaches. He was coming from the Patriots and, you know, the standard of the Patriots organization at that time was crazy. So everybody was like, *We're okay. This is all right.*

KYLE CARTER: At the time, Patriot tight ends Rob Gronkowski and Aaron Hernandez were crushing it in the league. I was excited to try filling that Aaron Hernandez role.

STEPHON MORRIS: Joe was a great football coach, but he was very outdated, too. Our defense, our offense, everything was very vanilla. Very 1980. Once O'Brien came in, our schemes, the systems we had in place, finally matched the levels of the Ohio States and the Alabamas. We were getting challenged, brought up to speed, on not just things at the collegiate level, but what Bill O'Brien had learned in New England, as well.

ERIC SHRIVE: You see a fiery guy on the field. But, deep down, he's a players coach. I mean, we had more fun with Coach O'Brien. He always had some kind of joke. We'd bust him about wearing those damn long sleeves and sweatpants to practice in the middle of August.

He was a players coach, but, when it came right down to it, he wanted to get the best out of you and we all respected him for that.

VENITA PARKER, MOTHER OF JOHN URSCHEL: He treated them as men. He didn't sugarcoat anything. And he showed them how much he loved them. John said to me, "I would walk through fire for that man."

MICHAEL YANCICH: He was tenacious with us.

MATT STANKIEWITCH: It was nothing personal. He's one hundred percent about winning football games, the right way, but he's going to tell you the way it is. If you suck on tape, I mean . . . we once had a squad meeting. We were all in the room together. He pulls up a video of practice. And we're like, Oh, wow, Joe never did this. I mean, Joe didn't even know how to work a video. So Bill brings up a practice video, a one-on-one drill. One running back versus one linebacker.

On the video, the back was falling down before he got hit. Coach was just *reaming* him, asking, "Are you afraid to run the ball?" and adding, "If you're afraid to run the ball, you're not going to run for me."

This was a guy who thought he was hot shit, and O'Brien just called him out, right on film. "You're falling down before you got hit. That means you're afraid to get hit."

In one of the first games, a player on the kickoff return team didn't hit anyone. O'Brien kept rewinding the video and saying, "What are you doing? You didn't hit anybody. You're just standing around. I'm standing on the sideline and I'm doing as much as you."

He kept rewinding it.

He would just call people out. He hated mediocre, bad-effort plays.

If you give full effort, but someone else makes a play on you, that's okay. If you're in the right spot, doing what you're supposed to do, it comes down to ability. But if you are a coward or you're not doing your homework, he doesn't have patience for it.

JESSE DELLA VALLE, SAFETY AND PUNT RETURNER, 2010–14: He didn't care how many stars you had next to your name. Didn't care if you were a preferred walk-on coming out of high school. Didn't care if you were All Big Ten last year. He wanted to know who was there to play, who was there for Penn State.

MATT STANKIEWITCH: It was a big deal to be sitting in the squad room and have the whole team watching you on film. To be exposed like that. Allen Robinson is sitting over there and he's watching *me* trying to block Gerald Hodges and Hodges and I get into a fight. It was like, *Oh, shit, we're all watching this right now.* I was pretty taken back.

O'Brien wasn't picking on people. He was just making it clear that everyone's job was open. Don't be walking around, thinking you have things locked up. I'm one hundred percent about performance. I don't care if you're black, white, blue, red. I'm one hundred percent about performance.

MATT MCGLOIN: I've always respected that. That's all I ever asked for: Tell me where I stand, because I may not like it, but how do I get to the next step?

PAT ZERBE: I want a coach that's in my face, that expects greatness from me. Effort—every play, every down, every second you're on the field. As long as he's fair.

If you go up to O'Brien and ask, "Hey, coach, how do I get more playing time?," he will tell you straight up. "You're good at this, you need to work on this." You can't ask for anything more than that.

VENITA PARKER: He's probably the only person who could have done what he did with that team.

STEPHON MORRIS: Everything O'Brien did in the off-season was vital—to the point where, when the sanctions came out, it was an easy decision for me. If someone else was in that position, the program may have dissolved. He brought new life, a fresh breath of air. He cared, you know. Took time to meet with each individual. Not about football, just to learn about us in general.

BILL O'BRIEN: I made it a priority to have a relationship with every guy on the team. The first few months on the job was a whirlwind, trying to get everything organized and get us going in the right direction. But after spring practice, I met with every guy.

I also made sure the seniors were put into leadership roles, whether it was naming each guy a captain for a game or having each lead the stretch lines at the end of practice. I tried to make that a priority throughout the year.

Little by little, the players and others inside the program began to see the wisdom in those decisions, the emotional intelligence in the man who had stepped forward to replace the icon named Paterno. Before long, they felt transformed by him, both physically and emotionally.

STEPHON MORRIS: Our bodies were starting to change from the weight program. If you look at Penn State in the past, body-wise, we didn't look the part, to be honest. But when OB came, we started doing squats, benching, things our bodies needed to do to compete. We felt like it was a real program.

Kudos to Joe's strengths as a coach, because we didn't have any of that modern stuff under him, but we were still squeezing out nine wins a year.

SPIDER CALDWELL: When it was announced that Coach O'Brien was coming to head up the program, one of the first things I did was call the New England Patriots equipment managers to get feedback on what Bill was going to need. Now remember, he's still in the playoffs, getting ready for the Super Bowl. He's trying to get his staff in place and organize his team from afar. So he'd call the equipment room a fair amount, wanting this and that. I was calling New England to say, "Hey, Coach O'Brien said you had this timing clock . . . What do I got to expect?"

It was a whole new world for me. I mean, I'd been with Joe Paterno for twenty-eight years, so I'd never had to make a staff change. Under Joe, we literally changed one position coach about every six years.

Think about that. To have the whole staff change in a flash? It was tough. I even called Michigan and other schools to say, "Hey, give me help on transitioning a coach. I don't know how to do it."

They said, "Don't tell him what you used to do. Ask him how he wants it done." That was the big advice.

It was a difficult time. We were still in the midst of the Freeh Group's investigation of the Sandusky scandal, addressing the university's questions, and people were obviously being let go to make way for Coach O'Brien's staff, so you know, you're emotional. A lot of the people I had worked with for over twenty years are coming in needing boxes to pack up their things.

We're being investigated, interviewed by different groups—the attorney general's office and whatnot. Then Coach Paterno dies. Coach O'Brien's still in the playoffs. He's coming and going. And we're trying to do winter workouts. So, the morning of Joe's viewing, we come in at 5 a.m. to do this workout. The whole team gets showered, dressed, puts on coats and ties and goes to the viewing. That was brutal. I was an emotional wreck.

KAREN CALDWELL, WIFE OF SPIDER CALDWELL: We all were going through grief and shock. I mean, I saw grown men crying. Coach O'Brien was trying to hold everybody together. It was a horrible time.

SPIDER CALDWELL: We're starting to get a more consistent workout routine, but I'm still finding out what he wants, what he needs. We're getting yelled at because the buzzers aren't loud enough and the clock isn't working right and again this is all new to us. Because, you know, Joe was always the timekeeper on the practice field. He had his schedule, a real simple schedule. He blew the whistle when it was time to start or stop. If he needed to go longer, he'd let things go on. You just went on JoePa time. Now it was all segmented, everything's segmented, and all these clocks and horns had to be ready to go. It was very, very structured.

Before everything happened, there were twenty-nine people, including the coaches, in the Lasch Building. There were seven of us left when the smoke cleared. Two left on their own. So that left five of us. And we were told, you know, you're still in a probationary period. If something comes up in the investigation or Coach O'Brien wants to go in a different direction, you might be let go. So they were only guaranteeing us employment till June 30th, the end of the fiscal year. I'm going through spring practice not even knowing if I have a job.

But here's where I really appreciate Coach O'Brien. About three quarters of the way through spring practice, he came up to the equipment room. It was just me and my assistant Kirk Diehl at the window. And he said, "Hey, listen, I love you guys. I love the student managers. They're outstanding, hustlers. Don't change a thing. You're my guys. I want you to relax."

He knew we were uptight. He said, "You've done enough. Got to get ready for the season. So just hang with me."

Burden lifted. We were all in at that point.

THREE

BLINDSIDED

Summer days on the Penn State campus are tranquil. Without the frenzy of 46,000 students hustling to class, huddling on the lawns, and descending in waves on the pubs and dining spots along College Avenue, the place has a sleepy vibe. You can order a Long Island iced tea at Cafe 210 West and sit back in the sunshine, literally drinking in the peace.

For the players who had weathered the turmoil of the Sandusky scandal, the withering heat of tabloid media scrutiny, the death of their exalted head coach, and the first major shift in personnel and philosophy in close to fifty years, this dip in intensity was a welcome relief.

It gave them the space to focus on classwork and conditioning and little else.

That is, until NCAA president Mark Emmert stepped to the lectern at 9 a.m. on Monday, July 23, and issued his verdict on the Sandusky affair. Within moments, the precious stillness was shattered, replaced by the din of ruthless recruiters phoning, texting, and knocking on doors, looking to tear the team apart.

MICHAEL MAUTI: Coming out of spring practice in 2012, I don't think anybody on our team had any clue as to what was about to happen.

MICHAEL ZORDICH: We were completely blindsided by the sanctions. I mean, we thought we were going to play a regular football season.

CRAIG FITZGERALD: We knew the day before the announcement that something was coming. Not any of the details.

I got a call from our defensive backs coach, John Butler, who said, "Hey, this is going to be bad."

I'm like, "What does that mean?"

He goes, "I'm not sure. I'm just saying we've got to call some of the team leaders."

So I called Mauti and said, "Look, man, tomorrow's going to be bad. I don't know exactly what's going to happen, but, like, do you want us to change things up? Maybe do something on the lighter end for the morning workout? Because our heads may not be in it."

Max Day, the most important weight room workout of the year, was just hours away.

CRAIG FITZGERALD: Mauti's quote was, "Fuck no, we're going to blow the roof off that place."

So I said, "Okay, let's just do it at, like, 7 a.m. Then we'll have breakfast, go into the team meeting room, and watch the thing together."

And that's how it went. The guys did a tremendous job in the weight room and then we went in there and heard the announcement.

ERIC SHRIVE: We watched it on TV in the player's lounge. Mark Emmert, president of the NCAA, came out and placed the sanctions on us. We figured something was going to happen but didn't know the severity of it.

MATT STANKIEWITCH: Everyone was talking about the sanctions. "What were they going to be?" I was like, "What do you mean?" We, as players, had nothing to do with what had happened. It's not like we were cheating on tests or half the team got into a DUI accident. We didn't do anything. So I didn't think it was going to be as severe as it was.

STEPHON MORRIS: Mark Emmert dropped the news and the room went quiet for about three seconds. You could hear crickets. After that, it was like an explosion. So many emotions.

CRAIG FITZGERALD: Disappointment, anger, sadness, all the things you'd imagine.

SAM FICKEN, KICKER, 2012–15: No player did anything wrong. What are they going to hit us with? That was my mindset. When they announced the sanctions, my jaw hit the floor.

People immediately started walking out of the building, throwing water bottles in anger.

GENO LEWIS: I remember seeing dudes break down and cry. I remember seeing dudes looking flustered, not sure what to do.

STEPHON MORRIS: As a senior, I couldn't react the way I wanted to, because we had a very young secondary and I knew those guys were looking at me. I ended up getting them into the meeting room. The DB room. And me, Malcolm Willis, maybe Jake Fagnano, ended up telling the guys, "Hey, I get it: You've got the opportunity to go elsewhere. I totally get it. I'm not going nowhere. I would love to have all you guys commit to stay."

I'm not sure what went on in the other meeting rooms, but, like I was just saying, there were mixed emotions. We ended up going back to the locker room, and the whole team was in there. You could see guys with their heads down, guys kind of walking around lost, as if they didn't know what was gonna happen.

People don't realize. We were still young men. That was the first time we had to handle anything like this.

BILL O'BRIEN: We'd had a really strong spring practice, a really good summer training program, and all of a sudden here come these sanctions and these kids are like, "Wait a second, we can't go to a bowl, we can't play for a Big Ten Championship, and now they're saying we can transfer?" That's something people forget. Every kid on that team had a choice to make. Every single scholarship kid and walk-on had a choice to make. Not one of them had to stay at Penn State. They could have all left, gone and played somewhere else.

It wasn't the scholarship reductions, which were, you know, going to be tough, that really endangered us. It was the fact that we had to recruit our own team back.

MATT MCGLOIN: The NCAA tried to give the university a death penalty without calling it a death penalty. That's what it was. Let's be honest.

MATT STANKIEWITCH: It was like they wanted to see the program crumble. I don't know why.

ADAM BRENEMAN, TIGHT END, 2013–15: I don't think any school in America could have withstood what Penn State did and come out the other side of it.

JOHN URSCHEL: O'Brien had called a team meeting prior to the announcement to give us a heads-up—not to tell us what the NCAA was going to say, but to prepare us. We had another team meeting afterwards and O'Brien stressed that not playing for a national championship isn't a huge deal, because we were not a national championship team.

That shows you the honesty he had. He also said, every Saturday at Penn State, you play in front of 110,000 people. That's better than any bowl game.

He stressed that those are the things that are important, then he released us.

ERIC SHRIVE: We were in summer school, preparing for camp to get started, and you had players leaving and players announcing that they were leaving. It was just a crazy time.

At that point in the year, Penn State coaches—outside of the strength and conditioning staff—were not permitted to interact much with the players, according to NCAA rules. But coaches from opposing teams now had sweeping access to those athletes to entice them into abandoning O'Brien's program. In fact, rival coaches had even been granted the liberty to surpass the NCAA's cap on scholarships to make room on their rosters for Penn State transfers.

SILAS REDD, RUNNING BACK, 2010–11: It was open season. Everybody was getting hit up.

BILL O'BRIEN: We could have lost the whole team.

MICHAEL MAUTI: For the NCAA to say it was doing us a service by allowing us to transfer with no holds barred, no rules, is—I'm going to choose my words carefully—a joke. An absolute joke.

ERIC SHRIVE: Instantly, the phones were ringing. All of our phones were ringing.

It was a tough time. You didn't know what to do.

JOHN URSCHEL: We were all nervous, because if we each were getting that level of interest, everyone else was, too. There was this concern like, what if I stay and everyone else leaves?

STEVE JONES, PLAY-BY-PLAY ANNOUNCER, PENN STATE FOOTBALL: It became a recruiting meat market. Other schools were recruiting, following Penn State players to class, following them to their apartments, getting ahold of them on their phones.

MICHAEL MAUTI: Coaches hounding our players. Like, ten, twelve calls a day. On our campus, outside of our apartments, outside our classrooms. To me, it just didn't seem right.

MALIK GOLDEN, WIDE RECEIVER AND DEFENSIVE BACK, 2012–16: They were ruthless.

BILL O'BRIEN: It was like NFL free agency without the rules. They could do what they wanted, as long as they told our compliance office that they were contacting kids.

GENO LEWIS: They had coaches at the Lasch Football Building, sitting outside the doors. People from all different schools. It was like a grocery store. They were trying to get everybody out of there.

KAREN CALDWELL: Spider would come out of the locker room and there were people from other teams literally standing there, trying to catch our young men, recruit them for teams across the country.

STEPHON MORRIS: We were *all* fair game. We had college football experience and we had played in one of the game's top conferences.

ADRIAN AMOS, DEFENSIVE BACK, 2011–14: It became a little overwhelming. All the coaches and people selling the dream, saying you can play for a national championship now, come in and start for three years.

KEITH CONLIN: I don't blame the schools. I blame the NCAA for making such a *stupid* rule. You know, people say Tim Beckman of Illinois deserves a lot of crap for what he did. Yeah, he probably does. I mean, he brought ten Illinois coaches to State College. But that's a guy fighting for his job, so he thought, okay, I may be able to pluck one or two guys and maybe save my job.

MATT STANKIEWITCH: Alabama, Georgia, and Nebraska were after me. There were a bunch of others, but those were the top three. Alabama's offensive line coach called my high school. My brother works at the school and told him I had made a commitment to Penn State and I was going to stay. But Alabama's idea was to bring me down and move center Barrett Jones to tackle, because he didn't want to play center. He thought he was a better draft prospect at tackle.

That was a big moment in my life. Alabama thought I was good enough to be the starting center on a national-championship-caliber team.

STEPHON MORRIS: My dad was getting contacted by schools—not top SEC schools, but Missouri had just got to the conference, Ole Miss, some mid-level SEC schools. Michigan reached out to me personally. And then, me and Amos, we had some Illinois coach knock on our apartment doors. We lived in Nittany Apartments. It happened to Amos first. He ended up coming to my place, saying, "Some coach knocked on my door." Ten minutes later, he's knocking on my door.

We ended up going to the football offices, me and Amos together, to tell Coach Butler. I wasn't a big Twitter person then. I'm still not. But John was like, "This is what you're gonna do."

That tweet wasn't from me, it was from John Butler, but it was on my account. It got a lot of reaction.

The tweet read: We have chosen to stay at PSU & other opposing coaches are outside our apartment. Was that the intentions of the NCAA. #Leave-UsAlone #WeAre

CRAIG FITZGERALD: The amazing thing isn't that some people left. It's that the core of the guys stayed. Because the things they had to look forward to had now been stripped away.

After a few guys left, I thought, Man, it's going to be tough to keep the team. Because if so-and-so leaves and I play such-and-such position, that's going to affect my position. If this receiver leaves, that's going to affect me as the other receiver. Now I'm getting double-teamed. If this running back leaves and I'm an offensive lineman, I'm not looking as good to the pro scouts. So, you know, I was like this may be a trickle-down-to-nothing scenario.

MICHAEL MAUTI: That's when this thing really affected us personally. Like, our careers, the course of our careers. Some really big decisions had to be made. We turned that resentment into let's take the bull by the horns. This is our show. If we don't do it, who is going to do it?

FOUR

THE ONES WHO STAYED

IN THE END, *it would not be Bill O'Brien, the athletic director, or even the university's president who decided the fate of the program. That all-important call would fall to the players themselves, the young men who had opted to play for Joe Paterno in the team's better days.*

Amid all the madness, it was those college "kids" who saw most clearly what Penn State had to offer—and committed themselves to preserving Paterno's Grand Experiment. It was by no means a simple decision. In fact, for many, it required serious soul-searching.

BILL O'BRIEN: When the sanctions came out, people had this program left for dead. The so-called experts said this program would never survive. We all looked at each other and said, that's not the case. We might not be able to win a national championship or go to a bowl game, but we had a lot of good players—pro-caliber players. So we thought we could win. And that's what I'm most proud of: In some ways, we went out and proved people wrong.

BOB MORGAN, PRODUCER, *SAVING THE ROAR* DOCUMENTARY: Everybody tags millennials as not really caring about anything, but those players gave up dreams, potential pro careers, to fight for one another. That really strikes a chord with people, particularly in today's age of the transfer portal.

BILL O'BRIEN: The people involved at that time, such a critical time for that university, were unbelievable. The coaching staff, the administrative staff, the athletic department staff, but most importantly the players. They were just driven to overcome the odds.

JOHN URSCHEL: We had a player meeting and a few guys started saying, "I'm staying."

Mauti was sort of the main person.

At the time, I was kind of certain I was going to stay, so I was saying, "Let's stay. We're a team, we're going to work this out."

MALIK GOLDEN: It was a tug-of-war, people whispering in my ear, you got five years and the bowl ban is for four. You're not going to play in a post-season game until your redshirt senior year.

People were just telling me to leave.

MICHAEL YANCICH: Schools asked me to visit and friends from my home-town were saying, "Why don't you entertain this?" I said, "What kind of man would I be if I walked out on these guys? On the promise I made four years ago? How am I supposed to teach my children about integrity?"

GENO LEWIS: The older guys, man, they did a hell of a job, just trying to keep everybody together, keep everything above water.

CRAIG FITZGERALD: Those guys basically said the shit stops here.

Mauti put his foot down. He was getting recruited by everybody, be-cause he's an All-American player. If he left, game over. Game over. Game over. Not only because he was a great leader, but because he was a great player, too. If other players saw him leave, they'd be like, "Well, I'm out of here, because now I've got to look out for me."

KEITH CONLIN: Fitz, Mauti, Michael Zordich, Gerald Hodges, and Jordan Hill, they all sat down and said, "Okay, I'll take care of these guys, you take care of those guys. Get a feel for who's going, who's staying."

MALIK GOLDEN: Those dudes held it together. They were some badasses.

MICHAEL MAUTI: We were fortunate in that we had a senior leader in each position group that kind of took charge of their flocks. Those first couple days, everybody was making house calls. I was calling parents. We were calling everybody.

STEPHON MORRIS: I said, "I'm not leaving." But, of course, I got to make that decision based on everyone else, because I want to continue to play college football.

People think most of the guys weren't entertaining calls. That's BS. We didn't know if we were going to have a team. People were leaving. Jumping ship. So it was crazy for us NOT to entertain. I was entertaining Michigan, because of the way they were making it seem. [laughter] They were saying, "Well, you sure? Because you're not going to have a team this year."

I was like, "No, guys are staying."

But Silas Redd ended up leaving. I said, "All right, boys, if a big-time player like Silas leaves, there's going to be a few more."

I didn't expect wide receiver Justin Brown to leave. Now, I'm like, okay, well, this thing is getting shady. We really may not have a team.

GENO LEWIS: My roommate, Akeel Lynch, was set to go to Iowa. I said, "Listen, man, like, let's just thug this out. Let's rock this out for one year. See how it goes. They might need us now, because guys are leaving."

We said, "All right, we going to do it." That's how I ended up staying.

MATT STANKIEWITCH: It was pretty big macho-wise in the locker room to say, "Oh, who got the biggest offer? Who rejected the biggest offer?"

Not that I was trying to be pompous. I was kind of using it to make a point to the younger guys.

"You're thinking about going to Maryland? Oh, I got an offer from Alabama and I didn't go."

"So, where are you going to go? Illinois? Good luck. Have fun. You're a loser."

I'd make it seem like your offers were insignificant.

STEPHON MORRIS: There were some guys, big-time names, that I talked to personally when the sanctions dropped and they were like, "Man, I'm thinking about leaving."

So, I was not necessarily going to Michigan, but they wanted me to do an official visit. And I said, "Well, if I come on campus, can you keep it out of the media?"

But I think Mark Emmert required any team that hosted a player to put the word out. So I got a little frightened. Never went.

I ended up meeting with Maryland head coach Randy Edsall and offensive coordinator Mike Locksley, because I wanted to make sure I had a backup plan. But that was it.

KYLE CARTER: Are you familiar with the Super 6? It was a group of recruits that included myself, Bill Belton, Adrian Amos, Deion Barnes, Allen Robinson, and Donovan Smith. We were all tight. Always hanging out, training together, eating together. After the sanctions dropped, we went back to our apartment, sat in the living room, and had a roundtable discussion.

Adrian was already playing as a freshman. Bill and A-Rob, too. Donovan wasn't playing yet, but he had a lot of interest from other schools. I had committed to Penn State kind of early, so there weren't a bunch of schools that knew me and tried to poach me.

But coaches were hitting the other guys up—calling, texting. Some had places like Alabama reaching out. There was even an opportunity for all of us, including tight end Jesse James, to visit Arizona State. At the time, that sounded amazing. Nice and warm. A chance to get out of the cold.

We all were sitting there, literally thinking about taking that visit. Like, it wouldn't hurt, right? But after talking it through, we decided, hey, you know, we can be legends at Penn State, if we stay here and turn this thing around.

We made that decision and stood tall on it.

SAM FICKEN: I called my high school coach and was like, "Based on what I'm seeing, I don't know if we're going to have a football team next year. Can you make a couple phone calls?"

At that point, a lot of the guys in my recruiting class had the same mindset. Hey, we love it here, but if we don't have a team, we have to figure something out.

It was kind of a mad scramble for that first forty-eight hours.

We fully expected the seniors to leave, because they had offers to play at almost any school they wanted. And then, they called us all together—it was like a senior-led meeting. Sat everyone down and said, "We've got a group of eighteen seniors. We're not leaving."

That was the turning point. The seniors all stood up and said, "We ain't leaving."

They put everyone's mind at ease. Like, hey, we're going to have a team.

SPIDER CALDWELL: Mauti and Zordich were extremely key in this. I know they've been praised for it, but it's so true. Tight end Jesse James was literally on Interstate 80 heading to Pittsburgh. And they were like, "Get your ass back here."

They were actually yelling at guys. Telling them to stay, stick with us. Junior linebacker Mike Hull was transferring to Pitt. They talked him out of it. That's how key those guys were.

MIKE HULL: When Mauti found out I was thinking about leaving, he said it would mean the world to the program if I stayed. I loved Penn State. That's why I decided to stay.

PETE MASSARO, DEFENSIVE END, 2008–12: In the situation we faced, the most important thing was not bowl games, not reduced scholarships, it was, is the guy next to me going to stick around? Once we conquered that issue, all the pieces fell into place.

KYLE CARTER: Bill O'Brien wanted to know who was fully committed to the team, and I'd say the vast majority of the players were, but some seniors wanted to go somewhere secure, a place where they could get the numbers they needed to go to the next level.

Guys like Justin Brown and Silas Redd made decisions that were best for their careers. Those of us in the Super 6 didn't look at those players any differently. Those were business decisions.

ERIC SHRIVE: Everybody's situation was a little different. Some of us had fully committed our lives to the Penn State way. We had friendships and credits toward a degree. Some of the younger kids had never played in a bowl game, never had the experiences we had, and they stayed committed to the program, knowing they were never going to play for a championship.

Guys like Christian Hackenberg and Adam Breneman, big-time prospects still in high school, stayed committed to the program, knowing that they were not going to have a chance to play for a championship, not going to go to a bowl game. Man, that shows what Penn State's about.

MICHAEL MAUTI: I remember sitting in front of our squad room, talking to the underclassmen. It was like, "Look, we've got the easy decision. We're staying, but we've only got like six more months. You guys have got two, three, four more years. This thing is going to get harder, not easier."

BILL O'BRIEN: It's not like me to tell people what I speak about in team meetings, but I will tell you that, number one, I talked to the players about the education they were receiving at Penn State, a world-renowned institution. Six hundred thousand alumni will tell you about that.

I talked to them about their commitments to each other.

I talked to them about the bond they had formed with a fantastic football staff.

I talked to them about adversity. Gave them my own story, the story of my wife and I and our son Jack, who suffers from a rare genetic disorder called lissencephaly.

I talked to them about how each one of them had adversity in their lives, how our coaches had adversity in their lives. The measure of a man is how you overcome adversity, I said.

CRAIG FITZGERALD: In the first year in a new job, everybody's busy, all the coaches, setting up databases, running workouts, putting the offense in. That's why people often say, I just want to stay in this job, I don't want to start over.

So we were there late, every night, that summer.

You know who was there with us? Mauti.

Coming back and forth with his yellow legal pad, logging the scenarios.

Who's going to stay? Who's on the cusp of leaving? What do we need to do to get that guy to stick around?

He was like a recruiting coordinator.

Mauti and Zordich came into my office one night. It was like 10 p.m. They've got a pad full of names. Not like, "Hey, what do we do?" More like, "Hey, here's what we got."

And I'm like, "Well, let's talk." After about ten minutes, I said, "We need to call Bill."

So, I called his office and Bill came right down. He said, "Okay, let me see the list." And then, "Okay, okay, if we lose this guy, we'll lose this guy. I think this guy is going to stay. We have to get on him. We've still got a shot."

Bill had to make decisions on where to focus our energy. But Mike and Mike already had that lined up. It was amazing. You're talking about guys who are twenty-two years old. What they should be thinking about is where are we getting our burger tonight? Who's got a case of beer?

They were thinking about things far beyond that. They were doing coaches' jobs.

MICHAEL ZORDICH: It was really the four of us—OB, Fitz, Mauts, and me. You know, OB had this way of being brutally honest. It was like a whole new world to me, talking with him about stuff like that. There's no sugar-coating anything—it's, this is what it is.

We got into the whole social dynamics of the team.

"This guy is friends with these four. If he leaves, they're going to go."

We were breaking the team into cliques. There's 120 of us—you hang out in groups of friends. And we were like, "If this guy goes, this one's going to go, so we've got to make sure he stays."

It was really cool. Talking with your head coach, figuring out the dynamics of your team, how to keep things together. Not that we were making the decisions, but OB was listening to us.

It's so easy for a head coach to be like, this is my decision, but for the situation to be so insane and him to be . . . not vulnerable, but open about how to handle this thing.

That was the thing: We had the benefit of knowing the locker room and OB knew that, so he would come to us and ask, How are guys feeling? What's going on?

What a wild time.

BILL O'BRIEN: Thank god we had developed strong relationships with those kids from February through July. There was trust that we were gonna do right by them.

MICHAEL MAUTI: The sanctions were announced on Monday. On Tuesday or Wednesday, Zordich, Fitz, OB, and I were up in OB's office, watching the ticker on ESPN. They're listing like the twenty guys that are leaving. It's like 10:30 at night and we're sitting there gassed, after a full day of texting and calling people, trying to re-recruit our team, and after like ten minutes of silence, OB says, "Mauts, you ever play offense?"

That's when it registered.

Like, *what?* We might have twenty-two guys—literally.

That was the moment for me. Okay, this is getting real.

CRAIG FITZGERALD: We needed a lot of help, a lot of hands on deck, and the whole place came together.

KEITH CONLIN: Mauti, Zordich, McGloin, Jordan Hill, Hodges. I believe I'm missing one. Maybe Stankiewitch. He was a fifth-year senior. Those guys deserve a *lot* of credit. They worked their asses off to keep their friends here.

JOHN BACON, AUTHOR, *FOURTH AND LONG: THE FIGHT FOR THE SOUL OF COLLEGE FOOTBALL*: They go to their apartments, their dorm rooms, they knock on doors, they talk to girlfriends, they call parents at home, making their pitch for these guys to stay.

It is an all-points bulletin, trying to stop them at the county line.

STEPHON MORRIS: The guys that stayed—we have a brotherhood stronger than any other in the history of college football. We went to war together, we cried together, we were vulnerable together. And, you know, most young men don't know how to be vulnerable, don't know how to show it. But we got through it all together.

JOHN URSCHEL: To our credit, almost everyone who mattered stayed—with the exception of Silas and kicker Anthony Fera. Maybe a freshman or sophomore left, but no one that mattered.

When you look at the core group—the fifty or so key players—we only lost two people.

Anthony got a chance to play for Texas in his hometown, to be closer to his mother, who was going through some health issues.

And, Silas, I mean, USC rolled out the red carpet for him. I don't know if this is true, but I heard they flew him out there. I heard Snoop Dogg picked him up at the airport or something like that. I don't know, that's what I heard. Obviously, he was really looking at his pro football potential at the time and he thought USC would give him the best chance to get there. I mean, I personally can't fault him for that decision.

It definitely hurt, though. I loved blocking for that guy.

FIVE

RALLY TIME

As THE HOURS passed, Bill O'Brien and his staff members found themselves in the absurd position of having to re-recruit their own players. Coaches from the country's top programs were pushing Penn State kids to jump ship, serenading them with a pageant of promises: more playing time, starting roles, beach weather, playoff glory, a bigger showcase for their talents, better odds of making the NFL.

Tim Beckman, the first-year head coach at Illinois, sent not one, not two, but eight members of his staff to State College to lure players from O'Brien's program. According to reports circulating among Penn State's players—and later denied by USC and Silas Redd—the Nittany Lions star running back had been shuttled from the airport in Los Angeles to USC's palm-tree-lined campus in a limo owned by rapper Snoop Dogg.

"It's like NFL free agency without the rules," said O'Brien. "They can do what they want as long as they tell our compliance office they're contacting these kids."

To demonstrate what Penn State had to offer, beyond a rich football and academic tradition, O'Brien and his associates sent out a distress call, requesting help from the program's former players and longtime fans. In a public show of support, roughly three thousand Nittany Lion faithful flocked to campus at 6 a.m. on a midsummer Tuesday to essentially watch the players work out. Dubbed the Rise and Rally, the event was coordinated with the *help of lettermen Keith Conlin and Tim Sweeney, hosts of the internet radio program* The Goon Show.

The pep talks concluded later that afternoon with a private sit-down, featuring many of the biggest names in Penn State's 125-year football history.

KEITH CONLIN: Craig Fitzgerald and John Butler, the defensive backs coach, are lifelong friends. I've known John since I was in kindergarten. And, Fitz, we've been best friends since early in high school.

We did a radio show that week, downstairs at Damon's. My cohost Tim Sweeney was president of the Letterman's Club. And Fitz and Butler came on the show and said, "Listen, guys, you don't understand: The water's coming aboard, the boat is sinking. It's gonna go down if we don't do something."

John Butler's on the radio, saying there are Big Ten coaches—coaches from every school in this country—in State College right now, actively recruiting these kids on our campus.

That hit me hard. It pissed me off that the NCAA would allow that.

The Rise and Rally was six days later. It was literally launched that night on the show.

CRAIG FITZGERALD: It was a last-minute thing. Hey, we're going to have an event. Come on out!

KEITH CONLIN: I never got involved in the politics of who did what, why the university accepted what it accepted. I mean, there's no way to even comprehend what was going on there.

Our thing was, what's going to happen to these kids?

CRAIG FITZGERALD: We drew up a little workout for the guys at the practice fields and Keith and Tim Sweeney emceed it. They did the radio show from there.

TIM SWEENEY: The rally was mostly about the players in that locker room, showing them we're here to support you. But there's a bit of me, a bit of Goon, I think, and a bit of every Penn Stater that wanted to give the NCAA the single finger salute. Say, you know what? You're trying to destroy this program, and it's a hell of a lot stronger than you think.

And so, the call went out, businesses in State College donated coffee and donuts, and a throng of fans showed up on a weekday in July, lining the walkways to the practice field.

JESSE DELLA VALLE: I lived in Nittany Apartments, which neighbors Holuba Hall, where we worked out and, man, there were thousands of people lining the street at six in the morning. That speaks volumes on the support we had.

It wasn't like we're going to be playing in an empty stadium, playing for nothing. It was like, this is Penn State football. We are what we are.

CRAIG FITZGERALD: It was like, hey, look at all these fans. I mean, the guys couldn't even walk to the field. The fans were side by side as the players walked through the tunnel, handing out high fives, slaps on the back.

KEITH CONLIN: The players needed that. If you ask them, to a man, it was the most exhilarating two hundred yards of their life, walking up to the practice field with all those people cheering.

ALLEN ROBINSON: It gave me the chills. It was almost like a game day, coming through the tunnel, seeing all the fans.

MICHAEL ZORDICH: The freshmen players had just joined the program two weeks before the sanctions announcement. So they hadn't experienced the real Penn State yet. For them to see all that support for a forty-five-minute workout was kind of mind-blowing. It gave them a taste of what Penn State fans are like.

KEITH CONLIN: We had some guy on the air. He'd driven to campus from Lake Michigan or somewhere out in the Midwest. He goes, "I just felt like I needed to be here for this."

People needed it. The players needed it.

Bill O'Brien had an even greater show of support in store for the players that afternoon. With the help of Sweeney and Fran Ganter, the longtime director of the Letterman's Club, he reached out to every program alum and urged them to return to campus for a team meeting.

KEITH CONLIN: Tim wrote a letter to the football lettermen—pretty much an SOS—saying Coach O'Brien was calling on all the guys to come back.

TIM SWEENEY: At that time, we had over a thousand dues-paying members. I sent the email out Friday morning, inviting everybody back on Tuesday, and I think close to three hundred guys showed up, some getting private jets to fly in for the event. The response was overwhelming.

MICHAEL NASH, DIRECTOR OF THE *SAVING THE ROAR* DOCUMENTARY: After the sanctions came out, there were discussions of thirty to forty players leaving. Many people within the university thought Penn State football was over with, at least from a competitive level.

That's why so many of the lettermen flew in to talk to the kids.

SPIDER CALDWELL: O'Brien put out an all-points bulletin to the lettermen. Said, listen, I need your help. We need to keep these guys here. I need you to talk to them. We had over three hundred lettermen drop everything—vacations, business trips—to get here.

TOM PANCOAST, TIGHT END, 2013-17: I wasn't there at the time, but I've heard the stories. They had guys who went on to win Super Bowls and guys who ended up crushing it on Wall Street. They all flew in on a few days' notice and there was a big meeting in Holuba Hall, where all these lettermen stood up and talked to the players, told them what it meant to be a Penn State football player.

LANCE LONERGAN, QUARTERBACK, 1986-88: They reached out to the lettermen on a Friday and asked us to join a team meeting the following Tuesday, so it was short notice.

A day or two after that outreach, I got a call from Franny Ganter about speaking to the team about my experience as a player and, more importantly, my experience afterwards—the impact of being part of the program, being a letterman. Obviously, I was flattered.

I asked who else was going to speak. He said Todd Blackledge, Matt Millen, Adam Taliaferro, and Franco Harris.

CRAIG FITZGERALD: You don't get that at other schools. You know, those guys showed up. I'm putting myself in their shoes. It's July, you're on vacation, and now you're going to State College. Drop everything. It's not an easy place to get to if you don't live around there, right?

That said a lot to our players.

What do they say about a loyal friend? He just shows up, man.

KEITH CONLIN: Guys on vacation broke away from their families. Flew up, drove up, got there any way possible. And again, they had, like, a four-day window to get this done. So there were a lot of people in important positions in this world who dropped what they had to do right then and there and got it done.

LANCE LONERGAN: Left their families and their jobs in the middle of the week and somehow got to Pennsylvania.

LYDELL SARGEANT, DEFENSIVE BACK, 2005–08: They canceled stuff and said, "Hey, I gotta go to State College on Tuesday."

It was a scramble for everybody. But it was a no-brainer, too.

MICHAEL NASH: They showed up on their own dime. It wasn't like the athletic department was paying for this. The airport was filled with private jets.

CRAIG FITZGERALD: They weren't going to a game. Going to a game's kind of easy. A good time, right? This is summertime in State College and there's not much going on other than a heart attack from working out. So it says a *lot* about those guys. And the players, because they're smart kids, that was not lost on them.

MICHAEL YANCICH: Like Michael Mauti said after the sanctions broke, one man didn't build Penn State and one man is not going to tear Penn State down. In that moment, that was so true.

When you looked around, there wasn't just one man standing there. There were three hundred men standing there, looking at you, saying, "Hey, we got you, we're right here with you, you're not going through this alone."

LYDELL SARGEANT: The Letterman's Club is the largest dues-paying football alumni association in the country. One of the things that makes it special is that you've got fifty years' worth of guys who played under the same coach—Coach Paterno. So guys like myself from the early 2000s had the very same experience as guys who had graduated in the '60s and '70s. It's very unique.

MICHAEL MAUTI: That's why I went to Penn State. To be one of those guys. Every day you walk through that hallway in the Lasch Building and see all those pictures of the All-Americans. That's all I thought about for five years. I wanted to be one of those guys. Be remembered for how I played the game. It just became so much more than that.

The buy-in factor was so high that season from walk-on to starter to coach. And it just meant so much to so many people. I think we realized that that summer, when we had three thousand people show up for a morning practice, lettermen coming back on a couple days' notice. That's when it became clear this is bigger than us. To be remembered for how we acted in the public eye, not just saying it, but doing it, and playing at a high level. That's really special.

MATT STANKIEWITCH: I don't want to throw anyone at the university under the bus, but the only people that really supported us were the lettermen. They had our backs from day one. The nation, the university, even the university president were all kind of watching to see what we were going to do. Everyone was tiptoeing around, because no one wanted to be the face of the scandal. They wanted to keep the spotlight on Sandusky and Joe Paterno. So no one really had our backs.

MICHAEL NASH: The administration had kind of caved on them, so it was up to the warriors who had spilled blood on those fields in years past to tell the players that this may not make a lot of sense to you right now, but in time you will realize the value of sticking with this program.

TIM SWEENEY: We've never had three hundred lettermen on the sidelines for a game. That's never happened. The max you're going to get is one hundred and maybe seventy sprinkled throughout the stands.

KEITH CONLIN: I think that's when Coach O'Brien really realized, wow, this is pretty important to people.

Me and Tim, our houses were full. I had fifteen to twenty former players here in my home that night. It was very similar to when JoePa died. Like, hey, we got to get there. And it was only lettermen. It wasn't bring your father, your cousin, your eight kids. Just lettermen. They really, really stressed that. It was strictly for ex–football players and the current team.

CHARLIE FISHER, QUARTERBACKS COACH: I've been a head coach at a couple of places, been in some great programs, and I've never seen a program that embraced its guys, former players, the way Penn State does. And those people were so supportive in that situation. There was no finger-pointing. It was okay, we're all in this together. Let's find a way to get it done.

SPIDER CALDWELL: We had the event in Holuba Hall, closed the doors, no media.

CRAIG FITZGERALD: We had a team meeting and I think Bill surprised everybody. He said, "Look, guys, we're having dinner tonight with some alumni and it's going to be in Holuba Hall. I want you here."

SPIDER CALDWELL: We set up a small set of bleachers for the team.

LYDELL SARGEANT: Literally just your everyday, junior-high, aluminum bleachers.

SPIDER CALDWELL: And we had all these chairs, rows of chairs, like a theater, for the lettermen.

Bill had the lettermen come in and sit down.

KEITH CONLIN: O'Brien talked for about fifteen, twenty minutes, just to the lettermen, then he brought the team in.

LYDELL SARGEANT: It was a bittersweet moment. You're all there together, but not for the reason you want to be together. That's when Bill O'Brien became Coach O'Brien. At the time, we needed somebody who was very direct, knew how to control the room, how to get the attention of men.

LANCE LONERGAN: Coach O'Brien said, "Hey, guys, I really, really, really appreciate you being here. It's important for these young guys to hear stories about the impact this program has had on your lives, how important it will be to them in their lives, if they can find a way to hang in there, protect each other, stay on the team.

"The players' heads are spinning from the sanctions. They don't know what to make of it.

"We have college coaches running around the parking lots, looking to talk to them, trying to recruit them as they walk between classes, between our football complex and our workout facility. I just walked out of a meeting with our best player and his parents and he's transferring to USC. The players don't know that yet. But that's what's happening.

"We got to keep the team together."

LYDELL SARGEANT: That's as evident as it gets that the threat is real. Not only are guys on the bottom of the deck targets, but some of your best players, too, and they're being enticed in ways you can't counter.

LANCE LONERGAN: And then the young guys came marching in and sat directly across from us, grown men with baby faces, staring at us, like, we can't believe how many guys are here.

CRAIG FITZGERALD: We walked into Holuba Hall and all those veterans, all the alumni, gave the guys a standing ovation. They were already standing up. Unbelievable, right?

SPIDER CALDWELL: O'Brien had a guy from every era speak—the '50s, '60s, '70s, '80s, '90s, 2000s. I'm trying to think who all spoke. I can't remember half of them. Lydell Sargeant spoke for the 2000 era. Lance Lonergan, who was a backup quarterback for us in the mid-'80s, spoke.

CRAIG FITZGERALD: It's amazing the people that talked. Amazing the people that *didn't* talk. Like, there wasn't time for them to talk. You're like, wow, there's some really good players standing right there. They're just here. Very humble.

TIM SWEENEY: The message the lettermen delivered was about Penn State being a family, a brotherhood, more than just a place to win football games and get an education. The network that's there after you graduate is unrivaled.

The only university with something similar would be Duke, where Coach K had success for so many years. That's the only example I can think of right now, at least on the male side of sports. I mean, you've got Geno Auriemma up in Connecticut, too.

But, you know, when you have a football program with twenty to twenty-five new kids per class, decade after decade, you end up with a large organization. That's what we wanted to impress upon the players in that room—and that was done in no uncertain terms that evening.

ERIC SHRIVE: That's one thing about Penn State—the lettermen are tight-knit. I remember them talking about their life experiences: why you should stay, what Penn State means to each of them. As a young player, even a twenty-two-year-old, you get caught up in the moment sometimes and all that stuff goes out the window.

CRAIG FITZGERALD: I think, if I remember right, there was a mic.

LYDELL SARGEANT: I'm not sure if we had a mic, but we stood in front of the guys and told our stories.

LANCE LONERGAN: I forget who led it off. Everybody had a different spin. Franco focused on a year the Steelers started really slow. I think they were oh-and-three or something. They got together in the locker room and said, "This is over, we're not losing again, we're going to get this done as a team." And they went on a run. I think they ended up winning a Super Bowl.

Todd Blackledge got up and said, "You guys can't go to a bowl game, but you have an opportunity to play your bowl game every Saturday in the greatest stadium in the country." He said, "I've played in or broadcast from every venue in the nation and that place across the street is hands-down the best place to play a football game."

Matt Millen spoke about young guys in the military. He told one specific story about a young guy who protected a few of his teammates on the battlefield. That kid was his son.

Adam Taliaferro said Penn State's football program, the people in the Penn State community, saved his life after a spinal cord injury nearly left him paralyzed for life. That's how strongly he feels about the program and the people associated with Penn State.

My spin on things was, "Hey, guys, all of us come to Penn State with some expectation of playing in the NFL and at the end of the day most of us don't get that chance. But we do have an opportunity to take what we learned here, the relationships and the bonds, and use that to leverage a positive experience for the rest of our lives.

"Every time I've had a big celebration in my life, I've shared it with my Penn State brothers, and every time I faced a difficult challenge, they were the first ones I went to for help.

"What you can prove here to everybody is our program at its essence. It's about protecting each other, trusting each other, staying together as a team. And if you do that, you can send the strongest message ever to the world about what this program is about. It's a decision that will have a lifetime impact. If you stick together, we've got your backs on everything."

SPIDER CALDWELL: Basically, what the guys were saying is Penn State is so much more than Xs and Os. We take care of each other.

LYDELL SARGEANT: There were some very personal stories shared that day and we were able to explain what makes Penn State special, what makes the brotherhood of the lettermen special.

Coach Paterno always said, whether or not you play in the NFL, at some point you're going to stop playing football. And what you do after that is very, very important. Even if you play fifteen years in the NFL, you're gonna have, God willing, another forty, fifty years of life. And so, life after football is just as important as life in football.

That afternoon, we had the opportunity to tell those guys, hey, this is what's going to be meaningful once you leave this institution, to pinpoint for them what exactly this brotherhood meant to us in the times when we needed it.

STEPHON MORRIS: Most of the lettermen brought up points we already knew. The reasons we had committed to Penn State: Success with honor, getting a Penn State degree, the alumni network, the Nittany Lion brotherhood—we knew all of those things. But it did help some of the younger guys to see how much the lettermen cared about the program.

CRAIG FITZGERALD: They had some food afterwards. There was a nice buffet spread and everyone got their plates, steaks, burgers, whatever you wanted. Hung out, talked, and had some laughs. Alumni matched up with players, just talked to them as a friend, not a coach. A coach is different. It really doesn't matter to a letterman's livelihood if this guy stays or not.

KEITH CONLIN: It was just a way for the older guys to talk to the younger guys. You know, you always look up the guys who once played at your position, the ones from your hometown. So you had a lot of that going on. The defensive backs gravitating towards the defensive backs, receivers to receivers, quarterbacks to quarterbacks. All the fat guys looked up the fat guys. We all took care of each other.

LANCE LONERGAN: And after that, everybody spread out, went downtown for dinner and down to the G-Man. A couple of guys came down. Mauti, Zordich, and a few of the captains. We just sat around, had a couple beers, and said, "Hey, guys, this is your time to prove something."

And they turned around and did it.

SPIDER CALDWELL: That night, Coach O'Brien had a conference call with the parents. He said, "Listen, what can I do to keep your son here? I promise you, I'm gonna make it a fun year. But, please, I need your help. Just hang in there. We'll get through this."

One of the parents said, "Well, can we do something special for the team? The guys that stay, something that's really recognizable?" And one of the other parents said, "What about putting names on the jerseys? That's never been done in Penn State history."

O'Brien said, "Boy, that's not a bad idea. I'll check on that. See if we can get that done."

———

SIX

GOING PUBLIC

Two days after Mark Emmert's sanctions announcement, Penn State's *players, led by Michael Mauti and Michael Zordich, stepped from the relatively safe confines of the team's training complex to address the nation. Given the rampant speculation about the likelihood of the program collapsing, they wanted to share what the core of the team was thinking.*

With Bill O'Brien's blessing, they reached out to ESPN and arranged to deliver a public statement on camera. For a media-averse institution like Penn State, it was a striking shift in reasoning. In fact, O'Brien had originally instructed the players not to speak to the media at all, but after talking things over with Mauti and Zordich, he gave them the go-ahead.

The two leaders tried to compose their remarks in advance, even reportedly running a draft by the athletic department. When it came time to speak, though, they tore up the script and spoke straight from the heart. It was risky, but precisely what the moment called for: two young men, sons of former players, standing before their teammates and the world and pledging to rescue the program, preserving what those before them had built.

"We're going to fight for Penn State, fight for each other," said Mauti.

MICHAEL ZORDICH: We had such a tight-knit group and there was so much chaos around us that we instinctively built a bubble. As everything was going on around us, we were so calm. Not calm. I guess, collected. We knew who we were and what we needed to do.

MATT MCGLOIN: That's what I always go back to—the friendships we had, the trust we had in one another, the way we held each other accountable.

If you haven't seen the *Saving the Roar* documentary, it's about the 2012 team, the ins and outs of that season. When I watch it today, it's like, *Wow, I can't believe what we had to deal with. How did we get through it?*

For me, it's because of the people—that senior class, O'Brien, Fitz, the coaching staff.

MICHAEL MAUTI: We had thirty-plus seniors on that team, a bunch of guys who stuck together.

BILL O'BRIEN: It was a very special group. Our assistants will tell you the same thing. They loved to practice, loved to lift weights, loved to condition.

STEVE JONES: When you have a crisis, you're always looking for individuals with guts. This university could not have asked for better ambassadors than that senior class.

BOB MORGAN: As Franco Harris said, it's like they had the legacy of the program on their shoulders.

MICHAEL NASH: Not only the history and the tradition—all the lettermen who had taken the field before them—on their shoulders, but also the history that had not yet been written.

SAM FICKEN: A lot of the guys had parents that had played. They knew what that tradition meant.

MICHAEL ZORDICH: We didn't know the impact we were having. It took seeing the film to fully realize what was going on. It shows what can happen when you believe in something bigger than yourself. Because all we wanted to do was play football together. We did everything we could to make that happen.

The whole university ended up jumping onto those shoulders and then you saw this cascade effect.

On July 25, 2012, flanked by roughly two dozen players, Mauti and Zordich exited the Lasch Building, walked up to an ESPN camera, and boldly defended the school and its football program.

"We have an obligation to Penn State and we have the ability to fight— for not just a team, not just a program, but an entire university and every man that wore the blue and white on that gridiron before us," said Zordich. "We're going to embrace this opportunity and make something very special happen in 2012."

"This program was not built by one man," added Mauti. "And this program sure as hell is not going to be torn down by one man."

It was a pronounced show of force, considering the silence that had preceded it. In the eight months since Joe Paterno's undoing, no one else had dared to defend the school with such conviction. Not the athletic director, the university president, or a single member of the board of trustees. That left it to the media to tell the story. And the tale the media told was universally damning. If you supported Penn State, you were evil. End of story. That left the players, the whole student body, in a precarious position, vulnerable to all manner of slings.

AUDREY SNYDER: The university is so protective of who talks to the media, but at that point it was like anything goes. If the players want to talk, they can talk. I mean, hell, you've got coaches camped out at the back of the Lasch Building trying to get them to leave.

BOB MORGAN: If you're a Penn State fan, you know that everything about the football program had been tightly controlled for years, so to see those guys walk out there and take charge like that was a significant shift.

When you talk to the players, though, they tell you they had no choice, because nobody else was saying anything. The university didn't want to communicate.

MICHAEL NASH: The grown-ups in Penn State's administration were making bad decision after bad decision, and these kids came together and did things society has deemed millennials incapable of doing. The fact that all the grown-ups were running around making bad decisions and the kids were doing the right thing is a story that needed to be told.

LANCE LONERGAN: It was so impressive the way they stepped up, took control when the university had essentially gone silent. The only strong positive communication to come out of the school was from those players. It was incredibly mature, given that most of the guys were nineteen or twenty years old.

MATT MCGLOIN: I was a guy who had split time at quarterback, so I couldn't be this vocal leader. I had to lead by example. Thank god we had Mauti, who had played a ton of football. Everybody looked up to him. It was like, we support what this guy says. We have his back.

JOHN URSCHEL: I cannot stress enough how important Mauti was to that football team. He was more or less the driving force behind us saying, no, we're not leaving.

MICHAEL MAUTI: Penn State was part of my family, the way I was raised. I'm a second-generation Penn State kid, so all those things that made Penn State great—the people, success with honor, living the right way on and off the field—those are things I live by. As a player, I just wanted to be remembered for doing things the right way.

MATT MCGLOIN: Mauti was my roommate during my first training camp and I'll never forget this. I walk in, Mauti's already in the room, he's standing there, and he's got a sleeveless shirt on. I'm probably like 180 pounds at the time. I'll bet you Mauti's 235 or 240—as a freshman. He's absolutely massive. And I remember thinking, *Look at the size of this guy.*

Mauti's probably thinking, *Hey, bro, are you lost or something?*

But, when I walked into that room, I thought to myself, *All right, that's a Penn State football player. This is what Penn State football is all about. I have to do everything I can to match this guy. That is the standard.*

BILL O'BRIEN: The first time I met Mauti—the day of the press conference introducing me as Penn State's new coach—he came right up to me and had a lot of questions about our strength and conditioning program. I knew right away that he was a passionate football player.

MICHAEL NASH: Mauti's a warrior. You can see it in his eyes, see it in his reaction times. That's what makes middle linebackers great—they make smart split-second decisions.

What's interesting, though, if you talk to people, is that Mauti could never have done what he did without Zordich.

Zordich was Mauti's balance. Mauti would probably have handled things differently if Zordich wasn't there to work out the details with him. In fact, Zordich was the first to say, "I'm not going anywhere." And Mauti was like, *Yeah, what am I thinking?*

Many schools wanted Michael Mauti. He was a star, so he was getting a lot more attention. But Zordich said to him, back in their apartment, "I'm not going anywhere, bro."

ERIC SHRIVE: Mauti and Zordich led the charge. What they had to say at the press conference represented everybody.

MICHAEL ZORDICH: At first, it was supposed to be just the two of us. But the whole team was there in the locker room that day. It was like, "What the hell are we doing? Get behind us. Let's go!"

I just remember opening those doors and getting the biggest surge in strength.

Because, at the time, it truly was us against the world.

ERIC SHRIVE: We were fortunate to have leaders like Mauti, Z, and Jordan Hill. They had what was best for Penn State in mind. They had their teammates' best interests in mind, too.

PAT ZERBE: Mauti, Zordich, Hill, Mike Farrell, McGloin, Mike Yancich— they were just a bunch of hardworking, blue-collar guys who said, "Hey, we're gonna dig our feet in. We're not gonna let anything get in the way."

MATT STANKIEWITCH: It was a short and sweet speech, only about five minutes long, but it got the point across, the fact that we were going to remain together as a team.

BOB MORGAN: That speaks to the relationship they had with Coach O'Brien. They had such admiration and respect for Joe Paterno, but they quickly fell in love with Bill O'Brien, and he had the wherewithal to trust them. He let those players take a leadership role. In most programs, you would never have that. It wouldn't be allowed.

MICHAEL NASH: Several times in that summer of chaos, Bill O'Brien allowed his captains to make key decisions, and I don't know if many coaches would have listened to their players in that way.

In that instance, Mauti and Zordich went up to him and said, "Look, Coach, you told us to stay away from the media and we have, but now the press is defining who we are and they don't know anything about us. We need to get out in front of this."

They actually wrote a speech. It was all kind of impromptu. They went into the weight room, collected some players, and said, "Hey, we've got this news conference." And when they got to the door, Zordich and Mauti looked at each other like, "No, man, this isn't us." Whatever was on that piece of paper wasn't what was at the depths of their hearts. So they ripped the paper up, threw it in the trash, then walked out the door and spoke from their hearts.

CHARLIE FISHER: I'm a Pennsylvania kid. Grew up fifty miles from State College. Sat in the wooden bleachers in the old Beaver Stadium in the late '60s. So, for me, to coach at Penn State was a dream come true. I remember having tears in my eyes the first day I walked into the building. What a blessing it was to be around those kids—a group of young men that galvanized people, brought them together, saying no matter what you throw in front of us, we're going to find a way to overcome this adversity.

It really speaks to life, what you've got to do in life, and for that experience, I'll always be grateful. I mean, I loved those kids. I don't know how to explain it.

I get emotional just thinking about what an inspiration they were, how they said, "No one man built this program and no one man is going to tear it down."

Those words, I hear them to this day.

SEVEN

LOST BOYS

WHILE MANY PLAYERS *were vocal about their plans to stay, others quietly wrestled with the decision. Foremost among them was the team's star running back Silas Redd, who was coming off a sophomore season that placed him among the sport's elite. Instead of celebrating his good fortune, Redd found himself struggling to make sense of what had become of the program he loved.*

And so, when USC—a preseason favorite to win the national championship—approached him about transferring, Redd was willing to listen. Head coach Lane Kiffin did not stalk the back on Penn State's campus. He flew across the country with five assistants in tow and applied a full-court press at the Connecticut home of Redd's high school coach. The three-hour presentation ended with an invitation to visit the school's sunny Southern California campus.

For Redd, as tempting as it was to play for the program that had produced O.J. Simpson, Marcus Allen, and Charles White, it was not a simple call, as painless as changing uniforms. It meant uprooting his life. Moving to a new home, transferring credits, learning a new playbook, and ultimately shifting his allegiance. Many close friendships were destroyed in the process.

MATT STANKIEWITCH: The big target for me and senior Mike Farrell was Silas Redd. At that time, he was our only proven running back, so I met with him. Me, Bill O'Brien . . . I don't know if Mike was there. I just remember me, O'Brien, Silas Redd, and Silas's dad. He looks identical to Silas and shook my hand super hard.

We were up in the main office, trying to convince Silas to stay.

I was like, "Silas, you had over a thousand yards last year. If anything, our offensive line will be better this season and you're going to get all the carries. Why would you want to go anywhere else?"

Bill O'Brien was echoing my thoughts.

"Listen, we're going to really open up the running game, we're going to have a passing game . . ."

I'm shaking the dad's hand. We're kind of chest bumping. It was a rah-type meeting. I was like, "Oh, my god, that went great. There's no way he's going to go."

A day or two later, he went to USC. I was shocked.

SPIDER CALDWELL: O'Brien loved Silas. In the spring, he was like, "Oh, man, he's incredible. We'll be great with him." He was crushed when he left.

MICHAEL NASH: USC was the number-one team in the country going into that year and needed a running back. Silas Redd was a contender for the Heisman Trophy in a program that might not even field a team in six weeks and USC, a tailback school, is ready to plug him into the lineup.

MALIK GOLDEN: Who wouldn't want to go to USC? If I was in his position, I might have gone, too. Same with Justin Brown, who went to Oklahoma. Some guys left and we didn't blame them.

JUSTIN BROWN, WIDE RECEIVER, 2009–11: It was a difficult decision, but it was the decision that was best for me and my family. No disrespect to Penn State or the players—I still talked to them, they were still family.

DAVID JONES, COLUMNIST, HARRISBURG *PATRIOT-NEWS*: What people don't understand is that players are trying to make a *living*. Guys at that level are doing the best they can to make it to the NFL. And back then, before the

NIL [name, image, and likeness] policy was introduced, you had to get a contract in the NFL to make money for your family.

GENO LEWIS: Justin Brown was a big influence on me. When I'd visit Penn State as a recruit, he was like, "Hey, man, we need you, hurry up and get here." Every time I went, he sat down and talked to me.

JUSTIN BROWN: It was all very difficult, very emotional. I talked to my teammates before I made the decision, and they told me to make the best decision for me. They were going to support me either way. That meant a lot, that approval. I'd been playing with them for three years.

SPIDER CALDWELL: We don't curse those guys. They made the decision they had to make. If you see *Saving the Roar*, Silas is interviewed in it. He's in tears. When Franco Harris and other lettermen saw that, they were like, we got to reach out to that kid, welcome him back.

It was a tough thing.

Anthony Fera's mother was ill. That was a good reason to go back to Texas.

ANTHONY FERA, KICKER, 2009–11: Shortly before I arrived on campus at Penn State, my mother, the most important person in my life, was diagnosed with multiple sclerosis, making it more and more difficult for her to travel from Texas to see me play.

I was afforded the opportunity to give back to my family, make their lives a little easier, by transferring to a university closer to home.

MATT STANKIEWITCH: Fera was a big loss. He was our kicker and our punter, too. So Alex Butterworth had to step up and be our punter that season.

ALEX BUTTERWORTH, PUNTER, 2010–13: When Anthony left, I was really sad, but I understood the situation with his mom. It would be hard for anybody to say no to what he was saying yes to.

MATT STANKIEWITCH: Khairi Fortt? He wasn't going to be a big-time line-backer for us, but he was a big-enough name to make the news when he transferred. We didn't really miss him, because Mike Hull was a lot better than we thought. But we did miss Silas and Justin Brown.

SILAS REDD: I played football from the time I was six. I was an aggressive kid, always running around. My pops was a former Marine, so I had a real disciplined childhood. A Pop Warner coach of mine went to Penn State and he'd bring me back jerseys and stuff. I came to like the Nittany Lions, went to their camps from eighth grade through my junior year of high school. Once they showed interest in me, I committed.

DAVID JONES: He was the most talented back on the roster. I mean, he leaves and all of a sudden Penn State's featured back is Zach Zwinak. It's not quite the same.

SILAS REDD: I had led the nation in rushing the previous October, so I was getting some heavy press, having like a small run as a Heisman dark horse. It's crazy, because my grandmother had died that month, so that was a roller coaster. It happened to be the best collegiate month in the four years I played. The line was clicking, the offense was clicking. We were rolling.

And then, all hell broke loose. Jerry Sandusky was arrested, the press descended on the campus, the nation rushed to judgment, and Redd and others were left to fend for themselves, thrust into the spotlight by a situation well beyond their control.

SILAS REDD: It was like they punished Joe and then they punished us. You know what I'm saying? It's like you punish the one reason I came to this school. Fire him. Then he dies that January. He died of cancer, but if you ask me, he was heartbroken, too.

You do that to that man and then a few months later you punish us, when we were in first or second grade when those awful things were happening. My twenty-year-old head just couldn't wrap itself around that. I felt like I had no protection from the people I was playing for. I had given my everything to that program. And it just felt like we were getting the short end of the stick.

ADAM RITTENBERG, COLLEGE FOOTBALL REPORTER, ESPN: Redd found himself in a different situation from most Lions players. He had two years of eligibility left, and likely would face an NFL decision after the season. He also played a position where a transition to a new team, even just a month before the opener, wouldn't be overly dramatic.

SILAS REDD: Winter workouts were fun. Coach Fitz made it fun. The camaraderie was there. But I was still dealing with the emptiness from the season before. And, I guess you could say, I was still upset. Trying to mask it. Because by that time I was getting a lot of attention from the media. It was hard to handle this duality of feelings—dealing with the emptiness, but also having to be one of the faces of the program.

ADAM RITTENBERG: The NCAA made it as easy as possible for Penn State players to transfer without penalty. USC's Lane Kiffin came calling, and Redd, after visiting USC's campus during the weekend, accepted the invitation.

SILAS REDD: When I first told my parents I was thinking about transferring, I don't think they wanted me to go. A few friends made it very clear they thought I should stay. One of my best friends spoke about legacy. And, you know, I really thought about that conversation.

I didn't make a decision for a few weeks. I decided to just take a visit to USC. That was the only school that intrigued me. Nick Saban of Alabama had called my dad. Coach Richt at Georgia. A lot of schools called my dad. But the only school I wanted to give any play to was USC.

Why? [exhales] Cali.

When they said I could come out for a visit, I was like, let me just go see. I'm not milking twenty other schools. I want to see one and that's it. I will make my decision after that.

I fell in love. I'm not gonna lie. I fell in love with the atmosphere, the weather, the school. You know, they have just as much tradition as Penn State. So the visit went well.

And after that, it was decision time.

ADAM BRENEMAN: I remember every day turning on ESPN and the story was what's Silas Redd going to do? What's Silas Redd gonna do? Is he going to transfer? I can't imagine the weight that had on him. He was like twenty years old at that time.

SILAS REDD: The consensus in my family was for me to stay, but I don't know. As an athlete, I was never high-maintenance, never wanted for much. I just wanted to play for a school that protected its players, the people who gave their whole lives to the organization, and I didn't like the . . . I can't even remember the dude's name . . . I was not a big fan. I didn't want those guys representing me anymore. That was very, very hard to come to terms with, because I loved Penn State. I'd wanted to go there since I was seven years old.

ADAM RITTENBERG: This isn't a case of a cocky kid looking for the next best thing. Any Penn State fan who knows Redd or has read about him knows he's humble, hardworking, and extremely classy. He comes from a terrific family and earned everything that has come his way.

SILAS REDD: When I decided I was going to transfer, I tried to do everything to a T. I didn't want to have a big-ass press conference. Some LeBron-decision-type moment. I come from a pretty blue-collar family. Both parents work hard. So it wasn't in my nature to add more fuel to the flames.

I had a private meeting with Coach O'Brien. I felt I owed him that.

MALIK GOLDEN: I can only imagine the conversations those guys had to have—with Coach O'Brien, the dudes they came in with—so you can't fault them. It's heavy.

SILAS REDD: I didn't address the whole squad. I'm not going to say they rushed me out of the building, but I wasn't about to linger around after I told the head coach I was transferring. So I didn't get to say goodbye to Spider and Kirk and those guys. But that night I did get to have one last hurrah with some close friends on the team. I went back to my room, the apartment I was living in with Jordan Hill and Justin Brown. I started packing and I cried like a baby. Afraid of what was to come. I knew I was not going to be the most popular person in that region for a while.

BOB MORGAN: When we interviewed Silas Redd for the documentary, you saw the devastating effect of losing those bonds. That was one of the more powerful elements in the story.

MICHAEL NASH: When I talked to him on the phone, I said, "Look, Silas, we're doing this film about the people who stayed. You obviously did not and I don't know if you'll even be in the film if we do the interview, but I'll tell you this, I will not make you look like an asshole. You have my word on that."

He goes, okay. So, he shows up, and once we got into it, I mean, his interview is a film unto itself. Once he broke down and started crying, he explained things no one had ever heard before. When I got done interviewing him, he hugged me. You could tell a big burden had been lifted.

EIGHT

RUN-ONS

As a COACH with NFL experience, Bill O'Brien was uniquely qualified to handle Penn State's biggest challenge—the limits in manpower that would hinder the team in the years ahead. Under the school's agreement with the NCAA, he had two years to trim his roster from eighty-five to sixty-five scholarship players. In the four years after that, he could award up to fifteen new scholarships per class instead of the standard twenty-five.

The logistics were far more complicated than that. Any Penn State player under scholarship when the sanctions were handed down could quit the team without forfeiting the financial support, essentially earning room, board, tuition, books, and academic help without the drudgery of workouts and practice. (Three players took that deal.)

And then, you had scholarship players who were technically active, but sidelined with injuries, some for weeks at a stretch, others for a full season or more.

And, finally, there were the true freshmen who optimally take a redshirt year to add much needed practice, conditioning, and muscle before officially taking the field. The prolonged transition gives them a chance to acclimate themselves to the rigors of college life before assuming the pressures of game prep.

Needless to say, keeping track of the numbers and the variations in status is a chore. O'Brien spent a good bit of time dipping into the NCAA handbook for guidance.

"Data really isn't out there in the public realm to see how something like this unfolds," one athletic department official told the Harrisburg Patriot-News. *"Compliance people usually aren't in high demand, but here we pretty much talk about football scholarship numbers on a daily basis."*

For the new head coach, though, it was less of a burden than one might expect. In the NFL, where rosters are limited to fifty-three active players, O'Brien was accustomed to working with far fewer athletes. Still, in the era before the transfer portal, he didn't have a deep pool of free agents to help him plug holes. And, unlike in the NFL, he could not reward those willing to join him at Penn State with a paycheck. To the contrary, they often had to pay their own way—room, board, books, and tuition.

And yet, thanks to the success of the program, there were willing recruits throughout Pennsylvania. To find them, O'Brien and his coaching staff crisscrossed the commonwealth, visiting schools, soliciting emails, scouring the highlight videos that accompanied them. As an added incentive, he changed the job title of these would-be gems from walk-on to run-on.

AUDREY SNYDER: The people who walked on were viewed as heroes, because they were willing to come help the program and they were not even getting a scholarship.

ZACH LADONIS, LONG SNAPPER, 2013–16: The way people in Pennsylvania responded to the call to arms—I mean, I don't think we've ever seen anything like it. There was this influx of talent, kids that didn't have opportunities to play anywhere else were willing to step up to the plate, play with the best.

TOM PANCOAST: One of the big selling points was the chance to play, because of the limited scholarships. Under O'Brien, walk-ons made up, like, fifty percent of the special teams. That's rare.

BRANDON SMITH, LINEBACKER, 2013–17: I didn't come to just sit on the bench. I had aspirations of getting on the field. Everybody on the team was competitive. We wanted to contribute as much as we could.

BILL O'BRIEN: You're looking for guys who can play a number of positions. Offensive tackles who can play guard, centers who can play guard, safeties that can play linebacker, guys that can contribute on special teams, maybe a running back who can run down on the kicking team.

GREGG GARRITY, WIDE RECEIVER, 2013-16: In 2011, when the Sandusky news broke, I was in my junior year in high school—a receiver getting mostly D3 looks. And then, in my senior year, I started breaking out a bit. Got some one-double-A looks, and to be honest with you, I got some letters from Penn State, interest that probably wouldn't have happened without the sanctions. So the sanctions, for me, were a blessing and a curse. A blessing, because I got an opportunity to go to Penn State, but a curse, because of, you know, the whole situation.

VON WALKER, RUNNING BACK, SAFETY, LINEBACKER, 2013-16: I grew up in Lock Haven, thirty minutes down the road from Penn State. Wasn't really recruited much. I had a small offer from Lycoming College. Almost went to Villanova to play baseball. I remember Coach Mac McWhorter, the offensive line coach under Bill O'Brien. He came to my high school a few times. We built a relationship. The next thing you know, my parents and I are in the office with Coach O'Brien.

They sat me down and Coach O'Brien ran me through what he was probably pleading to a bunch of guys. "Hey, listen, we don't have as many scholarships. I'd love to help you out, but I can't. I promise you, if you come here and commit yourself to the program, I will give you a shot to play. Give you your chance."

And, I mean, I'm a small kid from a small town. I said, yes, on the spot.

GREGG GARRITY: I came in with, like, thirty walk-ons. At the time, there were over a hundred kids on the team. So a third of the team was freshmen walk-ons.

BILL O'BRIEN: When you have sixty-five scholarship players on your roster, you're hoping these run-ons can run downfield on the kickoff, run downfield on the punt team. That's part of the challenge.

VON WALKER: My freshman year, we had the old locker room with the wooden lockers. As soon as you walked in, there was this little corridor that led back to this little square, these lockers way outside the main area. You can ask Hack, ask Garrett Sickels, they were in the main area with all the big-name guys. The run-ons were back in what they call the Ghetto. These cruddy lockers in this tiny square of a room. So, yeah, it kind of forced us to be close. We *all* became close really quick.

GREGG GARRITY: That's where our bond started. We were thirty walk-ons, plus a handful of scholarship kids in the way back corner of the locker room, just kind of goofing around.

PAT ZERBE: The scholarship players hung out with each other, because they were recruited together, met on their official visits. The preferred walk-ons were pieced together after the fact. It's one of those things you grow out of, but for the first half of your freshman year, even when you're on the field, you're in your little divisions of walk-on and scholarship.

SPIDER CALDWELL: Yeah, that was the Ghetto. Those guys kind of had to earn their way out to the front. We used to put all the freshmen back there, scholarship or not, and the walk-ons. But during the Bill O'Brien era, we were putting scholarship players out front, because there were fewer of them.

GREGG GARRITY: When I first got there, it was just a bunch of unknowns. They told me coming in, "Hey, you know, we'd love to have you, but we don't know if we'll have a roster spot for you. We're going to bring you into camp, but you have to work your way onto the team." So I just went into it that summer with my head down. Just wanted to make a name for myself. Work hard and not fly under the radar, but not be, like, too loud or anything, either. That was my mindset.

I remember our first workout. It was just the freshmen class. We were outside on the turf field at the Lasch Building. And at that point, I knew a lot of the guys in the freshman class, but there was one older guy there. I had no clue who it was. He was tall, ripped, athletic, and I was like, jeez, that must be like Deion Barnes, a huge D-end or a linebacker. It was Allen Robinson. I couldn't believe it. He's a receiver and I'm a receiver.

I look nothing like Allen Robinson. So I'm like, *Jeez, I got my work cut out for me here.* One of the first days in study hall, I remember one of the older guys walking in. Same thing. *Oh, jeez, this guy must be like a linebacker or D-end.* It was Adrian Amos. A safety. I'm like, *Oh, my god, he's gonna be hitting me when I come across the middle.* So I was kind of starstruck by the size and the athleticism of the older guys, but my mentality didn't change. I still wanted to work hard and make a name for myself.

TOM PANCOAST: On our third day in camp, one of the scholarship kids was like, "Man, I don't know if I want to do this anymore."

Then he looked at us.

"You guys are paying to get your ass kicked."

We're like, "Yeah, I guess we are."

It's tough, especially when you know you're taking on a lot of student debt to do it and the scholarship kids are getting stipends, going out to dinner and stuff like that.

In the summer, we had to be there on campus for workouts. The scholarship kids, their classes and everything were paid for, but as a walk-on, you had to foot your own bill. So I did all kinds of random jobs. I was a bouncer at the Den, while working at the Creamery one summer. The next summer, I did landscaping jobs and started a window-cleaning company. Ended up making way more money than working at the Den and scooping ice cream.

PAT ZERBE: Every now and then, you'd have a scholarship guy who was cocky and arrogant. He'd be like, "Oh, you're just a walk-on." And you're like, "Dude, I'm here just like you and I'll go toe-to-toe with you." You have to have that mentality. As a walk-on, you're expendable. I didn't really party much when I was a walk-on. I was very cautious. I never wanted to get in trouble. If a scholarship guy gets in trouble, his leash is a lot longer than yours.

I never told anyone that I played football. You know, people always joke: "Oh, you go to parties, you see girls, and you just tell them you're a football player." I never told anyone that. I mean, you could assume it, because I was hanging out with all the football guys. But I'm not telling anyone that, because you never know what's going to happen.

TOM PANCOAST: As a walk-on, you get put at the bottom of the depth chart at the start of every training camp. When new scholarship kids come in, they put them ahead of you on the depth chart, no matter how old you are—until you earn a scholarship, which is pretty rare.

VON WALKER: The week before our first game against Syracuse at MetLife Stadium in 2013, our punt returners just weren't catching the ball in practice. Coach OB used to walk around with a megaphone. So I'm standing there and he says, "Get Walker! Walker needs to catch the punt returns!" So the next thing I know, I'm catching punts. I catch one. Then another. People start to look and I keep catching them. I can't tell you what number I got to. It was like seven or eight maybe. And the next thing I know, Coach O'Brien's like, "He starts." My stomach drops. I'm eighteen years old. I figured I would redshirt like my buddies. That didn't happen. The night before the first game in my college career, I did not sleep a lick. We played in Giants Stadium, MetLife Stadium. That's where it started for me. My career kind of bloomed in special teams.

GREGG GARRITY: Before every practice, they would have the JUGS machine shooting balls up and people catching them. At the beginning of camp, there were maybe ten of us there, freshmen to seniors. And to be honest with you, I was probably the only one that didn't drop any balls. Week one, I was in the bullpen. On the depth chart for the punt returner, you have the starter, the backup, the third-string, fourth-string, and then bullpen. I was way down at the bottom. The second week, I worked my way up to fourth-string. By the end of camp, I was the backup behind Jesse Della Valle. It's not like I did anything special. I just caught the punt.

PAT ZERBE: You need to go out and work that much harder than those scholarship guys every day, because, at the end of the day, the university is invested in them. It's essentially paying them to be there. With walk-ons, if you work out, it's like, "Oh, man, great, we got bang for our buck." Hopefully, they reward you with a full scholarship.

TOM PANCOAST: We used to have these "dirty show" scrimmages, with, like, freshmen scholarship kids and walk-ons. It was during practice on Monday. We had just had this all-out brawl of a scrimmage and then it would just be the older walk-ons and freshmen that kept going. The idea was to give the younger scholarship kids a rest.

The older walk-ons would just get their ass kicked in, because they'd take a million reps.

If you ended up getting playing time—on special teams, offense, or defense—and earned a scholarship, it was like a badge of honor. Because everyone on the team knew it was a huge uphill battle.

GREGG GARRITY: Coach OB's mentality was like, "Hey, I'm gonna play the best guy. I don't care if you were a five-star coming out of high school. I don't care if you weren't rated at all. I'm going to give you a fair shot." And that's really how it was. If you outperformed a senior as a freshman, you were gonna play. That kind of continued with Coach Franklin.

VON WALKER: I can remember being in a home game, weighing like 185 pounds, my freshman year. I'm standing in the end zone pregame, catching kicks, the music going, the fans starting to roll in, and all the recruits would be down on the field, like, "Who the hell is this little white kid returning kicks? Why don't we have someone better back there?" I could literally hear people saying that. And it was like, *Man, what am I getting myself into?*

GREGG GARRITY: At receiver, my whole life, my mindset was to be a route-running technician. I was never the biggest guy, strongest guy, fastest guy, but I really prided myself on getting separation, running good routes, and just making the catch. Most of the one-on-one sessions we had were against younger guys. And the whole first week and a half that I went one-on-one, I beat the linebacker, the safety, the cornerback every single time. And that caught the eye of a few coaches. I remember going into a team meeting before one of our practices and, as we're walking in, Coach O'Brien just kind of said, "Hey, is anybody gonna stop Garrity today in one-on-ones." I just chuckled, but that was pretty cool.

PAT ZERBE: I played with a lot of walk-ons that were really good players in the same situation as me. They could have gone somewhere else—a William and Mary, a James Madison, or any other D-1AA program—and played right away, but they wanted to challenge themselves and go to Penn State, be at the top level.

GREGG GARRITY: Towards the end of the year in 2013, we had two punt returners on the field at one time: Jesse Della Valle and Von Walker. And Von ended up getting a concussion in the Purdue game. So I actually got in the game. The first time I got on the field, I caught a punt. I think I got like nine yards. I don't really remember it. I remember the ball going up and I just blacked out. Like I caught it, I guess, ran nine yards and ran out of bounds.

VON WALKER: I'll be completely honest. If I came to Penn State now, I don't know if I become the same player. There were opportunities given to me right off the jump, because of the situation we were in. They were just looking for guys willing to give them everything they had.

PAT ZERBE: The locker room has since been redone. They redid that whole building. It's beautiful now.

NINE

THE WALK-ON QB

MATT MCGLOIN LOVED *nothing more than to prove people wrong. He'd been doing it since the first day he set foot on campus. In three seasons at West Scranton High School, he had thrown for close to 5,500 yards and fifty-eight TDs, leading the team to two district championships and one league title. And yet, he arrived in State College with no fanfare, not a single scholarship offer from a Division I program.*

At six-foot-one, he didn't have the height recruiters covet or a big arm to make them swoon. And so, he joined Penn State as a walk-on, starting his career as the scout team QB. But, true to his blue-collar, coal-country roots, he refused to give in, no matter how deep Paterno's staff buried him on the depth chart. "I always thought that if I packed up and went home, I was letting other people win," he said.

Through force of will, he scaled his way to the third string, then caught a break when true freshman Rob Bolden—one of the most celebrated recruits in Penn State history—was sidelined by a concussion in 2010. Bolden's backup Kevin Newsome was battling a stomach bug. McGloin, a redshirt sophomore, didn't wait long to show what he could do. His first career completion—a forty-two-yard strike to a sprinting Derek Moye—gave the Lions a 21–7 lead against Minnesota en route to a 33–31 win.

It wasn't enough for the kid from Scranton to throw touchdown passes and rally the team, though. He was forever proving himself, only to be upstaged by passers with richer pedigrees. After splitting time with Bolden for much of the 2011 season, McGloin finally claimed the starting job, right around the time the Sandusky scandal erupted. In the days leading up to the TicketCity Bowl, he was knocked unconscious in a locker room scuffle with receiver Curtis Drake. He missed the season finale.

Bolden took the field instead.

When Bill O'Brien arrived, fresh off coaching Tom Brady in the Super Bowl as the New England Patriots' offensive coordinator, Matt McGloin had just one season of college football left. He was determined not to spend it on the bench.

BILL O'BRIEN: When we started spring practice, it was obvious to me after about nine or ten practices, that this was the starting quarterback. The guy was smart, accurate—he worked hard to improve.

CHARLIE FISHER: There was a lot of turmoil there before the bowl game in 2011. And, a year earlier, Matt had thrown five interceptions against Florida in the Outback Bowl. After that, a lot of the fan base was really down on him. He wanted to rectify that.

That's what I love about the kid—he overcame the odds. When you walk on, the odds are against you. They brought Rob Bolden in there and all these star recruits. It was like, Hey, man, you're going to get left behind.

He never did. He kept fighting. It was like, Screw you, I'm going to find a way to get this done.

BILL O'BRIEN: When I first saw him, I knew right away we had a competitive kid. The way he was on the field, the way he was in meetings, the way he took notes, the way he listened—you have to have those traits to be a successful quarterback. You have to have a brain that can work fast, you have to be competitive, you have to have a huge desire to win. And he had that.

ERIC SHRIVE: Matt really flourished under Bill O'Brien. Going on to win the starting quarterback position, making it to the NFL. Nobody gave him a chance coming out of high school. He was arguably one of the best quarterbacks in the Big Ten his senior year and didn't even get invited to the

Combine. He ended up starting eight or nine games as a rookie for the Oakland Raiders. Even guys that get drafted in the first ten picks don't start eight or nine games as a rookie.

He's got the chip on his shoulder, that's for sure.

MATT MCGLOIN: The recruiting process always drove me crazy. When I played in games at Penn State, I'd think to myself, *All right, you didn't recruit me. I'm going to show you what a big mistake that was.*

CHARLIE FISHER: I had recruited Matt when I was at Vanderbilt. He was a good player. Not the most highly recruited guy on the team, though. West Scranton also had this tackle Eric Shrive and a big tight end named Hubie Graham, who went to Illinois.

Matt was a bit of an afterthought. He wasn't the biggest guy, but he was really productive, so we evaluated him. He just didn't fit what we were doing at Vanderbilt. Jay Cutler had graduated and we had shifted to kind of a spread offense with a dual-threat quarterback. And so, I wrote Matt a note and wished him the best. "It's not going to work out here at Vandy," I said, "but you keep grinding—good things happen that way."

In 2012, I took the job as Penn State's quarterbacks coach. I'd been there about a week. I'm sitting in the office and my phone dings. I've got a text. I open it and there's a picture of this letter I sent to Matt. "Hey, Coach, funny how things work out."

I think he always respected the fact that I didn't just cast him aside.

MATT MCGLOIN: We had a lot of guys being recruited at different positions, so there were coaches constantly coming to the high school and to this day I think I got caught in the middle: The bigger schools thought I couldn't play at that level, and the smaller schools thought I was going somewhere else. I still scratch my head over it.

It was tough, because I knew I was capable of playing at a high level. And I didn't want to go to a Lehigh or a Holy Cross. Nothing against those schools, they're great, but I didn't want to play in front of 1,500 people. Didn't want to work my tail off every single day just for that.

I wanted to play on ESPN. On ABC. I wanted to run out in front of a hundred thousand people.

CRAIG FITZGERALD: Not many people had him on top of their recruiting lists. But not just *anyone* could lead that 2012 team.

Matt played great at quarterback, but he also brought the leadership that team needed. It was like, "I don't care how many scholarships we got, I don't care how many points we're down—it doesn't matter."

Matt McGloin is going to jog out on the field. He's going to give Bill a look like, I got this. And here we go.

AUDREY SNYDER: He was the perfect guy to quarterback that team, because he was brutally honest and that aligns so well with Mauti and Zordich.

CHARLIE FISHER: Nothing scared him. Nothing bothered him. There was nothing he didn't believe he could do.

Did he have a chip on his shoulder? Absolutely. Did he play with an edge? Absolutely. It was like, Whatever you're going to throw at me, bring it on.

You know how you always hear about quarterbacks with stars? This is a five-star guy and this is a four-star guy . . . he'd always remind us: I beat out guys worth seventeen stars.

MATT MCGLOIN: You had Paul Jones who was five stars, Kevin Newsome who was four stars, Bolden who was four stars, and then me who was zero.

AUDREY SNYDER: When I first started covering the team in 2010, I emailed Matt McGloin using the Penn State directory. I was like, "Hey, I'm a student reporter, I see that you're a journalism major, can I talk to you?"

I remember sitting in my dorm room at the end of sophomore year, talking to Matt. I got the impression right away that this guy was so confident, so sure of himself, he thought he was going to win the job. I remember thinking, Oh, this is interesting.

And he was spot-on. Here's a guy you wouldn't think in a million years is going to be your starting quarterback and yet he is. He just meshed with Bill. When O'Brien got hired, people thought he had his work cut out for him. It's Matt McGloin. Who knows what you're going to get? He was viewed as this gunslinger. It was such a fascinating pairing, because both of them could fly off the handle at any point. But they were so good for each other.

BILL O'BRIEN: In a meeting in spring practice, I put him up on the board and I said draw this up. This play. And he drew it up in about three seconds. Neatly. Knew the read, knew what everybody did. Drew up the front, drew up the coverage. Knew the protection, knew where it was supposed to go. It was Gun Trips Right 64 Special H Sneak, I'll never forget it.

It was bang!

I knew at that point we had a kid who wanted to be the starting quarterback.

CRAIG FITZGERALD: There were a million excuses for that season to be unsuccessful. But Matt McGloin wasn't going to let anyone make excuses. In the weight room, all season long, he was one of the hardest workers. He might not be lifting the same weight as the linebackers, but he was straining just as hard. There was a work ethic that filtered through the team because of him.

MATT MCGLOIN: I hate the term walk-on. I've always felt it's ridiculous to label somebody as a walk-on, a run-on, or a scholarship athlete. Let me tell you, when you're one of a hundred and ten guys on the football team, you're a Penn State football player. At the end of the day, this game we play is performed in space, so it doesn't matter if you're five-star or one-star. If you don't deliver on the field, you're not going to play.

I didn't have fifty offers. I needed to earn the respect of everybody around me every single day. Needed to be the hardest-working guy in the film room, on the practice field, in the weight room.

I needed to make a name for myself. I was a big self-promoter, because I had to be.

CHARLIE FISHER: He had no trouble telling you what he thought—by any means.

MATT MCGLOIN: I'm sure I rubbed people the wrong way with the way I approached the game, how intense I was, but for me, it was always about self-promotion, because—guess what?—no one else was promoting me. I had to do it myself.

CHARLIE FISHER: By that time in my career, I had matured and our personalities meshed well. Bill's a high-end, emotional, get after it kind of guy. I've got some of those qualities, but my role was different. I wasn't the head coach, wasn't the coordinator, I was the quarterback coach. So I had to find that junction between me, Matt, and Bill. I always tried to take the calm approach, get Matt to play under control.

That's one of the biggest steps he made that year. He was able to take all that made him good and compartmentalize it, not let it work against him. By just being calm. Let's think this out, find ways to do what we need to do.

And, listen, so there's no debate: He was the best quarterback on campus—hands-down. It wasn't close. He outplayed the other guys in the spring. It's that simple. He was the best quarterback on campus. And when we made him the starter, he really embraced it. Okay, this is it, my opportunity to go out the right way.

O'Brien announced the decision on June 1. Redshirt sophomore Paul Jones was named the backup. On August 1, Rob Bolden announced that he was transferring to LSU. Jones left for Robert Morris three months later, after surrendering the second-string role to true freshman Steven Bench.

TEN

CHARLIE MIKE

FOR ALL THE *pep talk—the emotional pleas from teammates, coaches, and stars like Matt Millen—the words that mattered most to the players were delivered by an obscure figure in Penn State history.*

In the autumn of 1997, he had walked onto the team as a twenty-nine-year-old defensive tackle. By his own account, he logged just one play in his three-year career. But he knew firsthand what it takes to succeed at the Division I level and he knew the value of a Penn State education, particularly one infused with the rich tradition of the Nittany Lion football program. He also knew something about exhibiting courage in the face of adversity. After the terrorist attacks on the Pentagon and the World Trade Center on September 11, 2001, Rick "Hawk" Slater had reenlisted in the military, serving five tours of duty in Iraq and Afghanistan as a Navy SEAL.

He carried the lessons he learned in Happy Valley with him onto the battlefield, he explained. In fact, he was preparing for yet another overseas assignment when his old teammates asked him to return to campus to speak to the 2012 players. And, while he was literally needed on the other side of the world, he agreed to rush back to State College out of loyalty to the program.

RICK SLATER: I was stationed out in San Diego at the time, and a good friend of mine, Justin Kurpeikis, gave me a heads-up that the lettermen were coming back to campus to speak to the players. It was all hands on deck.

I could not make it, because I was leaving in about a week for Australia. I was going to be attached to the Australian military, basically on loan to the Aussies for three years.

So I wrote a letter, and Coach O'Brien read the letter after everybody spoke. And after he read it, he turned to Justin and said, "Hey, any chance you can get this guy back here to speak?"

Now, I'm days out from going overseas, but I said, "Roger that—this is an important mission."

I wrote up this speech and flew to State College on a Friday. I think it was in August. The guys were in camp.

SPIDER CALDWELL: He was a Navy SEAL. He did several tours as a Navy SEAL. And then he came to Penn State, used the GI Bill to go back to school when he was like twenty-nine years old. Went to tryouts, walk-on tryouts, made the team. So he was basically with us for three years.

The players *loved* the guy. But he . . . I mean, he was different.

RICK SLATER: I did twenty-four years of service in special operations with the SEAL teams. Nine and a half of that was pre–Penn State.

When I got out, I walked on the football team. I was a bench rider. Still out there on the practice field, though. Still in the meetings. It was the most impactful portion of my life.

BOB MORGAN: I've seen lettermen from that era interact with Rick. They absolutely love that guy. He's legendary for his work ethic. That's why Paterno loved him.

RICK SLATER: After I left Penn State, I was living in Brazil and then 9/11 happened. So I returned home to serve again. Was going to do four more years; I ended up staying another fifteen.

BOB MORGAN: He reenlisted with the Navy SEALs after 9/11. I mean, it's rare to meet somebody with that much drive, someone who pours his heart and soul into everything he does.

MATT STANKIEWITCH: He felt it was his duty to come back to the United States and go after the enemy. There's nothing more compelling than that.

He wasn't in the Navy SEALs anymore, and he felt it was his duty to come back.

For a man who prized duty and honor, playing football at Penn State was a life-changing experience. It wasn't the on-field heroics that moved him so much as the relationships with his fellow players, the standards they set for one another in their time together.

RICK SLATER: The friends I made on the team—that's a lifelong bond. It doesn't work like that in the military. Yes, you're on the battlefield with somebody who becomes your brother, but the bond with the Penn State football players, I still have that to this day. And it will be there till the day I die.

In the military, you want to train perfect because your life depends on it. In college football, especially at one of the tier-one units, you want to train perfect to win the national title. Obviously, one's more high-stakes than the other. But there's just something different about the drive of a tier-one athlete, the perfection I saw at Penn State. It was very unique.

I went through a tryout with a bunch of people from the student body and was the only guy picked up. It wasn't because I was a standout. I got one play in during my years at Penn State. I was on the practice field, given the best look I could get, but there was no way I was good enough to be up there with the starters or the second-stringers.

I think Joe Paterno liked that I was older. He could sense that he'd get an honest day's work from me.

Little did the coach know that Slater would play a pivotal role in rallying the team more than a decade later, returning to deliver a pep talk in the program's hour of need.

SPIDER CALDWELL: So we're in the squad meeting room, which is like a theater. Coach O'Brien introduces Rick and sits down. As Rick's walking down the steps, the team gives him a standing ovation. Well, Rick's just, you know, real nonchalant.

STEPHON MORRIS: You couldn't tell he was a Navy SEAL. You would have thought he was a WWE character, the way he carried himself. At that point in time, everyone was a bit afraid of Fitz, because Fitz was just crazy. You know, high-energy. And [laughter] I remember watching Rick walk past Fitz and not give one shit who he was.

Me and Gerald Hodges were like, "Did you see that?"

TIM SWEENEY: When you view Rick at face value, he looks disheveled. I think the players were kind of smirking, until he started to speak. OB was like, *Who the hell is this?* I mean, he invited Rick to come talk to the team sight-unseen. When OB saw him, I think he was like, *Oh, boy, I hope I picked the right guy.*

But after Rick got done speaking, there was no question he had picked the right guy.

SPIDER CALDWELL: To give you some perspective, here's what he does. He walks up to the lectern. [Spider removes his wallet, keys, and various items from his pocket and places them on the lectern one at a time, then he pauses to straighten them out.]

STEPHON MORRIS: He's rearranging his keys, taking stuff out of his backpack, taking off his belt. He was silent for like five minutes. He commanded the room with his eyes. We're all looking at this dude like, *What the hell?* Then he proceeded to talk.

SPIDER CALDWELL [DROPPING HIS VOICE TO A WHISPER]: "Gentlemen, it's an honor to be here."

[Ha!] That's how he set the tone. And you're just like . . . [Spider drops his jaw.]

Coach O'Brien's like this [Spider opens his eyes wide]. He just *mesmerized* the guys.

PETE MASSARO: You couldn't hear a sound, everybody was on the edge of their seats.

STEPHON MORRIS: The way he talked, the way he went about it—he just looked us in the eyes. It sent chills down my body.

RICK SLATER: I'd had enough years in leadership positions, where you learn to get your message out and you're not shy about it. So that was just me—just my style, I guess.

SPIDER CALDWELL: He pulled off his belt. It's an old web belt—a Boy Scout belt that we gave the players to hold up their football pants. He said, when he left Penn State, he wore that belt *everywhere* he went. On every single combat mission.

He held the thing up and said, "Because I always wanted to be reminded of what Penn State meant to me, what it did for me."

MICHAEL NASH: When he held up his practice belt, this blue practice belt, and told them, "I've worn this belt on every mission, every battle I fought in Afghanistan and Iraq—the same practice belt I wore on these fields," I think the guys realized bigger battles have been fought on this planet than the one they found themselves in. The only way to get through it—and this was really at the core of Rick's speech—was to rely on the man to the right and to the left of you. No one else has your back.

The media's trying to destroy you. The administration hasn't made the best decisions. And there's a lot of chatter about everybody in the program leaving. The only thing that's going to get you through this is everybody in this room coming together.

STEPHON MORRIS: That was kind of the turning point in training camp. I'll take what he said and carry it with me for the rest of my life.

RICK SLATER: The speech was about loyalty, how it can wane in a really bad situation and why it should not. I said, "You guys are in a battle right now and it's not looking favorable. You have a lot of better options if you abandon ship. You can do that or you can stay on this sinking ship. But you're going to need some good leadership, all hands on deck." That kind of stuff.

MICHAEL YANCICH: I have a quote from the speech in the notes section on my phone. I saved it. It gives me goosebumps reading it right now. It says, "You are now either by coincidence or design, the few on a mission to accomplish what no others have ever been asked to accomplish before. Regaining the honor and tradition of Penn State. Keep your core straight, carry the weight, do not waver, and let history remember you as the greatest generation."

SPIDER CALDWELL: We didn't film the speech. We regret that. But we did get a copy of it afterwards. Rick talked about the call sign Charlie Mike, which stands for Continue the Mission. He explained what Penn State means to him and said, "You're here now and you need to continue the mission."

STEPHON MORRIS: Charlie Mike, Continue the Mission. He left us with that. We ended up putting Charlie Mike on our workout shirts. That's the motto we went by the entire season: Charlie Mike.

I still have my Charlie Mike shirt.

MICHAEL YANCICH: After our loss to Ohio U—Charlie Mike; our loss at Virginia—Charlie Mike; our loss against Ohio State—Charlie Mike; and then our loss in Nebraska—Charlie Mike. I think many of us probably still use that phrase as inspiration.

I'll be sitting on a job site, and, you know, if something doesn't go right with a subcontractor, I say to one of my coworkers, "Hey, man, Charlie Mike." They're like, "Who's Charlie Mike?"

GENO LEWIS: The whole Charlie Mike thing—I still use that today, man. Like, now that I'm in the Canadian Football League, I tell them boys, man, we burning the ship. There ain't no way you leaving.

BOB MORGAN: When you hear his story, you realize that whatever adversity you're going through is nothing compared to what Rick Slater has gone through.

He gave the team perspective—encouragement. Yes, it's bad, but you got to Charlie Mike.

Keep going.

Don't quit.

STEPHON MORRIS: He commanded the audience, which was kind of hard at that time, because we were tired of all the speeches. We just wanted to play football.

Usually, when speakers come in, the coaches duck in and out. That's the first time I'd seen everyone quiet. He had their full attention.

TIM SWEENEY: If that guy doesn't make you proud to be an American, proud to be a Penn State football player, proud to be a Penn Stater, nothing will.

GENO LEWIS: Guys bought into it. They really understood.

Like, this is Penn State University. We're going through adversity right now, but we're not going to change the fact that this is Penn State and we have a standard here and we're going to do everything we can to uphold that standard.

RICK SLATER: At the end, everybody lined up and shook my hand. There were three standouts. One, I can't remember his name, I wish I could. But the other two were Mike Mauti and Mike Zordich and I could tell straight away that they were key leaders on that team, the type that go up front on the battle lines. That was their leadership style.

Those are the guys that stepped up. I just said a few words.

Three or four days later, I was in Australia. And about two months after that, I was on the battlefield in Afghanistan. I couldn't keep up with the news on how they were performing. But there on the far side of the world, I was always thinking about those guys.

ELEVEN

NAMES TO REMEMBER

PENN STATE LEGEND *John Cappelletti, who Joe Paterno once described as "the best player I ever coached," rushed for 1,522 yards and 17 touchdowns in 1973, logging three 200-yard games in the final stretch to cap a perfect 12–0 record for the team. At season's end, he won the Heisman Trophy, awarded annually to the most outstanding player in college football.*

In his tearful acceptance speech, immortalized in the made-for-TV movie Something for Joey, *the running back heaped praise on his eleven-year-old brother, who had bravely battled leukemia for six years. "If I can dedicate this trophy to him tonight and give him a couple days of happiness," said John, "this is worth everything."*

Forty years later, Penn State honored Cappelletti's contributions to the program by retiring his number twenty-two jersey. The most remarkable thing about that jersey? Cappelletti's name never once appeared on the back.

As any Penn State fan will tell you, none of the greats in the Nittany Lions' storied 125-year history enjoyed that privilege. Not Franco Harris, Matt Millen, or LaVar Arrington. Not Todd Blackledge, who quarterbacked the team to a national championship in 1983, or John Shaffer, who led the way to national championship number two in 1987.

At Penn State, putting a player's name on the uniform is viewed as sacrilege. "The name on the front of the jersey is what really matters," Joe Paterno explained, "not the one on the back."

Over the years, this had evolved into the program's signature statement. Black shoes, basic blues. No names, all game.

And so, it was big news in 2012 when Bill O'Brien elected to part with tradition and put his players' names on the back of the team's iconic jerseys.

SPIDER CALDWELL: After that meeting with the lettermen, Coach O'Brien calls me.

"Spider, what do you think about putting names on the jerseys?"

I was like, "Ah, coach, there might be a mutiny."

KAREN CALDWELL: My husband comes home and says, "Oh, my word, Coach O'Brien was asking me what I thought about putting names on the jerseys.

I said, "Holy cow, the lettermen will go crazy."

SPIDER CALDWELL: I mean, our lettermen, they really . . . they were not happy when bowl patches started appearing on jerseys, because of corporate sponsorship. In the contracts for bowl games, they start fining you if you don't put a patch on. Lots of money. Not millions, but thousands of dollars. So we gave in and put the patches on.

After five years or so, the players were like, "Ah, okay." But that was a big deal.

STEPHON MORRIS: I get tradition, but people got to realize, too, that at that point in 2012, we were going through a transition. We wanted the program to have a little flair, be a little more modern. People think O'Brien was going in a different direction, but that's not the case at all. He did that to honor the guys that stayed. It wasn't purely OB's decision. He took the senior leaders aside and asked us if we wanted last names on the back of our jerseys.

GARRY GILLIAM, TIGHT END, OFFENSIVE TACKLE, 2009–13: It was time for us to move on to the next chapter and for the community to know which players decided to stick it out in a tough time.

MALIK GOLDEN: That was big. It had never happened before, so a lot of the older guys were hyped, the younger guys were hyped.

BILL O'BRIEN: Those kids made a *huge* decision in their young lives to stay there at Penn State. Donovan Smith had like fifty scholarship offers. *Fifty*, not fifteen. Five-*oh*. And he chose to stay.

Mauti could have gone to Florida.

Zordich could have gone to Ohio State.

All those guys could have gone to other places. That's what people have to remember about that time. I did it because I wanted the fans, the alums, and the former players to know the names of the kids who stayed with the program. I wanted them to know those names.

SPIDER CALDWELL: Early on, some of the former players were pretty upset. I'd say, "There's a reason for it. I totally understand where Coach O'Brien is coming from. We need to throw him a bone here."

MICHAEL YANCICH: Black shoes, basic blues, no names, all game. That was the motto of Penn State forever. But Coach O'Brien sat down and said, "Listen, I'm doing this because I want everybody in the college football world to know who decided to stay and work this thing out, turn this tumultuous situation into a success." In hindsight, I couldn't agree more. I think the names deserved to be there on the back of the jerseys for that short period of time.

SPIDER CALDWELL: I said, "I understand the concept. It's a great reason to do it. But you will get some fallout." I said, "I'm in uncharted territory, but I'll give it a shot." You know, by now, we're almost in August, so the only way to get the jerseys done is to do them ourselves. So Nike sends me blank panels. And all the letters. That's it, a whole box of letters.

Our time constraints were so tight. I said, "Well, okay, I'm going to take these to one of the screen-printing companies downtown and heat-set 'em. Fry them on."

And then, I went to my wife and said, "Hey, dear, what do you think about . . . ?"

KAREN CALDWELL: It kind of came with the marriage, because I had a sewing machine and liked to sew, and with him taking care of the equipment, jerseys had to be repaired. Sometimes they'd tear right by the sleeve or where the shoulder pads would . . . you know, where someone grabbed ahold of them. And so, to have the jerseys looking good in time for the next week's game, why they were running into problems. Sometimes they couldn't get the turnaround time they needed and sometimes the jersey would go missing, because you know everybody likes a souvenir.

And so, Spider asked me. "Could I bring them home? Try it out. See what you think."

SPIDER CALDWELL: She always sewed the bowl patches on for me. Repaired rips and stuff, too. A lot of times, the jerseys would go missing if we sent them to a reconditioning company, so my wife said, "Bring them home, I'll fix them." She started doing them, sewing little holes and stuff. You know, eight or ten jerseys would get ripped during a game. It was nothing major.

But then, we started doing the bowl patches. And she's like, "Well, yeah, I'll put the patches on." So, we started sewing patches, and it just kind of morphed into, you know, being a team seamstress. I would take stuff home as needed. Paterno's wife, Sue, was like, "Can she sew Joe's pants?" Then we start sewing all the coaches' pants. My poor wife, I'm amazed we're still married.

KAREN CALDWELL: Oh, yes. That was kind of fun for me, too. Spider would take all the measurements. Nike would send the famous khaki trousers, but they were not hemmed, so Spider would take all the measurements and have this big chart: what size trousers and what inseam. I mean, I can probably still remember some of the sizes.

Spider's not that tall, and I'm holding these trousers up above my head, thinking, *Wow.* I mean, Todd Kulka, he's an academic counselor who once played football and those were tall trousers. We had some ones that were pretty big around, too. You know, the waist size.

But, anyways, yes, I did some hemming, including JoePa's trousers. I think Sue always liked turning them up. I guess she didn't want the early ones getting muddy, so she would tack them up and then it became a tradition. So to do JoePa's trousers and then see them on TV, out on the field, I'd take my binoculars and look to see, you know, how they looked, hoping the legs matched. So, yes, that was fun.

SPIDER CALDWELL: But, anyway, that summer I said, "Do you think you could do this? We're running out of time." And my wife said, "Yeah, I can do the panel—zip it on there, no problem."

So I started taking the jerseys home, twenty-five at a time, in a bag. And she'd sew the panels on. And then, I'd take those twenty-five back and bring twenty-five more. I was doing the blue ones first, because the first game's at home.

KAREN CALDWELL: Nike would send out a strip of cloth that's—I don't know—three inches high and, you know, however long the name is. If it's a blue jersey, it's a blue background cloth. Nike rushed them through to us, but it was a quick turnaround.

Spider said, "Don't feel like you have to do this, because he knew. I was as upset as anybody with all the stuff that had been happening. But the name strips came, he brought them home, and I said, "Let's see what we can do."

I always had my sewing machine set up on this table, but this was going to be a big job, so I reset things, placed the table in front of the TV in our downstairs area, where I could just leave things set up and go for it.

He would bring the jerseys home in a big cloth bag. And they're heavy. I mean, thirty jerseys weigh a lot. So he'd come dragging them down to the basement, along with the strips of names, which he had charted out.

He said, "Boy, I hope they got these spelled right."

And I said, "I can check the spelling. I'm a schoolteacher, so don't you worry about that."

Before I sewed the strips on, I had to pin them on the jersey and hold it up. Make sure the panel was straight. It was challenging, because the cloth is so movable.

But, wow, I remember that very first jersey.

I got it laid out, pinned on, and all of a sudden it struck me. *Oh, my word, we never had names on these jerseys before.*

I got up and I'm pacing around. My arms were shaking. I said, "Holy cow, what's JoePa going to think of this? Names on jerseys."

Brad and I, we'd been talking about this a lot. Some of the lettermen were understanding. Some were in there begging, "No, Coach, don't break the tradition." I really did understand that we were supporting this group of men, the 2012 team, these young guys who had decided, *Okay, I will stay with Penn State no matter what.*

But my arms are shaking. I can hardly see what I'm doing. All these emotions. And I thought, *Okay, Coach O'Brien, I'm supporting you. I want you to have a successful season.*

I'm literally talking to myself as I sew that first one on.

I wish I could remember which one I picked. I don't know what name was on it. But I got that thing sewed on and from then it was fine. I mean, I was actually proud.

Holy cow, I'm making Penn State history.

It was humbling. Made me think of the ladies who worked in the office, the trainers, the team doctors, every coach and assistant. As wives, we felt like part of that team, too. If we won a Bowl game and the guys got a ring, the ladies got a nice pendant. The Paternos would do that for us. After Joe-Pa's four-hundredth win, we got a ring that said, Paterno 400. They treated us like part of the team.

Spider would take those twenty-five jerseys back to work and bring me another twenty-five. I was going to school during the day, so this was kind of an evening thing. After supper. I worked until I got tired.

But we got the things done. They were ready for that first game.

SPIDER CALDWELL: Now, during that first game, I noticed that a few letters were starting to peel off. They didn't *fall* off, but they were definitely . . . I said, "Ah, this ain't working. They must not have heated them enough." So after the game, I reheated them, the ones that were kind of funny.

Then we go to Virginia with the white jerseys. Well, it was real humid. And I don't think they heat-set them as hot as they had done the blue ones. And letters are falling off all game. If you watch it, you'll see it was Derek Da instead of Derek Day, because his Y fell off. Mauti's letters were flopping. There were letters flopping in the wind. I'm like, "Oh, my god, no!"

KAREN CALDWELL: I'm watching on TV and I think, *Holy cow.* Day's Y came off and it's flapping. And see the difference with those—there was no time for Nike to send us the sewn panels. They sent Spider the letters and the strips of cloth, but we had to get the job done. So they were sent to somebody in town with a heat press, and it's no fault of theirs. They had never done this before. You can't have the press too hot or it will burn the fabric, but it's still got to be hot enough to stick the letters on good.

So here it is on TV, and I'm standing up, yelling at the television. "Oh, no!" And then, of course, they start talking about it, you know, the broadcasters, making a big joke about it. They said, "Oh, JoePa's reaching down, peeling those off."

It did kind of make me laugh. But yet, I'm saying, "Oh, my word, my husband's going to be in big trouble. Spider is going to hear about this."

SPIDER CALDWELL: On Monday, Dave Joyner calls me. He's like, "Spider, that was an embarrassment. Why don't you get those fixed?"

I'm like, "I know, Dave, here's what happened . . ."

KAREN CALDWELL: Sure enough, he comes home feeling bad.

SPIDER CALDWELL: I'm like, "Karen, what do you think?"

She said, "Bring them home. We'll just sew every letter."

KAREN CALDWELL: He said, "You can't do that."

I said, "You bring them home, I'm stitching those doggone things on so they're not coming off."

SPIDER CALDWELL: We didn't have time to take the panels off, sew the letters on them, and put the panels back on, so we just sewed right through the whole jersey. Those letters were sewed right onto the jersey.

I would take them home again, twenty-five at a time. We did the starters first, because it would take her about fifteen minutes per jersey, especially for guys like Stankiewitch, Obeng-Agyapong. She really busted her rear end.

KAREN CALDWELL: So here comes everything back again. I would sit in front of the TV till, you know, one o'clock, two o'clock in the morning, when I just started to get cross-eyed. With the zigzag on the sewing machine, I went around every crazy letter. And oh, boy, I was really happy when the guys had short names. I remember seeing Hull and thinking, *Oh, good, what a relief.* Let me think, there was Hull and Hill, Jordan Hill.

I think he was a tackle. And then, there were names like Hodges and McGloin. But I'll tell you, there were a couple like Stankiewitch.

Matt Stankiewitch was our center. Man, that name stretched clear from shoulder to shoulder.

I did Obeng-Agyapong, too. That one actually went over the seam of the sleeve. I was like, *Why did I say I was doing this?*

MATT STANKIEWITCH: My great-grandfather was blinded in the coal mines. He had to play the violin to make money for his family with only a third-grade education. Another great-grandfather had his leg damaged in the mines. So, yeah, if you want to talk about oppression and hard times, my family knows it. I know some people were upset when Bill put the names on the back of the jerseys, but I was just so honored to represent my father's father and mother, who both died very young.

One of my family members posted on Facebook that I have broad shoulders for a broad name and my grandparents were sitting on those shoulders, looking down on me. I get teared up when I think of it. The idea was to represent my family, all that they went through in the coal mines, the immigration process, working for two cents an hour, going into the coal mines when it was dark and coming out when it was dark.

I was proud to honor them, honor that family name.

SPIDER CALDWELL: So the next game, we only had the starters sewn. The other ones were still just heat-set, but those guys didn't play a bunch, so the letters weren't peeling off in the game. You didn't notice it. And then we did the same thing with the white ones. By game four, I think we finally had them all done.

KAREN CALDWELL: I don't always remember the numbers. My husband, he can remember a player's head size from fitting the helmets. He often knows shoe sizes. I mean, he can probably look down at your feet and say, "You know, you're a ten and a half." He just . . . I don't know . . . Everybody has their specialty, but I always marvel that Spider can remember so many things.

When I first saw the racks of jerseys that had been freshly laundered and sorted . . . And then, there's the practice jerseys and the backup jerseys and backup shoes . . . I actually had somebody at my school saying, "Well, what do you bother with sewing them for? Why don't they just pull out a new jersey?" But, I mean, there's a lot of money tied up in those things. And so, you're conservative with them. At Penn State, they repair things and repair them well. You know, I didn't want a guy getting tackled because somebody got their fingers in a hole, pulled on his jersey and tackled him. You know what I mean?

In July of 2015, just prior to his second season as head coach, James Franklin would remove the names and restore the tradition. "This is something I've had a lot of conversations with Spider about," Franklin explained. "I had a lot of conversations with [defensive recruiting coordinator] Terry Smith about. I've thought about this from day one. I think people are excited with the direction of the program and the future of the program, but also want to be very respectful of our past traditions and our history."

MATT MCGLOIN: It's funny, because every time I see number eleven on TV, I have to say, they're still selling my jersey there. They're still selling my jersey.

_____

TWELVE

ROUGH START

IN TEN MONTHS' _time, they had weathered more than any team in history—the jolt of the Sandusky news, the heat from the public outrage, the death of their longtime coach, the crippling rebuke from the NCAA, and the loss of their star running back, snatched from the fold and installed on a national title contender—and now at last they were ready to resume playing football._

After studiously strengthening their bodies and their resolve, they were eager to show what they could do. On the eve of the season opener, fifteen thousand fans emerged at Beaver Stadium for a Friday night pep rally. For many attendees, it was the first real look at the new head coach.

Bill O'Brien didn't disappoint. He took the microphone and turned on the charm. "This is a very, very special group of players, led by a very special senior class," he said. "Our guys have worked extremely hard. . . . They're tired of hitting each other and can't wait to get going."

In a made-for-TV special, it would be the perfect cue for a stunning revival. But in reality, the players had yet more punishment to endure—at the hands of two surprisingly stout nonconference opponents.

AUDREY SNYDER: The day the sanctions came out, I was standing in the airport in New York, getting ready to hop on a plane to London to cover the Olympics. I remember seeing the announcement, then getting on the flight and being like, *Whoa, that's a lot. By the time I land, who the heck knows what's going to happen?*

But at that point, it was like, Hey, I just graduated from Penn State. This isn't my story anymore.

Sure enough, by September, it was my problem again, because I took a job covering the team for *PennLive*. So I had a unique vantage point. I had covered what had happened in 2011 as a student reporter and then I came back to it. I've seen it pretty much the full way through.

I accepted the job with *PennLive* in late August and I was still waiting for the paperwork to clear, so I couldn't cover the early games. But I remember watching and being like, *Oh, my god, this is really bad. What am I getting myself into?*

How do you cover a team when you don't know what the expectation should be? You have all this crazy stuff going on. You don't know who's going to stay, who's going to go. And then this thing goes south in a hurry on the field.

STEPHON MORRIS: Once we got our team, the team we knew we were gonna have, you could still sense some animosity about everything—the fact we couldn't challenge for the Big Ten title, couldn't go to a bowl game, and players we had formed relationships with, hosted on visits to Penn State, had left. We were still dealing with betrayal. We were just so high-strung going into training camp, you know, limited as to what we could do, because of the depth of our squad.

CRAIG FITZGERALD: Our camp was about getting twos and threes ready to be starters. New running back, new kicker, new receiver, new line, new linebacker. There were a lot of players that had never started before.

The team also had a brand-new offense and a brand-new defense.

AUDREY SNYDER: It was like, Are people still going to show up to support this team? Are they still going to care? In hindsight, it's interesting, because the fans did show up, but it was hard not to wonder if people might get burned out on the scandal, mad at Penn State because of how things were handled. You still had that sideshow going on while the season was unfolding.

On the Friday evening before the home opener, the diehard fans—many of them students—hiked across campus to Beaver Stadium, filing into the stands behind the south end zone, for the pep rally. With the players seated on bleachers behind him, shoulder to shoulder in navy blue warmup suits, Bill O'Brien took hold of the microphone and addressed the crowd.

STEPHON MORRIS: That pep rally gave us chills. I almost shed a tear. I really think I almost shed a tear. It was just so emotional. Like, Damn, we done went through *everything* that, you know, Louis Freeh, former head of the FBI, could throw at a program. Emmert and the NCAA, too. We lost Paterno and were pilloried for being assaulted by Sandusky, because some people didn't *read*. They thought, because we went to Penn State, stuff happened to us, too.

It was just so emotional, just to finally get to that Friday.

When the sun rose above the Allegheny Mountains of Central Pennsylvania the following morning, the Nittany Lion faithful came out in force once again, eager to turn the page on the darkest chapter in Penn State history.

The players came streaming onto the field from the tunnel with names on their jerseys and light blue ribbon stickers on their helmets to recognize victims of child abuse. Moments later, the PA announcer asked the 97,000 fans in attendance to take part in the tribute by observing a moment of silence. Many later held hands in a ring around the stadium in a show of support for Sandusky's victims.

But deep down the team was not quite ready to move beyond the tragedy. O'Brien's Lions lost a heartbreaker to the Ohio Bobcats and then a second heartbreaker a week later to Virginia.

MATT STANKIEWITCH: Starting off oh-and-two was rough. A lot of people looked at us like, *Wow, you guys really stink.* But those of us inside the locker room knew how good we were.

MICHAEL YANCICH: It didn't seem real at first, losing to Ohio and Virginia. I think everybody was just so caught up in what had happened a few months earlier.

It was Penn State versus the world.

"Look at Penn State, they lost to Ohio. Look at Penn State, they lost to Virginia. Those are easy nonconference games. They're supposed to walk away with a win."

At that time, we all thought, this is it. We got to buckle our chin straps.

JOHN URSCHEL: The game against Ohio, I don't even remember. I must have blocked it out.

DARIAN SOMERS, 2015 PRESIDENT, NITTANYVILLE STUDENT GROUP: They're not even losing to Ohio State at this point—they're losing to *Ohio*. It's like, *How bad are things gonna get?*

KYLE CARTER: I remember Bill Belton scoring the first touchdown of the season. After everything that had happened, it was wild. But it was a tough game. We had a lot of new guys and just didn't know how to finish games yet.

It was a good kick in the mouth.

JORDAN HILL: We lost the fire a bit. They got the momentum and kept it.

With Joe Paterno's wife and children watching from a suite atop the stadium, Penn State moved the ball okay in the first quarter, but struggled the rest of the way, slowly, dishearteningly surrendering an eleven-point halftime lead to a well-coached foe.

There were flashes of promise. Sophomore receiver Allen Robinson made nine catches. And freshman linebacker Nyeem Wartman-White set up the team's second touchdown by racing through the heart of Ohio's line to block a punt. Tight end Matt Lehman, a junior playing in his first game for the Lions, scored a few plays later on a short pass from McGloin.

But the squad made costly mistakes, too. Sophomore Bill Belton, who moved from receiver to running back to replace Silas Redd, spoiled an impressive opening drive with a fumble on the Bobcat twenty-one-yard line. And linebacker Gerald Hodges muffed a punt on the Penn State thirteen. (Yes, the team had a linebacker fielding kicks.)

In the end, the defense simply could not stop Bobcat quarterback Tyler Tettleton and Ohio's fast-paced passing attack.

DEREK DAY: It was an emotional day, but as a team we tried not to get into that. We had one goal and that was to come out and win a football game and we weren't able to get that done. A loss is a loss, and that was unacceptable in our eyes.

The veteran Bobcats team, guided by former Nebraska coach Frank Solich, put the game away in the fourth quarter with a seventeen-play drive that started on its own seven-yard line.

CRAIG FITZGERALD: That Ohio team had a lot of fifth-year seniors, playing at their very best. And so, it was like the perfect storm. We had a team trying to grow and build. And when push came to shove, they just outplayed us. You can't snap your fingers and say we're going to get hardened. You've got to go through the process, get tough by playing.

That's one of the moments that sticks out to me. It was like, This is going to be hard.

STEPHON MORRIS: The support, the love, was there on game day, but we weren't ready for it and it showed. We were excited to play football, but that emotion got the best of us. It drained us real fast.

CRAIG FITZGERALD: What kind of team are we?

We didn't know.

Our guys had to learn what's *good* in the second half, figure out what that means.

STEPHON MORRIS: We felt like we'd let the world down. We were going to keep fighting, but we didn't know if we'd be any good, because McGloin wasn't McGloin yet; Allen Robinson wasn't Allen Robinson yet; Zach Zwinak wasn't Zach Zwinak yet.

We really didn't know how to trust the process, because that was our first time going to war with Bill O'Brien and we had lost some pieces we'd usually use to fill those roles.

In week two, the magnitude of the shift to a new head coach was still evident, particularly on offense, where the team struggled to execute on

O'Brien's vision. With the coaching staff working feverishly to address per-sonnel issues, even calling plays in a timely manner proved to be difficult.

The defense came up with four takeaways. The offense converted them into just three points.

As the gut-wrenching drama unfolded on TV, all eyes turned to nineteen-year-old kicker Sam Ficken, who would come to epitomize the Lions' early-season shortcomings. In all, the slim sophomore missed four field goals: a forty-yard attempt late in the first quarter . . . A thirty-eight-yard try mid-way through the second quarter . . . A twenty-yard kick late in the third . . .

An extra point attempt after the team's second touchdown drive was blocked.

Ficken's final miss of the day—from forty-two yards out, as time expired—let the Cavaliers escape with a 17–16 win.

MICHAEL YANCICH: Ficken is a fantastic placekicker, but he was a sophomore and we asked him to fill really big shoes.

SAM FICKEN: Me and senior Evan Lewis had battled it out my freshman year to see who was going to start. He won the competition and then went through some struggles of his own.

I got put into a game, had a kick blocked, and they put in Anthony Fera. From that point on, Fera had a tremendous year. When he was named All Big Ten for kicking and punting, I was under the impression I'd be red-shirting the next year. That's where my head was at.

Let's get bigger and stronger my sophomore year.

Once the sanctions were announced and Fera left for Texas, I was like, *I guess that's out the window.*

I actually had a tremendous camp. I kicked really well.

I think it was just the jitters of getting in there and being like, It's my job now—anxiety over some fundamental flaws in my kicking and the perfect storm of the Virginia game.

ALEX BUTTERWORTH: There are certain games where, for one reason or an-other, things don't go right. It happens to every kicker, every punter, and you remember those situations well. If you play another position, a skill position, you can get up, brush it off, and keep moving.

With kicking, it's much more mechanical, much more mental. And so, it's easy for those negative situations to compound. That's one of the things we always talk about on special teams—short memory. You have to have a short memory.

SAM FICKEN: I had a tremendous warmup. I don't think I missed a kick. I was like 13-for-13, all the way back to the fifty-five. And then, you know, I missed that first field goal.

Okay, no big deal. I feel like I know what I did.

Then I missed the second one to the opposite side.

Okay, let's get this under control.

ALEX BUTTERWORTH: Everybody misses, but you miss two in a row and that third kick is gonna be the hardest of your career.

SAM FICKEN: Right before the fourth quarter, I missed a twenty-yard field goal, a tremendously short field goal from the right hash, which is actually more difficult than people give you credit for, because you've got to angle it so much on those college hashes. But, mentally, I was kind of exhausted.

And then, I had an extra point blocked.

JOHN URSCHEL: On offense, we were getting into the red zone, but we were really having trouble there and Ficken was just not having a good day.

JOE JULIUS, KICKER, 2014–16: That's the life of a kicker. It's often just one moment that defines you.

SAM FICKEN: I finally made a field goal with eleven minutes left to put us up by six points. Virginia hadn't moved the ball on us all game, so I take a sigh of relief.

And then, they storm right down the field, go up by one.

Our offense does a good job moving the ball down the field and, unfortunately, I missed the game-winner as time expired.

MATT MCGLOIN: It happens. That's not what won or lost us the game. A couple plays here and there lost it.

BILL O'BRIEN: We had some plays in the red zone we could have called better. I could have called better plays, we could have executed better, so it's never on the kicker alone.

SAM FICKEN: You sign up for that. That's part of the deal of being a kicker.

If it hadn't been so early in my career, it would not have happened, but because of the firestorm with the sanctions, the national media everywhere, coaches recruiting people on campus, it was just wild. And then, you go out and lose the first game.

It was kind of the perfect storm, in terms of my failure and the way it aligned with the outcome of the game. No one cares if you miss four kicks and win by twenty. But people *really* care if you miss four kicks and lose by one.

KYLE CARTER: Losing was rough. But we needed those losses to understand what it takes to win.

STEPHON MORRIS: Going into Navy, we needed to turn things around, which we did. We ended up winning five straight games. So we started to trust the process with O'Brien. Some guys that weren't on anyone's radar—like A-Rob—ended up breaking out.

That first game, we just weren't ready. We were prepared, but weren't ready emotionally. Week two, we were prepared and we were ready emotionally—we just had some tough breaks.

CRAIG FITZGERALD: We knew our team was tough. They were on the road, playing their asses off, and we just didn't know how to win the game yet. But that was a turning point, because if you remember, that's where Bill stood up for Ficken. A bunch of people were writing things on the internet—*internet champions*. And Bill spoke up for Ficken. said, "I'm going to stand up for my kicker." The whole team rallied around Ficken and, of course, Ficken paid us back big time.

BILL O'BRIEN: If you look at the game, should it really have come down to that last kick?

We had four turnovers. We got the ball inside the fifteen-yard line, I think, three times, inside the twenty-yard line once and came away with a field goal.

SPIDER CALDWELL: After that game, Gerald Hodges went up to Ficken in the locker room and said, "Listen to me. Everybody, listen. We're sticking by this guy. This guy's our brother. Don't look down on what he did today, because we could have done other things better."

He was yelling, "We have your back and we're still going to need you this year."

Ficken ended up having a great year. Now he's kicking in the NFL.

SAM FICKEN: Right after the game, I was pretty devastated, keeping to myself. But a ton of guys came up and patted me on the head. Like, "Head up, dude."

STEPHON MORRIS: We told him to keep his head up. We were all going through the same thing.

MATT STANKIEWITCH: People called it Stickin' with Ficken. I remember my family and friends calling it Stickin' with Ficken.

JOHN URSCHEL: At that point, we were oh-and-two and we really sort of . . . O'Brien was stressing not to panic, not to lose our minds, keep doing what you're doing.

I'm sure he was stressed, but panicking doesn't do anyone any good.

BILL O'BRIEN: The guys were learning a new system on offense and defense and a lot of the things we were doing football-wise were different from what they had done in the past.

There were some growing pains. And the guys were frustrated, because we all knew we had the makings of a good football team.

I'll never forget the Monday after the Virginia game, when we came back to work, our guys practiced really hard. We knew then as a coaching staff that we had a resilient bunch of guys.

THIRTEEN

BATTLING IN THE BIG TEN

WITH BACK-TO-BACK WINS *against Navy and Temple, Penn State's players exhibited their grit, but they still had a lot to prove before anyone would consider calling the 2012 season a success. It's one thing to beat the Midshipmen and the Owls and yet another to conquer the challenges that awaited them in the Big Ten Conference, where even a perennial underdog can make you look foolish.*

While tight-knit and physically fit, the team had glaring weak spots. Bill O'Brien had not yet found a reliable back (or two) to replace Silas Redd. He had not resolved his kicking-game issue. And he was still struggling to rein in the miscues—fumbles, dropped passes, penalties—that kept the Nittany Lions from capitalizing on favorable field position.

There were dozens of things to straighten out before the coach could hope to challenge the Big Ten's premier programs. But, to his great fortune, he had a team of hardworking, high-character guys. And, as they prepared to board a flight for their first conference showdown, they had an extra incentive to play well: They were off to Illinois, home of Tim Beckman, the coach who had worked so feverishly to raid their roster in July.

KAREN CALDWELL: JoePa had this saying: Take care of the little things and the big things take care of themselves. I used it in my classroom a lot.

Coach O'Brien, he had a saying, too: Know your job, do your job. Real simple . . . Know your job, do your job.

MATT MCGLOIN: When you look back, everyone knew what their job was. Big or small, everybody embraced their role. Just accepted it. And that's hard to do in college football or the NFL: have guys willing to contribute, even if it's on special teams, even if it's playing just a little defense here and there, not getting a lot of carries, not getting a lot of reps. Guys just wanted to be part of that 2012 team. That's what was really special.

BILL O'BRIEN: It's always been part of my philosophy, even when I was a player.

I wasn't great, I just loved to play. If they asked me to switch positions, I'd do it at a moment's notice, just to help the team.

When I went to Georgia Tech, that was a big part of what we did; and at Maryland with Ralph Friedgen; and in New England—that's where I really saw what that sort of thinking meant for a successful season.

At Penn State, guys like Mike Yancich, Mike Hull, Ben Kline, Michael Zordich, Brandon Moseby-Felder—they went in there and accepted their roles on special teams. Maybe they started some games, backed up other games, but at the end of the day, they helped the team win.

ERIC SHRIVE: One game, we didn't even have a running back. Mike Zordich—a fullback—ended up playing tailback. And he was successful. Very successful.

It was just win-by-committee.

ALLEN ROBINSON: We had Gerald Hodges, a linebacker, catching punts!

MATT MCGLOIN: I think they even asked Mike Mauti if he'd ever play offense.

ERIC SHRIVE: You had young guys like tight end Jesse James stepping up. Receiver Allen Robinson was born that year. Some of those guys are making big money now in the NFL. Robinson, safety Adrian Amos, defensive tackle DaQuan Jones, left tackle Donovan Smith. That team had a lot of talent.

TIM SWEENEY: The way OB and his coaching staff got those guys to grind every week with that us-versus-the-world mentality—when everybody thought they probably wouldn't win a game—it's arguably the most incredible season in the history of college football.

MATT MCGLOIN: That's something O'Brien talked about all the time—ignoring the noise. One day at a time, just continuing to march forward.

MATT STANKIEWITCH: I wasn't on social media. My brother and my parents filtered things for me, made sure I wasn't hearing anything that would distract me.

I was so focused on what we needed to do to win. Bill made that very simple.

By week five, O'Brien's "game-plan offense" was beginning to blossom. Rooted in the pro-style alchemy he had learned from Ralph Friedgen at Georgia Tech and Maryland, it relied heavily on players to read and react to the defense, shifting schemes, assignments, sometimes even roles, based on what they saw.

ALLEN ROBINSON: My rookie year in the NFL, we didn't have any sight adjustments on blitz.

I'm like, there's no sight adjustment in this offense?

And they're like, nah.

I'm like, in college, I ran sight adjustments off the will linebacker and the free safety. I knew how to adjust my routes, based on protections.

BILL O'BRIEN: The system we ran requires a quarterback that could think fast. You had to process stuff very quickly, pre-snap and post-snap, and Matt McGloin worked at it. Guys that are good in that system love it, because it's a challenge. Every day is a challenge, every game plan is a challenge. Every week is different.

MATT MCGLOIN: If you ask Coach O'Brien, he'll tell you, he just calls the play. It's up to you to see what front they're in, see what coverage they're in, and basically get the offense into the right play. The main objective is to run good plays. We didn't want to go out there and run any bad plays at all.

It's a very difficult and challenging offense, but we worked so hard on it throughout the spring, throughout the summer, throughout camp, until we hit our stride and got comfortable with it.

One wrinkle O'Brien introduced to the attack was an up-tempo, no-huddle "NASCAR" scheme used to put defenders on their heels. In an instant, even mid-drive, the Lions might shift into high gear, forcing opponents to abandon substitutions. The players believed this gave them a slight edge, thanks to Fitz's off-season workouts. "They get tired and we continue to push," said Matt McGloin.

In a dramatic departure from Joe Paterno's conservative, field-position approach to football, O'Brien often opted to leave the ball in McGloin's hands on fourth down, too. In the first four games, he went with his veteran quarterback instead of his young punter or his placekicker ten times and the Lions converted on seven of them.

KYLE CARTER: They often talk about analytics now, but O'Brien was early to that train. We appreciated it as players, because we were only there for so long. We didn't have a bowl game. So let us go out there and try to win as many games as possible.

MATT STANKIEWITCH: Bill let us know at the beginning of the season that he'd go for it on fourth down. His thinking was, if we didn't get the first down, we had a defense powerful enough to get the ball back and an offense that could go right down the field again. If you had a passing game, which we established throughout the year, you could go down the field in less than a minute. So going for it on fourth down was not as risky.

BILL O'BRIEN: Once we got close to the fifty, I was not going to punt. We were going to go for it, unless it was fourth down and forever. We prepared the kids for it.

MICHAEL ZORDICH: We loved it. It was an attitude kind of play.

We wanted touchdowns. That's what offense is about. If we needed to go for it and we were in the right field position, that's what we were going to do.

ALLEN ROBINSON: We looked at fourth down as a *redeem* play. If we did not get a lot of yardage on first down or second down, we could make it up on fourth down.

MATT STANKIEWITCH: I had two guards next to me—Urschel and Dieffenbach—that would fire off the ball very nicely. But Matt as a quarterback knew how to ride the center, too.

He was very good at reading how I was going to fire off the ball, making sure his hands were there, so there was no fumble. If I snap the ball and I'm trying to reach a nose guard. Let's say the nose guard is shaved a bit to me. So we're looking eye to eye, but he steps over and now he's on my shoulder. Well, my snap is going to be at a different angle. If Matt doesn't follow with his hands, he's going to miss that snap.

But Matt also changed a lot of those fourth-down calls from Bill O'Brien to a quarterback sneak, using the code words "dog, dog."

There are two things we know on offense: the play call and the snap count. We don't come up to the ball and use the same play every single time, so why use the same snap count? We're not just saying, "Hey, how are you today?" It all means something.

The cadence we used was "dog, dog." I don't know why it's called "dog, dog." You'll have to ask Bill O'Brien. But "dog, dog" means quarterback sneak and "blue go" was the cadence. The rhythm and cadence has to be in sync for all of us to fire off the ball at the same time. So some of those fourth-down play calls were changed by Matt to a QB sneak. Most of the time, he'd sneak to the left side, between me and Urschel.

The team would continue to employ the tactic to great effect, converting on nineteen of thirty-four fourth-down attempts in 2012.

ILLINOIS—SEPTEMBER 29, 2012

With a 10–7 victory against the Fighting Illini in 2011, Penn State's players had secured win number 409 for Joe Paterno, inching him ahead of Eddie Robinson of Grambling as the winningest coach in Division I football history. Seven days later, Jerry Sandusky was arrested, sending Paterno and his program into a spiral.

And, as the players on the 2012 team remembered well, the Illini's first-year head coach Tim Beckman had seized on that chaos, sending not one, not two, but eight assistants to State College in an all-out effort to siphon talent from their locker room.

For Michael Mauti, in particular, the September 29 matchup between the two teams—both with 2–2 records—was an opportunity to settle the score.

STEPHON MORRIS: You should have seen him before the game. He was amped. Banging his head against the locker and all this stuff. He had the defense going.

ADRIAN AMOS: When Mauti gets revved up, it gets the whole team revved up.

GERALD HODGES: He really took this game personally. He showed how personally when he stepped on the field.

In the highlight of the afternoon, the team's fiery leader intercepted a pass at the goal line and returned it nearly the length of the field. "Ninety-nine yards without a touchdown," he joked. "That one's gonna hurt."

In all, the linebacker recorded six tackles, a forced fumble, and two pivotal pickoffs versus the Illini. The Lions ran off with a 35–7 win.

MATT STANKIEWITCH: We hit the pedal and didn't let up.

MICHAEL MAUTI: It was sweet.

Matt McGloin had a solid day at quarterback, completing eighteen passes, including a twenty-one-yard strike to tight end Matt Lehman for the Lions' third touchdown. He added two more scores with QB sneaks. But the big breakthrough came in the rushing attack, where redshirt sophomore Zach Zwinak—the son of a high school track star and a Virginia Tech nose tackle—emerged as a go-to back, rumbling through would-be tacklers for one hundred yards and a pair of TDs.

CHARLES LONDON, RUNNING BACKS COACH: Going into the season, Zwinak was probably fourth on the depth chart, but he just kept working, kept getting better, and waited for his opportunity to come. We always told him, when it comes, you need to take advantage of it. In mid-September, he had an opportunity and never looked back.

MATT STANKIEWITCH: We were able to run the ball in the middle of the field, because Zwinak really fit our offense nicely. He was bigger and stronger than Silas.

BILL O'BRIEN: He's a tough kid, faster than people think, and 235 pounds—a punishing runner.

MATT STANKIEWITCH: Losing Silas was a big blow. He was good on contact—would always get yards after the first hit and fall forward for two to three extra yards. With his speed, we could run the ball outside, too.

We tried Derek Day at running back that season, but he just didn't have the speed or size. When we finally figured out that Zwinak was our back, running the ball outside was not an option. So we had to do a lot of play action, which suited Matt nicely, because the defense was worried about Zwinak running the ball up the middle.

After the Illinois game, it was like, now we know we can run the ball. That opens up our passing game.

When the contest ended, Bill O'Brien raced out to midfield, barely pausing to acknowledge Tim Beckman, much less shake his hand. For all the ill will he generated, the Illini coach had just one souvenir from his midsummer raid in State College—and lineman Ryan Nowicki would not play a single down in Illini gear before transferring to Northern Arizona, where he finished his career less than 140 miles from his childhood home.

The Illini coach lost his job after the 2014 season, closing out his tenure with twelve wins and twenty-five losses.

NORTHWESTERN—OCTOBER 6, 2012

Bill O'Brien's players faced a much stiffer challenge when they welcomed Northwestern to Beaver Stadium for the homecoming game. The 5–0 Wildcats were coming off their most potent offensive performance in school history, a seven-hundred-yard outburst against the Indiana Hoosiers. In an inspired bit of brinkmanship, head coach Pat Fitzgerald had turned a talented junior named Kain Colter into a triple-threat quarterback, shifting him from passer to runner to, yes, wide receiver throughout the game. His passing numbers were ho-hum (one completion for two yards), but he logged fourteen carries for 161 yards and nine catches for 131 more.

DARIAN SOMERS: Northwestern was ranked number twenty-one in the country and a Penn State player had gotten ahold of then-Nittanyville president Troy Weller days before the game, saying, "Hey, we really could use your help this week—what can we do?"

Weller and the other Nittanyville execs were like, "Let's have a student White Out."

That Wednesday night, we went through East Halls putting up banners, any campus building that was unlocked at nine or ten o'clock, and hung those banners.

If you go back and watch the videos of that game, everybody in the student section was wearing white. They all got the message. It was such a grassroots moment.

BILL O'BRIEN: We asked the students to be out there early. They were there, in force, standing up.

ALLEN ROBINSON: This was a game we needed to get. A statement game. They were undefeated—good offense, good defense. We knew it was going to be a challenge and we were excited for that challenge.

DONNIE COLLINS, COLUMNIST, SCRANTON *TIMES-TRIBUNE*: That game went, until the end of the third quarter, exactly as you'd picture it. Penn State used a lot of Zach Zwinak, took an early lead. Northwestern comes back. Then Penn State takes the lead. Then Northwestern got it back. And, at the end of the third quarter, the one play that can't happen for Penn State happens.

After leading 17–14, the Lions had surrendered a rushing touchdown to Colter on an eleven-play drive, and then—after an uninspired four-

play response from Penn State—the Wildcats scored again on a seventy-five-yard punt return, jumping ahead eleven points with the final quarter looming.

"I think the punter outkicked his coverage," said Pat Fitzgerald. "Nobody touched the return man."

VENRIC MARK, NORTHWESTERN RUNNING BACK/RETURN MAN: You could tell the Lions did a lot of film study. They knew we were going to go right. I knew they knew we were going to go right, too, so I went left. There was no one there but the kicker and one other guy.

We had them 28–17 after that return.

KYLE CARTER: It took a lot of the air out of the crowd.

BILL O'BRIEN: We had to gather on the sideline and point out that there was a lot of time left. Think there were about fifty seconds to go in the third quarter. Our kids really bowed up and played some good football in that fourth quarter.

CHARLIE FISHER: That game stands out as a turning point for Matt Mc-Gloin, because we were behind, fighting for our life, and he played well in the second half, made a lot of really good decisions.

KYLE CARTER: At that moment, as a team, we just needed somebody to say something, do something, and lo and behold, Matt comes into that huddle during a TV timeout, looks everybody in the eye and says, "I live for these moments. I don't know about you all, but I love this."

MATT MCGLOIN: We had a full quarter to play and we'd been able to move the ball all day—we had just stopped ourselves a few times. The crowd was still into it. We were, too.

MICHAEL ZORDICH: A lot of things went the Wildcats' way in the third quarter, but nobody on the team put their heads down. We just kept moving forward.

ALLEN ROBINSON: Coach O'Brien preached all week about keeping plays going, putting drives together and points on the board. We knew we needed to put points on the board to win.

The Lions' off-season conditioning once again played a role in the outcome.

MICHAEL ZORDICH: We were calling the same plays, doing the same things, but they were starting to break. That's what offense does to defense. You keep moving and hopefully wear them down.

PAT FITZGERALD, HEAD COACH, NORTHWESTERN: We were on the field for a long time. When you get worn out on defense, you're going to give up plays. In the first half, our defense kept us in the game. But the time of possession, as the game wore on, obviously wore us down.

MATT STANKIEWITCH: I think we had like ninety plays on offense. In a college game, you're generally looking at seventy to seventy-five. So, if you're up in the nineties, you're really controlling the ball.

With Matt McGloin and Zach Zwinak chipping away at the Wildcats' resolve, Penn State moved the ball seventy yards, setting up a fourth-and-four on Northwestern's six-yard line with 9:49 remaining. The team had already converted four of five fourth-down attempts. McGloin's next pass made it five-of-six.

CHARLIE FISHER: He hit Allen Robinson in the back of the end zone. That was a huge play. Matt scrambled around a bit, stayed patient in the pocket, and found Allen on the back line.

ALLEN ROBINSON: I ran an in-route, and Matt had a lot of time in the pocket. There was no one in the middle of the field, so he was able to give me a good ball.

O'Brien decided to try for a two-point conversion. Michael Zordich took the handoff from McGloin, sprinted left, then broke quickly toward the end zone, and powered his way in from the three-yard line to cut Northwestern's lead to three.

The defense took the field, looking to stop a Wildcat attack that had piled up 394 yards rushing and 310 yards passing one week earlier.

MICHAEL MAUTI: We knew what we needed to do. It just came down to executing our assignments, making the plays when we needed to make them.

GERALD HODGES: We were going to keep pushing forward and come out with a victory.

Northwestern gained four yards in three plays.

Penn State had the ball back on its own fifteen-yard line with eight minutes to go. McGloin got right to work, hitting Brandon Moseby-Felder, Allen Robinson, Kyle Carter, and Matt Lehman in a fifteen-play drive to the Wildcat five-yard line.

CHARLIE FISHER: Then Matt had that scramble—one of the worst quarterback slides of his life, down near the goal line. He had this big knee brace on and did a hook slide towards the pylon. The brace stuck in the turf and he flipped over. Not the most aesthetic play, but that's kind of who Matt is, you know? The ultimate grinder.

MATT MCGLOIN: When I make the turn and I see the pylon, I know I'm going to run. I'm thinking the whole time, I'm diving, man, I'm diving.

BILL O'BRIEN: Somebody blew the protection and Matt made a nice instinctive play, scrambled to his right and scored.

CRAIG FITZGERALD: When you had Matt McGloin, you felt you always had a chance, because he was going to will the offense to score. Watch the Northwestern game. I mean, that's Matt. Eleven-point deficit and here you go. He was Never Say Die. Tough as shit.

You couldn't have just a big-time talent at quarterback that year. If the guy didn't have grit, it wouldn't have worked. You needed a guy that played tough, played hurt, accepted no excuses.

Leading 32–28, the Lions added one last touchdown, after another defensive stop and a twenty-five-yard run by Michael Zordich. One play later, Zordich crossed the goal line from three yards out to seal the win.

BILL O'BRIEN: What impressed me about that team and that coaching staff through six games, training camp, and spring practice is the poise, the ability to focus, to understand the task at hand and not worry about all the things you could not control.

IOWA—OCTOBER 20, 2012

Iowa City, home of the Hawkeyes, had long been a trouble spot for the Nittany Lions. They had not left the place with a victory in more than a decade.

Kinnick Stadium seats 69,000—roughly 40,000 less than Beaver Stadium—but the stands sit so close to the field the fans are right at your back when you're on the sideline. And on this night the crowd was pumped up, spurred on by a prime-time TV matchup pitting the 4–2 Hawkeyes against the 4–2 Lions.

Over the years, Penn State had struggled to muster offense here, losing 24–3, 24–23, 26–14, and 24–18. But things would be different this time. With Bill Belton, fully recovered from an early-season ankle injury, slashing through the line and Matt McGloin adding big chunks through the air, Penn State raced out to a fourteen-point lead and didn't let up, stretching the margin to 38–0 before yielding a pair of late touchdowns in the fourth quarter.

By then, the Kinnick Stadium fans had moved on to booing the Hawkeyes.

STEPHON MORRIS: Winning the Iowa game was the turning point of our season. That's when we really began to gel as a team. In the first half of the season, we didn't play anybody we couldn't beat. But that rivalry with Iowa, especially a night game, can go either way, and the way we put our foot on their necks for the entire game, that was a turning point. You could just see, when you got back to that locker room, how joyful everyone was. We thought we were special.

CRAIG FITZGERALD: Nobody goes to Iowa and lights them up, right? We did that.

MATT STANKIEWITCH: That was a night game. Really hostile stadium. They're right on top of you. Really close to the sideline. And don't care that you're a college athlete.

"Stankiewitch, what type of name is that? F-bomb, F-bomb, F-bomb."

They call it the Beehive. They have a black stripe, yellow stripe, then black strip all around the stadium.

We got booed so hard coming onto the field, everyone's dropping Sandusky slurs, and we shut them up so quickly, it was awesome.

Gracefully gliding around the pocket, sizing up the defense, and stepping into his throws, Matt McGloin directed Bill O'Brien's offense like an ace fighter pilot, connecting with nine different wide receivers before the night was through.

MATT STANKIEWITCH: For the first time since, like, Kyle Brady in the '90s, we were utilizing our tight ends and all sorts of wide receivers. Matt Lehman, a guy who probably never would have seen the field under Joe Paterno, caught a lot of passes that year. Allen Robinson made big plays for us. And Brandon Felder, who's probably not a first-string guy if Justin Brown is around, really stepped up.

KYLE CARTER: I was a redshirt freshman. I hadn't played in college at all. Had to really earn my stripes from the start of spring ball. Bill O'Brien came in there and said everybody has a fair shake and, like I said, I started at the bottom of the depth chart.

I tried to make a play every opportunity I got. And by the end of spring ball—shoot, five weeks—I was the starting F tight end. Playing in that Aaron Hernandez role used by the New England Patriots.

Once I got that starting F role, I held it down.

BILL O'BRIEN: Here's a guy—a young player—that came in trying to learn a very difficult position. Offensively, it's the second hardest position to learn behind quarterback. You're involved in the running game, protection, route running, you have to recognize coverage. There are so many things you have to know, and, as a young player, he came in and did a really nice job.

At Iowa, playing in his first night game, Carter made six catches for eighty-five yards—all in the first half—en route to Big Ten Freshman of the Week honors. Thirty-four of the yards came on a fourth-down catch-and-run play in which he deftly reached over a defensive back's head, plucked the ball from the air, tucked it under his arm, and rumbled to the eleven-yard line. That set up the touchdown that put the Lions ahead 14–0.

KYLE CARTER: Once the conference season rolled around, I was making plays left and right. Matt McGloin and I had a great relationship. We had the same feel for space. Saw the field the same way. If he was running around, I'd get open and he'd throw me the ball. We made a lot of plays that way, Matt scrambling around and finding me when the defense was blitzing. I was there for him as a safety outlet.

OHIO STATE—OCTOBER 27, 2012

The Penn State campus practically hums the week of the Ohio State game. You can feel the excitement in the air. And this go-round was no different. Students showed up in record numbers to camp outside the stadium a full six days before the kickoff.

The Buckeyes, led by sophomore quarterback Braxton Miller, were ineligible for a bowl bid, too, serving a one-year ban after eight players from the 2010 team (coached by Jim Tressel) had been caught swapping Buckeye memorabilia for tattoos and money.

Penn State took the early lead after Mike Hull zipped unblocked through Ohio State's line to block a punt and Michael Yancich recovered the ball in the end zone. Less than a minute later, the Lions had the Buckeyes pinned in a fourth-and-eight on their own twenty-seven-yard line, but a questionable defensive holding penalty put the ball back in Miller's hands. Eight plays after that he handed the ball off to Carlos Hyde for the tying touchdown.

The game was deadlocked at 7–7 at the half.

Matt McGloin, pressured all night long by a formidable Buckeye front seven, threw an interception returned seventeen yards for an Ohio State touchdown on the opening drive of the second half, then steered the Lions downfield for a Sam Ficken field goal.

Moments later, Adrian Amos intercepted Braxton Miller at the Buckeye forty-four, but the Lions could not capitalize on the miscue. After a one-yard run by Zwinak, McGloin was sacked for an eight-yard loss. He got those yards back on a pass to Zwinak.

On fourth-and-nine from the OSU forty-three, Bill O'Brien called a fake punt, but the pass from Alex Butterworth landed short of its intended target. "We had it," said O'Brien. "We just didn't execute it well."

Penalties and mental errors doomed PSU drives the rest of the night. As Braxton Miller settled into his role as quarterback, the Buckeyes rattled off back-to-back touchdown drives to put the game away. Final score: Ohio State 35, Penn State 23.

The team rebounded one week later at Purdue, despite arriving late to Indiana on Friday night because of plane trouble. Disheartened by a lack of energy in the players, strength coach Craig Fitzgerald stripped the shirt from his back during the pregame stretch, started running, and launched himself arms-first into a bellyflop on the turf.

In an instant, the players were at his side, laughing, cheering, and leaping up and down.

That seemed to do the trick. With Zach Zwinak and Matt McGloin pacing the offense on the ground and through the air, the team rolled past Purdue 34–9.

The win was especially sweet for Sam Ficken, born and raised in nearby Valparaiso. It took twenty-seven tickets to get his family and friends into the game. He ended the day two-for-two on field goal tries.

NEBRASKA—NOVEMBER 10, 2012

On the second Saturday of November, the players got another chance to prove themselves—on the road against the No. 18 team in the country. A program they admired and had battled in a highly emotional contest in 2011, just three days after the university had dismissed Joe Paterno.

Before the kickoff, players from both teams had gathered at midfield in Beaver Stadium, taking a knee and holding hands as Nebraska running backs coach Ron Brown led them in prayer. The game essentially ended on

*a fourth-and-one stop on Penn State's thirty-seven-yard line with 1:49 re-
maining. Silas Redd had fallen short.*

The bewildered Lions lost 17–14.

*In Lincoln, Nebraska, the 2012 Lions opened with a 20–6 lead, then gave
up back-to-back touchdowns. The Huskers took their first lead of the game
on a five-yard toss from Taylor Martinez to Jamal Turner with 10:57 to go.*

Nebraska 27, Penn State 23.

*Four plays later, Allen Robinson slipped behind the Husker secondary
and McGloin hit him for a thirty-eight-yard gain. After another Robinson
catch and a few runs, Penn State was looking at second-and-goal from the
three.*

That's when the referees intervened.

MATT STANKIEWITCH: Nebraska was pretty good back then. I don't know
what they're doing now, but when we faced them in 2011 and 2012 they
were pretty good.

Awesome stadium, awesome atmosphere. We were able to move the
ball.

BILL O'BRIEN: We had some good drives there in the second half. We just
didn't come away with touchdowns. We either turned it over or kicked
field goals.

*In this case, it was a contested turnover that burned the team. On
second-and-goal from the three, O'Brien went with an empty backfield. Mc-
Gloin took the snap and threw a quick swing pass to Lehman, who caught it
and knifed between three Nebraska defenders. At the goal line, the ball was
knocked from his outstretched arms by a defender's knee.*

Nebraska recovered it in the end zone and the referees called it a fumble.

*The replay on ABC showed the tight end breaking the plane with the ball
in his hands.*

*"I think that's a touchdown," said play-by-play announcer Sean Mc-
Donough. "What do you think?"*

"I think you're absolutely right," replied analyst Chris Spielman.

KYLE CARTER: To this day, I say Matt Lehman scored that touchdown.

MATT STANKIEWITCH: As they're reviewing the play, we're all standing on the sideline and the Penn State crowd is chanting, "Reverse it. Reverse it."

They show the replay on the Jumbotron, the side view, looking down the goal line, and clearly he had possession of the ball when it reached the top of the goal line. All it needs to do is break the plane. He had it in his hand.

The whole crowd goes silent, because they know it's a touchdown. We're all slapping hands on the sideline.

Well, the ref comes out and upholds the call on the field.

The crowd didn't even know how to react. All 85,000 or whatever knew it was a touchdown, because they saw it on the Jumbotron.

I can't believe the refs could get a call like that wrong.

MICHAEL YANCICH: I won't go into specifics, but I think someone *did* cross the goal line with the ball intact. But that play received a Big Ten official review and they said he didn't. You've got to just put your head down and keep playing and that's what we did.

BILL O'BRIEN: We thought it was over the goal line, but the referees did not think they could reverse it. There wasn't enough evidence to reverse the call.

Nebraska took possession, then pinned Penn State down at the two with a sixty-nine-yard punt. On second down, under pressure in the end zone, McGloin stepped to his right and threw the ball away. The referees flagged him for intentional grounding. The safety put Nebraska up 29–23.

Penn State got another crack at offense with under three minutes left, but turned the ball over on downs, leaving the Huskers in position for one last field goal.

STEPHON MORRIS: That game hurt us more as a team than losing to Ohio, because we fought like hell. We fought, we fought like hell that game. I'm not a crier, but afterwards, I went into the locker room and saw Mauti crying, banging against a locker, and I'm just in *tears*.

I can't even tell you what we were crying for. We were just . . . We wanted that game. We felt like we had to have that game.

If you remember, we held hands with the Huskers on the field the year prior. To lose to them twice, to lose the way we did, where Matt Lehman scored and they called it a fumble. It was just . . . we were hurt. We felt like all season long the referees were not calling things our way. So that Nebraska game just . . . it crushed us. It really did.

The locker room was just . . . we were hurt.

It was quiet on the plane ride back. Bill O'Brien wasn't speechless, but he didn't have much to say.

MATT STANKIEWITCH: Bill was watching the game on an iPad. I remember talking with my brother on the phone. He's snapping out, saying that was a touchdown.

I said to Bill, "They're talking about it on ESPN, how that call was such bullshit."

He's like, "Yeah, that's bullshit."

AUDREY SNYDER: After the game, we were in this cramped, visiting-team media room and it was my job to take videos. I remember Matt McGloin going off. He's like, "We're not going to get that call. Not here, not anywhere."

The players had this legitimate belief that they weren't going to get the benefit of the doubt on calls. They were like, "Yeah, we knew we were never going to get a call like that, because of what had happened at Penn State."

Is there truth to that? You can never get the answer, because Big Ten officiating, as we've seen over time, is its own mess, but it's a really interesting theory.

I remember getting on the plane the next day, flying out of Lincoln, and that was the picture, front and center, in the newspaper. Matt Lehman, reaching across the goal line and the ball right there. It was one of those moments where, yeah, you could definitely see how that call probably should have gone the other way.

FOURTEEN

LOSING MAUTI

WITH THE NEBRASKA *showdown behind them, the end was near for Penn State's seniors.*

With no bowl game to round out their college careers, they tried to savor each moment, steep themselves in the fleeting bonds of sport and youth and autumn afternoons in Beaver Stadium.

"You've got to make the most of every single Saturday," said Michael Mauti.

But football's a fickle sport. It rarely lets you decide for yourself when to call it quits. All too often, the frailty of the human body conspires to wrest that judgment from your hands.

Mauti was acutely aware of this enigma. In the summer of 2009, his sophomore season was cut short by a tear in the anterior cruciate ligament in his right knee, and in 2011 a similar tear in his left knee abruptly halted a promising redshirt senior season. And so, it was truly devastating for the linebacker and his teammates when the fragility of flesh and bone ended his final season—the most storied of his career—just two games shy of the curtain call.

MICHAEL MAUTI: Dealing with injuries is just part of the game. You've got to be a little lucky to stay healthy, especially playing a position as physical as linebacker.

MICHAEL ZORDICH: It's a funny game, a crazy game, and things are going to happen. You have to bounce back, have to keep going.

Penn State was at home against Indiana, a team that had lost six of its first ten games, including a 31–30 squeaker to Navy. Midway through the first quarter, with the score tied at zero, the Hoosiers' Isaiah Roundtree took a handoff from quarterback Cameron Coffman and rushed for four yards. Mauti had his feet squared, arms wrapped with a lineman, as the play unfolded. Roundtree's lead blocker launched himself at Mauti's legs, buckling the linebacker's left knee.

Mauti collapsed in a heap of bodies. As the players rose one by one from the pile, their spirited leader remained flat on his back, hands gripping the top of his facemask, obscuring his eyes.

The crowd went silent.

CRAIG FITZGERALD: Tim Bream gave me a look when he came off the field like, *This isn't good*—and I said, "Oh, jeez."

MATT STANKIEWITCH: I was on the bench looking through offensive stuff. I didn't even know who was hurt until someone said it was Mauti. Then, of course, you get that feeling in your stomach.

JORDAN HILL: My heart dropped. It was just like, Here we go again. It's hard to think about it.

MICHAEL YANCICH: It was like, What do we do now?

MATT MCGLOIN: You cannot replace a guy like that.

GERALD HODGES: I gave a quick prayer. Told him I loved him—loved him like a brother.

STEVE JONES: I thought, *Oh, no, of all the kids to have this happen.* He'd already gone through two ACL tears. Eighteen to twenty months of rehabilitation in his lifetime at Penn State.

The players hovered on the field as the team doctors attended to their fallen leader.

Mauti left the arena on a cart.

To those in Penn State jerseys, he was more than just a trusted voice. He led the team in tackles, interceptions, and forced fumbles, anchoring a defense that had been called on time and again to help the players on offense and special teams overcome early struggles.

MICHAEL YANCICH: When we got together as a team, we said, Hey, listen, we're going to make this thing work. It's a crazy loss, but it's not about one person. Like Mike said, One person didn't make Penn State, one person isn't going to bring Penn State down.

JOHN URSCHEL: We gathered together to say we have to get this done. Even though we've lost our senior leader, we have to go out and play hard to get this win for him.

GERALD HODGES: We had to lift each other up.

Junior Mike Hull took the field in Mauti's place. The defense soon forced the Hoosiers to punt and Matt McGloin directed the offense through a ninety-one-yard scoring drive, one that culminated with a leaping, fourth-down catch by Allen Robinson.

Indiana answered with a field goal and a touchdown of its own, but McGloin and Robinson went to work once again, connecting on a fifty-three-yard pass play—the longest of the season.

Penn State led 28–13 at the half.

CRAIG FITZGERALD: In the locker room, Mike was devastated he couldn't play with his teammates. He wasn't thinking about his NFL career, why he stayed there, none of that.

Mike stayed in the program for everybody else. He could have left and had first-line talent all around him, but he didn't. And so, Mike sat around saying, "Hey, Fitz, keep these guys going. We need to win this game."

He's got tears in his eyes.

STEPHON MORRIS: It's heartbreaking. But, if you dwell on it, you're going to give up plays. We just had to keep going, play for him. We were all thinking, *Just play for Mauti.*

By game's end, the team had put together four long scoring drives for a season-high 546 yards in total offense. The defense surrendered 454 passing yards but held the Hoosiers to twenty-two points. Hull finished the afternoon with a career-high eleven tackles.

All the while Mauti wrestled with what comes next.

MICHAEL MAUTI: Yeah, every time you get hurt, that thought goes through your mind—is it time to stop? For me, it was, I know I can play. I know I'm good enough. And if there's a way to get over this hurdle, then that's all it's going to be when I look back on it. The rest is just problem solving.

After the first injury, it's like, Okay, it's just one ACL. After the second, you play mind tricks on yourself, because you've got to get back to the level where you can stick that foot in the ground. That's a whole other mental challenge. The third ACL? That was probably the most difficult.

MATT MCGLOIN: Everyone is tough physically. You play football, you've got to be tough. Got to be a different cat. But, mentally, it's different. There are certain levels of how tough you can be.

MICHAEL MAUTI: I'd had two previous knee injuries, so it was . . . well, frustrating is not the word. I was playing the best football of my career and here we were having one of the most memorable seasons and I couldn't finish it. That was a tough pill to swallow.

STEPHON MORRIS: It was tough, because he was one of our leaders, but also because of his injury history. Defensively, we knew we were going to have some drop-off, but we trusted Mike Hull. You remember how good Michael Hull was, right? And, of course, we had Gerald Hodges.

Losing Mauti was tough. But the motto was the same.

Mauti would say it himself: Continue the Mission.

Hull—whom Mauti had convinced to stay at Penn State—took his place on the field and responded with not just a career-high eleven tackles, but also one sack and a pass breakup. With the 45–22 victory, the Lions clinched a winning record for the season.

Mauti returned to the sideline on crutches in the fourth quarter. He joined the team in singing the alma mater in front of the student section at Beaver Stadium.

CRAIG FITZGERALD: In the locker room after the game, he was hugging the guys, congratulating them. He was tearing up, because he was sad and he was hurt, but he was fired up for the team.

He participated in everything that next week. On Thursday night, we had a team meeting with the seniors, let them get up and speak. It was something John Butler had brought with him from his days as a coach at Harvard. On the Thursday before the Yale game, the seniors would get up and speak. Talk about their careers. Five minutes, twenty, whatever.

For the coaches, it's an unbelievable experience. It reinforces why you do what you do.

Mike went last. It was all about how happy he was that he stayed, how proud he was of the group, how he was going to be on the sideline coaching, how he wanted to win this next game more than any other game. I mean, that's the kind of guy he is. He turned it into a rally.

MATT MCGLOIN: To see Mike out there, supporting his teammates, after what happened, you couldn't help but realize how special a person he is.

MICHAEL ZORDICH: It's a testament to the type of man he is, the leader he became.

BILL O'BRIEN: He came and saw me that Sunday. I met with him and his parents. It was tough for him. When you're that engrossed, you know . . . he's just a football guy. He loved Penn State, loved his teammates, so it was difficult. I've been around that. I've seen Tom Brady with a knee injury, Wes Welker. For guys that live and breathe the game, it's a difficult thing.

CRAIG FITZGERALD: Mike's parents were there at that Indiana game. They came up from New Orleans. They were going to stay for the Wisconsin game, too. It was Mike's last week of Penn State football, so they wanted to stick around.

They were planning to host a Sunday night dinner for the coaches. They wanted to treat them to jambalaya. They had all the stuff brought up from Louisiana. Gator meat, everything. So Bill calls Mike's dad, Rich Mauti, and says, "Don't worry about all that. Just take care of Mike." And Rich goes, "No, no, Bill, me and my wife and my kids are going to host you guys. We're doing it tomorrow night and there's no getting out of it. We need to do this. We need to have some fun."

And so, we're there. We felt bad for Mike and his family and they're hosting the coaches, telling jokes. They're all about trying to help the coaches relax. The whole time. That's what the Mautis are all about. They were trying to help that team that week. Unbelievable.

The whole week they were hanging out at the football building. Mauti's sisters were in the weight room, working out on the heavy bag. His brother was in there. Rich was in there. They weren't like, we're going to huddle up and be all sad about the knee injury. They were like we're here to support, man. Here to be positive.

Mauti's teammates had something special in store, too.

SPIDER CALDWELL: Jordan Hill and . . . Who came with Jordan? It must have been Zordich. They came to me and said, Spider, is there any way we could put Mauti's number 42 on the side of the helmets? And I said, "Guys, that's more of an administrative decision, you have to go to Coach O'Brien. And then he'll probably have to check with our athletic director."

I said, "I can get this done. But I need to know quickly."

And so, they went to talk to Coach O'Brien and, I guess, he was like, Absolutely. Because he loved Mauti, too. He didn't have a problem with it.

He said, "Well, check with Spider to see if we can get this done."

And they said, "We already did."

I think it was almost Wednesday before I knew for sure. Tuesday or Wednesday. So again, time constraints. I called our sign shop. We have a sign shop on campus. A lot of those signs you see posted around the stadium—they're all made in-house. I knew I couldn't get the things from a sticker company soon enough.

So I said, "Hey, can you guys make me a bunch of 42s? I need at least 125 or 150. I'm just going to put them on one side of the helmet."

"Yeah, yeah," they said, "we can do that for you."

But, like I said, I only had 125 or 150 made. When they got here a couple days later, I was playing around with one and the material they used was real thin. I'm like, son of a gun, these are really hard to put on, especially on a curved helmet. If I have my students do this, they're going to get all crooked and funny and then rip if you try to move them.

So I'm like, All right, it's too late to make any more. I just got to do this myself.

I'm not trying to blow my own horn, but the night before the Wisconsin game, I spent five hours putting those stickers on myself. Because I needed to keep them straight. Keep them looking right.

I just took my time. I said to my wife, Karen, "I'm not coming home. I'm just going to work here and get this done."

When the team gets to the stadium the next day, Mauti and Zordich get off the bus first. Zordich has his arm around Mauti. He brings him into the locker room. I'm just standing there as they come around the corner. They stop and Mauti's looking around. I had all the helmets lined up on the bench with the 42s facing out. His head dropped and he sprinted to the bathroom. Started bawling.

MICHAEL MAUTI: I just folded, man. Took a hard right into the shower and was a basket case.

SPIDER CALDWELL: Zordy's with him. By now, the team's coming in.

Mauti comes back. Comes up to me and gives me a big hug. I said, "You better appreciate this, you son of a bitch. I spent five hours here last night putting these on."

He laughed. Gave me a big hug.

MICHAEL MAUTI: When you're up every day, that's just what you do. That's your role. You don't realize the impact it has on the guys around you. I felt like we all had that mentality.

But that was special. I wasn't dead and wasn't dying, so I was giving them shit for it. At the same time, I appreciated the respect. For me, that was one of the ultimate humbling moments in my career.

SPIDER CALDWELL: That's Bill O'Brien appreciating the commitment those players made. That's why he let it happen. I know it may be weird to do that for one player, but people don't realize how instrumental that one player was—those two guys, Mauti and Zordich, were—in holding this thing together. They deserved it.

BILL O'BRIEN: I've coached the greatest. I've coached a Hall of Fame quarterback, Hall of Fame receivers, great players. Mauti's one of the most special. He embodies what Penn State is all about: tough, grind it out, smart. He's just a fantastic kid.

With Mauti on the sideline, Gerald Hodges became the team's leading tackler. In their four years together at linebacker, the two young men had pushed each other to excel, gently ribbing one another about highlights and stats. Mauti was the emotional one, Hodges more laid-back. But they deeply admired one another.

And so, Hodges felt compelled to offer up a tribute of his own.

CRAIG FITZGERALD: Gerald Hodges wanted to wear jersey number 42 for the game. Which is unbelievable, right? Hodges is a pro-caliber linebacker. He's not thinking, I want them to see my number. He's like, I want to wear 42, I'm going to wear 42.

SPIDER CALDWELL: I forgot about that. Yes, Hodges asked me about it. I said, "Check with Coach."

BILL O'BRIEN: Hodges texted me and called after the Indiana game to ask me if he could do that. I thought we should check with Michael first and he was all for it. It was a great gesture.

GERALD HODGES: I just wanted to go out there and rep my brother. Be out there his last time on the field. Wear his number and represent how he would want to be out there and play.

MICHAEL MAUTI: When they told me that, I couldn't help but cry. I mean, it's the biggest sign of respect.

FIFTEEN

SENIOR DAY

THE LAST PRACTICE *of the 2012 season landed on Thanksgiving Day. To honor the senior class, Bill O'Brien had the younger players form two lines side by side on the field and instructed their elders to walk single file between them through a gauntlet of high fives and pats on the back. A short time later, the whole team sat down to a white-tablecloth feast in Pollock Dining Commons: cheese and crackers, shrimp, stuffing, green beans, mashed potatoes, and—by one report—the meat from twenty turkeys.*

After a walkthrough on Friday and a night at the Penn Stater, the Lions boarded the team's iconic navy blue buses for one last drive to Beaver Stadium. Thirty-one seniors in all would be introduced by PA announcer Dean DeVore a half-hour before kickoff. The list included familiar names like McGloin, Zordich, and Mauti, but also those of veterans who had gamely manned the practice squads and special teams, guys like Michael Yancich, backup quarterback Shane McGregor, and former walk-on Jacob Fagnano.

After posing for a group photo, the crew was asked to look up at the stadium's eastern facade. On a gray band between the banks of private suites, there's a string of blue numbers honoring each of the Penn State teams that had finished a season with a championship or a perfect record. To the far right, the university had hung a white cloth.

As the players watched, the cloth was stripped away, revealing a blue

2012, a nod to the pivotal role the 7–4 team had played in rescuing the program. All that remained now to complete the mission was one last task: a pitched battle with Wisconsin.

MATT McGLOIN: When you look at 2012, I don't think anything about that year was normal for us. We had twelve opportunities to put on the Penn State helmet, to put on a Penn State jersey, and that was it. Your season at Penn State was over, your career at Penn State was over. I mean, we knew what was at stake for us every single week.

BILL O'BRIEN: Those guys went through a lot off the field. They went through the death of their former head coach—a legendary coach. They went through things off the field that don't need to be repeated. They hung tough, dealing with the NCAA and the sanctions. They had to lead this football team and keep these guys together. At the age of twenty-one, twenty-two, or twenty-three, that's heavy stuff.

SAM FICKEN: They might be the best leaders I've ever been around, peer-wise. If they didn't do what they did, I don't think we'd have had a football team.

I really believe that.

MATT McGLOIN: Guys cared about one another, they respected one another, they were behind each other no matter what—the senior class was truly something special.

STEPHON MORRIS: We wanted to go out on top, wanted to be among the greatest teams in Penn State history.

We weren't thinking about college football history; we just wanted to be one of the greatest teams in Penn State history, because of all the turmoil we'd had to go through.

That was a weird week. We seniors knew it was our last game. Some had NFL dreams and, for some of us, that was the last snap. It's already an emotional weekend, but we put pressure on ourselves to get a win—for the seniors.

It was freaking cold as hell that day, too.

MATT STANKIEWITCH: It's always tough facing Wisconsin. The year before, at their place, Russell Wilson had chewed us up and spit us out. We always talk about the running back Montee Ball, but quarterback Russell Wilson was the one who crushed us. It was horrible.

It was raining. No one wanted to be there. Jay Paterno, the quarterbacks coach, got in a fight with wide receiver Derek Moye on the sideline—horrible.

MICHAEL YANCICH: When they unveiled the 2012 alongside the years of the most successful teams in Penn State history, it was enough to bring everyone to tears. Some players held it together better than others. I was crying.

MICHAEL ZORDICH: They put those numbers up on the stadium because of football at its purest form. It's what this game is all about.

We just loved each other, stood by each other.

MATT STANKIEWITCH: Not a lot of people get the opportunity to be a part of something bigger than themselves. Some join the military. Some go to work for Tesla or SpaceX. That's the first time in my life I was a part of something I could not have accomplished by myself.

I was so proud to be part of the group of guys that battled that adversity. It was a great way to put a stamp on that year, because so much blood, sweat, and tears went into that season.

That team was the tip of the spear for the university, the state, maybe even college football. It was young men triumphing over adversity, looking it straight in the eye and conquering it.

Everyone was waiting to see what we were going to do, how we were going to react. Were we all going to transfer?

I'm proud of what my teammates did. We played football to the highest degree we could. We were good teammates, good people, good leaders in the community.

That's what Penn State football is all about.

MICHAEL YANCICH: To see the signs the fans had in the stands for Senior Day . . .

"You stayed with us, dot, dot, dot, we stand with you."

That set the tone for the game. I don't think anything was going to stop us at that point. We refused to lose.

Russell Wilson had graduated, moving on to the NFL's Seattle Seahawks, but Montee Ball was still a potent threat in the Wisconsin offense. A year earlier, as a junior, he'd scored four touchdowns in the lopsided 45–7 win against Penn State, finishing fourth in the voting for the Heisman Trophy.

And with Ball in the backfield, Wisconsin scored twice in the first seven minutes of the 2012 game—the first on a fifty-seven-yard strike from quarterback Curt Phillips to receiver Melvin Gordon and the second on a seventeen-yard run by Ball himself. It was the seventy-ninth rushing touchdown of his career, making him the NCAA's all-time leader.

The Lions scored on their first drive as well, but gave up a forty-seven-yard return on the ensuing kickoff, setting the stage for Ball's record-breaking TD. They then moved the ball just thirty-three yards in six plays on their second drive.

The Badgers had come ready to play. Had Penn State? That was the lingering question.

CRAIG FITZGERALD: You go down 14–7 against the best rushing team in the country. The star running back sets the all-time rushing touchdown record on the second TD. [laughter] That's not going to be easy to come back from, right? But Wisconsin didn't score again until late in the game.

RON VANDERLINDEN, LINEBACKER COACH: They came out smoking in the first two series, which caught us off guard. But after that, we stepped up and really played well.

TED ROOF, DEFENSIVE COORDINATOR: They were getting out on the edge, and we weren't doing a good job of setting the edge. We had talked all week about that. Our kids did a great job of making adjustments and battling back.

CHARLIE FISHER: That game just epitomized what that team was about. I mean, we're down 14–7 before you can blink. They're moving the ball pretty much at will. And then we had a big stop on a third or fourth down, and just like that the game kind of turns.

MICHAEL YANCICH: Wisconsin was a really, really good team. It almost seemed like they had our number, but we came out of the locker room in the second half and were ultimately successful. It's like Bill O'Brien said, you're a bunch of fighters and we're not going to falter under pressure. We have way too much invested in this university and this team to let Penn State down on Senior Day. We're going to win this game.

MATT STANKIEWITCH: Their defensive line was so big. They outweighed us by like thirty pounds each. I remember the nose guard. He got drafted by the Eagles. He outweighed me by like thirty-five to forty pounds. He was a strong dude, too.

CHARLIE FISHER: That was a good Wisconsin team. Big as hell. Maybe one of the biggest teams I've ever seen walk onto a football field. And it was like, *It doesn't matter.* It's just the epitome of that team.

"It doesn't matter. We're going to find a way to beat you."

Penn State added two Ficken field goals in the third quarter to trim the Wisconsin lead to 14–13.

MATT STANKIEWITCH: Wisconsin's middle linebacker Chris Borland didn't play that game—I think he had a hurt hamstring or something—and that was big for us, because he was really good. Probably the number-one middle linebacker in the country.

His backup was terrible. On one play, I pancaked him and stayed on top of him. The ref goes, "Fifty-four! What in the hell is wrong with you?" Because I kept shaking him while I was on top of him.

Little by little, the Lions exerted their will.

MATT STANKIEWITCH: I couldn't believe we were able to establish a running game against them. It took a lot of time off the clock. A lot of guys stepped up, too.

CHARLIE FISHER: Zwinak had a bunch of yards—I can't remember exactly how many—but in typical Zwinak fashion. I don't know if he made anybody miss, but he sure as hell bruised them up. He was tough as nails running the football.

He does not get near enough credit for how good he was as a player at Penn State. He wasn't Saquon Barkley, he wasn't flash, but he was tough and he was productive and at the end of the day that's all that matters.

On a fourth down and six early in the fourth quarter, Matt McGloin took the snap from Stankiewitch just beyond the fifty-yard line, looked downfield, and waited patiently for tight end Jesse James to come streaking into view. Early in the half, the quarterback and receiver had connected on a thirty-seven-yard pass play. This time, James caught the ball in stride and rumbled into the end zone from forty-one yards out.

BILL O'BRIEN: It was a play called "special." We ran it quite a bit and Matt McGloin had a great feel for that play. Jesse did a nice job of weaving through some traffic there and coming open.

CHARLIE FISHER: Jesse straight-armed a guy out on the left side, I think, then raced down the sideline and the place went crazy.

MATT STANKIEWITCH: Jesse runs well for a guy his size. He's a big dude. A legit six-foot-seven.

Zach Zwinak converted on the two-point attempt and Penn State had a 21–14 lead with 13:32 left in the game.

The Badgers were not ready to give in yet. They mounted an eleven-play drive to the Penn State twenty, only to have Jake Fagnano—the onetime walk-on—intercept a fourth-and-eight pass.

JAKE FAGNANO: We were creeping up on the red zone there inside the thirty and the quarterback was giving us a couple of reads we liked. So we decided to check to a bit of man-to-man coverage and basically spy off the quarterback's eyes. Backyard football. I made the correct read and broke on the ball.

Once everything settled down, I said, "Hey, look, we're going to have to do it again." We knew how much time was on the clock, the caliber of the team we were playing, and we were going to have to go back out there one more time.

Sure enough, Penn State's offense moved the ball three yards in three plays and promptly punted, downing the kick on the Wisconsin thirty-four. The Badgers lined up with 3:43 to go.

James White rushed for four yards, Melvin Gordon for nine, and Montee Ball for six. As the clock ticked, Wisconsin kept moving forward. A fourteen-yard pass to Jordan Fredrick put the ball on the twenty-six.

Jordan Hill sacked Curt Phillips, pushing the Badgers back to the thirty-three.

The seesaw battle continued until Wisconsin was staring at fourth-and-goal from the four with eighteen seconds left. Phillips took the snap, rolled right, and found a receiver at the goal line surrounded by three blue jerseys. He released the pass.

Touchdown.

The teams were tied at 21.

MATT MCGLOIN: Earlier in the week, I'd said to Charlie Fisher, "You know, I never played in an overtime game here." And, sure enough, in the last game of my career, we go to overtime.

I mean, you can't make that up. Can't write that any better.

In college football, the rules shift in overtime. The referees place the ball twenty-five yards from the end zone and give each team a set of downs. If the first team scores, the other team gets a chance to respond. McGloin threw incomplete to Brandon Moseby-Felder, handed the ball to Zwinak for six yards, then missed a toss to Zordich. On fourth down, Sam Ficken strutted onto the field.

CHARLIE FISHER: It was only fitting that it came down to Sam Ficken, a guy who was cast aside after the Virginia game. He goes out there and nails the final thirty-seven-yarder in the snow. There's an iconic photo of this, the ball coming off his foot, the light snow coming down, and the ball headed towards the pipes. It's hard as a coach to watch those kicks, it really is, but I learned a long time ago, that by gosh you worked way too hard not to watch.

He hit it true.

BILL O'BRIEN: I'm Irish-Catholic from Boston. I said a Hail Mary and an Our Father. I'm not sure that worked. I just know our kids played hard and I was hoping Ficken hooked it and that's what he did.

MATT STANKIEWITCH: That was like redemption for Sam Ficken. He got the field goal and the other guy missed, so we won. It was just awesome to get that eighth win.

We should have been like 10–2.

SAM FICKEN: I would have been so disappointed if I had let the seniors down, especially after what had happened earlier in the year. They all had my back. For me, that was such a key moment. It was like, Okay, I have an opportunity to put us up.

It was not technically a game-winner, but, obviously, it takes a lot of pressure off Wisconsin if I miss that first kick. After I made it, I let out a sigh of relief. I still might have had to go out and make another kick, though, so I stayed locked in.

I think they went three-and-out and sent their kicker onto the field.

On first down, Montee Ball rushed for one yard. On second down, Curt Phillips was sacked for a three-yard loss. He fumbled the ball, but Wisconsin recovered. A third-down pass was nearly intercepted by linebacker Glenn Carson. That sent kicker Kyle French onto the field to attempt a forty-four-yard, game-tying field goal.

MATT STANKIEWITCH: On the last play of the game, we put Jesse James on the field goal block team. I don't know whose idea that was. They put him in because he's six-foot-seven and he could jump really high.

SAM FICKEN: I was standing at the very back of the sideline, as far from the play as anyone on the team. I've got my helmet in my hand.

The second I saw him miss, I ran onto the field and threw my helmet. Just utter joy to know we could send the seniors out the way they deserved.

MICHAEL YANCICH: I sprinted across the field and started ringing the victory bell. I feel bad for the camera guy right next to it. I'm pretty sure his ears were bleeding after I was done. I just had a crazy amount of energy.

The laughter, the happiness, the tears of that season—all came rushing back in that moment. Every part of the journey was returning in flashbacks.

I don't think there was a person in that stadium—player, spectator, reporter, cheerleader, band member, coach—who didn't feel the same way. Everyone's blood was mixed. There was such a sense of accomplishment.

CRAIG FITZGERALD: We certainly lost some key players after the sanctions, but everything happens for a reason. If the kicker doesn't leave, Sam Ficken isn't Sam Ficken. Zach Zwinak had a thousand yards. Bill Belton developed into a good back. Allen Robinson had his coming-out party, because somebody left to play wide receiver somewhere else. I wouldn't change any of the personnel we had at those positions.

MICHAEL YANCICH: I'll never forget that feeling, running out onto the field with all your teammates one last time as the clock comes to zero. You look at each other and say, "Hey, we did it! We just showed the world Penn State's still here."

BILL O'BRIEN: The experts said we weren't going to win *any*. So to win eight games was pretty good.

MICHAEL MAUTI: I mean, that's better than any bowl trip I've been a part of.

STEPHON MORRIS: The emotion in that locker room after the game—the jumping around, cheers—it was awesome. I can't really explain it. It was just raw emotion.

It's a feeling I wish I could get back, but I've never experienced it again.

MICHAEL MAUTI: I can count on one hand the best post-game locker rooms in my career and that was number one by far. It really was. And I didn't play in the game.

The way that season ended, it was storybook, man. It really was. Having O'Brien in the middle of that mosh pit, his hands in the air, eyes closed. Just unbelievable.

MICHAEL YANCICH: They wanted to talk to us in the media room. I was sitting at my locker and I didn't want to leave. I knew that was going to be the last time I was inside that locker room as a player. I think it was Jeff Nelson, the communications director, who kept going, "Mike, we got to go. They're waiting for you."

I'm sitting there like, Just give me one more minute, *please.*

JORDAN HILL: That whole game really told the story of what we went through all year, being knocked down early and being able to get back up.

BOB MORGAN: Twenty-two players from that 2012 team ended up in the NFL. That's a staggering number for any program.

MICHAEL NASH: There's almost a divine circle in this story and it started when Joe Paterno was in his prime and coached a couple kids—one with the last name Mauti and one with the last name Zordich. They were stars on campus in their days, but when they graduated, they went different ways—one to Philadelphia, one to New Orleans—and both had great professional careers. They raised their children with the ethics and morals they learned from Joe Paterno, and their kids grew up with those ethics and morals. And when Joe was removed from his job and died and Penn State was in its darkest hours, when thirty to forty players were thinking about leaving, these two kids steeped in the character instilled in their fathers by Joe Paterno took it upon themselves to keep the team together, to walk out in front of those cameras on ESPN and say, "One guy didn't build this program; one guy's not tearing it down.

"We're not going anywhere. In fact, we're going to raise hell every Saturday."

When Joe's beliefs were most needed, those two players raised by parents who became men through his program used those very lessons to save it. Joe was no longer there, but those ethics and morals were still echoing across the campus.

SIXTEEN

THE QUARTERBACK
OF THE FUTURE

FOR BILL O'BRIEN, *the man hired to replace Joe Paterno, the Jerry Sandusky scandal brought untold challenges, and those challenges multiplied the day the NCAA issued the sanctions on his program. If it was hard to convince high school kids all of seventeen years old to commit to joining the disgraced institution in early 2012, it got significantly harder once you stripped away the chance to compete for college football's biggest prizes. No national championship, no conference title, no berth in one of the sport's thirty-two postseason bowl games.*

In the aftermath of the NCAA's announcement, it was unclear if O'Brien would even have enough players to field a team come September.

"The NCAA stopped short of shutting down Penn State's program," wrote Pete Thamel in The New York Times, "but officials insisted the breadth and significance of the penalty were nearly as debilitating. It is expected to be almost a decade before Penn State will be in a position to attempt to regain its place as one of the sport's elite programs."

Into the fray stepped a young quarterback the likes of which Penn State had never seen. A polished, handsome, NFL-style signal caller with the talent and football intelligence to start as a true freshman. Born in Pennsylvania, he moved with his family to Richmond, Virginia, at age six, blossoming into a three-sport athlete. By his junior year in high school, he was the number-one QB prospect in the nation, according to ESPN.

Even better, Christian Hackenberg was open to the idea of playing at Penn State; not only open to it, he genuinely relished the notion of playing for Bill O'Brien, the man who had coached New England Patriots superstar Tom Brady in Super Bowl XLVI.

MARK BRENNAN, EDITOR AND PUBLISHER, *LIONS 247*: You have to give Bill O'Brien all the credit in the world. I mean, that has got to go down as one of the greatest recruiting efforts ever. And when O'Brien came in, he wasn't really known as a recruiter. He had been in the NFL for so long, everybody's wondering, can he recruit? Somehow he was able to convince those kids in 2012 to come to Penn State. There was zero used car salesman in Bill O'Brien. With him, what you see is what you get. And that worked. At that moment in time, at Penn State, with that group of players, it worked.

BOB FLOUNDERS, PENN STATE BEAT WRITER, HARRISBURG *PATRIOT-NEWS*: Because of his success with the Patriots, there's a bit of a Pied Piper effect. "Come to Penn State. Get a great education. And we're going to develop you." That's what O'Brien was selling.

His recent background was all about the NFL, but he knew quite a bit about what goes into developing a college program. And he had recruited in the past. So it wasn't quite foreign to him. It was a little bit like riding a bike, right? He just needed to shake off the rust.

CHRISTIAN HACKENBERG: When Bill got there, that place really checked all the boxes for me—especially on the football side. Being able to come in there and run a pro system would prepare me to take the next step in my career. At that age, it was always, "I want to play in the NFL." That's the end goal for all of us.

BILL O'BRIEN: Hackenberg's the perfect fit for what we were trying to do offensively. He's big, tall, strong. He can run. He's got a good arm, he's accurate, he's smart. We had an offense that fit his talent level and that would be a big part of his decision.

BOB FLOUNDERS: They've had some quarterbacks that developed over time at Penn State. Pretty talented kids. But I don't think there was ever, *ever* the buzz around a quarterback recruit like there was around Hackenberg. Kerry Collins was a good player. But he took a while to establish himself. Todd Blackledge was a first-round pick, but we're talking apples and oranges. In terms of perception and flat-out physical talent, I think it's safe to say Christian Hackenberg to this day is the most celebrated quarterback recruit in Penn State history.

In the end, Hackenberg was the gem in a recruiting class that included some high-caliber talent—future stars like wide receiver DaeSean Hamilton, offensive linemen Brendan Mahon and Andrew Nelson, linebacker Brandon Bell, and defensive end Garrett Sickels. But it was tight end Adam Breneman, a five-star recruit from Harrisburg's Cedar Cliff High School, that truly united the group.

MARK BRENNAN: I think it starts with Breneman. If they don't get Adam Breneman, they don't get Hackenberg. He was as important in recruiting Hackenberg as anybody.

ADAM BRENEMAN: My recruitment started early. After my sophomore season of high school. At the end of the day, I had an offer from everybody in the country. I could have gone anywhere I wanted. It's hard, man. When you're fifteen, sixteen, seventeen years old and you got Alabama's Nick Saban and Notre Dame's Brian Kelly and Texas A&M's Jimbo Fisher showing up in your high school. There's a lot of responsibility, a lot of attention thrown your way.

BOB FLOUNDERS: Adam's high school coach Jim Cantafio knew early that he had a special athlete, one who was going to be physically and mentally superior to anyone that tried to guard him on the high school level. He was essentially a big wideout. Not really a tight end. But he flourished in Jim's offense. No one could handle him. He could run with just about any DB and he was bigger than anyone.

CHRISTIAN HACKENBERG: I was fortunate to get an offer after my sopho-more year in high school from Virginia, which was right in my backyard, and then everything kind of blew up for me.

ADAM BRENEMAN: We were both looking at UVA. That's how Christian and I got to know each other. This was when Joe Paterno was still at Penn State. Before Bill O'Brien was even known to Penn State fans.

CHRISTIAN HACKENBERG: I didn't even have an offer from Penn State. I didn't get anything back from Paterno's staff. When I had started laying out the schools that would be good fits for me, I was like, Well, I've got Virginia. We can start looking at that together.

ADAM BRENEMAN: I'm like, Dude, I've got Alabama, Florida State, Georgia.

BOB FLOUNDERS: Breneman and Hackenberg bonded pretty quickly on the recruiting trail. They got very close. And you know in today's age, when a school gets an early commitment from an elite athlete, he almost immediately becomes a recruiter. He will do everything he can to con-vince other kids to come with him. There's no question that Adam and Christian were able to do that.

Those two developed a friendship. They committed and other players fell in line. There were some very good players in that 2013 class: Garrett Sickels, Brendan Mahon, Will Fuller.

CHRISTIAN HACKENBERG: I grew up in Northeastern Pennsylvania, up in the coal regions, so everyone around me was a Penn State fan. I knew a lot about the program, but I wasn't recruited by the old staff. It sort of devel-oped with Coach O'Brien.

ADAM BRENEMAN: Penn State was obviously my hometown team. I was waiting for a Penn State offer for a while—this was Joe Paterno's staff—but eventually got one. And to be honest, I didn't really know where I was going to go. For a while, it was, I want to be different. I want to go out of state, go to a different part of the country, and spread my wings. But once Bill O'Brien got to Penn State, it didn't take much convincing. I fell in love with Bill O'Brien. His vision and the offense he was running. He did a great job recruiting me and didn't just recruit me, he recruited my parents, my head coach, and everyone around me. It was a pretty easy decision.

CHRISTIAN HACKENBERG: I sat with them in February of 2012. Got to know the staff, got to know the system. O'Brien really laid it out for me and that was a big selling point. I remember calling Breneman about that. Just being like, "Dude, this is going to be great for us."

ADAM BRENEMAN: I was there with my family and my high school coach. We're with the whole staff watching Patriot tight ends Rob Gronkowski and Aaron Hernandez on film and O'Brien's like, "Man, I'm going to feed you the rock when you come here."

I'm not even committed, but literally on cloud nine. Could you imagine a better place to be as a high school football player? O'Brien's like you're going to wear number eighty-one, because I'm going to use you just like Aaron Hernandez.

MARK BRENNAN: The quarterback with New England—a guy named Tom Brady—was pretty good back then, too. Even so, it's different saying, "Hey, I produced this guy and that guy," and then sitting in a seventeen-year old's living room and convincing him to go to Penn State. That's the amazing part. That O'Brien was able to pull it off. Yeah, he obviously had the bona fides. The credentials. But being able to go and recruit the way he did, there's something to be said for that.

Getting a five-star tight end is one thing. Getting a five-star quarterback is quite another. That's not to diminish the importance of a tight end, but now you're bringing in a kid six-foot-four, 220 pounds, good-looking, rocket arm, all of these things that can make him the savior of the program.

CHRISTIAN HACKENBERG: I remember driving home from my visit to Penn State. It was snowing and we're driving and I looked at my dad and I was like, "Dude, I want to come here." My dad played college ball, so he had gone through the recruiting process. He was like, "Just sit on it for like a week." He goes, "If you feel the same way in a week, pull the trigger."

GARRETT SICKELS: As a recruit in high school, coaches just give you lip service. Tell you, yeah, you're going to play as a freshman. We could see you being a possible starter your freshman year. You know, I'm not putting limits on myself, but I see what these guys look like that play D-end in the SEC and the Big Ten. I was just six-foot-four, 230 pounds. I'm like, *What are you guys talking about?*

O'Brien said, with a straight face, in the way he always did it, We think you could be a player for us here and you're going to have every opportunity to contribute early. But if you're not ready, you're not ready. We still want to give you an offer. I was like, *Wow, that's pretty incredible.* It was the first time I'd heard something like that.

We had visits to Ohio State and Notre Dame planned for probably a month later. My dad and I were going to drive out there. I remember that whole trip back from Penn State, very similar to Christian, I was saying, "I want to go here." And my dad said, "Write out a hundred reasons why you want to go to Penn State and not take other visits."

I wrote like a hundred and twenty-two reasons. And the main one was there's so much more to play for at Penn State. To show that this guy and the scandal wasn't going to define the university or inhibit its progress. Penn State's a legendary program and I want to be a part of that.

CHRISTIAN HACKENBERG: So, I got home. I was getting ready for baseball season. I worked out at the school, did some stuff in the batting cages, threw a bullpen or two, and then came home. We were eating dinner. I was like, *Hey, man, I'm going to do it. I'm going to pull the trigger.*

I remember, I was upstairs, I had just gotten out of the shower, in a pair of underwear or something, and I called Bill while sitting on my bed. I was like, "Hey, man, I'm coming to Penn State." And then I just shot that little tweet out. Because I guess that's what you've got to do now as a recruit. Get the information out there.

So far so good. Cut to July.

CHRISTIAN HACKENBERG: I verbally committed February of my junior year. That July the sanctions were placed on the program.

ADAM BRENEMAN: Joe Paterno had been fired. Bill O'Brien's there. And we had been hearing there might be sanctions. But what we're hearing is it may be a slap on the wrist. It may be a fine. O'Brien said don't worry about it. So none of us knew what was going to happen.

CHRISTIAN HACKENBERG: My dad and I were returning from the Elite 11 quarterback camp in California. We landed in Richmond and when we got in the car we turned on the radio and that was like the first thing on ESPN. They were talking about the sanctions and how Penn State got hammered. I was like, *Ughhhhhh.* Because everything we were being told—all the information we'd been gathering—was that it was just going to be a slap on the wrist. Because the Sandusky stuff didn't really have anything to do with the football program. But all of a sudden, it had everything to do with the football program.

GARRETT SICKELS: At my high school, we had practice in the morning. I'm like, "Hey, let's go have some breakfast." I was sitting there with my dad and my buddies and NCAA president Mark Emmert was on TV and the first thing he announced, I think, was the bowl ban for four years. That hit me, but I wasn't choosing a college to play in a bowl game. Then he said guys could transfer anywhere. It was like I just got punched in the stomach.

ADAM BRENEMAN: I was walking in to rehab my knee, because I had just torn my ACL. I'm going to rehab and Mark Emmert is on the radio announcing the sanctions and the chaos just starts immediately. For a few days, we were getting calls from literally every media outlet known to man.

CHRISTIAN HACKENBERG: Every outlet and every school.

ADAM BRENEMAN: The Anderson Cooper show from CNN called my family's house and was like, "We want to have Adam on the show to talk about Penn State." I'm like, "Whaaat?" My mom's like, "You are not going on CNN to talk about Penn State." It was a crazy time, man. We were seventeen years old.

GARRETT SICKELS: All these schools started hounding us. Not the way they were hounding the players on Penn State's campus. What they did to the players at Penn State was just disgraceful. You know, like we were still in high school. We hadn't signed on the dotted line.

ADAM BRENEMAN: Really, at this point, it was like everyone's going to leave Penn State. Bill O'Brien's probably going to leave Penn State. The place is going to be dead. I mean, there's no way we could ever go to Penn State. We have all talked to Bill O'Brien, but it's up in the air. Like, *What's going on?* The frenzy of the media. The media just swarmed on Penn State. It was like the perfect storm.

BOB FLOUNDERS: There was blood in the water. It was open season on Penn State talent.

With all the sanctions, guys are free to leave right away and we don't know what the future's going to hold. No post-season. Limited scholarships. How is Bill O'Brien going to get not only his current players, but the 2013 class to stay? Why would they stay when there's no post-season? They can't compete for conference championships. It was a very, very daunting task.

STEVE JONES: It became a recruiting meat market here. Other schools were recruiting, following Penn State players to class, following them to their apartments, getting ahold of them on their phones.

BILL O'BRIEN: We could have lost the whole team.

JOHN BACON: If you lose twenty or thirty players, you can't run a practice.

GARRETT SICKELS: I remember texting Penn State defensive end Anthony Zettel, because I had met him a few times and had his number and he was like, "Yeah, dude, I'm thinking about transferring." He and tight end Jesse James were on the way out of State College to visit Michigan.

ADAM BRENEMAN: No one in the country thought we'd still go to Penn State. Literally, no one.

GARRETT SICKELS: Everybody was calling me crazy for going to Penn State after everything that happened.

CHRISTIAN HACKENBERG: Breneman, Garrett Sickels, and Brendan Mahon—those are the guys I contacted after I had committed to Penn State. To really get on them. Get them to come with me. So when that all happened, we had already been talking.

GARRETT SICKELS: I called Brendan Mahon and I was like, "What are you doing?" He's like, "Dude, I committed to O'Brien. I'm not going anywhere." And I felt the same way. My dad was like, "Hey, take some time." He's like, "I'm going to reach out to Mr. Breneman, Mr. Hackenberg, Mr. Mahon. I'm going to see what they're thinking. We need answers." So my dad's online. It's like fifteen minutes after the sanctions. And he sees that Brendan Mahon and Garrett Sickels have reaffirmed their commitment to Penn State. And my dad's calling me like, *"What are you doing?"*

ADAM BRENEMAN: About a week later, Bill O'Brien said to us—all the commits—"Hey, before you guys do anything, I need you to come visit me in State College." So that Saturday, we go visit Bill O'Brien. It was a pretty emotional day.

GARRETT SICKELS: That's when he said if you commit to us, we'll commit to you.

CHRISTIAN HACKENBERG: We had the meeting in the team room. Just us and our parents. And Coach O'Brien kind of laid out what was coming. It was a brutally honest conversation. That's what's funny. In this business, you don't find a lot of brutally honest people and one of the things I give Coach O'Brien credit for is that he is a brutally honest guy. He didn't sugarcoat things. You kind of knew what was going on and what was going through his mind. He never really held anything back.

ADAM BRENEMAN: Yeah, that was an emotional room. I never saw so many grown men crying. And I remember O'Brien giving us that speech. It's the parents and the commits and Bill O'Brien, and O'Brien said something like, "If you guys stay, I promise you, you will be remembered forever for coming to this school at this time." And then he said, "I'm going to let you guys talk it out. I'll be upstairs when you're done. Come get me."

CHRISTIAN HACKENBERG: He went upstairs and we sat there with our parents and talked for a bit. And then we were all like, "Dude, we're staying." Like, "We're staying." You know what I mean? It was pretty unanimous. I know our parents were a wreck at the time, but . . .

ADAM BRENEMAN: I have this vivid memory of Garrett Sickels's dad standing up after O'Brien spoke to everyone. I don't remember exactly what he said, but I remember seeing him tear up.

That was an impactful moment for me. That was the moment for me where I was like, *Okay, everyone's coming after us again, but I want to go to Penn State. No matter what, I want to be with these guys. I want to play for Coach O'Brien. I want to play with Hack, and Garrett, and Brendan.*

I always look back to that day, because if we didn't have that Saturday in State College, I don't know if we all would have stayed together like we did.

GARRETT SICKELS: Who didn't have doubts? I had doubts. But I was like, *As long as O'Brien's here and there's a team, I'm going to go here.*

My dad stood up and my dad's a pretty emotional guy, but you wouldn't think that to see him. He's got that big white mustache. And he stood up and he said something along these lines. "You guys are seventeen years old and you should never have to make such a hard, life-defining decision." And I think he said, "There's so much more to play for here at Penn State." He's like, "I'm not promising anything . . ." I mean, he never played college football. But he goes, "You guys will be remembered here and what you play for here you cannot play for anywhere else."

That's just how I felt. I remember looking around and everyone was on the same page. Our parents, our fathers, all came together. We were all in agreement.

ADAM BRENEMAN: Our parents stood up. I think Mr. Hackenberg said something. My dad said something. Mr. Sickels got up and started tearing up. I never saw Mr. Sickels cry before. But it was an emotional time. We just said, "Screw it, we're going to go to Penn State." And then we walked upstairs and told Bill O'Brien.

GARRETT SICKELS: We all went up to his office and told him we were staying. It's funny, but you look back and you realize that that decision really could have backfired, if things did go south. But you think everything's always going to work out when you're seventeen.

So we went up to Coach O'Brien's office. He sat at his desk and I think Brendan cracked a joke. Like, "We're all going to Florida."

ADAM BRENEMAN: I remember that. We went up there and we messed with him first. We all walked in and someone—I think it was Brendan—was like, "I think we're going to go to Florida, man." The joke didn't last long, but it was pretty funny.

GARRETT SICKELS: Yeah, Brendan started laughing, of course. O'Brien stood up and gave us hugs. Our parents were like, "Where did you go?" And it was like, "We just told O'Brien we're staying."

I think my dad was crying. Easy E, Erick Hackenberg was tearing up. Big Bob Mahon was a little emotional. Just because that whole week. I mean, we weren't even there yet. Our recruiting experience just got turned upside down and there were so many questions that had to be answered. That was a wild time. A wild summer going into your senior year of high school.

ADAM BRENEMAN: It's cool looking back to think of what we did together. Christian said this a lot, but I don't know if we'll ever fully understand the impact that those commitments had on that school. We could talk for hours and hours and hours about all this stuff.

CHRISTIAN HACKENBERG: The other thing that stuck with me is that O'Brien said he'd see us through. Throughout the process. After we did that, he did say he'd see us through.

ADAM BRENEMAN: I remember him saying, "If you guys come, I will stay for your entire career." I vividly remember that—and we all know what happened after our freshman year. Coach O'Brien left and went to the Houston Texans. Bill O'Brien leaves and our world gets turned upside down. Again.

SEVENTEEN

ENTER HACKENBERG

CHRISTIAN HACKENBERG ARRIVED *on campus in June 2013, roughly two months before the season opener against Syracuse, and was immediately thrust into a pitched battle for the starting role at QB. His chief rival, Tyler Ferguson, had arrived in January, after one stellar season—2,600 passing yards and twenty-two touchdowns in ten games—at a California junior college.*

If the transition from senior prom to college stud was difficult, Hackenberg certainly didn't show it. Barely four months removed from his eighteenth birthday, he donned Penn State jersey number fourteen—formerly worn by Todd Blackledge and John Shaffer, who both had led Penn State to national championships—and got right to work demonstrating what could be.

For more than a year, talent scouts had been eyeballing his every move, weighing his innate potential against that of fellow phenoms Jared Goff, Mitch Trubisky, and Baker Mayfield. In short order, Hack—as he would soon be known to Penn State faithful—showed why he had been ranked ahead of all three.

CHRISTIAN HACKENBERG: The most challenging part for me was just being able to handle all the expectations that come with being a quarterback at a program like Penn State. You know, you really don't understand the bigness of it. I was playing high school football in Central Virginia, so stepping into this new environment was a change. The more you experience it each week, the more you grasp how big it is.

CHARLIE FISHER: You don't ever promise anything to anybody—anything good has got to be earned—but he had a very good preseason camp. Made some wow-factor type throws. I remember thinking, Man, this guy is good. He's even exceeding expectations.

JOHN URSCHEL: There was a whole lot of media coverage on the recruits in his class talking about restoring the roar. As players, we thought, who are these guys? They haven't played a single down of college football.

When they came in, we gave them a hard time about that. But it became apparent extremely quickly that Hackenberg could play. He worked, he studied, and he honed his craft. The guy was doing everything he could to help the team win.

I mean, I loved blocking for that guy. He was a quarterback—the way he prepared, the way he carried himself, what he put into football, what he gave of himself. Yeah, as an offensive lineman, I wanted to protect that guy. I really, really wanted to protect that guy.

BILL O'BRIEN: He won the starting job about the second week of training camp when he led our team down the field at Beaver Stadium on a two-minute drill that ended in a touchdown.

TYLER FERGUSON: I came in as the number-two junior college player in the country. Well, we had the number-one high school player in the country come in at quarterback. And Christian was really good. There weren't a lot of guys I'd been around at that point in my career that I thought, Wow, this guy is good. I always thought I could throw with anybody.

I got there in January. Hackenberg came in the summer. So I had a little leg up. He came to fall practice and I called my dad and I'm like, "This guy's legit. Like, this guy is really good."

CHRISTIAN HACKENBERG: It was Tyler and myself. He had been there all spring and I came in the summer, because I wanted to play baseball my senior year of high school.

Like I said, Bill never promised me anything. I had to work my way up. So *every day* it was, "Just do the right thing. Just do the right thing. Learn, apply, yada, yada, yada."

The one thing we talked about was mindset, your aptitude for staying levelheaded and, I guess, wise. I think I was just dumb. And I mean that in a good way.

I was just dumb to the stage and what was coming, because I came from a very small school in Central Virginia, a military academy kind of isolated in its bubble. I just wanted to play football, man. Like, that was really it. I didn't think about the articles. I didn't think about the stats. I just wanted to play football and win the game.

TYLER FERGUSON: Coach O'Brien and I had gotten close. We had a unique relationship. He was teaching us an NFL playbook every single day. That was his big selling point in recruiting: "Look, you're going to learn the Patriots' offense from the Patriots' former offensive coordinator." And we did—to a T. It was extremely complex, and that was the whole reason I went there.

CHARLIE FISHER: Tyler had a gunslinger mentality. We were looking for a junior college bridge guy to compete with Christian. So it was a healthy competition. They had a great battle. And Tyler didn't have a bad camp. But there was a lot of investment, a lot of high expectations for Christian Hackenberg.

He was like a first-round draft choice. He and Jared Goff were the two heaviest-recruited quarterbacks in the nation in 2012. So if he was ready, he was going to get the opportunity to show what he could do.

CHRISTIAN HACKENBERG: I think it was perfect timing for me. I mean, my sophomore year at Fort Union, the team had two seniors and I had to beat them out. And I did. We won a state championship that year. So I had experience competing with older guys as a young cat and having to prove my worth.

Subliminally, that helped. But I was also just dumb to the stage and the expectations. Just numb to it. And that really helped me. Because that's all I cared about—the football. I was watching film every second I could.

Trying to absorb as much as I could. And, fortunately, I was able to do that and apply it quickly. As camp went on, I took advantage of the opportunities that had been given to me.

JOHN URSCHEL: He's the most talented quarterback I've ever had the pleasure of playing with. Just an amazing guy, amazing competitor. I can't stress enough how much I loved playing for that guy. Even though he was a freshman, I'm telling you, he was truly a leader.

We had Allen Robinson, but he's not going to help us if no one can get him the ball.

CHARLIE FISHER: Once Christian committed, he was all in. I've always respected that. He never flinched, never wavered. That had a lot to do with holding that recruiting class together.

He was a great fit for the system we were running. His personality, his leadership ability, his ability to learn—he checked all the boxes.

CHRISTIAN HACKENBERG: I think it just got to a point where Bill trusted me and saw that I was making the right strides, processing information and applying information and minimizing catastrophic plays to the point where he thought we could trust this kid.

I give him a ton of credit. A lot of coaches out there would have never made that decision, even if it was the right one. For him to do that in the situation we were in—in terms of the limitations, the sanctions . . . I mean, we played with like forty-five scholarship guys that year. Fortunately, a lot of those guys were older. They had a year or two in the system. It was a good supporting cast for me. But had we had a couple of injuries, it would have been tougher. So that was a very—for lack of a better term—ballsy decision, but he stuck with it, and ultimately you know I did my part, too. I think I made it easier with how I prepared and how I attacked it.

MARK BRENNAN: At one of the Friday night get-togethers before a road game, we were sitting with Bill O'Brien and he puts his fingers up like he's showing you how thick a book is. He puts them like two inches apart and says, "In our offense, this is the tight end's playbook." Then he takes both hands. He puts them about a foot apart and he says, "This is the quarterback's playbook." So think about the fact that he had the confidence in Hackenberg to give that playbook to a true freshman. I mean, that tells you something about how smart Hackenberg is. He was able to come in and pick up something that a couple of quarterbacks in the program prior to him had struggled with. He was in the program for a month and was able to cut it.

CHARLIE FISHER: He wasn't flawless. That's why you practice. But he showed that he had a great ability to grasp things and, when he did make a mistake, he learned from it. It was more than just snap the ball and throw it to this guy. He had a lot of reads and checks at the line, making sure our run IDs were correct to get us in the right situation.

JOHN URSCHEL: Bill and Christian were together all the time. They would meet all the time, watch film all the time, go over things all the time. I still don't know how Christian found time to go to class. I can't stress how much preparation Christian put in, always following NCAA regulations, of course. But he spent so much time preparing.

He and O'Brien really connected and O'Brien was great for him. When you're in your first year of college and you really, really connect with a coach, it's special.

KYLE CARTER: O'Brien gave Hack all the tools he needed to be great at quarterback. He had the weapons—the receivers, the tight ends, and the running back—you need to be successful. But the mental side was all Hack, man. He had to have tough skin, because Penn State's fan base can get a little crazy. No matter what the circumstances, they expect wins. So he definitely did a great job keeping a level head.

GENO LEWIS: Coach O'Brien really had Hackenberg locked in. He would talk to him like, "Listen, you're the one playing out there. I can direct you, but I need you to tell me what you see."

CHRISTIAN HACKENBERG: That system was very dependent on me being an extension of him on the field. So he needed to get reassurance every day, every practice rep, every meeting that I was thinking the same way he was thinking and able to get us into the best play for the look that was presented.

That was his big thing: He hated wasting plays. He was like, "If I call something, Hack, and you see something that's going to be better, because I can't necessarily see the angles and the leverage from your perspective, go for it."

So, yeah, we spent a ton of time together. And it's funny, I still laugh about this, but, like, the first time I sit down with him, we just start talking football. So it's football, football, football, football. Week one, week two, week three. And then, all of a sudden, week four I come in and he starts bullshitting with me about class, and then life, and the meetings end up getting longer. We got our football in, but we started to enjoy our relationship. And that really helped me. You know, I knew who he was, I knew what he stood for, I knew the type of guy he was, the father he was. That made me trust him even more.

I think it was the same way for him, too. You know, you only get to know a kid so much through the recruiting process. But he got to know what made me tick, what buttons to press, whether or not I was paying attention. Like, that was always funny.

He'd be like, "You always look like you're confused as shit."

And I'm like, "Nah, I'm just internalizing it."

He'd be blown away that everything he'd say, I could apply at that next practice.

He'd be like, "You looked at me like you had no idea what I was saying and then you went out and did it." And I'm like, "Yeah, man." But you don't get that without spending those extra hours building that relationship.

The knowledge I gained from him from an Xs and Os standpoint, studying defenses and understanding his philosophy for offensive football, the way he saw things—it really meshed well with my game. And it got me to a place mentally where I was playing very, very free. Kind of operating in the subconscious. I was just thinking about how to get us into the best play within a twenty-to-twenty-eight-second time frame, after we broke the huddle and got to the line of scrimmage.

We were definitely *very* close. And we got closer as the year went on.

It even carried into the way we talked on the sidelines. He was always a bit more fiery than I was. I always tried to be even-keel. I had my emotional moments, but I would never let it get too high. I'd make sure I came back down to try and stay in that zone.

Bill would come over all fired up and I'd give him a very clean answer. Like, "Yeah, they were giving us this look, this is what the guy did, I think we can maybe try this after that." I'd just talk about what I saw and how we could adjust to it. And he'd look at me and be like, "That's great!" And I'd be like, "Yeah, so let's do it."

He'd come in all hot and I'd be flatlined. We balanced each other out really well. That's something I always enjoyed. I'd sit there waiting, like I can't wait to hear what he's going to say. But, as the year went on, he'd come over to me very calm, because he tried to match me. And we'd get more accomplished that way. There wasn't always that shock-and-awe moment.

"How are you so relaxed?"

"Why are you so upset? First quarter."

We got all that out of the way early in the year.

JOHN URSCHEL: O'Brien did a great job with him. By the end of the season, I'm telling you, he gave Christian lots of freedom . . . he was asking much more of Christian. And Christian had matured into a real leader.

The seniors, the upperclassmen—Hackenberg had all of our respect.

EIGHTEEN

LIVING UP TO THE HYPE

AT THE START *of a new season, every program wrestles with uncertainties, but as they prepared for Syracuse in 2013, the Nittany Lions had a daunting list of unknowns.*

Their opponent, a longtime rival, had a new head coach and two unfamiliar quarterbacks: a sophomore with a dangerous arm and nimble feet and a pro-style transfer, who had arrived from Oklahoma after serving two years as the backup to fourth-round draft pick Landry Jones.

Which one would be playing? That was the first big question.

The next was how the two teams would respond to squaring off in a showcase game on the NFL turf of MetLife Stadium, home to the Giants and Jets and soon-to-be site of the 2014 Broncos-Seahawks Super Bowl.

And then there was the heat: The temperature on the field before kickoff was a soul-sapping one hundred and four degrees.

The Lions had a new center and a new left tackle on the offensive line, a new coordinator for the defense, and, of course, a quarterback who—as Bill O'Brien joked—was only a few months removed from his senior prom. Hackenberg was one of thirty-one freshman players (sixteen true and fifteen redshirt) on the team's seventy-four-man travel squad.

MARK BRENNAN: All of a sudden, you go through this gigantic change—a sea change for Penn State football. It was incredibly rare for the school to play a freshman quarterback.

Against Youngstown State in 2010, Rob Bolden had become the first in a hundred years to start a season opener. Wally Richardson started a game against Temple back in 1992 due to injuries.

But to anoint a true freshman the starting quarterback before the season started?

Hackenberg immediately becomes the face of the program.

And not only does he become the face of the program, but he lives up to the hype. That's not to say he didn't have some growing pains, but overall, he lived up to the hype. He was that good as a freshman under Bill O'Brien.

CHRISTIAN HACKENBERG: Pregame, I had some nerves, but it is what it is. I'm in the bathroom in the locker room and I hear someone throwing up in the toilet next to me. I'm at the urinal and there's a stall right there. The door opens, Bill comes out, slaps me on the ass, says "Good luck, kid."

I'm like, that's my head coach, throwing up next to me. What the hell's going on?

BILL O'BRIEN: We went into MetLife Stadium with a true freshman quarterback. I think it was a hundred and four degrees on the field. We didn't have our best wide receiver in the first half.

GENO LEWIS: A-Rob got suspended.

I remember Bill O'Brien calling me up to tell me you're starting this week. He said, "I wouldn't start you if I didn't think you were ready."

So, yeah, that's when I made my first real catch.

CHARLIE FISHER: That's right, A-Rob was suspended. He and safety Adrian Amos got into a little scuffle in preseason camp.

CHRISTIAN HACKENBERG: Not having Allen that first half was tough for me, because I'd put so much time into working with him and he was such a focus for Bill. Bill was like, "Listen, if stuff goes awry, and you need a safety outlet, just find Eight." So not having that option was tough.

That's kind of why we were just slugging along.

With Zach Zwinak running the ball and Hackenberg making safe throws, the Lions picked up just one first down in each of the first two drives. On the third series, as planned, O'Brien gave Tyler Ferguson a chance to show what he could do. The backup quarterback handed off to Bill Belton for a five-yard loss, completed a twenty-yard strike to sophomore Matt Zanellato, then fumbled the football on a sack. Syracuse turned the mishap into a field goal for a 3–0 lead.

Hackenberg returned and promptly threw an interception at the Syracuse thirty-seven-yard line.

Two plays later, safety-turned-linebacker Stephen Obeng-Agyapong stripped the ball from running back Jerome Smith and recovered the fumble at midfield to put the offense back in Hackenberg's hands.

The freshman drove the team thirty yards for a game-tying field goal.

On the next series, he led an eight-play, forty-one-yard drive for a second field goal.

BILL O'BRIEN: The Syracuse defense threw a lot of stuff at him and overall the way he handled it was pretty good.

CHRISTIAN HACKENBERG: They brought a lot of pressure. It was relentless, all game, but our offensive line did a great job picking that up.

GARRY GILLIAM: As time went on, you could see him get more comfortable in the role.

TY HOWLE, CENTER AND OFFENSIVE GUARD, 2009–13: He showed a lot of poise.

CHRISTIAN HACKENBERG: Overall, I felt comfortable with what I was doing. The offensive line gave me a ton of time with the ball, the backs did a good job running the ball for me, and the receivers made plays.

To keep Penn State in the game, O'Brien leaned heavily on his defense, now coached by John Butler, who had assumed the coordinator role in January when Ted Roof left for Georgia Tech. Defensive tackle DaQuan Jones had a team-high nine stops. But Stephen Obeng-Agyapong, who grew up in the Bronx, just fifteen miles from MetLife stadium, was the star of the day.

In the spring, he'd shifted from defensive back to outside linebacker. And in a venue filled with family and friends, he delivered eight tackles, the first-quarter fumble, a pivotal fourth-quarter sack, and his first career interception. The two takeaways led to Sam Ficken field goals.

Penn State ended the half leading 6–3.

In the third quarter, with Allen Robinson back on the field, Christian Hackenberg started to show flashes of the promise that had earned him the starting job at quarterback.

CHRISTIAN HACKENBERG: Everyone saw what happened when Allen came into the game. We throw him a bubble screen, he takes it twenty-five yards. We throw a friggin' bubble-and-go, he takes that for a fifty-one-yard touchdown. It was off to the races from there.

CHARLIE FISHER: Two plays after Robinson came in, we were in the end zone.

KYLE CARTER: He had, like, two catches in a row—big plays—and we were rolling.

CHRISTIAN HACKENBERG: Allen made my job so much easier. I mean, he was unbelievable. With his frame, catch radius, ball skills, route-running ability, he was a great outlet for me. The guy always won battles for the ball. He understood how to set DBs up, how to win in one-on-one situations, how to win with double moves when the defense was trying to cloud him. He was very good—very, very good.

He had a knack for creating openings for teammates, too, luring safeties away from Penn State's other receivers. Early in the fourth quarter, he drew double coverage on one such play, leaving redshirt freshman Geno Lewis wide open on a deep post route. Hackenberg saw Lewis streaking toward the end zone and pounced.

CHRISTIAN HACKENBERG: Geno ran a great route, really dipped the corner, and the safety bit on the wheel that A-Rob was doing, so I threw it up to Geno.

BILL O'BRIEN: Zach Zwinak blocked the blitzing linebacker and allowed Christian to step up.

GENO LEWIS: Hack let that thing go, man. I just remember running the post route and the ball being in the air for so long. I'm like, Hurry up, hurry up, hurry up! Drop! Because I saw the defenders coming.

Everything worked out. The ball dropped in there. I made the play.

The completion—Hack's second fifty-plus-yard pass play of the day—put Penn State up 23–10. At times, though, the young quarterback's inexperience was evident, too. On a third-and-eleven play late in the game, Hackenberg overlooked a Syracuse lineman dropping back into coverage and threw an interception that was returned for thirty yards. The Orange quickly scored on a one-yard run, trimming the lead to six.

"He made a mistake, but I put him in that position," said Bill O'Brien, second-guessing the aggressive play call.

But, all in all, Hackenberg left the Penn State folks who watched the game from the stands and on ABC feeling hopeful, completing the day with two big touchdown plays and 278 yards passing. By contrast, Drew Allen, who got the start for Syracuse after transferring from Oklahoma, threw for 189 yards without a touchdown, but tossed two interceptions.

CHARLIE FISHER: You never know what to expect until they get out there and play. Obviously, Christian had the hopes of the fan base riding on him. For an eighteen-year-old kid, he had a lot on his plate. And he handled it beautifully. He made a lot of good decisions.

CHRISTIAN HACKENBERG: After the game, that Monday or Tuesday, we were doing center-quarterback exchange drills in practice and Bill walks over to me.

He's like, "You know, man, about week three or four, you're gonna go back and watch this film and be, like, 'What the *hell* were you doing?'"

And I'm like, "What do you mean?"

"You're gonna sit there and go, 'Why was I making that check into this look?' Things like that."

He was one-thousand-percent right. He predicted my growth even before I could see it.

I was like, Damn, if he isn't right.

That game was me just making stuff happen, taking advantage of a couple of big shots. A young kid trying to figure it all out. It just so happened the good outweighed the bad.

MARK BRENNAN: For years and years, Penn State didn't allow true freshmen to speak to the media. Not until the spring semester of their freshman year. Joe had a couple of rare exceptions—Derrick Williams and Justin King. But after his first game, Hackenberg was up there on the podium. At the Meadowlands. Talking to the media.

He wasn't a fiery interview like McGloin, but he carried himself extremely well. Like a pro quarterback, when he was a freshman—let's put it that way.

He carried himself like an NFL quarterback when dealing with the media, fans, and stuff. That's why I'll always respect him.

CHRISTIAN HACKENBERG: I've still got one of the tickets to that Syracuse game. Someone gave it to me. It's in my truck. I keep it in my side console.

NINETEEN

RUN-ONS: TAKE TWO

As the 2013 *season unfolded, Bill O'Brien was still looking for clever ways to fill the holes in Penn State's roster. He had opened the year with sixty-seven scholarship players and, to comply with the NCAA sanctions, he would have to trim that figure by two in 2014.*

Adding to the challenge, players like Steven Bench, who had transferred to South Florida after losing the quarterback battle to Hackenberg, still counted against the coach's scholarship total.

And so, the Lions' talent pool had thinned significantly, leaving the receiving corps, linebacker unit, and secondary with little depth, even before early-season injuries to linebacker Mike Hull and tight end Matt Lehman.

Given the limited rotation and the rigors of the game, it didn't make sense to have starting middle linebacker Glenn Carson snapping footballs on punts—as he did in the Syracuse game. Better to preserve his legs for pursuing quarterbacks and ball carriers.

But how does one replace a long snapper on short notice?

With a student-body walk-on tryout.

ZACH LADONIS: After high school, I didn't have many opportunities outside of DIII, DII schools. I had the grades and the desire to be an aerospace engineer, so I told George Curry, the legendary coach of Berwick High School, I was not gonna play football.

"Well, if you want to go to Penn State," he said, "I know a guy. Just come down to the field after school and long-snap a bit."

I had played a little in ninth grade, tenth grade, eleventh grade, twelfth grade, but was never really the guy—even on my high school team. Midsummer, before my freshman year in college, we had a guy with scholarship potential and Mac McWhorter, Penn State's offensive line coach, came to watch him practice.

I was out there long-snapping and George did his thing, kind of pointed me out to Mac.

GEORGE CURRY: I told him, "I got a kid you want to look at—as a walk-on. He's a heck of a long snapper. He'll run down and tackle for you, too."

ZACH LADONIS: When McWhorter came over, I said, "Hello, how's it going? You coach at Penn State? That's cool—I'm going to Penn State. Already been accepted."

He said, "Come try out for the team."

My first weekend in State College, I'm in the East Halls dorms. Not where the football players stay, more like Pollock Commons, with the generic freshmen. The run-on tryouts are September 16, I believe. So I'm preparing. Not like everybody else on the team—I'm a regular college student who goes to the generic gym.

One thing leads to another and a couple of college buddies are out catching snaps for me at the tailgating field near the Arboretum. I went on runs, did the whole workout routine.

That run-on tryout was the oh, crap moment—as in, this could actually be a thing.

Fitz put everyone through the ringer. We were running conditioning drills and I was super winded. I'd already snapped about one hundred times to show the staff my stuff. Then we started running suicides and I could feel it in my quads. Next he put us through NFL bag drills and beat us down as far as we could go.

They basically took the top ten out of eighty to a hundred kids. My number was called and I thought, This is a blessing, I'm one of ten people that get to do even more of a workout.

That one was even more intense. I'm running through these drills dog-tired. They finally call us together. Ten of us.

A lot of the other students had stayed to watch.

They said, "All right, if we call your number, we want you to stick around."

Once again, a blessing: I'm one of three people whose number gets called. I'm standing there talking to Coach Fitz and Bill Kavanaugh, the director of player personnel. They're like, "Zach, we really like what you have. Practice just ended. We want you to snap for the coaches."

I was like, You want me to snap more? I'm dead tired.

As a long snapper, you usually come in fresh, snap the ball once, and go back to the sideline. This was not normal, to be dead tired, barely able to squat down, jelly legs all over.

I'm snapping to one of the other guys who got his number called. All the coaches from Bill O'Brien down to, I think, Larry Johnson are feeding me balls. And I'm throwing them through my legs, hitting the target every single time. After a while, I was amazed. I was so tired, there was no nervousness anymore. No, wow, I've been coming to Penn State games since I was three or four years old. This was survival.

Eventually, they told me, "You did great today. We'll get back to you."

BILL O'BRIEN: I personally timed him and thought he did a really good job.

ZACH LADONIS: I was ecstatic. Went back to my room and started telling my roommates, calling my high school coach, my parents, my trainer, everybody.

I was like, "I think I just made the team! I think I just made the team!"

Three or four days later, I get a call from Kirk Diehl, the player personnel guy. He says, "Zach, you made the team. We want you to come in. We've got some things to discuss."

During that whole stretch, I was going to games as a regular student. I think there were two games before I tried out and then they couldn't start me for another two games.

Kirk Diehl called me into the office. He's telling me all this stuff about the meetings. And everybody's saying you can't really start playing for two weeks, but we'll get you in, kind of let you be around the team—in the locker room, out at practice—if you want to come.

Obviously, if you're trying to make the team, you go to practice when they say if you want to come. It was a very surreal moment, every kid's dream.

My first practice was at the start of a bye week and then we played at Indiana. I practiced all through that first week and on Monday, Tuesday, Wednesday the next week. After Wednesday's practice, my position coach said, "Hey, keep your phone close to you. We're not sure how the depth chart's going to work out. We have a game against Indiana, but like, you just joined the team two weeks ago, so we're not sure what's going to happen."

That next morning, I was up, getting ready. I think we had a workout at 6 a.m. The coach called me, left a voicemail. I think I still have it on my phone.

"Hey, Zach, you're starting this weekend, we're taking you to Indiana. Here's how travel works . . ."

At seven o'clock in the morning, I get out of the workout, I'm freaking out inside. Like, how do I handle this kind of news in the locker room? It was very big for me, but everybody else is just like, whatever, man.

You get to go and actually play in the game. You're one of the guys, you know.

I remember calling my parents.

"Hey, they're taking me to the game. They think I'm gonna play. I don't know what else to tell you."

They packed up, got in the car, and drove to Indiana.

Given the nature of special teams, it's not uncommon for a walk-on to earn live reps in a game. It's not often, though, that a kid who was sitting in the stands for the home opener against Eastern Michigan finds himself down on the field in Indiana a few weeks later.

ZACH LADONIS: My first snap was a little high. All I could hear from the crowd was oooh and aaah. I was like, Oh, no, I really messed this one up! But I settled into the game, actually made a tackle on a return. It was pretty cool. I think I got like four plays. We punted four times.

The next game we played Michigan. That was the first time I ever stepped foot on the field at Beaver Stadium. It's a White Out game. We're warming up. I'm literally looking back at our punter, Alex Butterworth, and can't find him amidst all the commotion in the student section.

It was like, Where did he go? It's a wall of white and like his little blue jersey. I just snapped it straight back, he caught it, and I heard the thump. I was like, Okay, this is how this one's going to go.

That game was absolutely insane. That's the one where we went into four overtimes.

TWENTY

NITTANY NATION

ONLY ELEVEN STADIUMS *in the world have the capacity to seat 100,000 people. One of them sits atop a bluff on Penn State's campus, visible from two miles away as you approach the school on Route 99. On football Saturdays, the venue draws so many fans that State College becomes the fourth largest city in the state, surpassed only by Philadelphia, Pittsburgh, and Allentown.*

Needless to say, the passion for Penn State football runs deep. You see it in the countless blue-and-white lion's paw magnets that dot cars throughout the Northeast; in the impromptu exchanges between perfect strangers decked out in PSU slickers or T-shirts; in the swarm of Nittanyville kids who camp out the week before the big game to be first in line for the seats in the student section; and in the tricked-out RVs and tailgate tents that stretch as far as the eye can see in the fields surrounding the stadium in the hours before kickoff.

And then, of course, there's the stunning spectacle of 106,572 ivory-clad fans pumping ivory pom-poms and roaring in support of the team at the annual White Out game. Urban Meyer, who witnessed the fervor of this raucous celebration up close for six seasons as head coach of the Ohio State Buckeyes, called it the toughest environment in the country to compete.

For people unfamiliar with the Penn State program and its storied traditions, it may be hard to fathom how anyone could rally around the coach, the team, and the university, given the scope of Jerry Sandusky's malfea-sance—as if it's impossible to separate the crimes of the monster from the morals of the larger community.

For those who know Penn State well, the heinous acts—and the ques-tions they raised—were no less disturbing. But the rush to judgment in the outside world left no time for genuine answers.

How much did Paterno and university administrators know? Did they plot to conceal the facts?

There's no way to say for sure. The media stormed in and trampled the crime scene before the evidence could be collected. The executioners on talk radio, cable TV, and Twitter weighed the facts and convicted the accused based solely on the details in a grand jury report. The story dropped on a Friday. By the following Wednesday, Joe Paterno, the head coach of forty-six years, was gone without so much as an inquiry—dismissed by the univer-sity's bunkered board of trustees with a handwritten note delivered to his door in the dark of night.

When you view the fallout that followed from that vantage point, it's easier to understand the confused reaction from the fans, the angry out-bursts from teenage students. Their campus had been invaded by a hostile force. Their longtime leader beheaded without a trial.

DARIAN SOMERS: I guess you could say my allegiance to Penn State started prior to birth. I was in the womb for my first game, so, you know, the al-ternative was not really an option in my house. It was like, do you want to root for another team or do you want to get fed?

Every happy childhood memory I have is tied to Penn State football. When it was time for college, I applied to one school. I started an applica-tion to Robert Morris, but said, "Screw it. There's no way I'm *not* going to Penn State. It's too big a part of my life."

SARA BUTCHER, PRESIDENT, NITTANYVILLE, 2016–17: There was never any other option for me. My whole family—my dad, all my aunts and uncles—went to Penn State. My great-aunt and -uncle lived in State College.

My great-uncle actually worked in the university's Old Main building for almost two decades, if not more. So I had been coming to State College since I was a kid, going to games with my dad from like seven years old on, walking around campus at the age of thirteen. I knew that's where I wanted to be when it was time to choose a college. I didn't apply anywhere else.

That was probably dumb in hindsight, but it worked out well.

We'd be at the games and I'd point to the student section and say, "Dad, I'm going to be over there one day. You're going to be waving at me from across the stadium."

And that's how it worked out.

DARIAN SOMERS: On the day Joe Paterno was fired, I played hockey—Altoona High against State High—in the Greenberg Ice Pavilion. The game must have been at eight-something at night and we probably got out of there at 9:45. When my mom and I got on I-99, there was virtually no one on the road. We're driving south and coming north are seven or eight cop cars in a flying V formation.

My mom and I looked at each other like, that's weird.

At 10:17, I get this ESPN text alert saying Joe had been fired.

Penn State had always been such a pillar in my life and a lot of that had to do with Joe. It was unimaginable to think he could be fired. He was everything to Penn State.

We were at the game where he got his 409th win. We kind of lucked into tickets. We were offered tickets to the Nebraska game two weeks later—the one right after he had been let go—and passed on them. I remember how I felt sitting on the couch that day, watching the team walk out of the tunnel. You never saw that. You only saw them run.

It was like, Is this going to be the Penn State I know and love in the future?

Obviously, there's so much more to a university than football, but to an eighteen-year-old kid who spent not every Saturday, but a lot of them, in State College, it really was everything.

ROB NELLIS, NITTANY LION MASCOT, 2011–13: I remember the day Joe Paterno was let go, because it was my birthday. I remember getting the news and being in shock.

I went to a friend's apartment off-campus. I didn't want to get caught up in all the hubbub.

I needed time to reflect.

MICHAEL WEINREB, AUTHOR, JOURNALIST, ALUM RAISED IN STATE COLLEGE: For many Penn State people, the university becomes part of your identity. It's such a fun place to go to school that people just embrace it—the idea of it.

TOM HANNIFAN, COHOST, *PAYDIRT* PODCAST WITH MATT MCGLOIN: My mom would play the Penn State Blue Band in the house on a tape, once upon a time when tape decks existed, so I got indoctrinated very early.

RYAN JONES, EDITOR, *PENN STATER* ALUMNI MAGAZINE: If you're an alum and you had a good experience at Penn State—it set you up with relationships, jobs, and all that—there is a strong emotional connection there.

A lot of that is tied to football and, for a *lot* of people, it's connected specifically to Joe Paterno and his teams, because he was there for so long and he was so successful. Because of everything he represented, the way he seemed to live his life.

MICHAEL WEINREB: To have all those pieces shaken up so suddenly, it was hard. A lot of us who went there felt a certain way about the school. Now how were we supposed to feel?

RYAN JONES: It was emotional. I mean, it hit people.

And so, identity was one of the angles we addressed in that first issue of the alumni magazine after the scandal broke. What does it mean to be a Penn Stater? To love Penn State?

That's the thing people were wrestling with.

Because so much of that identity had been undeniably positive for people. Like, Oh, hey, our football coach is great; he gives a lot of money to charity; he's got a big family; he's humble; and his team's almost always good. And, you know, he cares about the whole university community.

There was no reason to think all of that wasn't valid.

ROB NELLIS: I was asking myself, what's the Nittany Lion's role in all this?

I think everyone was a little confused. People were very down, very angry, but the Lion is always a beacon of positivity and respect. So the fact the Lion can't talk was a huge benefit, because there was no pressure to come up with a public statement.

MICHAEL WEINREB: The visceral anger from the nation was so high I stopped wearing Penn State stuff for a while. I was living in New York at the time and just didn't want to deal with it.

ROB NELLIS: Ultimately, I doubled down on my efforts to make appearances at student functions, because I sensed that the students just wanted to be students. You know, people sometimes refer to State College as a bubble, but that idea was amplified in 2011. People were really keying on the student body as a community, because there was a lot of animosity coming from the outside. And so, as the Lion, I wanted to be as engaged as I could in student activities, kind of show the university's support for those activities, show people that Penn State is not just a football school.

DARIAN SOMERS: I grew up in Altoona, so my allegiances for the most part align with the western side of the state. When it comes to sports, you were taught to respect the Rooneys—the family that owns the Pittsburgh Steelers—and respect JoePa.

In 2012, the year Paternoville was renamed Nittanyville, even though I was new to the group, I knew—we all knew—that what we were doing was big. It meant something to the people who care about the football program, care about the players, and it meant something to the players and coaches, too.

After all that had happened, people still truly cared about Penn State football. I'm sure you remember a lot of the columns and articles where people said ten thousand people are gonna show up at one-hundred-thousand-seat Beaver Stadium in the fall. Going to the games was, for lack of a better term, kind of a big eff-you to those people. Like, We're here, we still care about this school, we still care about this program. It doesn't matter who the head coach is. This is what we put our pride in.

SARA BUTCHER: I had camped out every game but one my freshman year and fell in love with it. Didn't want to be anywhere else. Seemed like all my friends were equally excited to be there. I didn't feel like I was missing out on the college experience, because you could go to class, you could live your life, but Wednesday, Thursday, Friday, there was always a reason to be at Nittanyville. Whether it was players visiting, other people from the university dropping by to deliver food and hang out, the culture was great. There was a sense of community there.

DARIAN SOMERS: The Ohio State game in 2012 still holds the record for the most campers at Nittanyville. Twelve hundred people slept outside the stadium in the days before the game. That shows that people were still passionate about Penn State football.

GERALD HODGES: A thousand people camping out for a week straight to show their support—that's truly amazing.

JASON CABINDA, LINEBACKER, 2014–17: That says so much about the fans we have, the craze about Penn State football.

SARA BUTCHER: You'd wake up outside the stadium and it was just people everywhere. I'd go to sleep every night on an air mattress but wake up on the concrete. It was part of the experience. My parents would laugh. Be like, You're paying rent to live in an apartment downtown and for six weeks out of the year you're living outside in a tent.

DARIAN SOMERS: One night, we look over and Carl Nassib, the team's starting defensive end, is walking up to the tents.

We're like, "What are you doing here?"

He's like, "Nothing! I just came to hang out."

He sat there with us for probably an hour and a half, playing cards. I think, for him, it was just a way to be a normal student for a bit. You never would have known he was on the football team.

SARA BUTCHER: Each week, a different group from the team would come and hang out. The players would eat dinner, then go to study hall, so they couldn't stay too long. But I distinctly remember hanging out with Carl Nassib, a great player, great guy. Very humble. He actually hung out with the Nittanyville exec board for about an hour after the team had left. We were just playing cards. A game called Spoons. I beat him like four times. It didn't seem like he needed to be there. To me, it felt like he wanted to be there. Had no reason to stay. Just wanted to hang out with fellow students. I will never forget that.

DARIAN SOMERS: Things like that would happen all the time. Matt McGloin used to stop up. Shane McGregor, the backup quarterback with the incredible hair, would show up all the time.

You'd get to know some of the guys and, later in the year, you'd go to a party and there would be Donovan Smith or Adrian Amos. It wasn't Donovan Smith, the football player. It was Donovan Smith, fellow college student.

The players drew strength from that bond with the community, too.

GENO LEWIS: Even though we weren't playing for a bowl game, NCAA championship, or Big Ten championship, we still had 100,000 people coming to those games, man. Not a lot of people can say they played in front of 110,000 people, you know what I mean?

I know what those White Out games are like. It's incredible. Something you can't totally understand if you've never experienced it before. So, that helped a lot of guys, man. That crowd, the people who were at Penn State supporting us, that's what we were playing for. That's all we really needed.

At the end of the day, we were still out there playing the game we loved, the game God gave us the blessing to go out there and play each day. You just had to find a bigger purpose, understand who you were doing it for.

Of all the participants in Penn State's athletic programs, not one is more in tune with the fans than the Nittany Lion mascot—or rather the student granted the honor to don the suit and commune with the masses, skillfully leading a stadium filled with human beings of every age to chant, cheer, and rejoice at the wonders of life on campus, without speaking a single word.

To preserve that mystique, the identity of the student is carefully concealed from the public—much like the true identity of Batman or Superman—until it's time to name a successor.

As a result, generations of spectators have come to see the Lion as a living, breathing symbol of the university, a figure worthy of tremendous affection in and around State College and tremendous vitriol in the stadiums of Big Ten rivals, especially during the sanction years.

ROB NELLIS: There were a lot of alumni who, even as sweaty as I was, just wanted a hug from the Nittany Lion. They'd come from out of town for a football game, feeling all these emotions, and here's the Nittany Lion, able to embrace them in person. That meant a lot to them. It was a reminder of the positivity of the Penn State experience.

JACK DAVIS, NITTANY LION MASCOT, 2015–17: The Nittany Lion's a great mascot, a member of the first class inducted into the Mascot Hall of Fame, but it's hard not to be good when you've got fans who are that passionate. All you have to do is walk into a room and everyone goes crazy. The bar is pretty low for firing people up, because they're so passionate about whatever it is: the football team, Relay for Life, THON, all these student interest groups on campus, the alumni chapters off-campus. It's incredible, even outside of game day, the passion Penn Staters have for whatever it is they're doing.

When the guy dressed up like an animal thinks the other person is crazy, you know you have some intense fans. I once met two kids before a game in Columbus, Ohio. One was named Bryce and one was named Jordan. It took me a second to put together that the couple that introduced them had named their children after former university president Bryce Jordan.

ROB NELLIS: I remember going to football games my freshman year and seeing the Lion down on the field. I kind of looked up to the Lion as a symbol. To be honest, though, I wasn't really thinking about being the mascot. My older sister, Kylie, was a cheerleader, two years ahead of me at Penn State, and she kind of mentioned that the trials for the Lion were happening, but I was still, you know, getting used to college life. I was like, That seems like a big commitment.

But the opportunity came around again towards the end of my junior year. By chance, I met Max Levi, the Lion before me, and he let me know he was graduating. "You seem like a good fit for the Lion," he said. "I encourage you to try out."

JACK DAVIS: I never thought being the mascot was on the table for me. I always assumed it was a gymnast or a cheerleader who got the role.

I was primarily a wrestler in high school. In my sophomore year in college, I was fooling around and taught myself how to do a backflip and that's when I thought, Hmmm, I'm going to nearly all the sporting events anyway—could I actually fill that position?

I researched it and learned that Michael Valania, the current Nittany Lion, was graduating and there was going to be an open tryout.

I spent about six months going to club gymnastics and dance groups on campus. Thankfully, in the spirit of Penn State, everyone was very open to having an amateur gymnast and very goofy dancer join in and learn from them.

ROB NELLIS: After talking to Max Levi, I was like, That seems like a really cool idea, so I tried to learn more about it—the Lion's role at the university, what it's like schedule-wise, what's required physically.

It was a three-stage tryout process. First, there was a written application, where you submitted your GPA and answered some high-level questions.

Why do you want to be the mascot? What would you bring to the position?

JACK DAVIS: It's about five pages long. What does Penn State mean to you? That kind of thing. They might make a couple of cuts there. Generally, though, you only get about ten applicants.

ROB NELLIS: From there, they select a number of candidates for interviews.

I sat on one end of the table, surrounded by, I think, nine or ten interviewers: one or two of the cheerleading coaches, a representative from the Alumni Association, a representative from the Blue Band, one or two previous Lions, as well as a couple of other people with a vested interest in who was selected to be the Lion. It was kind of cool, but also a little intimidating.

JACK DAVIS: You don't get to put the Lion suit on until the actual tryout, and I really wanted to do a backflip in the suit. To prepare for that, I'd wear three coats and blindfold myself at gymnastics and see if I could still do a backflip. And, thankfully, that practice paid off. I was able to land one in the tryout. Of course, there's a big interview component to it as well. They're looking for someone they trust to represent Penn State and the Nittany Lion off the field.

ROB NELLIS: I made it through the interview process and they selected candidates to do a physical tryout, which had three main components. There was a skit or a dance component, indicative of what the Lion might do at a football or basketball game. It had a two-minute time limit.

And then, there was an improvisation portion, where you picked an item out of a duffel bag and had thirty seconds to entertain the judges with it.

And, lastly, you had to do fifty one-arm pushups on command, which are obviously a big tradition for the Lion.

JACK DAVIS: The criteria is fifty one-arm pushups. That narrows the field a bit.

ROB NELLIS: There's a lot of endurance required, because you never know what's going to happen.

JACK DAVIS: At Purdue in 2016, we ended up winning 62–24. That's the most one-handed pushups I ever did—one for each point scored after each touchdown. I remember getting heckled by a Purdue fan towards the end of the first half about how we were going to have that hangover loss after the Ohio State upset.

ROB NELLIS: Only one student at a time is selected to be the mascot. On the main campus, at least. Penn State is pretty unique in that sense. There's a formal backup, someone who can fill in temporarily if you get injured or something. But, yeah, it's your main commitment.

It adds a sense of responsibility.

Hey, this is my role. The Lion is going to be whatever I make it personify.

It allows you to step into that role, not only while you have the suit on, but also as a regular student on campus, knowing that anything you say or do should reflect the Lion, even though I took good care to keep my identity anonymous.

With the campus being so large, with so many students, most people didn't know I was the Lion and I really liked that, because it took the pressure off a bit. At the same time, I made sure to conduct myself in and out of the suit with the highest degree of respectfulness.

That may be one reason I was selected to take on the role—that kind of came second nature to me: the responsibility and the humility it required. Recognizing the position for what it is, more of an honor than one person can totally grasp. You're essentially responsible for personifying the university and its values.

JACK DAVIS: It was a good fit for me. I have a bit of goofiness in my character and a bit of seriousness and that's one thing we talked about with the Nittany Lion, always carrying yourself with that pride and that swagger, but not taking yourself too seriously, especially if a kid runs up. You can't be too big-time to get down and play.

ROB NELLIS: At events where you interact with alumni, away football games and things like that, I was always the guy who disappeared from the room right before the pep rally. So, yes, some of the alumni members caught on that I was the Nittany Lion. But I went through pretty good lengths to remain anonymous.

When I was in the suit, I was very visible. But when I went to change, I'd sometimes linger in the locker room longer than I needed to, just to make sure nobody who saw me go in to change was standing around waiting for me to come out. I'd put the suit in a bag, just casually walk out, and go about my business as if I'd just gone to the gym.

JACK DAVIS: I grew up watching the Phillie Phanatic. He's definitely on one end of the goofy spectrum. As the Nittany Lion, you have to strike a balance, try to be intimidating, fierce, doing one-arm pushups, some acrobatics, but also having fun, being a bit silly with some of the skits.

There are more smartphones around these days. When you talk to older Nittany Lions, they've got much better stories than I do, because they weren't worried about everything finding its way onto film. Even in the uniform, they had things they could do without worrying about it getting recorded and sent around. They could have more fun pushing the boundaries. I was very careful at all times to avoid doing anything that could go viral in a negative way.

TWENTY-ONE

FOUR-OT WIN

THE PLAYERS PRIDED *themselves on their resiliency. In two years' time, they had withstood wave after wave of unprecedented challenges—from the NCAA, a hostile press corps, unscrupulous recruiters, the cutthroat crowds at Big Ten stadiums, and the venomous know-it-alls on Facebook and Twitter.*

They kept pressing forward.

Linebacker Glenn Carson called it a bend-don't-break mindset.

"If things don't go your way," he said, "you just keep playing."

On October 12, 2013, the team's resolve would be sorely tested when 5–0 Michigan, ranked eighteenth in the country by the Associated Press, ventured to Beaver Stadium for the Homecoming Game. In prior weeks, the 2–2 Lions had suffered painful losses to Central Florida and Indiana, two teams that could once be counted on to concede without much of a fight. After falling eighteen points behind Central Florida in the third quarter, Penn State had rallied with two rushing touchdowns from Zach Zwinak and a five-yard touchdown catch by Allen Robinson, but John Butler's beleaguered defense was no match for quarterback Blake Bortles, who completed one big play after another en route to five hundred yards of total offense.

The bout with Indiana—a conference foe with an 0–16 record against Penn State—was even more dispiriting. Trailing 21–17 after three quarters, the Lions' defense went into free fall, giving up twenty-three fourth-quarter points. Final score: 44–24.

The roster depth issues that had hampered the team in early 2012 seemed to have resurfaced. But the players raised their play once more, bending but not breaking against a resourceful Michigan team—one that had rallied for white-knuckle victories over uncharacteristically strong opposition from Akron and UConn. The White Out showdown between the Lions and the Wolverines produced so many big moments in the waning minutes that the first three quarters barely register in most fans' minds. Everyone remembers the four-overtime duel that decided the outcome and the famous catch that launched all that drama—by Allen Robinson, a Penn State kid born in Detroit, roughly forty miles east of Michigan's hallowed campus.

BILL O'BRIEN: That's a game I'll always remember—four overtimes, back and forth, great crowd. It was a five o'clock start, so the sun was just setting. A beautiful day and 107,000 fans were watching. It was a four-hour game. I mean, it went forever.

CHRISTIAN HACKENBERG: It was a White Out game, Beaver Stadium, five o'clock—you knew it was going to be a brawl.

ALLEN ROBINSON: I had Michigan marked on my schedule since the day I set foot in State College.

My family came to see the game. My buddy, Juwan Howard's son, came.

I remember the bus ride to the stadium. The route was packed. As we're making the drive, there are tens of thousands of people there.

ADRIAN AMOS: The crowd was crazy.

BILL O'BRIEN: I'll never forget the feeling of that stadium. The ground was actually shaking.

You could feel the ground shaking.

SAM FICKEN: That was a huge, huge moment for us as a team.

ERIC SHRIVE: Hackenberg played out of his mind.

CHARLIE FISHER: He just made throw after throw.

JOHN URSCHEL: Before the game, he kept saying he had a really good feeling about this one.

CHRISTIAN HACKENBERG: At that point in the season, I was really seeing things, not only commanding protections and understanding where I needed to go with the football in the pass game but hitting a stride with my understanding of the run game, too. Throughout the night, I made checks from pass to run or run to run. From a maturation standpoint, that was cool.

BILL BELTON: He was calm, never got rattled, no matter what happened.

The team played well from the start, forging a 21–10 lead midway through the second quarter. Hackenberg threw a touchdown pass to Brandon Felder to get the Lions on the board, then connected with tight end Jesse James for a second score—one play after an interception by defensive end Anthony Zettel—and hit Felder again with a pinpoint twenty-four-yard toss while on the run.

Michigan came storming back in the second half, returning a Zach Zwinak fumble twenty-five yards for a score on the opening drive, then adding a pair of touchdown throws by Devin Gardner to push ahead 34–24.

A Sam Ficken field goal trimmed the Wolverine lead to seven points with 6:35 left in the game, but the Lions' hopes faded as Michigan advanced the ball to the Penn State twenty-seven. A delay of game penalty on third-and-nine pushed the ball back to the thirty-two and, given the time on the clock and the field position, Wolverine coach Brady Hoke opted to pin Penn State deep with a punt instead of attempting a lengthy field goal.

Matt Wile's boot landed in the end zone.

That put the ball back in Hackenberg's hands with fifty seconds, no timeouts, and eighty yards to go for a game-tying touchdown.

PAT ZERBE: People always ask, "Were you nervous? Did you think you were going to lose?" And for some reason, I don't know what it was about that day, but I never had an inkling we were gonna lose that game. It was surreal.

BILL BELTON: We used to practice the two-minute drill all the time, so it felt routine. I'm like, all right, our backs are against the wall, we've got this amount of time, we've got to go down and score.

ALLEN ROBINSON: From the time camp started to that day, we'd probably run a hundred two-minute drills, with thirty seconds remaining, zero or one timeout.

BILL O'BRIEN: We'd try to mix up the situations, hoping two or three times during the year those situations would come up and our players would have an idea how to react.

PAT ZERBE: O'Brien would yell out, "Forty seconds left! You're on your own forty! One timeout! You need a field goal to win!" And then we'd go against the defense.

I swear, the situation on that Thursday before the Michigan game was we're on our own thirty-five. Like, a minute-thirty left. One timeout. We need a touchdown to tie the game. I'm almost positive that was the situation. I just remember thinking, *We just did this. We literally just practiced this.*

CHARLIE FISHER: We'd talked about that scenario in a Friday staff meeting. We'd just sit around and randomly talk about situations and somehow we'd talked about that exact thing, almost foretelling what was going to happen.

PAT ZERBE: That's what O'Brien always preached: situational football. Knowing the down and distance, where you are on the field, the time on the clock, everything encompassed in that play.

CHRISTIAN HACKENBERG: This was our chance to go out and execute it—do it for real.

PAT ZERBE: On the first play, Allen Robinson ran like a fifteen-yard out route to the left sideline and made a great catch. As soon as that first play hit, I was like, Oh, we're scoring!

BILL BELTON: That was probably the best catch I've seen. The ball was damn near the players standing out of bounds and Allen ended up putting his foot down in bounds and getting his body and his hands out there to catch the ball.

CHRISTIAN HACKENBERG: One thing Bill always stressed is, when you start a two-minute drive, a successful first play is huge in getting things going. And when I threw that come-back to Allen, I was like, Shit, I left it wide, and he *caught* it.

That was the best catch of the drive.

After watching the play at full speed, the officials ruled the catch out of bounds, but instant replay confirmed that Robinson, soaring across the sideline, arms thrust out like Superman, had indeed gotten one big toe down with the ball in his grasp.

JOE TESSITORE, ESPN ANNOUNCER: An incredible job of balance by Allen Robinson. Left foot down, the right foot still floating.

PAT ZERBE: Then Brandon Felder caught a nice pass on the right sideline.

CHARLIE FISHER: Great catch. Safety was closing on him and whacked him right when he caught it.

CHRISTIAN HACKENBERG: Felder had played great that game. And that free safety was kind of getting nosy. I don't know if it was because we had some big plays up the seam, but he was kinda expecting Felder, I think. I just snapped into a hole shot to the field. Felder caught it and I was like, Well, I got away with that one, so I want a heater.

I should never have completed that throw. Like, not in a million years.

JOE TESSITORE: Penn State's in business folks. Watch out!

Hack spikes the ball to stop the clock with thirty-five seconds left.

MATT MILLEN, ESPN ANALYST: He needs maybe fifteen yards and then you can think about taking a shot. You don't have to eat it all up. You've got thirty-five seconds. The clock stops as they move the chains. Put yourself in a better position to make a throw.

CHRISTIAN HACKENBERG: The next signal was all-go. I looked at Allen and he didn't have to say anything. When I called it, he just looked at me and I looked at him and we kind of nodded. Pre-snap, I'm like, I'm putting this bitch up to Eight. I'm putting it up to Eight. If he makes a play, great. If he doesn't, we'll figure it out.

I vividly remember being like, I'm throwing this football to Allen. There's nothing on Planet Earth that's going to stop me from throwing this ball to Allen.

PAT ZERBE: And then Hackenberg launches the ball.

CHRISTIAN HACKENBERG: I took the snap and looked at that free safety. I went to hitch and I felt our left tackle Donovan Smith getting pushed back, so I took that little step forward. That safety kind of stopped for a second and I just let it go.

VON WALKER: That was it. That was the story. That play right there reflected our year.

You had a bunch of talented people, a bunch of older guys, just throwing Hail Marys, working their asses off and hoping something sticks.

That one stuck.

When Allen caught that ball on the one, it was kind of over. I felt we were going to win.

ALLEN ROBINSON: We had run all-go on the prior play, too. Hack threw to Brandon Felder and the pass almost got intercepted. When he called it again, I just had a feeling he was going to come to me. Once I got down there and saw him throwing the ball, I just wanted to make a play.

It's funny because I feel like I was in the perfect position. Right behind the DB. In the perfect position to catch the ball.

MATT MCGLOIN: It was like, A-Rob is down there somewhere, I'm just going to throw it up. But knowing O'Brien, it was probably supposed to go to

Allen. Bill always did an awesome job of putting you in a position for the ball to go your way.

CHRISTIAN HACKENBERG: I figured I'd give the guy with a thirty-eight-inch vertical a shot and he went up and got it.

JOE TESSITORE: Six-foot-two cornerback Channing Stribling went all the way up and somehow, some way, Robinson hauled it in.

PAT ZERBE: That catch will live in fans' heads forever. That guy, he thrives in big moments, so you knew what was gonna happen. He's coming down with it. The fact he kept his body in bounds is unbelievable. But we knew he was coming down with the ball.

ALLEN ROBINSON: Every time I see that play, I get the same feeling. It's definitely surreal.

CHARLIE FISHER: I still have the picture in my office. It's signed by Allen. I'm looking at it right now. Allen going up over the DB to make a catch, which is—I don't want to say the greatest catch in Penn State history, because there've been a lot of great catches—but it's right up there in the top five.

Christian slid forward in the pocket, bought just enough time, and let it rip and, you know, Allen being Allen—a great high-point guy—went up and made the play. I mean, the kid from Michigan, God bless him, he wasn't in bad shape. He's nearly got his hand on the ball, but it was just enough above him for Allen to pluck it right off his fingertips.

CHRISTIAN HACKENBERG: I thought Allen had scored. I was running downfield like, he scored! He scored! He scored! And Bill's like, *He didn't score! He didn't score! Get on the line!* Yelling at me. The place has friggin' erupted. That was nuts.

The officials stopped the clock for a replay review, eventually confirming yet another clutch Robinson catch and placing the ball a half-yard from the end zone. Michigan coach Brady Hoke used his last timeout to talk with his defense.

When the teams returned to the field, Penn State lined up in I-formation with Pat Zerbe at fullback and Bill Belton at tailback.

JOE TESSITORE: This looks and smells to me like play-action to the tight end.

PAT ZERBE: Hackenberg runs a QB sneak.

CHARLIE FISHER: That big rascal snuck it in. Used that big body to get it in there.

PAT ZERBE: If you look back at the tape, I'm yelling at the guys, because I wasn't sure he got in. I'm telling them to get back on the line, get back on the line!

And then the refs come in, say, It's a touchdown.

That left Penn State one extra point away from tying the game at 34.

SAM FICKEN: I had a new holder that week. Adam Geiger, a true freshman. He'd held for me one day in practice and they put him in the game. I was pretty nervous about that.

The snap was good, Geiger fielded the ball cleanly and placed it on the turf for Ficken's kick. The ball sailed through the uprights.

CHRISTIAN HACKENBERG: After that drive, I snapped out of the whole thought process for a second, the laser focus. I looked around and I was like, *Man, this is pretty cool.* It was the first time I took in the greatness of Beaver Stadium.

PAT ZERBE: Long story short, we go into overtime and it was a battle. I think their kicker missed like, what, three field goals?

ERIC SHRIVE: It was like a game that was never-ending.

AUDREY SNYDER: I was down on the sideline, thinking, Well, my game story, sidebar, whatever I was planning to write that day has blown up in my face ten times over.

These storybook moments just kept unfolding.

Michigan's ace kicker Brendan Gibbons tried to seal the game with a fifty-two-yard field goal at the end of regulation, but the ball fell just short of the crossbar. It was his first miss in seventeen tries.

Sam Ficken had converted two of three field goal attempts earlier in the day, but his kick in the first overtime period missed wide right from forty yards out.

MATT MILLEN: That was a squirrelly kick, like a knuckleball.

JOE TESSITORE: It didn't have the perfect end-over-end rotation.

Michigan played it conservative once again, rushing for just two yards in three plays, while keeping the ball near the center of the field for a field goal try, then sent Gibbons out to kick the game-winner from forty yards out. The ball was blocked by defensive tackle Kyle Baublitz.

"The kicker had been kicking it low," he said, "so I pushed the line back, waited for a second or two, then put my hands up. It hit me in the arm."

The two teams traded field goals in the second overtime.

ERIC SHRIVE: And then, O'Brien—I don't know what the hell he was doing—ran some sort of horseshit reverse and we fumbled.

On first-and-ten from the twenty-five, Hackenberg faked the handoff to Belton, then gave the ball to Robinson sweeping right and the receiver dropped it, right into the hands of a Michigan defender.

MATT MILLEN: It was the right call. The field was wide open on that side. It was a good handoff. Allen Robinson just never got the handle.

JOE TESSITORE: Michigan would win with any score.

BILL BELTON: The third overtime was the most tense. Michigan had a chance to seal the game. But our defense came out and played well. We did a good job getting after the field goal kicker, too.

ERIC SHRIVE: Michigan's kicker missed the field goal.

The snap was good, the hold was good, Gibbons just pushed the ball left from thirty-three yards out. When he saw the ball drift wide, he lowered his head in his hands. It was his third miss in four tries.

BILL BELTON: That gave us the opportunity to go to the fourth overtime and seal the deal.

Michigan got the ball first. On first down, Devin Gardner had to throw the ball away under pressure from defensive end Deion Barnes. On second down, the quarterback overthrew his receiver. On third down, Michigan got called for delay of game for failing to snap the football in time. On third-and-fifteen, Gardner was forced from the pocket and scrambled for a few yards.

Gibbons made the forty-yard kick on fourth down to put Michigan up 40–37.

Penn State's offense took the field.

On first down, Bill Belton rushed for five yards.

CHARLIE FISHER: On the next play, Belton had a great hole and he slipped. Otherwise he might have taken that one inside the five.

MATT MILLEN: He had a hole, just wasn't able to get there.

Instead he picked up one yard. On third-and-four, Hackenberg gave him the ball again and he came up a half-yard short of the first-down marker.

JOHN BACON: Bill O'Brien looks around. He sees the field's all torn up. He says, "Man, we got to win it or we got to lose it now. The gas is out of the tank. Let's go for it."

PAT ZERBE: O'Brien just said, for lack of better words, "Eff it, we're going for it."

That was his mentality.

We loved it. It fueled our fire.

He's like, "We're gonna get this."

And, you know, when you have a coach with full confidence in you, it comes out on the field. Everything we accomplished in that game springs from him. His confidence in his players.

On fourth down, O'Brien called on Belton for a fourth straight run.

PAT ZERBE: For some reason, Bill Belton and I really jelled together. He knew how to read my blocks. He was a patient runner, sneaky powerful. People didn't realize when they were tackling him how strong he was. At the same time, he was pretty elusive. Where Zwinak was straight power, Bill had good breakaway speed, but he was a bull, an absolute bull.

KYLE CARTER: Bill Belton, man, what a weapon. Came into the program as a receiver who had played quarterback in high school. Just shifty, he knew how to play in space. He made the decision with Bill O'Brien to shift from receiver to running back, which is tough to do, because a receiver doesn't get hit on most plays. Being a running back means having to bulk up, having to start taking that punishment play after play after play.

PAT ZERBE: It was like, *All right, we need to get this, there's no other option.* Bill and I looked at each other in the huddle and Bill's like, "I'm following you, man."

I was like, "Let's go. Just run up my back."

The hole opened up right off Urschel. Between Urschel and I believe Adam Gress at right tackle. I kind of dove at the linebacker just to get him out of the way and Bill dove right behind me, if memory serves me correctly.

MATT MILLEN: Let me tell you something, that's a gutsy call.

On the next play, Hackenberg threw to Robinson in the far corner of the end zone and the ball slipped through his hands.

MATT MILLEN: That should have been six.

On second-and-ten, Belton had a short carry to the eleven-yard line.

On third-and-eight, Hackenberg tried to zip the ball to Robinson between four Michigan defenders in the end zone and the Wolverines got called for pass interference.

MATT MILLEN: The kid did not lack for confidence. He trusted that arm. Threw it into a *tiny* window.

The ball was placed at the two-yard line. Penn State lined up in the I-formation with Zerbe and Belton behind Hackenberg. Belton took the hand-off with Zerbe leading the way.

ERIC SHRIVE: Pat Zerbe made a huge block, Billy Belton scored the game-winning touchdown, and the place went nuts.

PAT ZERBE: The play was Zero Sword Boss, which goes to the right. And we had an alert. If they were overstacked on that side, we're running Lamp on the backside, which is basically a left outside zone. So in the film you'll see Hackenberg tapping his helmet, going, Alert! Alert!

I turn back to Bill, just letting him know. Alert! Alert! Then we go off the left.

CHRISTIAN HACKENBERG: I handed that ball off, I saw we had the edge, and I was already running towards the tunnel before he got in.

PAT ZERBE: Jesse James is playing tight end. He's helping Donovan Smith, the left tackle. My job is to take anyone that's not touched. The first person that shoots through that gap, I'm hitting him.

So Bill and I had a really good connection. He knew how to read my blocks and I knew what he was doing. I knew he was going to try and get to the outside. So I'm going to try and block the defender inside out. If the guy plays over top of me, Bill's going to come up inside me. If the guy jumps inside, Bill's gonna go outside. He's reading me the whole way.

And that defender, I still don't know his name. He hesitated for a second. And it gave me enough time to get my hands on him. And then, as Bill's running around me, I gave him a nice slow-down, pushed him down, and followed Bill to the end zone.

AUDREY SNYDER: Belton scores and the place just erupts.

CHARLIE FISHER: The roar of 107,000 people.

BILL BELTON: When I crossed the line, there was a feeling I can't even describe.

AUDREY SNYDER: It's this massive moment, one you could not have expected a couple years earlier, because of everything that had gone down.

VON WALKER: I remember tearing up. Thinking like, Man, somebody is really watching over us. It felt a lot like the Ohio State game in 2016, that feeling that the only reason these things are happening is because somebody is watching. Like, there's got to be something greater making this happen, right? It's an out-of-body experience.

PAT ZERBE: That's what it's all about: Taking a shot of adversity straight to the face and being like, Hey, I'm gonna beat you.

CHRISTIAN HACKENBERG: It's a testament to the type of kids we had—a bunch of guys who just wanted to fight. Didn't care what the score was, what the outcome was, what obstacle was in front of us. We just worked hard and fought.

And, you know, we don't talk enough about the impact that game had—the kids that were there. Like, I think that was the first time I met Mike Gesicki.

Gesicki, a future star at tight end, was invited to the game as a recruit. He was there with fellow high school standout Jason Cabinda and a young running back named Saquon Barkley.

SAQUON BARKLEY: At the time, I was committed to Rutgers. But being there and watching Allen Robinson, Bill Belton, and Christian Hackenberg play really well, a hundred thousand people screaming. I remember going home, thinking, *Wow, this is what I want to do. This is where I want to play.*

BILL O'BRIEN: He came into the locker room after the game, very excited to be there.

I said, "Yeah, but you're committed to Rutgers."

I think he said, "No, no, no."

TWENTY-TWO

HITTING THE BOOKS

JOE PATERNO HAD from the very beginning envisioned his program as a temple to higher learning. He wasn't interested in coaching football zealots. He wanted guys with a thirst for education, too.

He never bothered to recruit Joe Namath, born and raised in Western Pennsylvania, he said, because Namath was no scholar.

In his forty-six seasons at the helm, the Brooklyn-born, Ivy League–educated coach trumpeted this Grand Experiment, championing the idea that you could win games— ultimately more games than anyone else in the sport's top ranks—with bona fide student-athletes. When Mike Reid, his star defensive tackle, asked for permission to leave the locker room for a year to study theater instead of blitz packages, Paterno gave the kid his blessing. When Bob White, a highly coveted recruit, decided to play for Penn State, his scholarship offer came with a caveat: He had to read twelve novels chosen by Joe's wife, Sue, and file twelve book reports before coming to campus.

"We try to remember," Paterno once said, "football is part of life—not life itself."

Bill O'Brien was hired to steer the program in a new direction. He arrived from the world of professional football, where grade-point averages have little bearing on minutes played. But he quickly embraced Paterno's views on education. From the get-go, he sold his recruits on the chance to play football in a 100,000-seat stadium while earning a "world-class degree."

As living proof of that statement, O'Brien had on his roster a six-foot-three, three-hundred-pound offensive lineman with a gift for solving numbers problems. And, like his predecessor, O'Brien allowed John Urschel to indulge his twin passions—football and figures. Before leaving campus for the NFL in 2014, Urschel would own three degrees: a bachelor's in math, a master's in math, and a master's in math education. Because why not make the most of your college experience?

Paterno passed away before O'Brien had a chance to meet him and collect his thoughts on football and life, but his Grand Experiment lived on in the hearts and minds of players like Urschel who flocked to Penn State because they wanted to do more than don the helmet.

GRANT HALEY, CORNERBACK, 2014–17: I'm a guy that loved school. It's always been a big, big thing in our family. My parents really drove me—*academics first, academics first.* That was one of the reasons I chose the schools I did during the recruiting process.

MICHAEL MAUTI: Football and academics—you can't have one without the other. You've got a hundred and five guys out there playing on Saturdays and no one does that without going to classes, no one does that without passing all their classes and making good grades and holding a certain GPA. So we really were student-athletes. It's something we hang our hats on.

BRIAN IRVIN, DEFENSIVE END AND TIGHT END, 2008–12: We were all told from the time we got here that academics is first. You can't play without keeping your grades up. That's like the single most important thing here—getting your degree and keeping your grades up so you can stay eligible.

TODD BLACKLEDGE, QUARTERBACK, 1980–82: It has always been that way. I'm proud to be a part of that. When you play here, you work to play for championships, you work hard in the classroom and graduate and go on to be successful in the community. You're a well-rounded person, not just a football player.

MICHAEL MAUTI: That degree goes a lot farther than football in life.

ANDREW NELSON, OFFENSIVE LINEMAN, 2013–17: My parents instilled in me the idea that football will end someday for everybody—and when that day comes, it's what you know that makes you successful. So, during the recruiting process, I always tried to keep my eye on the prize, the value of education.

It was easy to see that education came first at Penn State. On Junior Day, we sat and talked with the academic advisors longer than we did with any of the PSU coaches.

John Urschel's parents had raised their son to see the value in education, too. His mother, Venita, wanted him to be an aeronautical engineer. She herself had earned a master's in biomedical science while working nights in Cincinnati as an operating room nurse. His father, John, was a thoracic surgeon. The two divorced when young John was three, settling on opposite sides of the U.S.-Canada border, but together they instilled in their child a lifelong interest in learning.

Venita later earned a law degree. John Sr. pursued a master's in economics.

For their son, football and math were a captivating mix.

MAC MCWHORTER, OFFENSIVE LINE COACH: He was really bright—a three-year grad in mathematics, with a 4.0 GPA. He and I were on two different wavelengths about mathematics, I promise you. We got on the same wavelength with football.

VENITA PARKER: John grew up in Buffalo, New York. Close to the border. I was an avid hockey fan, so as soon as he was age-eligible, I signed him up. I want to say he was six or seven. He did that for a year—did not like it at all.

He wanted to play football—his father had played in high school and college—but John couldn't do Pop Warner because of his height. He was always a big kid. So he played soccer instead.

In middle school, he went out for the football team and made it, but they didn't have a helmet that would fit his head. So he tried lacrosse. *Loved* lacrosse. At one point, he was on, I want to say, three different teams.

When it came time for high school, I sent him to a Jesuit program at Canisius High.

I thought, okay, he's gonna play lacrosse. And then, he tries out for football.

Instead of putting him on the freshman team, they put him on junior varsity. Even though he'd never played in elementary or middle school, he did quite well. It's who he is. If he likes something, he gives it his all.

I didn't know much about sports and scholarships. But his coach sent out tapes and colleges started recruiting him. John had quite a few offers, to the point where my head was swimming. I was like, You gotta stop. I literally went to his coach and said, "Stop sending out tapes. We have too many schools."

I was focused on academics and then this football thing comes out of left field. So we narrow the list to a few schools. We looked at Princeton and Stanford. There were others, but I wasn't interested in those. If Stanford and Princeton are interested, we're taking one of those offers.

So we've done our visits and now Penn State assistant coach Mike McQueary calls. The team had just gone to a bowl game and it was the last weekend for visits.

"We'll need an answer from you before you leave," Mike said.

Okay, let's go to Penn State.

It's the second weekend in January. There's supposed to be a humongous snowstorm, so instead of driving from Buffalo to State College on Friday, we go on Thursday and walk around campus. On Friday night, we do some stuff, and then on Saturday night, the players take the recruits out and the Paternos host the parents at their house.

It was a very personal interaction. Joe Paterno showed you how he'd take care of your child—academically in addition to athletically. I found that to be quite eye-opening. On our other visits, it was about the team, football. But Paterno added an academic component.

On Sunday morning, John and I were supposed to meet up and have breakfast. He dialed me and said, "Mom, what do you think? I *really, really, really* want to come here."

Once he got a feel for State College, the players, the program, he fell in love. He committed that weekend.

BILL O'BRIEN: At the end of the day, this is a very special place to play college football, because you can earn a world-renowned degree, choose from one-hundred-plus majors, and your degree can take you anywhere in the world, any occupation, any graduate school, and then, on top of that, you get to play football in front of 108,000 fans on national TV every week.

VENITA PARKER: John graduated from high school on a Saturday. We had a graduation party that night and then got up at like 4 a.m., because he had to report to Penn State on Sunday. I think it was at nine or ten o'clock. That means you should be there fifteen minutes before that, Mike McQueary said. If you're there less than fifteen minutes early, you're late.

I found that hilarious. But it shows how seriously they take things. You don't just drag in. "Hey, how's it going?" It's about responsibility, commitment, being prepared, being on time.

Urschel had no trouble adjusting to the demands of college life.

VENITA PARKER: Paterno made sure those boys walked away with an education, whether they walked away with an NFL offer or not. He made sure the staff wasn't just bringing kids in to use them, that they were giving them the tools to have a wonderful and meaningful life.

JOHN URSCHEL: For Paterno, this was not lip service. He was serious about guys graduating. The number of tutors we had at our disposal—I mean, people were tracking classes constantly. You had to work hard to not graduate.

BRADY ROURKE, ACADEMIC COUNSELOR: Our academic support service is right in the football building, so it's not hard for a student-athlete to meet with his position coach and two minutes later come down and see fellow counselor Todd Kulka or I for a class schedule and then work on a paper in the computer lab right in the same building.

VENITA PARKER: They knew everyone's strong points and weak points, on the field and off. The freshmen are required to study at the football building. After practice and dinner, they had to stay there. I think John said two hours a night. They brought in tutors to help everyone.

RICK SLATER: It was almost like the Uniform Code of Military Justice. You knew what Coach Paterno expected, and one of those things was going to class. He wanted all of his players to get an education and he wasn't shy about letting you know.

SAM FICKEN: If you missed class and they did a check, you were in deep shit. I don't think other places enforced that to the letter of the law.

JOHN URSCHEL: It was great to play for a coach like that. When I first got there, the academic staff had to pump the brakes on me a bit and say college is not high school. Maybe you don't want to be that ambitious.

But once they saw me succeeding, they said No, you were right. Take whatever you want.

I was taking PhD-level classes as a third-year student.

BRADY ROURKE: I'll never forget my first meeting with him. I said, "John, you're a first-year freshman. I don't think you should take Math 480."

He said, "I think I can handle it, Brady."

Long story short, he majors in mathematics and graduates in six semesters, with a perfect 4.0.

VENITA PARKER: I think his initial major was engineering—mechanical or aerospace—because he loved math. But once he got there, he was like, "Umm, I like this, but I don't know if I like engineering."

I said, "What's wrong with engineering?"

"When you go to the class and you're solving the problems, they give you the formula."

"Well, that's how things work."

"I want to figure out what the formula is, then work it out . . . I think I want to be a mathematician."

I said okay, because at the end of the day, your child knows what he loves and enjoys.

JOHN URSCHEL: Professor Vadim Kaloshin really took me under his wing at Penn State. He's the reason I'm a mathematician. I remember him coming up to me when I took his class, asking me to come see him in his office. He gave me a math book, told me I could be a mathematician.

VADIM KALOSHIN: I was teaching a second-year calculus class at Penn State. About two weeks into the semester, this big guy comes into my office and gives me an absent slip, saying he can't attend class on Friday.

Just for curiosity, I looked at his scores. He was acing every homework assignment.

I asked him if he'd be willing to read a book on mathematics. He said, Yes, he loved mathematics. I gave him a book I'd normally give to a graduate student. Thought it would take him two months to read. He came back in two weeks.

VENITA PARKER: When he was younger, John would just soak up information, especially with math. It just came natural to him.

JOHN URSCHEL: I was good at math, but didn't really know what I wanted to do. Once I got to Penn State and started taking the classes for an engineering degree, I realized the math classes were my favorites.

BILL O'BRIEN: If you give him the percentage of times a team blitzes, he wants to know the survey size, what games we looked at, and how many numbers related to . . . It's like, "John, just take it from us, they blitz a lot."

VADIM KALOSHIN: He was learning at least twice as fast as a PhD in mathematics. It was fascinating to see how he combined training with the football team—I think he said six hours a day—with getting great grades as a student. He also found time for research.

Penn State got invited to a bowl game one Christmas. I remember exchanging emails with John about a math project. He was with the team, I think, in Florida. And we exchanged maybe a dozen messages about his research.

VENITA PARKER: When they went on the road, John would take his books with him. After practice, he'd be in the hotel room, writing papers. He always had two or three papers he was writing. And it was not just, "Ahhhh, maybe I'll write about this or this." He was writing peer-reviewed articles. The first one he showed me, I was like, This looks like hieroglyphics. I don't understand a word of it. And I was a pretty good math student.

To him, it's just like one plus one. It comes natural to him.

VADIM KALOSHIN: Without any advanced math education, he dove into the book and came back two weeks later. He basically went from school-level math to PhD-level math in a few months. We had regular discussions in my office, we exchanged emails, I kept stimulating his interest by giving him math books, basically showing him a world where he could live until retirement age.

I haven't heard of another Penn State undergraduate who published a research paper. It happens at Caltech or MIT, but there we're talking about the cream of the crop, right? The guys at Caltech and MIT have been focusing on math for quite a long time to get to those places.

JOHN URSCHEL: Once Bill O'Brien got there—again—huge flexibility. I told the staff I wanted to teach some classes. I was a grad student, so I could teach in the math department. And they said, We need to check with the NCAA Clearinghouse to make sure that's allowed, but if that's something you want to do, we'll make it work.

While I was playing at Penn State, I taught two classes. I had to miss a couple practices to give tests. O'Brien let me.

VENITA PARKER: They had this schedule that showed who had what classes. It was color-coded—blue, yellow, green, whatever. O'Brien was looking at it one day and saw a patch of purple. He went to the staff and said, "Why is Urschel purple?" They said, "Oh, he has to be excused from practice, because he's giving an exam in the class he's teaching."

Even though he was a student, he was teaching a class and giving an exam and the football program worked around that. They let him choose any career path. A lot of schools tell their players to take fluff classes, so they can put everything into football.

JOHN URSCHEL: Education was important to the coaches. I really appreciated that, because obviously that's quite important to me. I mean, it still is. I graduated from the doctoral program at MIT. I'm now a researcher at the Institute for Advanced Study in Princeton, New Jersey, and I'm heading back to Boston next year for a postdoc at Harvard. I'm staying in academia.

TWENTY-THREE

BEATING THE ODDS

As THE WIN *versus Michigan demonstrated, Penn State still had significant talent, particularly at quarterback and wide receiver, but after a year
of defections, scholarship reductions, and injuries, the team was short on
manpower.*

*Against Ohio State quarterback Braxton Miller, the Lions' patchwork
defense—thin at linebacker and defensive back—yielded close to seven hundred yards, falling 63–14 in the worst beating a Penn State club had absorbed since a 64–5 drubbing to the Duquesne Athletic Club in 1899. A week
later, the unit gave up four hundred and eleven yards in a 24–17 overtime
win versus Illinois.*

*Against Minnesota, the sputtering offense converted only one third down
in four quarters, losing 24–10 after squandering late-game scoring opportunities with a fumble and failed passes.*

*Against Nebraska, after an impressive 45–21 win versus Purdue, it was the
special teams that faltered, costing the team a blocked punt, a ninety-nine-
yard kickoff return, and a missed extra point in an overtime heartbreaker.*

*And so, as the final game approached, Bill O'Brien modified his practice
routine, pulling his veterans from scrimmages to preserve their health. All
told, the coach had just forty-three scholarship players at his disposal for the
finale at 9–2 Wisconsin.*

The Vegas oddsmakers took note, installing the 6–5 Nittany Lions as a decided underdog, and let's just say that OB wasn't happy about that.

PAT ZERBE: I think we went into that game like twenty-four-point underdogs. O'Brien was heated. Oh, man, was he heated.

CHRISTIAN HACKENBERG: The whole week, that's all we heard. "Twenty-four-point dogs, twenty-four-point dogs, yada, yada, yada."

GENO LEWIS: People were basically saying we didn't have a chance.

PAT ZERBE: We were *all* heated, because of the disrespect.

Coach O'Brien's like, "We're going to Camp Randall and we're going to beat these . . ."

He used some words I won't repeat.

And we were like, "Hey, we got nothing to lose—we can't go to a bowl game."

MALIK GOLDEN: Let's just go out there and have at it.

GLENN CARSON: Leave it all out on the field. This is the last time we get to play for each other. Do it for the upperclassmen, do it for the younger classmen, so they can get back on track.

BRANDON BELL: Those seniors, they were going to go out with a bang. The younger guys wanted to win, to beat Wisconsin, not only for the seniors, but because the whole country didn't think we could. And, honestly, playing the spoiler role? I loved it.

JOHN URSCHEL: Wisconsin had a very good team that year.

BILL O'BRIEN: They had an unbelievable home record.

JOHN URSCHEL: Leading up to the game, they kept talking about how they should go to a BCS bowl. They weren't talking about us a lot, but there was a lot of conversation about why they deserved to be in the Rose Bowl. They were trying to make an argument for themselves. If they win the Big Ten Championship, they should go to a BCS bowl.

The team did have some very talented people: Melvin Gordon and James White at running back—two great, great players. Wide receiver Jared Abbrederis, who ended up becoming a buddy of mine. We trained together for the NFL Combine.

PAT ZERBE: They had Chris Borland at linebacker, who was a stud. He played in the NFL for one season and retired because he didn't want to risk getting any more concussions.

They had Beau Allen—a massive human—at nose tackle. He played for the Eagles for a while. And they had Derek Watt at fullback.

So they had a great team. And we went there to Madison, Wisconsin, and played them hard.

JOHN URSCHEL: We get the ball to start the game, get a first down, and Hackenberg throws a seventy-yard ball for a touchdown and we think, *We're ready to go!*

As it turns out, that would be the signature play for the two star recruits from the class of 2013. Hackenberg took the snap at the Penn State thirty-two, faked a handoff, and rolled to the right, zipping the ball downfield on the run. Tight end Adam Breneman caught the pass at midfield, shook a tackle, and rumbled to the end zone. Just like that, the Lions were ahead 7–0.

Wisconsin's defense had not allowed a single play longer than fifty-one yards all season. The Lions would end the day with four.

JOHN URSCHEL: The whole week leading up to Wisconsin, we didn't practice that hard. We didn't put pads on once. We didn't even watch the Nebraska film. We were single-mindedly focused on Wisconsin.

O'Brien really wanted to stress that no one's giving up on the season.

I've been on football teams where it shows that you're glad it's your last game. I mean, I played in the 30–14 TicketCity Bowl loss to Houston in 2012.

In this case, everyone on the team was focused on Wisconsin, not looking past the game to the off-season. That whole week of practice was sort of a chance for everyone to get healthy and really focus on mental reps. It really paid off in the game.

I mean, Hack had an *amazing* game. That guy was completing everything.

BILL O'BRIEN: He threw the deep ball better than I'd seen him do it all year.

JOHN URSCHEL: We were running the ball well. Zwinak was doing a great job.

On the offensive line, we were doing a good job with the line of scrimmage. It was very clear that we were the team that wanted it more.

Wisconsin would tie the game with an eleven-play drive capped by a four-yard toss to Brian Wozniak, then go ahead 14–7 on the team's next possession with another eleven-play drive. That one culminated with a twenty-yard pass to Jeff Duckworth.

Penn State answered minutes later with a Hackenberg throw to Geno Lewis, who strangely found himself standing all alone at the line of scrimmage, just a few steps from the end zone.

GENO LEWIS: Nobody came out and guarded me.

MIKE PATRICK, ESPN ANNOUNCER: There wasn't anybody within twenty yards.

BILL O'BRIEN: I think they were having trouble substituting.

GENO LEWIS: I was looking at Hack like, *Throw it, throw it, throw it, now!* Wisconsin's coach was trying to run onto the field to call a timeout, but we ended up getting the ball off right on time. Hack threw it to me and I scored from like the three-yard line.

Midway through the third quarter, Hackenberg completed a seven-yard touch pass to tight end Jesse James to retake the lead 21–14. The defense set up the next score with a thirty-five-yard interception return by defensive end C.J. Olaniyan, who literally plucked the ball right from the quarterback's hand. It was the first of three Nittany Lion interceptions that day.

Geno Lewis's second touchdown, a fifty-nine-yard beauty, put the game out of reach.

GENO LEWIS: The play was called Chicago. If the safety was high, I'd run a corner route. If the safety came down low, I'd run a go route. The safety came down and I just ran. Hack got killed, man, but he threw a perfect ball. A perfect ball. I caught it, broke a tackle, outran the next guy, and we scored.

The Lions had reeled off twenty-four unanswered points.

CHRISTIAN HACKENBERG: Yeah, we were seven-and-five that year, but really the only game we were clearly outmatched was against Ohio State. With two or three bounces our way, we could just as easily have been eleven-and-one.

Ohio State blew our doors out, but we were in every other game. Even the Indiana game. They had some big plays offensively, but that was close most of the way. Minnesota, you know, it was cold, but we had a lot of things go our way. We were still in that football game. Even the UCF game, like, we had them early in the season. I mean, that was my third start. And that team went on to win the Fiesta Bowl.

So we were in nearly every single football game that year. For the odds-makers to just throw us down, you know, as a complete underdog . . . Like, we knew we could play with those guys. That's how we felt every week.

When we got out there and started rolling, we knew we had to keep the foot on the gas and we did.

PAT ZERBE: After the third quarter at Wisconsin games, they play "Jump Around" and the whole stadium goes nuts. At that point, we were up. Our whole team was dancing on the field.

GENO LEWIS: They do the "Jump Around."

Jump! Jump!

And we were going crazy.

BRANDON BELL: We were more hyped than that whole stadium, just a few guys in white, jumping around, having fun.

CHRISTIAN HACKENBERG: It was one of those things where we had a ton of momentum. Things started going well and we just fought, scrapped, clawed, and took advantage.

The defense played great given the talent Wisconsin had in the backfield. And, obviously, Wisconsin's always gonna have great guys up front. That was a good team win.

The Badgers mounted a late comeback, scoring ten points in the fourth quarter to trim the lead to 31–24 with four minutes to go. That left one last gut check for Penn State's offense.

CHARLIE FISHER: Wisconsin was coming back. They had momentum. If they got the ball back and scored, they'd have a great chance to win it. They had us penned up in a third-and-nine on our eighteen-yard line and we ran a one-back draw into a full blitz. Honest to God, two kids are right there in Zach Zwinak's face and he breaks the tackle and off he goes. Sixty yards. Down to the Wisconsin twenty.

It was like, How did that happen?

But that's football. One kid missed the tackle. He ran right by Zwinak. Zwinak broke a tackle, made him miss in the hole, and took off.

We ended up putting the game away.

BILL O'BRIEN: We didn't eliminate all the mistakes, but we eliminated enough of them. Our defense hung in there, played a whale of a game, and our offense made enough plays to win.

Hackenberg finished with twenty-one completions for 339 yards and four TDs. He would soon be named Big Ten Freshman of the Year. His go-to target Allen Robinson was declared receiver of the year.

CHRISTIAN HACKENBERG: Bill O'Brien had pushed me subliminally all year long, careful not to give me too much credit. That was the only game I got a game ball for, the only game under Bill. I thought I had a few games there where I could have gotten one, but he waited.

PAT ZERBE: It was like a frickin' party in the locker room afterwards. Guys had cigars. We all took a long time to take our pads off.

JOHN URSCHEL: Everyone was dancing and celebrating. Two of the guys who played right next to me on the offensive line—Ty Howle and Adam Gress—had been growing their hair out all season. It . . . didn't look very good.

Both said they were going to cut it once the season was over.

We started cutting their hair off in the locker room right after the game.

It was something we had talked about earlier in the week. They said if we won, they'd let Glenn Carson do it in the locker room, because Glenn—their roommate—was very clean-cut, kind of straitlaced. And Ty's and Gress's hair bothered him.

There were a lot of conversations involving Glenn and Ty's and Adam's hair.

GLENN CARSON: I said if we win this game, I get to chop that hair off.

Before the game, they said they'd do it, so they were men of their words.

JOHN URSCHEL: I think Ty and Adam both realized that college football was about to be over and perhaps it's not the best thing to be walking around, trying to get a job, with long hair.

CHARLIE FISHER: Winning a football game is hard work, it really is. And when you win one like that, on the road, you cherish it.

PAT ZERBE: You have so many things in your head, so many emotions. You look back at all the work you put in for four or five years.

I don't know if those guys on the coaching staff knew they weren't going to be back. If they did, we never knew it, because they gave everything they had in practice and on the field.

AUDREY SNYDER: I remember covering that game and thinking, this team's going to be okay. The quarterback looks really good, the head coach has buy-in from the players, the young tight end looks like he's going to be a star . . . And then, everything just starts to fizzle.

You look at Bill and it's . . . I mean, you just never thought, this is how it ends, you know?

Adam Gress was such a big part of that team, this massive human being, and he died a few years later. John Urschel left the game in 2017 to get a doctorate in math and teach at MIT. And, Hackenberg, I mean, that becomes one of the games—if not *the* game—most people remember him for. The same thing goes for Adam Breneman.

It's like you had no idea in that moment how much things would soon change. That was the high point for that team, those players.

In little more than a month, Bill O'Brien would announce that he was moving on to become head coach of the NFL's Houston Texans, leaving the players to endure yet another round of uncertainty. In his post-game press conference, he praised them for their resiliency, noting the slim margin for error they had faced all season long.

"More times than not, we beat that margin of error," he said. "Could we be better? Certainly! But I think the program's in pretty good shape right now."

Good enough to weather another shift at the top? That was the big question.

TWENTY-FOUR

EXIT O'BRIEN

IN THE END, *Bill O'Brien's defection was not a complete surprise. The players had heard him speak of his desire to return to the NFL as a head coach, plus his need to provide for his family, particularly his oldest son, Jack, born with a rare neurological disorder. They also knew about the forces at play behind the scenes, the competing interests that invariably arise between the coach and others in a football program the size of Penn State's.*

Deep down, they could not fault the guy for accepting the offer from the Texans. But that didn't soften their disappointment. With their help, O'Brien had secured the first fifteen wins of his head coaching career. He had done it in a program left for dead two years earlier, with a team stripped of its star running back, top receiving threat, and tried-and-true kicker.

The players were the backbone of that success. They had paid for it with their blood, sweat, and tears. And now they were back to square one in the rebuilding process, forced to prove themselves again, to a coach who had not yet been named. It did not help matters that they learned of their change in fortune during the holiday break—on a night generally reserved for celebration.

MIKE GESICKI, THE TOP TIGHT END RECRUIT IN THE COUNTRY, ACCORDING TO *247SPORTS*: It was New Year's Eve and you see it come across the ticker on ESPN: O'Brien now the new head coach of the Houston Texans. You're like, Whoa, what does that mean for me?

VON WALKER: I was at a party at my friend's house and we got the news. I remember being a bit excited before that, thinking, Man, maybe I could earn a scholarship, you know? O'Brien and I had a good relationship.

So that was a hard blow. With James Franklin coming in, it was like hitting the restart button. As any player will tell you, it doesn't really matter what you did the year before. When a new coach comes in, it's a blank slate.

At that point, I had just finished my freshman year. I was back home. I had accomplished a lot. And I was having a blast, because it was the off-season. I remember being a few drinks deep and one of my buddies comes up to me.

"You excited to have a new coach?"

"What are you talking about?"

That's how I found out—an ESPN alert on one of my friends' phones.

I was shocked. Like, Man, that was my guy, the one who gave me a shot.

But as the night went on, I was happy for him. Because the guy came from the NFL, right? He was Tom Brady's quarterback coach. He's a genius when it comes to the offensive and, honestly, the defensive side of football. I can't ever be mad at a coach trying to get to the very top of his profession.

GREGG GARRITY: It's the off-season and I'm feeling really good about next year. I know the offense, I made a name for myself, I'm getting bigger, stronger. So I'm feeling good. And then the news breaks that Bill O'Brien is going to the Houston Texans.

It was bittersweet, because I loved Coach O'Brien. I still love Coach O'Brien. And, you know, if I were him, I would have done the same thing. His big goal was to become a head coach in the NFL. We all knew his son Jack had health issues and Houston had awesome medical facilities. So it was a no-brainer.

But it was bittersweet. My thoughts were, Well shoot, whatever coach comes in, I have to replicate what I did my freshman year and, I gotta be honest, I kind of surprised myself with how well I did. So I'm like, Crap, going into my sophomore year, I need to do the same thing and *more*. Because we're gonna have a new recruit class coming in. So I have to do that much extra to get more playing time and catch the coaches' eyes.

AUDREY SNYDER: There was no bowl game that year, so I got sent to Florida to talk to the recruits at the Under Armour All-America Game. Receiver DeAndre Thompkins, quarterback Michael O'Connor, receiver Chris Godwin—I remember talking to those guys and being like, So, I don't know what's going to happen with your head coach. I'm hearing he might not be here and some of you are enrolling at Penn State in the next week.

By the time I flew home, around midnight, it was clear Bill O'Brien was going to the Texans. I worked until like four o'clock in the morning. I was like, *Oh my god, what coach leaves on New Year's Eve—at midnight? This is terrible.*

CHRISTIAN HACKENBERG: Yeah, that was hard, man. It was such a conundrum for me, because I had gotten to know him so well. And I also knew how good the Houston deal was for him, how good it was for his family. If I separated myself from the situation, which I did—at least initially—I could see why he did it. I wasn't happy he made the decision, but I could understand it. It was like, I can't dwell on it, it's done. [laughter] You got to move on.

ADAM BRENEMAN: It was tough because O'Brien was such a pillar of that program. He meant a lot to the players on that team. He was really the perfect guy for that time at Penn State. We needed someone who was going to lead and take a no BS approach to being the head coach. And when we committed to Penn State, when I committed and Christian Hackenberg committed, there wasn't a ton of hope around the Penn State program. I mean, that's just the way it was. You know, we really were committing to Bill O'Brien, trusting in him and his vision.

When he left, it was difficult, because we felt like our commitment to him and that program during that time meant he would be there throughout our careers. I was definitely frustrated. My family was frustrated. The recruits in my class were frustrated. But, looking back, I don't blame him. You can't really fault another man for chasing his dream and doing what's best for his family.

DAVE JOYNER: Bill O'Brien was presented with a tremendous opportunity, one that, for his family and his future, he just could not pass up. I believe he always had Penn State's best interests at heart.

BILL O'BRIEN: The opportunity to go to Houston with great medical facilities for my oldest son, the opportunity to be the head coach of a first-class operation, the opportunity to work with Rick Smith, who I consider to be one of the best general managers in the National Football League—all of those things led my wife and I to make the decision.

While the parting was bittersweet, you could not help but respect the man for taking the Penn State job amid all the Sandusky madness, not to mention investing as much as he did in rescuing the program. As those who have watched Alabama, Florida State, and Nebraska struggle to replace coaching legends will tell you, it's mighty hard to get the call right.

AUDREY SNYDER: The guy's beloved here in State College, because of what he did. People will always snarl a bit about how he left but look at what he did in his time here. I mean, the whole thing was so remarkable, you can't nitpick the guy for taking an NFL job.

The players probably understood that best. That was always the thing.

GENO LEWIS: From the day he got there until the day he left, he was always honest with us. He always told us that his dream job was to be a head coach in the NFL. So we knew we only had about two to three years with O'Brien, because if we were successful, he was going to get a job offer.

The decision had to do with his kid, too, man. He has a son with disabilities and Houston had some of the best hospitals for his son. So it was all understandable.

ANDREA KREMER, CORRESPONDENT, *HBO REAL SPORTS*: I was once in his office, exchanging pleasantries, and he was showing me some things on his desk. He points out this picture, like a little school picture, of his son Jack. It's taped to the side of his computer. He says, "Remember when I told you I think about Jack and it keeps me grounded? That's why this picture's here."

AUDREY SNYDER: After Bill left, the players were like, Well, yeah, he always told us he wanted to be an NFL coach. We get it, you know? There was that level of honesty and trust between head coach and players—the understanding that they were working through an unprecedented situation— that helped make everything work.

LARRY JOHNSON, DEFENSIVE LINE COACH: He reached out to every player and talked to them personally and told them the situation. I do know he did that.

ALEX BUTTERWORTH: He left with as much grace as he came in. He called all the players, including me—I had just graduated—to let us know he was leaving. You can't ask for more than that. Obviously, I was bummed, but I knew the minute he said Houston that it was a great move for him. My younger brother has special needs, he has a rare chromosome disorder, and I know from being in a special needs family that Houston has health facilities that are second to none.

Shortly after learning of the coach's departure, David Jones of the Harrisburg Patriot-News *added a measure of intrigue to the online chatter, writing a column summarizing an early December phone call with O'Brien. Much of the conversation between the two men had been off the record. But when Jones noted that some people loyal to Paterno were likely to bristle at the departure of longtime linebacker coach Ron Vanderlinden, reportedly pushed out of his post, O'Brien erupted.*

"You can print this," he said. "You can print that I don't really give a — what the 'Paterno people' think about what I do with this program. I've done everything I can to show respect to Coach Paterno. Everything in my power. So I could really care less about what the Paterno faction of people, or whatever you call them, think about what I do with the program. I'm tired of it.

"For any 'Paterno person' to have any objection to what I'm doing, it makes me wanna put my fist through this windshield right now."

Striking in their candor, the comments left many to speculate who at Penn State had refused to move on. O'Brien later acknowledged that he regretted making those statements, adding that he had "good support" at the university, "especially from the student body."

But it was hard not to wonder what bad air awaited the next head coach.

DAVID JONES: I still have the tape from that interview, the entire tape. O'Brien said a lot more than I published. Some of it was off the record. But for the part I did use, he said, "You can print this, you can print this."

That was on December 4, 2013. Philly sportswriter Dick Jerardi and I were coming back from a Penn State basketball game in Pittsburgh. We had stopped off at the Flight 93 Memorial, because it was a nice day. I'd been working on O'Brien for two days and he finally called and said, "What are you calling me about Ron Vanderlinden for? Who cares?"

I just had a feeling it was kind of a tipping point for him, that he was getting *all* this shit. I had heard he was out the door. He could have been out the door the year before—very easily. I followed that storyline to the end. I was the only guy he finally did call. I broke the story that he was staying and it was very close. Let me tell you, he could have gone. He was called by eight different NFL teams. I thought it was four at the time. It was eight NFL teams.

He could have very easily been out the door after one year and he decided not to do it. But he could have gone. There was other shit involved that I'm not going to tell you about. That's all I'll say.

I was very certain he was seriously considering leaving, put it that way. He was sick of the shit. Sick of it. He couldn't get everyone to piss through the same straw. He's got to deal with these people who want to live in the past. He's got a hard enough job with the sanctions and everything else and he's got these dinosaurs trying to drag the program back. It was hard.

TIM SWEENEY: If I had to guess, I would say Dave Joyner's a big reason O'Brien left.

MARK BRENNAN: I know the AD rubbed everybody the wrong way. Dave Joyner. Like, *everybody*. And I'm not here to tell you that if there was a different athletic director O'Brien would have stayed, but I do know he had absolutely no time for Joyner.

TIM SWEENEY: OB came in wanting to hit the ground running. Coming from the NFL, he was used to being agile and responsive. And what he ran into at Penn State, as he explained to me, was like trying to turn a battleship on a dime. It was very hard for him to get the things he wanted to do done in a timely manner, probably more because of the administration at Penn State and the lack of leadership above O'Brien than anything else.

KEITH CONLIN: There are people out there who still shit on Bill, because they feel he deserted them. And I say he wasn't being treated right—from the start. He was told there was not going to be an NCAA issue: It was a criminal issue, not a school issue. So he accepts the job, but then all of a sudden he has to accept these sanctions.

DAVID JONES: I don't think he had *any* idea that any of that was about to come down. He was probably assured by Penn State that there would be no penalties, because it was criminal activity by a guy who was not really connected to the athletic program anymore. I mean, it's jail time for the perpetrator. It had nothing to do with the NCAA for Christ's sake.

KEITH CONLIN: Bill could have said there was breach of contract, a breach of honesty, whatever, and left, but he stuck it out. He deserves a lot of credit for keeping it together.

VENITA PARKER: He replaced a legendary coach and replaced him in the midst of a scandal. Who wants to step into something like that? Especially when you're talking about someone coming from a winning team like the Patriots?

The last thing I'd want to do is step into something where I got mass drama. And Bill O'Brien, it's not like he was the strength coach or the defensive coordinator—he was the face of the program, the guy who had to answer to the administration, to the media, to the boys, even to the parents. He stepped up and did what he needed to do.

DAVID JONES: I thought what O'Brien did those two years was a magic act. Nothing short of it. Especially the second year, because not only did he keep those guys on the team, but the second year he really didn't have much. The holdovers, some of them were gone. He couldn't really recruit many offensive lineman, and Franklin paid for that later.

KEITH CONLIN: I don't blame O'Brien for leaving one bit, because of how people treated him—on campus and in the athletic department. Bill deserves a lot of credit—and so does James Franklin—for taking the program to that next level.

BILL O'BRIEN: It was fun coaching there—and everything was a challenge. Just like any head coaching job. The biggest challenge was when the sanctions came out and all those kids had the ability to transfer without penalty, without having to sit out a year, and you're trying to keep that team together, trying to figure out how you're going to get down to sixty-five scholarships.

TIM SWEENEY: We all thought he'd be there for four years. I think OB wanted to be there for four years, to be honest with you, to see those guys through.

He had a really tough job, beyond coaching football. I mean, so many people in the administration believed Mark Emmert and the BS he spewed. And some people at Penn State said, We're never going to let another football coach become as powerful as Joe Paterno.

And that's from the top down—from the board of trustees right through Dave Joyner.

O'Brien's departure sent shivers through every player in the program, from high school recruit Chris Godwin to the walk-on Gregg Garrity to senior end C.J. Olaniyan, but no one paid a steeper price than Christian Hackenberg, who ended his first year of college football as the Big Ten Freshman of the Year. Like his injury-plagued pal Adam Breneman, the young QB would never again reach those same heights.

MARK BRENNAN: Obviously for Hackenberg it was a huge blow to his career. I mean, I don't think there's any other way to look at it, right? He ended up getting forced into an offense that didn't fit his skill set. But I think he understood that O'Brien had to do what was best for himself. He was trying to get to a bigger city, a place where his son could get better medical treatment, too.

CHRISTIAN HACKENBERG: That's the only *what if* in my college career. What if he stayed? Like, What if he stayed? How would we have done things differently?

I know from an Xs and Os standpoint the direction things would have gone. And I'm not going to talk in hypotheticals, but the guys we had there, the way Bill ran the program, and all that stuff . . . That's the only *what if*. The only *what if* I'll ever talk about.

Not just for me, I want that to be known. The way Bill handled himself, the way he carried himself—I don't think Nick Saban would have been able to do what he did. In the situation he was dealt. The hand he got dealt. And all the other BS he had to deal with from day one.

To have an eight-and-four season and a seven-and-five season back-to-back, to navigate those waters, waters that no one's ever navigated before in college football history, I don't think another man on this planet could have done the job he did.

I'm pissed off that it didn't work out for four years. But there's a side of me that's appreciative for the one year I got, because it tooled me with the ability to—mentally and from an Xs and Os standpoint—navigate the next two years.

It didn't work out great every Saturday, but it gave me a good foundation to fall back on.

TWENTY-FIVE

PATERNO PEOPLE

IT'S EASY TO *criticize the team's diehard fans for putting so much faith in a football coach, but when you grow up in the Rust Belt towns of Pennsylvania, that admiration is not unfounded. Despite the steeples that dot the commonwealth, the church bells that routinely serenade folks in Pottsville, Lock Haven, and Mt. Lebanon, there is no moral force to match Paterno. No politician, writer, or historical figure that did more in the last fifty years to champion the state and its way of life, the hardworking people who toiled year after year in the region's coal mines and steel mills, sacrificing their bodies to make a better life for their children.*

Paterno—the Ivy League–educated son of a Brooklyn law clerk—proudly stepped into that void in 1966, winning football games, yes, but challenging the team's supporters to strive for something even greater: success with honor. He quoted Virgil and Robert Browning. "Ah, but a man's reach should exceed his grasp . . ." And, little by little, he convinced folks that there was something noble in winning the right way, hitting the line and hitting the books, winning a national championship and using the spotlight to press for a bigger, better library on campus.

For half a century, the people of PA took pride in those shimmering victories. They celebrated the players who graduated from JoePa's program with degrees in finance and microbiology as much as those who played football for the Eagles and the Steelers. And so, it was hard to reconcile Paterno the legend with Paterno the man, the one who might have failed to do his duty when informed of a monster in his ranks. Was it enough to report the things he heard to his superiors, or should he have done more to bring Sandusky to justice? The world may never know, because Paterno was gone before the case was tried, silenced first by the university's trustees and then by a lethal illness.

SILAS REDD: He was already an older gentleman when I got there, so we never had a real one-on-one conversation, other than when I went for my official visit. But I can still hear him.

"Take care of the little things and the big things will take care of themselves."

That was one of his favorite sayings. I'd mess up in practice, fumble the ball, and I'd hear in my head, "You can't play if you can't hold on to the ball." In that Brooklyn accent. "If this guy can't handle the ball, he can't play."

That always drove me. Even at USC, I could hear that man in my head.

I was devastated when he got fired.

STEPHON MORRIS: Seeing JoePa at his last team meeting, tears coming out of his eyes, I will never forget that day.

NATE STUPAR, LINEBACKER, 2007–11: It was very emotional. Joe started to cry, the other coaches were really teary-eyed. I almost started to cry myself.

SILAS REDD: I was in my 10:10 class and got a text message. It said mandatory squad meeting at eleven. There are no happy thoughts when you get a text like that, especially during a week like that. You just knew something bad was going to happen.

MICHAEL MAUTI: It was a Wednesday, in the middle of Nebraska week. We were sitting in our apartment, watching ESPN, and they scrolled on the bottom of the screen: Joe Paterno's been fired. It was like ten in the morning and we all got a text summoning us to a squad meeting.

They had never scheduled a team meeting before 2:30, like in the history of this place, because we always had class. Your last class had to end before two. So it was like, "Woah, all right, this is real—something's about to happen."

That was the last time Joe addressed the team as the head coach.

SILAS REDD: The aura in the room was almost eerie. You could tell people were upset.

Joe started speaking to us. He didn't flat-out tell us right then and there. He kind of warmed up to it. I found myself looking around, at coaches, at my teammates, and there were tears, frowns. No one in that room took that news lightly.

What I took from what he said is that, as men, it's our job to stay in good character, treat people with respect, and treat yourself with respect. The values he instilled in us, I know I'll be telling my children about them. They'll be telling their children, too. It's not every day that something a man says sticks that far into your life.

MICHAEL ROBINSON, QUARTERBACK, 2002–05: When I met Joe, there was something different about him. He didn't lie to me. Not once. He didn't offer me money. He didn't promise me cars, as some at other schools did. He didn't promise me I'd be the starting quarterback my freshman year. He didn't even promise me I would always play quarterback.

But there were things he did promise. He promised that my education would be second to none. He promised me that I would have the opportunity to compete for the starting quarterback position. He promised me that I would play in front of the best fans in college football.

Again, Joe Paterno did not lie to me.

BILL O'BRIEN: I never said to myself, Wow, I'm following a legend. There were a lot of things in my mind. Number one was that I wasn't Joe Paterno. No one will ever replace Joe Paterno. As far as it relates to football and graduating his players, the guy was probably the best of all time. I don't think anybody will ever coach forty-seven years, sixty-one total, at Penn State again. That's just my opinion.

And so, I never thought about replacing Joe Paterno. I just tried to say to myself, Look, I'm going to do the best job I can. Put together a great staff, coach up our players, make good decisions based on what I feel is best for Penn State football.

CHIMA OKALI, OFFENSIVE TACKLE, 2007–11: It's criminal the way he went out, because he'd done so much for the university, had such a legacy, and that wasn't a fitting end to all the work he'd done.

MICHAEL ZORDICH: I never saw it coming. I didn't think he would have to step down.

KYLE CARTER: I'm from a very small state. I wanted to play Division I football, but knew nobody was going to come to Delaware to recruit me. I had to go to all these camps.

Back in the day . . . that sounds crazy saying back in the day, because it was only 2011 . . . But after my junior year in high school, we made a little highlight tape and my dad and I sent that tape out to every school in the Big Ten.

The one school that replied was Penn State.

Not Purdue. Not Rutgers. Not Illinois. The big boy in the conference— Penn State.

I went up there for a visit and Joe Paterno was having a Christmas party for the parents. My mom danced with him in their house. She's always had that little memory of him.

MICHAEL YANCICH: It wasn't just me who looked up to him. I still remember my grandfather, who passed away when I was ten years old, watching Penn State games, getting so into it. You were proud to call yourself a Pennsylvania resident, even prouder to call yourself a Penn Stater, because of Paterno.

MATT STANKIEWITCH: When I was in grade school, I wrote this paper: If I could meet one person in life, I'd want to meet Joe Paterno.

That's the magnitude of his influence. It goes beyond football.

With his charisma, his character, his reputation for making the right decisions, it was hard not to admire him. That's truly who he was, too. It wasn't like now that the camera's off, let me go smoke a cigarette, kick the dog. He really was a man of his word.

MICHAEL YANCICH: I still have a picture of Paterno hanging in my parents' room at home, with a quote that says, believe deep down in your heart that you're destined to do great things.

My parents got it for me when I committed to Penn State. It was in my apartment at school and in my dorm. It was something you looked to when facing adversity. It didn't have to be tied to football or sports. It could be about school or a social situation. You just knew you were going to make the right decision by looking at Joe in that picture. It kind of grounded you.

JAMES FRANKLIN: It's not about the wins and the losses. It's about all the players that came through here that he was able to have a positive impact on.

That's really his legacy.

KYLE CARTER: You just respected every word that came out of his mouth. He didn't do much speaking. He'd head down to the team meetings, but assistant coaches were running the show at that point.

STEPHON MORRIS: My dad is like a college football historian. Always talked about the teams on TV in his era—Penn State, Notre Dame, Ohio State. When I got my first offer, he was like, Wow, you have an opportunity to play for Joe Paterno. I *watched* him as a kid.

Joe was like a father figure. To all of us, especially the African American community. He *really* cared for us. I will always love Joe for that.

ROBBIE GOULD, KICKER, 2001–04: Being on time for things, doing homework, assignments, projects, helping your teammates, being accountable for the things you do. That's something we all learned from him. We became better people and better athletes by attending Penn State. That's why you go there.

MICHAEL MAUTI: It was a special opportunity to play for the same coach my dad had. I mean, that's why you see so many legacy guys. There were twentysomething legacy guys, father-son combinations, that went to Penn State. That's the kind of tradition they had.

STEPHON MORRIS: My family lived in Atlanta, SEC country. People would say, I hear you're playing for Joe Paterno. I'd be like, Yeah. It showed how much this man meant to college football. Every time I'd get asked about it, they'd go, "Oh, wow. I grew up watching him."

They always ask me about the things that went down and I'd tell them how Joe was present in my life and the lives of lots of other guys. The dude was more than just a football coach. He was a mentor, a leader.

KAREN CALDWELL: Developing young men, that was big for him. He wanted quality young men and he was concerned about their families. We saw it firsthand, and I have awesome respect for a man like that.

Spider would come home and tell me how Joe would sit down with young men and say, "We're going to work on these grades, because I want you to graduate."

It wasn't like, What can I get out of you for my football team? We'll fudge here or there to keep you going. No, it was like, We'll get you tutors. His wife worked with some young men, too, teaching them how to write essays and other things they needed to do.

He had a tough side, because he had to guard his time and privacy, but the stories of him encouraging students to graduate, that always stood out to me.

KEITH CONLIN: Chuck Noll was the '70s version of that: tough, hard-nosed football with the Pittsburgh Steelers. But Joe took it a step further with Success with Honor. Not just being a football power, but doing good in the classroom, doing good with graduation rates, going on to lead successful lives. That was the Grand Experiment to a T.

KAREN CALDWELL: Somehow, he'd heard I was an English teacher—I can't believe he'd remember that or even want to remember that—but he once saw me at a bowl game. There was always a hospitality suite where we could get, you know, coffee and tea or cold drinks and I was in there kind of late. The other ladies had left. Some of them had young children. And in walks JoePa.

He sees me and comes over with his cup of tea.

"Now, are you still teaching?" he said.

"Yes, yes, I teach high school literature."

"Literature? Do kids still know how to read?"

I said, "Well, we're sure trying."

He said, "Well, tell me. What books are you teaching them?"

At the time, it was *Robinson Crusoe* and Charles Dickens's *Great Expectations*.

He said, "Wow, you keep teaching." He was getting out of his chair. "I've got to get upstairs." He stood up, and there was that crooked finger he would point. He said, "And you keep teaching the classics. You keep at it."

Yes, I'll never forget that. I had chills. I just sat there stunned and thought, this man is for real. I almost get teary-eyed thinking of that.

MARK BRENNAN: I do think you have to look at what Paterno built. The academic success and the stadium—all that stuff. For as much of a hit as he took after the Sandusky scandal broke, any logical person would say you have to give him credit for the foundation he built. Because that's what sustained everything for the next couple of years. Now it took the right people to pull it off—the Bill O'Briens, Christian Hackenbergs, Michael Mautis—but that foundation was there.

MICHAEL YANCICH: Those are really, really tough shoes to fill, and Bill O'Brien did it with such class.

GENO LEWIS: I was at the 409-win game against Illinois. On a recruiting visit. It was crazy, going in there after the scandal with the uncertainty, man. Like, at that point, you're hoping they pick the right coach, somebody who's going to put you in the right situation to be successful.

STEPHON MORRIS: That 2011 team went through a lot. When they fired Joe, it messed our season up. We ended up losing two of the last three games.

There was a shift in the program. What's next? We were on the fence before the bowl game. Did we want to go? Did we want to play? So we had a team meeting.

We decided to finish things out. That's, of course, what we wanted to do. We love football.

But Joe would want us to do the same thing.

SPIDER CALDWELL: We're in Holuba Hall, our indoor practice facility, for one of the first practices in 2012 and O'Brien said, "Spider, come here. Why'd you lay the fields out like this? Why do I have two fields in here?"

"Well," I said, "Coach Paterno liked two fields, because he wanted to have an offensive practice and a defensive practice. Halfway through, the two teams would come together on one field or the other."

O'Brien said, "I want one big, long field down the middle, so I can throw a deep ball."

I said, "Well, it's seventy yards. If you back up to that blue track, you can wail the ball pretty good."

He said, "Well, I don't know. We're not gonna be inside anyway. I'm from New England. We're gonna be outside, through all sorts of weather. We're not even going to use this building."

What he didn't realize is that the grass fields near the Lasch Building, they're a swamp when it rains and they don't drain. The grading is not the greatest. We've always struggled with that, the water coming off Holuba. And so, we didn't get out as much as he wanted to, because it was a really wet spring.

Right before the Blue-White Game, one of our last indoor practices, he goes, "Spider, come here. You know, the old man didn't win 409 games for nothing. I'm keeping Holuba just like it is."

That was awesome. He always said, "Joe had everything in place to win here. I just got to guide the ship." And I'll always appreciate that. I felt bad for Bill, because he didn't have Joe's brain to pick. Joe died so fast, Bill didn't have a chance to get to know him. But I think Joe would have liked him. And Bill would have loved to know how and why Joe did the things he did.

TWENTY-SIX

ENTER FRANKLIN

For ATHLETIC DIRECTOR *Dave Joyner, there was little time to waste. With barely a month to go before national signing day, he had to find a new coach right away or risk losing talent. After assembling a search committee, identifying prime candidates, putting them through a series of interviews and extensive background checks, he selected his man—a silver-tongued, charismatic, forty-one-year-old ball of energy, who was schooled in psychology and had raised Vanderbilt, an institution renowned for academics, from the depths of the Southeastern Conference with back-to-back top twenty-five finishes.*

It took all of nine days to complete the process.

And before you knew it, James Franklin was rushing off to corral a pivotal class of recruits, some first courted by O'Brien's staff, others lured by Franklin's crew.

JASON CABINDA, THREE-STAR LINEBACKER PROSPECT: O'Brien called me—it was literally like New Year's Day—and told me he was taking the Houston Texans job, but really felt Penn State was the place for me. That I should stay. *Da, da, da.* But think about that: If you're going to change your mind about the school, you have one month to do it.

You thought you were all set with the decision and then the coach leaves. You don't know if the new staff is going to like you. As a player, you hear horror stories all the time: guys getting their scholarships taken away or a coach looking a dude in the face and saying, "If you come, bro, you're just not going to play."

We had a group chat. Imagine a bunch of high school kids, don't even know each other, talking every day, while the coaching search is going on. Every day, there's a new name coming up.

I'm trying to remember the names now.

ADAM BRENEMAN: Al Golden. Remember that one? From Miami.

JASON CABINDA: Al Golden. Yes, he was one. He was a candidate.

ADAM BRENEMAN: And Greg Schiano.

JASON CABINDA: The Rutgers coach. Yeah, Schiano. He was one.

We're talking about it and researching it every day. All right, who is this guy? Where is he from?

It was just a crazy time. I think it was like nine days. It's crazy that I remember the exact number. I feel like it took nine days for them to announce Coach Franklin.

James Franklin was named head coach on January 11, 2014, but the search did indeed get completed in nine days, according to Dave Joyner.

JASON CABINDA: It was just so random when it did happen. Because Franklin wasn't talked about until maybe the very last day.

It was like who is this? I didn't know anything about Vanderbilt football.

AUDREY SNYDER: James Franklin gets here in January and you've got to sign kids in February. And because of all the extra background checks implemented after the Sandusky scandal, he and his staff had to set up makeshift offices in the Penn Stater Hotel. They couldn't be on campus while waiting for the paperwork to clear.

JAMES FRANKLIN: It was a scramble. We were locked up in the Penn Stater, we lived in the Penn Stater, going through HR and everything. Half of our staff wasn't even allowed to come to the Lasch Building until they cleared all the background checks, so legitimately we were sequestered in the Penn Stater. It was basically me coming over, walking around Lasch by myself.

But it was a scramble, calling all those kids. We ended up recruiting a lot of guys we already had relationships with rather than trying to build new ones.

AUDREY SNYDER: During the introductory news conference for Franklin, I just kept thinking, Wow, you've got kids moving in across campus who have never met this guy in person before. They thought they were coming here to play for Bill O'Brien.

But, yeah, James came out selling hard, charging out of the gate.

KOA FARMER, THREE-STAR PROSPECT AT SAFETY AND OUTSIDE LINEBACKER: I was taking my official visits, set to go to Vanderbilt. My parents had bought their airline tickets. And I see on *SportsCenter* that Coach Franklin has gone to Penn State. I was like, Mom, Dad, it looks like we're not going to Vanderbilt this weekend.

GRANT HALEY: For me, it was between Vanderbilt and Florida and I ultimately chose Vanderbilt for the academics. They were on the rise in the SEC, so that was intriguing to me. I had gone to a couple of games my junior year. Me and Trace McSorley. We sat near each other and our moms made us have a conversation. Made us take down each other's phone numbers.

You know parents.

We were just awkward kids.

And then Franklin switched to Penn State. I had never really thought about going to Penn State, but my mother had graduated from there in the '80s, so I thought I might as well make the trip. It was her first time back to campus since she had graduated, so that was very special for me. I fell in love with the place.

CHANCE SORRELL, OFFENSIVE LINEMAN, 2014–15: In high school, I played wide receiver and tight end. Even though I was six-foot-six, 265 pounds, I was a slot receiver. A lot of my high school highlights are of me catching the ball.

I went to a few camps at Vanderbilt and visited quite a few times when Coach Franklin was there. I knew I wanted to play for him and his staff. Specifically, Herb Hand, the offensive line coach who recruited me. I was committing to that staff more than the program. But I did love Vanderbilt. I was committed there for, I think, more than a year.

I remember having a conversation with my dad about the success Coach Franklin was having—consistent nine-, ten-win seasons in the SEC—at a school that traditionally had not had much success.

BRUCE FELDMAN, COLLEGE FOOTBALL REPORTER, FOX SPORTS AND *THE ATHLETIC*: I think Vanderbilt had won ten SEC games in thirteen years before he got there, and the fact that they had back-to-back top twenty-five finishes after he arrived is remarkable. It's not like they had any great success till he got there.

He's very social media savvy and put a really good brand out there to elevate Vanderbilt football. I can see why that would be attractive to Penn State, because for a program that had taken so many hits, you want a guy, a Pennsylvania guy, that re-energizes the fan base.

CHANCE SORRELL: My dad said, "Look, with his success, Coach Franklin is going to be in demand. A larger, more traditional school may pick him up. Are you okay with that?"

And I said, "Yeah, I'm okay if I only get to play for him one to two years."

That's the level of commitment I felt for that staff.

When he flipped to Penn State, I freaked out a bit. Started calling all the coaches I had offers from, kind of gauging their interest in me.

In the morning, Coach Franklin announced he was taking the job at Penn State and that night he gave me a phone call. I remember sitting there with my parents, telling them to hush up. As soon as they saw who was calling, they got all giddy.

Coach Franklin said, "Chance, I want you to play for me here at Penn State."

And, without visiting campus, I said, Yeah. I immediately flipped.

I think I was the first commit he had as the coach at Penn State.

Coach Franklin had quite a few coaches listening to that call on the speakerphone. He almost made a joke of it—making me say multiple times, Yes, I, Chance Sorrell, am committing to play football for you, Coach Franklin, at Penn State University.

As soon as I did that, all the coaches on the other side of the line started cheering. It made me feel like a million bucks. And then, of course, with Coach Franklin being such a guru of social media, he's like, "You got to tweet it out." So I immediately did that.

KOA FARMER: Coach Franklin called me, if not that night, the next day, saying he was bringing everyone who was supposed to go to Vanderbilt that weekend to Penn State. Trace, Grant, Amani Oruwariye, they were all committed to Vanderbilt. And I was supposed to go on a visit with them. Instead we all went to Penn State.

GRANT HALEY: The first person I texted was Trace. I was like, "What's your plan?"

Later in the week, he reached out and said, "I'm going up to visit this weekend."

KOA FARMER: Long story short, we had a great time together. Coach Franklin actually locked us in a room. No parents. And told us all the things he wanted to do for the program, where he wanted to take us. We all looked at each other and said, "Well, it looks like we're going here."

My mom's from Hawaii. My dad's from Southern California. We landed in Philly from L.A. and I just remember having this big parka on. Jacket, fur. We walked through the sliding door and literally jumped back, because we'd never felt cold like that before. I want to say that was one of the coldest winters at Penn State. That's what I was told. Our taxi driver actually took us through Harrisburg and on to State College. He didn't get to frickin State College until about four or five hours later. It was a nightmare drive. It was snowing. I was like, Man, I don't know about all this.

GRANT HALEY: We discussed the academics, took a tour of campus, met with the coaches. It was cool, because I knew most of the coaches from Vanderbilt. So it wasn't a huge adjustment in that respect. The adjustment for me was the weather. I mean, I come from Georgia and it's January in State College. There's snow everywhere.

CHANCE SORRELL: It was very cold. Even though I grew up in Ohio, Pennsylvania was a different beast in terms of weather, especially in January. There was snow all over.

They drive you right up to the front of the stadium and you're in awe. You look up and see how big it is and imagine yourself playing there. It was all so beautiful.

GRANT HALEY: From a distance, I'm looking at the lights in the stadium. I think that was the moment I realized I was highly, highly likely to be going to Penn State. I was like, This stadium's pretty big. And there was just snow everywhere. It looked pretty cool—until the snowstorms started hitting my sophomore year.

KOA FARMER: The only thing I really knew about Penn State was the uniforms, the stadium, and, obviously, Joe Paterno. Did not know too much about the players that came through there. But the stadium is just incredible. I grew up going to the Rose Bowl and the Coliseum, which are really big, too, but there was just something different about Beaver Stadium.

But ultimately what sold us is what Coach Franklin was saying. You know, what he wanted to do for this program, the chance for me to be part of something that would be remembered for a lifetime. It was bigger than football itself.

GRANT HALEY: I really believed him, believed in what he was saying. I know it sounds kind of weird, but even when he was at Vanderbilt, saying he was going to take the program to the next level, it wasn't just talk. I saw it happening.

He's one of those coaches who has your best interest at heart—on and off the field. My family's still close with him. He reached out to me a couple months ago when my mom was getting surgery, so it's not just something he preaches to get you to come to his school. It goes way beyond the field. Beyond your time at Penn State or Vanderbilt.

ADAM BRENEMAN: It's just crazy to think about how impactful that recruiting class was.

GRANT HALEY: Yeah, it's crazy the amount of people that stuck with the class. It ended up being pretty strong.

MIKE GESICKI: I remember talking to Coach O'Brien the day after he accepted the Houston job, him telling me Penn State's the right place for me. I never decommitted, because I had committed to Penn State for more than Coach O'Brien. He was a big part of it, but there was also the people like Breneman, the people like Hack, the best fans in the world, Beaver Stadium, the opportunity to get a world-class degree, and being four hours from home. The stars kind of just aligned for Penn State.

Coach Franklin gets the job and comes to one of my basketball games with a couple of other coaches and we just hit it off. They came to my house afterwards, had dinner and all that, and I just let him know, "Hey, listen, I'm not going anywhere. I'm staying right here with you guys at Penn State."

It all paid off in the long run. I do remember being a little hesitant, because I didn't know how they were going to use the tight end. In the beginning stages, it was a little shaky, but everything ended up working itself out.

TWENTY-SEVEN

FIRST IMPRESSIONS

FOR THE PLAYERS *already inside Penn State's program, it was hard to know what to expect from the new coach. Beyond those two nine-win seasons at Vanderbilt, there was no body of work to examine, no storied offense to dissect, not even a video clip of him chewing out a legendary quarterback.*

And unlike rumored candidates Al Golden, Mike Munchak, and Greg Schiano, who had all played, coached, or done both for the Nittany Lions, James Franklin had no real ties to the university.

"I'm a Pennsylvania boy with a Penn State heart," he said in his introductory press conference.

What did that mean?

Who could say? The guy was raised by his mother in the suburbs of Philly, spent summers as a boy with his father's family in Pittsburgh, and entered the orbit of Joe Paterno's program just once—for a football camp, as a high school junior. "I thought I was good enough to play at Penn State," he joked. "I was not."

James Franklin ended up at Division II East Stroudsburg instead, where he was the starting quarterback in 1994 and '95 and set twenty-three school records, including the single-season marks for touchdown passes (19), passing yards (2,586), and total yards of offense (3,129). He graduated in '95 with a degree in psychology, but quickly discovered (not unlike Paterno) that he could do more good as a coach than a paid-by-the-hour professional.

It was a long haul, though, from East Stroudsburg to State College. Nineteen trips around the sun to be precise. Along the way, Franklin made stops at Kutztown University, East Stroudsburg (again), James Madison, Washington State, Idaho State, Maryland, Kansas State, Maryland (again), and Vanderbilt. He also served as the offensive coordinator of the Roskilde Kings in the Danish American Football Federation and the receivers coach of the Green Bay Packers.

To understand just how far he was from the game's lofty heights at the start, consider the thirty-seven-hour drive he made from Philly to Pullman, Washington, in 1998 with all his worldly possessions piled into a 1988 Honda Accord with more than 170,000 miles on it. Days before his departure, the vehicle had been stolen, pillaged, and then recovered. To keep the engine running, he had to insert a screwdriver in the ignition. When the state police in Montana saw the car and the license plate, they pulled him over and he had to explain that he was the owner of the automobile, not the thief.

Suffice to say, even with his striking success at Vanderbilt, Franklin was not a marquee figure in the sport. When he finally emerged as the man to replace Bill O'Brien, those in the locker room weren't quite sure what to make of the choice.

JORDAN LUCAS, CORNERBACK AND SAFETY, 2012–15: He came in and had a lot of energy.

ADAM BRENEMAN: You could tell how passionate he was about the game, his players, just from being with him for a couple of minutes.

CHRISTIAN HACKENBERG: He's an extremely high-energy person. He thrives on it, makes sure everybody in the building is maintaining that energy level throughout the day. Making freshmen dance in front of everyone before the meeting starts just to lighten the mood.

ADRIAN AMOS: He's a down-to-earth guy, but you can tell he's a competitor. Watch him on TV and he's a competitor.

O'Brien and Franklin had coached together for two years at Maryland under Ralph Friedgen. O'Brien had mentored the running backs and Franklin the wide receivers, and yet their styles were markedly different.

O'Brien was more hands-off with the players. As long as they performed on the field and in the classroom, he left them alone. Franklin viewed them more as unfinished beings. He wanted to mold them—as students, athletes, and members of society. To play for him, you kind of had to accept the whole package, embrace the role he created for you on the field and off.

He also had more flash to him. OB had no artifice: He told you exactly what he thought. Franklin was more inclined to embellish things. His program wasn't just great. It was unrivaled.

SAM FICKEN: O'Brien had to cater to the players, because they could up and leave at any time. Coach Franklin gets there and he's had a ton of success at Vanderbilt. I mean, if you're getting nine wins at Vanderbilt, you obviously know what you're doing. So he was super focused on the details. He cared about some stuff that maybe Coach O'Brien didn't and that sometimes ruffled feathers, but in terms of being a leader and seeing the big picture, what the program needed to be a legitimate title contender, no one could have expected a Big Ten Championship within what . . . three years?

CARLA NEAL-HALEY, MOTHER OF GRANT HALEY: At the time, James was making Vanderbilt not just an academic school, but more and more of a contender in the SEC. They were never going to be Florida or Georgia, but he was getting recruits into the NFL, getting to bowl games. And for the two years that Grant and I were on the recruiting trail, I said, "Look, this is the best of both worlds. You're still going to play in the SEC. The NFL is still going to look at you. But you're going to have the best educational foundation you can get in the SEC."

CAEL SANDERSON, HEAD COACH, PENN STATE WRESTLING: Both men love the game of football. Love to coach. To be the head coach of Penn State football, you've got to be pretty good at what you do.

O'Brien wanted to coach the team, call the plays. He was a great recruiter, but that's not really his passion. He'd say, "Hey, I'm going to take you all the way. Look at my track record." But he's not the social media type. And he was in a tough position, because when he came in the athletic department was obviously in a difficult position, so he had to take on more than just being the football coach. He did a wonderful job. We're fortunate he was here for those two years.

Franklin's more of the big-picture guy. He loves coaching, but he's more of a CEO.

DAVID JONES: He probably doesn't know as much about football as a lot of guys—certainly not as much about offense as Bill O'Brien.

He's the CEO in many ways.

He has a lot in common with Paterno there. Neither one's a genius about strategy. Their gift is in motivation and management. You hire really good assistants and let your coaches coach.

CHRISTIAN HACKENBERG: Their philosophies were very different. In the NFL, you don't have to go out and recruit—you're paying people. So when Bill got there, he took more of a pro approach. That's why he was able to be so transparent. He never promised us anything but opportunity.

Coach Franklin built a program at Vanderbilt, won some games in the SEC, the traditional college way. For him, it was about recruiting, presenting the place as irresistible.

And for us, at that age—eighteen, nineteen, twenty years old—that's a big shift. When all you know is a certain thought process, a certain way that things are run, and then it flips to the opposite end of the spectrum, it's hard to figure out how to maneuver relationships.

ALEX BUTTERWORTH: When Franklin came in, we had been beaten up by the media for months and months and months and months and months. Whether it be untrue statements or just trying to fight your way through the crowd of reporters to get to practice.

It was easy for us to generate a mutual hate for the press.

O'Brien saw that. He said, "Listen, I'm not going to be a friend of the media, the guy doing all this stuff on social media." He understood what we had just gone through.

And so, it was hard to swallow when Franklin came in and immediately embraced the media.

JAMES FRANKLIN: I was the fifth head coach in like twenty-seven months at Penn State, if you count interim head coaches. That's a lot of change in a short period of time. A lot of change for the community, a lot of change for the university, and a lot of change for our players.

ADAM BRENEMAN: No one will ever walk into a situation like the one Coach Franklin walked into. The older guys on the team had been through so much crap, going through sanctions and different coaches. You had Joe Paterno, Tom Bradley briefly, Bill O'Brien, and Larry Johnson briefly as your head coaches. And then Coach Franklin comes in and has to deal with a load of crap.

MICHAEL MAUTI: You've got some fourth- and fifth-year seniors. What are you going to tell those guys that they haven't already heard? Or haven't already experienced in their careers?

ADAM BRENEMAN: I remember sitting in a team meeting room with Coach Franklin and he said some harmless line. You know, in the two years under Coach O'Brien, we had seven or eight wins. Coach Franklin—again harmless—said, "You know, seven wins is never going to be good enough around here, seven wins isn't going to cut it anymore."

That's a perfect example of what I mean. In that locker room, the number of people that were so pissed off that he said that to us—to the seniors, especially—because, like, you don't know what we just went through. Seven wins was remarkable for those two years.

We had to go talk to Coach Franklin. Be like, "Hey, coach, we know you didn't mean anything by it, but that definitely struck a chord you didn't want to hit with people."

Then he addressed us and said, "Man, I was just making an analogy; what you guys did is amazing."

It's just an example of how sensitive a time it was.

MALIK GOLDEN: There was just a lot going on internally. I don't think the players and coaches meshed that well the first couple of years. That was kind of a reflection of us not winning those close games, because we did have a lot of talent.

It was unfortunate, because I think James . . . a lot of people were just overwhelmed.

VON WALKER: Coach O'Brien kind of treated the players like grown men, like he was coaching an NFL team. When Franklin came in, it was more of a family thing. He understood that he was coaching eighteen-, nineteen-, twenty-year-old men. We weren't just trying to win games, be respectful, and do the right thing. We were trying to be incredible student-athletes.

KOA FARMER: Coach Franklin really recruited guys that fit the program. You know, that's the thing to say. "He's a Penn State guy. He's a Penn State guy. He's a Penn State guy."

We were blue-collar guys from great families. Franklin had us do media training, but we knew what we were representing. We all took pride in our character. That might be the most important thing we instilled in one another: an appreciation for great morals, values, and character. Treat others how you want to be treated. Respect opposing players' locker rooms. Respect your opponent, your teammates, everyone in the building, because we're all on the same team.

VON WALKER: He's a genius when it comes to bringing in the right talent. So things kind of shifted. We were still hard-nosed football, but now super skill-oriented and super focused on the minute details, too.

MIKE HULL: I liked how he assigned everyone a role. Whether you were fourth-team or a starter, we needed everyone to pull together to win. He went everywhere—hockey games, wrestling matches. I think he really liked the Penn State spirit.

JASON CABINDA: We wanted to bring this culture of hard work. Wanted Penn State to be reborn. And obviously those first couple of years were tough. You know, getting over the sanctions. Either that first or second year I was there, we only had forty-six scholarship players on the roster, which is just absurd. College teams normally have eighty-five.

JAMES FRANKLIN: You talk about our core values—that's something I believe in. Number one is to have a positive attitude. People that approach their jobs, their work, their school, their opportunities with a positive attitude—that's the type of person others want to be around.

Number two is a great work ethic. You can't always control how big you are, how strong you are, and maybe how smart you are, but you can control how hard you work.

Number three is to compete. That's probably the biggest challenge nowadays, because our society has shifted. Everybody gets a trophy, everybody gets a smiley face.

And the last value, probably the most important one, is to sacrifice. Everybody says they want success, but very few people are willing to sacrifice to have the success they want. Are you able to give up small things now for big things later in life?

We talk about those things all the time, have them plastered all over our building, because in my short time on this earth, they've been really important, not just in football, but in general. If you can do those four things consistently, you've got a chance to be successful in any endeavor.

CARLA NEAL-HALEY: Given what James had done for Vanderbilt, taking them from being kind of a lame-duck program to being a contender in the SEC, winning some big games, I knew we'd be fine. Did I think we'd win a Big Ten Championship so quickly? I don't think I could have foreseen that.

I could see that we'd be part of rebuilding something. The way James framed it was enough for me. As a Penn State alumnus, I'm like, Can we bring our history back? Can we be the team we once were? Get the respect we once had? I'd love for my kid to be a part of that.

CHRISTIAN HACKENBERG: At that point in time, it was a lot bigger than football, if that makes sense. I was prepared to sacrifice anything just to make sure we saw what we had started through. I mean, I take pride in that—being a man of my word.

CARLA NEAL-HALEY: That made a big difference for the boys coming in. They're like, Look, we may not ever win a ring, but we'll keep life in the program, keep the legacy going.

I mean, it was hard as a Penn State alum to watch the program crumble over one man's ridiculousness. And way back when Joe Paterno was starting out, a coach was just a coach. Now you're a CEO, responsible for everything.

DAVID JONES: You can make the argument that O'Brien and Franklin were both exactly what the program needed at the time they were hired. O'Brien was a grinder, a motivator, a guy you wanted in your foxhole in a situation like that.

During that next step, the school needed somebody to rebrand the place, make everyone forget about Sandusky and Paterno, and who better to do that than James Franklin? I mean, really, when you think of Penn State now, what do you think about?

James Franklin.

You do. You don't think about Joe Paterno. You don't. And you don't think about Sandusky. You don't. Nobody talks about that anymore.

That stupid John Barr documentary, did you watch that? *The Paterno Legacy*? The whole premise is stupid. The whole premise is that ten years after the Sandusky scandal people are wondering what is Joe Paterno's legacy? No one is effing talking about Joe Paterno's legacy.

That's because of James Franklin.

He has rebranded the place in his own image, for better or for worse. I would not have believed he could accomplish that. But you cannot underestimate the importance of it. He was so full of shit, so over the top with promotion, that it was the best thing for the program.

It really was.

Give Dave Joyner some credit, because he hired two really different people at two different times, and they turned out to be the best possible coaches for those periods.

He made two incredible hires.

TWENTY-EIGHT

DUBLIN

FOR HIS FIRST official game at Penn State, James Franklin had to cross an ocean, touching down in Ireland some 3,300 miles away from the team's home locker room. In truth, any showdown with the University of Central Florida, coached by the resourceful George O'Leary, would present significant challenges. But this one brought a unique set of hurdles, starting with the fact that most of Penn State's players—roughly eighty percent, according to Franklin—had never once left the country. So, while he and his staff were sorting out the roster and introducing a new playbook, they were also applying for passports—dozens of passports—and worrying about packing lists, customs regulations, jet lag, nutrition requirements, and a million other things that can go horribly wrong when you venture to a foreign land with 118 college kids under your care.

SAM FICKEN: Bill O'Brien played a big role in getting that game on the schedule. He wanted to reward everyone for staying around. It was kind of his treat. "Hey, if we can't go to a bowl game, let's give these guys some cool experience."

It wasn't like a vacation. We were very focused on the game. But it was kind of cool to be able to hang out with your teammates in that environment for a week.

KYLE CARTER: I remember not loving the food, but that's the thing about football, man. It's about getting you out of your comfort zone. It was a great bonding experience for the team.

MALIK GOLDEN: We went to Dublin, stayed at a nice hotel, did a lot of great things—touristy stuff. I think we went to the Guinness factory.

GENO LEWIS: That was our bowl game. Like, that's literally why they set it up for us. So we could go somewhere, get a feeling for what a bowl game is like. Get some gifts, food, stay in a beautiful hotel. That was my first time out of the country, too. I wasn't sure what to expect. I remember this guy coming to a team meeting to explain the culture there.

He was like, "Listen, guys, if you go out on the streets and somebody asks, 'Hey, where's the crack?' In Ireland, crack means fun. Like, Hey, where's the fun at? Don't get caught off guard. They're not talking about drugs."

I remember everybody laughing.

JAMES FRANKLIN: We tried to keep the routine as consistent as possible. Obviously, flying to a different country makes it difficult to do that. That's why we sent a group over in the summer to scout everything.

MICHAEL HAZEL, DIRECTOR OF FOOTBALL OPERATIONS: When you go overseas, you're required to complete certain documents. You basically have to list every item you're taking with you. From a box of twenty-four pencils to 180 socks to 190 cleats, it needs to be listed A to Z.

The team packed more than nine thousand items, ranging from Post-it notes to blue index cards to 225 spare detachable metal cleats. All told, more than twenty thousand pounds' worth of cargo traveled from Harrisburg to Dublin. Only the Gatorade crossed the Atlantic by boat.

JAMES FRANKLIN: It was a massive plane. We had over three hundred people.

MALIK GOLDEN: You get to sit in first class. First class or business class. Six hours to Dublin. You get the nice seats that recline all the way. You get TV and good food.

Craig Fitzgerald overhauled the team's approach to training in 2012, winning the players over with his frenetic energy, T-shirts-in-January bravado, and the group-oriented exercises in his revamped weight room. *Courtesy of FightOnState.com*

Michael Mauti emerged as the 2012 team's spiritual leader, working tirelessly to hold the squad together, then anchoring the defense throughout the season. To honor his sacrifices, the players wore his 42 on their helmets for the year's final game. *Courtesy of FightOnState.com*

"Mauti could never have done what he did without Zordich," says documentary director Michael Nash. The fullback was the first to commit to staying in the program and backed Mauti up every step of the way. *Courtesy of FightOnState.com*

Bill O'Brien stepped forward to replace the legendary Joe Paterno and over two seasons made one momentous decision after another, shrewdly leading the program back from the brink of disaster. *Courtesy of FightOnState.com*

Spider Caldwell, the Lions' charismatic equipment manager, helped O'Brien steer the program forward, enlisting his wife, Karen, to get names stitched on the jerseys and working through the night to place those 42 stickers on PSU's helmets.
Courtesy of FightOnState.com

Fans rallied behind the players, showing up in force to greet Penn State's iconic blue buses as they arrived at Beaver Stadium for the 2012 home opener. Not even an 0–2 start to the season could deter them.
Courtesy of FightOnState.com

Matt McGloin exemplified the program's grit, all but willing himself to outduel more celebrated recruits for the starting role at quarterback. "He brought the leadership that team needed," says strength coach Craig Fitzgerald. *Courtesy of FightOnState.com*

For its pivotal role in rescuing the program, the 2012 team was added to Beaver Stadium's ring of honor, celebrated alongside squads that had finished with perfect records, conference championships, or national championships.
Photos by Chris Raymond

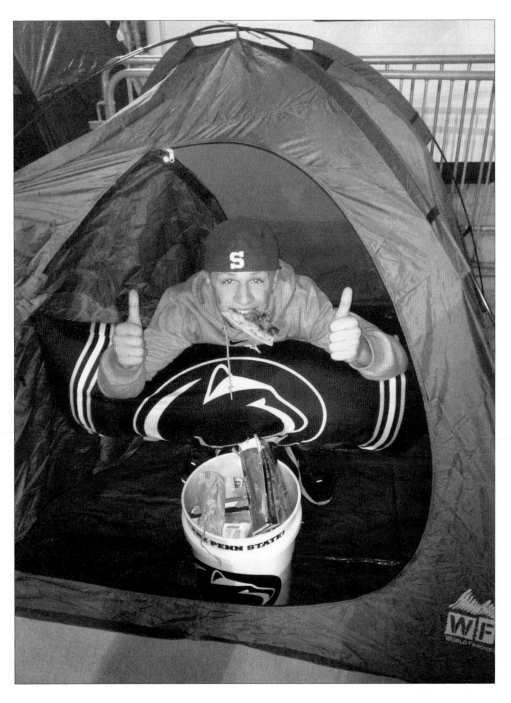

Darian Somers, a fan from birth, was among the student diehards who camped outside the stadium for the Lions' big games. He served as president of Nittanyville for the 2015–16 school year.
Courtesy of Darian Somers

In forty-five seasons as head coach, Joe Paterno steered the Nittany Lions to 409 victories and two national championships. And, as he liked to note, he fielded well-rounded athletes, including forty-seven Academic All-Americans on those teams. *Photo by Dan Oleski*

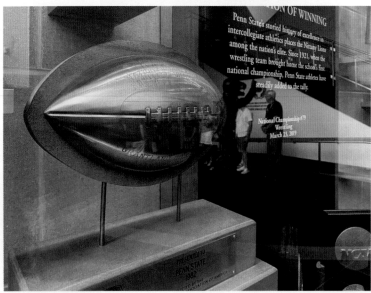

Paterno and his program became a point of pride for Pennsylvania residents, inspiring generations of players and fans with his commitment to success with honor. (Yes, that's the 1982 national championship trophy.) The sentiment burned bright long after the coach had passed, compelling others to rescue what he had built. *Photos by Chris Raymond and A. Greg Raymond*

Unlike O'Brien, James Franklin greeted the media with open arms, relishing each opportunity to pitch the virtues of his players and his program. His social media savvy turned his 1–0 posts into a mantra for the team and the last thing you see when exiting the locker room for the field. *Franklin photo courtesy of FightOnState.com. Locker room photo by A. Greg Raymond.*

Sam Ficken opened his storied Penn State kicking career with a horrific four-missed-field-goals day, but refused to let that be his legacy. With dogged work, he emerged as a rock-steady team leader, earning defining wins with clutch kicks against Central Florida and Boston College. *Courtesy of FightOnState.com*

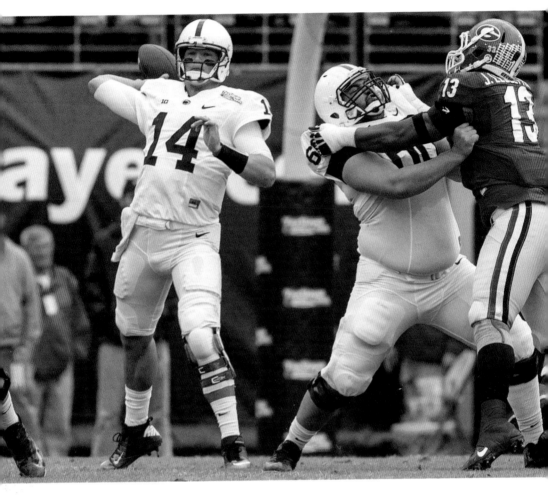

Christian Hackenberg arrived on campus as a star recruit and delivered on his early promise with a stellar freshman season, but challenges from the team's depleted roster thwarted his climb. He ended his run with a shoulder injury in the TaxSlayer Bowl. "The kid never complained," says QB coach Charlie Fisher. "He did his job. He showed up." *Courtesy of FightOnState.com*

With daring leaps over would-be tacklers, Saquon Barkley rocketed to stardom as a freshman, but always remained grounded off the field, dutifully putting in the legwork and agreeing to take on any task the team asked of him. *Courtesy of FightOnState.com*

Student songwriter Matty Fresh composed loving tributes to Saquon Barkley and Trace McSorley. The QB tune went viral. Uploaded to YouTube in 2018, it's been viewed more than 7.5 million times. *Courtesy of Matty Fresh*

Trace McSorley was named MVP of the Big Ten Championship Game in 2016, throwing for 384 yards and four touchdowns in the Lions' 38–31 win versus Wisconsin. He now owns nearly every major passing record at Penn State. *Courtesy of FightOnState.com*

SAM FICKEN: I got to sit in business class, so spread the legs. Really thankful for that, because I know there were a lot of people crammed into that plane.

AKEEL LYNCH, RUNNING BACK, 2012–15: It's crazy, man, where football can take you.

Franklin's roster featured fifty-four freshmen—some with a redshirt season under their belts, but many in their very first year in the program. By contrast, the Knights had a veteran team that had finished 12–1 the prior season, including a three-point win versus Penn State at Beaver Stadium and a ten-point win against sixth-ranked Baylor in the Fiesta Bowl.

"They had experience, confidence, and they knew how to win," said Franklin.

The Nittany Lion offense returned sophomore quarterback Christian Hackenburg and veteran running backs Zach Zwinak, Bill Belton, and Akeel Lynch, but the squad's vaunted playmaker Allen Robinson had declared for the NFL draft and was now a second-round pick for the Jacksonville Jaguars. Franklin was counting on sophomore Geno Lewis, redshirt freshman DaeSean Hamilton, and a group of promising-but-untested recruits—Troy Apke, Saeed Blacknall, Chris Godwin, and DeAndre Thompkins—to somehow replace him.

Adding to the drama, the phone up in the coaches' booth didn't work, so new offensive coordinator John Donovan had to call plays from down on the field. But the team responded well and Penn State led 10–3 at the half, prompting Central Florida's George O'Leary to switch quarterbacks, replacing redshirt freshman Pete DiNovo with sophomore Justin Holman.

That's when things got interesting. Holman rallied the team with three TDs in the final two quarters. And, with just over a minute to go in the contest, the Knights edged ahead 24–23, setting the stage for a true test of wills.

BOB FLOUNDERS: They left a little too much time on the clock for Hackenberg, and Ficken made them pay.

ED CUNNINGHAM, ESPN COLOR COMMENTATOR: In the last practice of the week, the last thing you do is the hurry-up drill. At the last practice in Ireland, James Franklin ran out and said a minute-twenty left, one timeout, and all we need is a field goal to win.

Well, now it's a minute-thirteen, three timeouts left, and a field goal to win.

Grant Haley returned the kick to the Penn State twenty-six-yard line and the Lions sophomore signal caller took the field.

The first-down throw to tight end Kyle Carter was batted away.

On second down, Hackenberg tossed a quick out to Geno Lewis for seven yards.

On third down, he overthrew Lewis deep downfield.

On fourth-and-three, Hackenberg took the snap, looked right, tucked the ball and started running.

CHRISTIAN HACKENBERG: It was fourth down. I knew if I was going to go, I had to *go*.

Eight yards later, Penn State had the ball first-and-ten at the forty-one.

A shovel pass to Belton added thirteen more yards. The Lions had now crossed midfield, earning a fresh set of downs, but there were just twenty-seven seconds on the clock.

CHRISTIAN HACKENBERG: Bill made a fantastic play to get out of bounds.

Geno Lewis followed with a juggling catch at the UCF thirty-seven. Seventeen ticks left on the clock.

Hack throws to Lewis, who sheds a tackle and sprints to the nineteen.

Three seconds left. Franklin calls timeout.

GENO LEWIS: Ficken ended up winning the game on that field goal. Trust me, if we had lost, that would've been a long flight back. Instead, it was one of the best flights ever.

SAM FICKEN: All three of my field goals before that big one were shorter kicks. I'd hit them all pretty solid. I was happy with how I felt, but, you know, it was eerily similar to the Virginia game in 2012. If I remember correctly, we were leading Virginia most of the game and they took the lead at the very end. The same thing happened here. The difference was that I was three-for-three going into that last kick. I had confidence.

The ball was placed on the right hash mark, thirty-six yards from the crossbar. Ficken, now a senior, was nearly two full years removed from that horrific Virginia afternoon.

SAM FICKEN: It wasn't a real difficult kick. The wind was blowing right to left. I asked them to get the ball to the right side of the field, so I could play the wind a little better. The snap was good, the hold was good, and, honestly, I didn't hit it great.

RYAN KEISER, THE HOLDER: I've got to keep my head down till he kicks it, but once the ball's off, I look and it's heading towards that right upright.

BOB FLOUNDERS: Dead at the right upright. But the wind is blowing to the left and it worked inside.

DAVID JONES: That's what Sam said, too.

SAM FICKEN: I was a little nervous it might clink, but the wind pushed it back in.
As soon as I saw it angle inward, I had a little fun running around. There are 310-pound linemen running at you and I didn't want to get dog-piled.

After sprinting around the field, Ficken jumped into Franklin's arms. The coach fought hard to contain his emotions during the post-game interview.

CHANCE SORRELL: We got to be 1–0, as Coach Franklin says—1–0, 1–0, 1–0.

JAMES FRANKLIN: That was a team win—offense, defense, special teams. It wasn't always pretty and, to me, that's a real positive: We found a way to beat a really good team, never stopped believing in each other.

CHRISTIAN HACKENBERG: It must have been something in the Irish air. Fish and chips? I don't know. But, yeah, it was fun. We played well. Getting that momentum early in the year was big for us. That set the expectations really high.

TWENTY-NINE

BYE BYE BOWL BAN

In the summer of 2012, at the urging of the NCAA, Penn State had hired former U.S. Senate majority leader George Mitchell to monitor its athletics program. It was his job to make sure the school upheld the "integrity agreement" it had signed with the NCAA and Big Ten Conference.

Mitchell had been handpicked for the role by the NCAA itself. According to Mark Emmert, he had "impeccable credentials as a fair and experienced negotiator." After leaving the Senate, the man had helped broker peace deals in Northern Ireland and the Middle East. He had also overseen a two-year investigation into steroid use in Major League Baseball and a two-month review of the International Olympic Committee's host city selection process.

Within a year of assuming his new duties at Penn State, Mitchell was encouraging the NCAA to step back its sanctions. Based on the swift actions taken by the school, "relief from the scholarship reductions is warranted," he said. And the NCAA agreed to restore five scholarships for the 2014–15 school year, with a promise of more to follow in the next two years.

In September of 2014, Mitchell issued another glowing report and the NCAA went one stride further, not only restoring the full scholarship count for 2015, but lifting the postseason ban, making it possible for Penn State to play in a bowl game and, yes, even the Big Ten title game.

Word spread fast. Within minutes, it seemed, students were celebrating on campus and recruits were applauding the decision. "Big day for Happy Valley," said four-star receiver Juwan Johnson. "No more worrying about sanctions."

The early retreat raised questions about the NCAA's response to the Sandusky scandal.

TRACE MCSORLEY: After our second game in 2014, they lifted the bowl ban. If we had the year we wanted, we'd be able to play in a bowl game. It motivated the guys on the team, especially some of the older guys. Now you're playing for something.

JAMES FRANKLIN: I found out on social media. That's just how it is nowadays. I tried to get a text out to the team as soon as I could, but the players were already aware of what was happening.

MIKE HULL: We were eating lunch at Chick-fil-A when we learned the news on Twitter. Like thirty seconds later, the coaches sent out a text message telling us to come to a team meeting.

MIKE HOOVER, PENN STATE ACCOUNTING MAJOR: Everyone got the ESPN alert and our whole class went wild. The professor was like, "What's happening, what's happening?"

GENO LEWIS: Over social media, news travels like hotfire. So we got a message from Coach saying we have a team meeting at three o'clock. He basically told us everything we were hearing was accurate. The sanctions were being lifted.

JAMES FRANKLIN: We brought the forty-nine guys who had stayed in the program after the sanctions announcement up to the front of the meeting room and the team gave them a standing ovation.

ANGELO MANGIRO, OFFENSIVE LINEMAN, 2011–15: I was happy for those guys, happy we were getting rewarded for our commitment. I said, "Let's go out, have a good year, and get to a bowl!"

GENO LEWIS: Everybody was like, "Listen, man, we got to get to a bowl." That was our goal. "We want to get to a bowl game."

That put some life into people, filled us with air.

In the hours that followed, some members of the media strongly objected to the decision. "The NCAA didn't put sanctions in place for four years because that's how long it would take for Penn State to right the ship," wrote Nina Mandell of USA Today. "It put them in place because Penn State had done the worst thing they could do as a university: Put the well-being of a football program ahead of everything—including protecting children from a predator."

Others were critical of the NCAA for the way it handled the case, questioning the organization's authority to intercede from the start. In a roundtable discussion on the Big Ten Network one year earlier, they had voiced their concern, after the NCAA's first retreat.

PAT FORDE, SENIOR WRITER, *SPORTS ILLUSTRATED*: I think this was a tacit admission that they didn't get it right the first time. Nobody said that on the NCAA teleconference. They all said this was going to be up for review anyway. They accelerated the timeline and reduced the sanctions, which tells me when Mark Emmert made his cowboy move, went totally outside of NCAA protocol, basically issued these sanctions on his own— devastating sanctions—one of the biggest NCAA cases since the SMU death penalty, they overreached and now they were dialing it back.

DOUG CHAPMAN, COLLEGE FOOTBALL ANALYST, BIG TEN NETWORK: Pat hit it right on the head: This is the NCAA retracting its false teeth. They acted too quickly, and this is their way of apologizing.

DAVID JONES: By the summer of 2013, I was hearing stuff about George Mitchell. That he was going to be able to lessen the sanctions, that he was in Penn State's corner.

PAT FORDE: This was a matter for the courts all along. It was never going to be the right thing to penalize the football players and the football program at Penn State. This was much more of an institutional issue than that. So, this was a good move by the NCAA, giving Penn State back its postseason hopes in a year when it looked like they could go bowling.

MIKE GROSS, COLUMNIST, LANCASTER NEWSPAPERS: They were closer to a level playing field than expected when this all came out. And we can argue about whether this is an admission that the NCAA overstepped its bounds—I think they did—in issuing the sanctions and also if it's acknowledgment of the diminishing power of the NCAA, as college football is increasingly run by the five major conferences, but it was certainly a good thing for Penn State's football program.

After the 26–24 win against Central Florida, James Franklin's Nittany Lions returned home to Beaver Stadium and treated fans to a decisive 21–3 victory against Akron. They still needed four more wins to be eligible for a bowl game invite. As enticing as a postseason showdown sounded, they had months of toil ahead before they could make the case that they truly deserved the honor. While thousands of students gathered on Old Main lawn to celebrate the day's big news, the players filed out of the team meeting room and quietly got back to business.

ANGELO MANGIRO: As soon as the meeting was over, me, Miles Dieffenbach, and the offensive line watched film on Rutgers.

MIKE HULL: We were excited, but still had to take it one game at a time.

JAMES FRANKLIN: Rutgers, Rutgers, Rutgers, Rutgers.

In January of 2015, the NCAA would restore the 111 victories stripped from Joe Paterno and his players, making him once again the coach with the most wins in major college football.

MICHAEL NASH: The fact the NCAA gave Paterno back all those victories is basically an admission that they were wrong after they dug deeper into Freeh's report and did their due diligence. This is my personal opinion— I'm not a Penn Stater—but had they found the proof they were looking for, those victories would never have been given back.

THIRTY

LOSING

DESPITE THE EARLY *retreat by the NCAA, the players were now facing their toughest battle yet, a campaign so grueling it left them staggered. Two and a half years of turmoil had taken a steep toll on the program, stripping the roster of much-needed talent. And what was missing could not be replaced with pep talks, walk-ons, or extra work in the weight room.*

The Nittany Lions needed a late touchdown to squeak out a 13–10 win at Rutgers. They handily beat 0–3 Massachusetts, then went into a tailspin, accepting a 29–6 whipping from Northwestern in the Homecoming Game followed by soul-crushing losses to Michigan, Ohio State, and Maryland. In a span of six weeks, it seemed, every flaw, every misstep, was suddenly exposed by the bright lights of the TV cameras and the prying eyes of social media.

The team stumbled past Indiana and Temple to earn the six victories required for a bowl bid, then succumbed to Illinois (still coached by Tim Beckman) and Michigan State to close the conference schedule. When the dust had cleared, Penn State was 2–6 in Big Ten play.

Needless to say, it was a trying time in Happy Valley, particularly for the team's young quarterback, who was singled out for much of the criticism on the program's failings.

CHRISTIAN HACKENBERG: That was probably my toughest year mentally, just riding the high—being in it, being in it, being in it—and then, you know, hitting rock bottom.

TRACE MCSORLEY: Once we got into the Big Ten schedule, we got hit hard. That's when things dropped off for us. We lost four straight.

JAMES FRANKLIN: We hadn't played pretty all year long and it caught up to us.

MALIK GOLDEN: We lost a lot of close games.

DAESEAN HAMILTON: On one drive we'd go down the field and score and on the next drive we'd start off with a penalty, get pushed back five yards, put ourselves in a hole, and struggle to get out of it. It had to do with consistency, playing disciplined football.

CHRISTIAN HACKENBERG: Those next two years, we were the youngest team in college football by a long shot. I remember going out to picture day. They had us line up by class. I was a true sophomore and I was in the minority.

We were lining up for pictures and we were like true sophomores and true juniors and then you look over at the true freshmen and the redshirt freshmen and that's like seventy percent of our team, eighty percent of our team.

That's insane.

ADAM BRENEMAN: We had like two fifth-year seniors.

CHRISTIAN HACKENBERG: That's what I think people have a hard time understanding: When you're out there trying to play games with guys who have to develop, it's really difficult, because there's a big jump from high school to college, no matter how you cut the cake.

JAMES FRANKLIN: The speed of the game, the complexity of the game is completely different.

MIKE GESICKI: I had no business being on the field my freshman year. I really didn't. It's not like I was blocking anybody. I wasn't making any plays in the passing game. It was a huge learning experience.

TRACE MCSORLEY: It was my first year, too. I was redshirting. To see how all that played out was eye-opening, just learning how much of a grind the college football season was.

BRANDON BELL: If the sanctions hadn't happened, we would have had more depth. We never used that as an excuse, but we all noticed it. It made things tougher, for sure.

ZACH LADONIS: We could never get it to click. Things were good some games, not so good others.

We didn't have the confidence we had in 2012 and 2013, when our backs were against the wall and we were just throwing haymakers into the darkness, landing some and feeling really good about ourselves for winning games.

In those '14 and '15 seasons, that didn't work. It was like, Okay, what's going on? We've been throwing haymakers for a while and nothing's connecting.

The scholarship reductions had an impact. We'd had a lot of experienced role players and locker room guys through the thick of 2011, 2012, and 2013, but those numbers started to dwindle, and I don't think we had the necessary experience in the glue guys those next two years.

JACK DAVIS: Under Bill O'Brien, Penn State was able to sustain some level of success. As James Franklin began his tenure, it was easy to forget that the sophomores, juniors, and seniors—players who would normally be leading your program—had arrived in these smaller recruiting classes. People underrated the impact the sanctions would continue to have.

Nowhere was the impact of those lean years more apparent than on the offensive line. After the season-ending win against Wisconsin in 2013, the team bid farewell to Adam Gress, Ty Howle, and John Urschel. Then right tackle Garry Gilliam passed up his final year of eligibility and joined the Seattle Seahawks as a free agent.

In the spring, Miles Dieffenbach tore his ACL, leaving the line with four first-year starters—tackle Andrew Nelson, center Angelo Mangiro, and guards Brendan Mahon and Brian Gaia—alongside left tackle Donovan Smith.

MARK BRENNAN: That was partly O'Brien's fault. Before the sanctions even hit, he was complaining about how many offensive linemen there were in the program. "In the NFL, we'd have like seven guys," he said. "Here we have like seventeen, eighteen."

Then he found out what happens when you lose your scholarships. In the NFL, guys come in as polished players. In college, offensive linemen are the hardest prospects to judge. You could have a six-foot-seven, three-hundred-forty-pound guy who just dominates in high school because he's bigger than everyone else. You get him on campus and he doesn't work out.

DAVID JONES: O'Brien couldn't recruit many offensive lineman, and Franklin paid for that. If you're capped at seventy-five scholarships, you've got to spend so many of them on skill-position players, simply because you need a dynamic product. You can't spend them on non-skill-position players, because they don't give you any boom power.

You've got to make tough choices.

JAMES FRANKLIN: We could have gone out and signed fifteen junior college players. The next year, we could have gone out and signed fifteen junior college players. But I don't think the administration or the fans wanted to do it that way.

Once you start doing that, you're going to have heavy turnover every year or two. And, like I said from day one, we wanted to build this thing the right way—for the long haul.

We needed a little patience.

The progress was there. Sometimes you just had to take a step back and look at it.

ANGELO MANGIRO: We had a lot of young guys, a lot of guys switching positions.

CHRISTIAN HACKENBERG: We had a lot of guys who hadn't played a lot of ball.

I mean, Brian Gaia and Derek Dowrey got asked two days before spring practice to play on the offensive line. They hadn't done that since high school.

Both had entered the program as defensive tackles under Bill O'Brien.

DEREK DOWREY, DEFENSIVE TACKLE AND OFFENSIVE GUARD, 2016–18: I spent that first year relearning how to play on the offensive line.

CHANCE SORRELL: Any position change is going to take time to get used to. The last time I had played on the offensive line was, I think, in middle school, so I was pretty well removed from it, but you just have to put in the time.

It's all about that extra work, getting your steps down and working on your technique. There's a little added incentive, because you've got to catch up to the guys who have been playing the position for years. You just have to put your head down and drive to catch up.

JAMES FRANKLIN: It's footwork, it's fundamentals, but there's an experience factor, too.

It's guys getting up to the line, getting in their stances, and making some calls. Seeing a front or a blitz they'd encountered before, being able to recognize things quickly, and then going out and blocking. When they thought too much, they didn't play as fast, as athletic, or as aggressive.

CHRISTIAN HACKENBERG: Ursh and Ty were gone. Gress was gone. Gilliam was gone. We didn't have a ton of depth. So now you're throwing a bunch of shit in the blender.

Allen Robinson's out and Brandon Felder's out. So you're trying to groom some young guys at receiver, too. It was a completely different team. A completely different thought process.

ANDREW NELSON: We rotated a lot. Guys were playing different positions, sometimes three in one game.

BRIAN GAIA: In practice, Coach Hand was always putting people here and there, in case a player went down.

HERB HAND, OFFENSIVE LINE COACH: Eight guys took the majority of the reps for us. Wendy Laurent, Derek Dowrey, and Albert Hall were our three main backups. Dowrey repped at both guard positions. Wendy repped at all three inside positions. And Albert repped at basically every position but center.

JAMES FRANKLIN: You lose your left tackle and your right tackle goes to left tackle, your center goes to right tackle and a new center comes in the game. That's a lot of moving parts.

Christian Hackenberg paid the price for that instability. In the season's twelve games, he was sacked forty-two times. With each successive hit, he seemed to lose a bit of his spark, the radiant confidence that had made him so successful as a freshman.

GENO LEWIS: Hackenberg was taking a lot of shots, man. A lot of hits.

MIKE GROSS: It starts to crawl into his head that he can't climb the pocket, he can't step into throws, he's constantly looking around for trouble, because trouble is almost always coming. I don't know that I'd ever seen a football team dragged down by one position group before.

DAVID JONES: Hackenberg was getting the crap knocked out of him on a weekly basis. Some of those sacks were his fault for holding on to the ball too long, others were just grotesque cave-ins.

JAMES FRANKLIN: He grew probably as much as any player in the country in terms of leadership, handling adversity, all the things he went through in a very, very short period of time.

CHRISTIAN HACKENBERG: Being considered a veteran leader on the team at nineteen years old, that's crazy—crazy as hell. Especially at a place like Penn State. But that's what it was.

JAMES FRANKLIN: Wins and losses, third-down percentage, and red zone—those are the areas where quarterbacks are usually judged. But, as we all know, playing the quarterback position is so much more than those statistics.

It's about leadership: how you handle yourself, from the time you wake up in the morning till the time you go to bed.

It's about making the guys around you better.

It's about how coachable you are, how confident you are, how much you believe in yourself.

All of those things.

TRACE MCSORLEY: Christian had just come off being Big Ten Freshman of the Year in 2013 and he was already being talked about as the number-one pick in the NFL Draft. He leads a two-minute drive to win the game in Dublin and everything's riding high, then we go on that four-game skid. And now every finger starts pointing at him.

JAMES FRANKLIN: I tried all season long to deflect that criticism, not because I didn't think Christian could handle it, but because he wasn't the issue. Everybody talked about Christian, Christian, Christian. We had to develop the guys around him. A lot of talent had left and we had challenges on the offensive line. We had one returning starter. And it all starts up front.

VON WALKER: There were nights where he couldn't even go out on campus. Like, we're all going out to bars, going out to parties. And, you know, thinking back on it, it was the ultimate sacrifice. He was trying to give everything he could to the program, bring it back, but there were people that wanted to fight him, cause trouble. So not only are you having a tough sophomore year, but the people you'd like to have backing you are putting you in the position where all you want to do is lay low.

TRACE MCSORLEY: He was able to handle all that, basically keep his emotions from getting too high or too low. He was still the same guy. He came to practice, meetings, everything, with the same mentality. That was something to see—my first exposure to how difficult it can be to be the quarterback at Penn State.

CHRISTIAN HACKENBERG: John Urschel, Ty Howle, Miles Dieffenbach, Donovan Smith, Adam Gress, and Garry Gilliam—that group of guys on the line was so instrumental my freshman year.

Allen Robinson, Jesse James, and Kyle Carter at receiver, too.

They made my job so much easier. I just had to understand my role and go out and execute. I knew they were going to do everything they could to help me be successful.

BRANDON BELL: That line was stout, man. We had some big-time guys up there, and obviously, when the whole line is a well-oiled machine, the quarterback benefits.

Ultimately, the coach does, too. As the losses mounted, the fingers started pointing at James Franklin as well. People inside and outside the program began to question his play calls, clock management, and offensive scheme. In an October press conference, he noted the criticism directed at him and his staff by disgruntled fans on Twitter—some of it constructive, some clearly not.

To make matters worse, Hackenberg did not have the deep personal relationship with Franklin that he once shared with O'Brien.

CHRISTIAN HACKENBERG: There were times where we got conservative offensively and there were things we needed to fix but didn't quite address. That was hard for the perfectionist in me. That's where I just hit a brick wall.

Throughout my freshman year, we ran the Patriots' system verbatim. I understood the run game, zone game, angles, leverage, box counts, all kinds of things. So when you see things on the field and you're not at liberty to shift into something else . . . It was like going from driving a Lamborghini to just a nice SUV.

And that's not a knock on Coach Donovan or Coach Rahne, who together oversaw the offense and the passing game. It was just a different philosophy.

That's why I got so frustrated. That's where I really let my brain get in the way. I knew the answers to some of the problems, but we just couldn't get there. It wasn't always a philosophy thing. It was certain limitations, too, trust in the entire unit top to bottom.

There were just so many things happening. That was the hardest part for me: knowing the answers, knowing how to put us in a better situation, but, like, continuing to do the same thing. I let that affect me. In my personal relationships. In the way I sometimes played.

ADAM BRENEMAN: We used to go to the Cracker Barrel off campus on Sunday mornings, get breakfast, and just hash it out—complain about what we wanted to complain about. I always think back to those Sunday mornings after the games where Christian had been sacked like sixteen times and the team was struggling and marvel at how much those conversations helped.

CHRISTIAN HACKENBERG: To be honest, that was the darkest place I've ever been. That season started on such a high note and ended on such a high note and there were some things in between that were good, but there was a lot of bad, a lot of darkness between those two games. And those Sunday mornings were therapeutic, man.

ADAM BRENEMAN: People were tweeting about me, what a bust, what a terrible recruit. I remember we would sit there and laugh about it, make jokes about it, but deep down, it wasn't funny at all.

CHANCE SORRELL: They always tell you to block out the noise, don't pay attention to it, but of course, as young men, you can't help but take a look. You go on Twitter and the critics have access to you like never before. So there wasn't much opportunity to escape the criticism.

ADAM BRENEMAN: Mike Gesicki used to delete his Twitter after games.

JAMES FRANKLIN: There is nothing better than having 107,000 fans when things are going well. When you have challenges, there are 107,000 critics, and as a coach you try to insulate the players and the staff from that as much as you can, but with social media, it's difficult.

VON WALKER: Passion brings out two sides. When you win and things are going in your direction, you're going to have people that love you. And when you find yourself in a tough situation, you have people calling for Franklin's head. They want him to get fired.

We're on the team, trying to block out all the noise, and we're all sitting there thinking, Man, do they even understand how a program is built? It's not easy.

MIKE GESICKI: You try to shake it off, but that stuff hurts—not what they're saying, but the reality of your play. At the end of the day, the idiots on Twitter know nothing about playing football. I could care less what they have to say. The problem is I wasn't backing up how I felt with how I played on the field, so there was nothing I could do about it.

VON WALKER: It's a weird spot to be in. Because you still have to go to class, you still have friends outside of the football team, and you hear stuff and become accustomed to it, but you have to have that little chip on your shoulder. At least, that's how it was for me. You have to just be like, You know what? It's going to be that much sweeter when we start winning and that same person flips the switch and starts loving us again. You have to take it with a grain of salt.

The veteran players also missed the hands-off way that Bill O'Brien approached things beyond the classroom and the football field.

Franklin's vision for the program was much broader. Like Paterno, he relished the role of molding men, not just football players, and so he cut them less slack. But that required another significant shift in culture—for what was essentially a band of brothers hell-bent on completing the mission it had started.

CHRISTIAN HACKENBERG: It was hard. He had this whole philosophy that had worked at Vanderbilt, right? But the situation Bill had stepped into was so unique. And it wasn't resolved yet. It was still super unique. And I don't think Coach Franklin realized just how different it was when he took the job, because we as a team didn't really let it out. We kept everything internal.

He had this vision and this messaging that he thought would mesh really well. And, when it didn't, he scrambled a bit, trying to reach and repair. And when you're trying to do all that, the focus on winning football games kind of gets put on the back burner, you know what I mean?

So there was this whirlwind of stuff. And there's only so much time in a day, only so much time on a head coach's schedule and a player's schedule with class and all the other administrative stuff. I just don't think the situation was what he had expected.

GENO LEWIS: There was a point in time where people didn't trust the systems we were using. I want to say there was a split between some of the older dudes and some of the younger guys.

The younger dudes didn't know anything else. Coach Franklin, that's all they knew.

Some of the older dudes had Joe Paterno as coach, then Bill O'Brien, and then Coach Franklin. Three totally different people.

JAMES FRANKLIN: Miles Dieffenbach told me this story. He said, when he showed up at Penn State, he was fifth-team on the depth chart and didn't get a rep in practice. When our freshmen showed up, they were second-team and taking almost as many reps as him.

There's usually a rite of passage. You're sent to the scout team for a year and you earn your stripes, then come up. With our guys, we didn't really have the ability to do that.

So, yeah, the older guys and the younger guys got to form a bond and connect, but I think some of the old guys viewed it like Penn State's a blue-collar program, you've got to come in and earn your stripes. That's a measure of the dynamics we had going on at that time.

GENO LEWIS: The older guys had been in three different offenses, maybe more depending on the offensive coordinator. And as you get older, start understanding the mental part of the game, you're like, Okay, I see why this makes sense, but I don't know why we're doing that, because you can see on the tape that it doesn't work.

Some guys felt like, Yeah, this'll work and this won't. And then you had other guys feeling like, That'll work and this won't. That's kind of what happened.

At the end of the day, we had to do what the coaches were asking us to do. That's all we could control—making the plays when we were able to make them.

BRANDON BELL: No one ever complained and said, "Oh, woe is me, we don't have this, we don't have that." We went out there and fought every day.

KOA FARMER: You know, we were just trying to do as much as we could to bring the team together, get everyone to buy in, believe in what Coach Franklin was trying to do.

Ultimately, that was the hardest part: getting everyone on the same page.

GENO LEWIS: Mind you, you're talking about kids who are eighteen, nineteen, twenty years old. Kids who are trying to deal with their emotions. There's so much going on in your head, you're trying to figure it all out, and it's just not coming out the way you expected it to.

JAMES FRANKLIN: We see these guys—they're six-foot-five, three-hundred-fifteen pounds, and they've got beards—and we think they're men and they're not. They're still growing. They have problems, issues with their families, with their girlfriends, with school.

At this level, it's not just football you're teaching, it's total development.

KOA FARMER: It was a tough situation for some of the guys there, man. They'd seen I don't know how many head coaches in three years. It's hard to be a part of something like that. I get it.

MALIK GOLDEN: There was a lot going on internally. I don't think the players and coaches meshed that well those first couple of years. That's kind of reflected in us not winning those close games, because we did have a lot of talent.

It was unfortunate. Those two years were definitely the toughest, because I think James . . . a lot of people . . . were just overwhelmed.

GENO LEWIS: At the end of the day, we did the best we could with that situation. We didn't let it become a cancer to our team. Did we know it was there? Yeah, for sure. But we all knew we were trying to accomplish the same goal.

CHRISTIAN HACKENBERG: Yeah, there were some losses we shouldn't have had and, yeah, we all wish we could have played better in certain situations, but when you look at it from a big-picture standpoint, the challenges we were facing, no one should hang their head.

Not one guy. Not one coach.

THIRTY-ONE

PINSTRIPE BOWL

I<small>T WAS NOT</small> *a must-see bowl game. Not the Rose Bowl, "the granddaddy of them all," according to late, great play-by-play announcer Keith Jackson. Not the Sugar Bowl or the Fiesta Bowl, which each had delivered a national championship to Penn State. Not even the Outback Bowl, site of rousing New Year's Day victories against Auburn and Tennessee.*

The Pinstripe Bowl barely merited a nod from most college football fans. In its first five years, it had hosted just one ranked team and, as you might expect, number twenty-five Notre Dame dispatched Rutgers with relative ease 29–16. But none of that mattered to Penn State's faithful supporters— the players, coaches, and fans who cheerfully embraced the opportunity to participate in postseason play, even if it did require a second-half rally against Temple to secure the six wins needed to qualify for the honor.

As a reward for their effort, James Franklin's players were invited to rainy New York City to play 7–5 Boston College. They had started the season in a hurling stadium in Dublin and they would close it out in a baseball stadium in the Bronx. The tickets, ranging in price from $65 to $235, sold out in a record thirty-six hours, according to Mark Holtzman, executive director of the event. "And Yankee Stadium is not a small place," he said.

The late December kickoff gave the team's stars a few weeks to recuperate from the strains of a challenging season. For the coaches, it meant extra hours of practice, not only to prep for the game, but also to tutor the younger players on the finer points of blocking and tackling.

As the showdown approached, training shifted from the Lasch Building in State College to the football facilities at Fordham University in New York.

CHANCE SORRELL: Bowl game practices are really used for resting the older guys. They provide a lot of development time for the younger guys.

ANGELO MANGIRO: We got the younger guys work that they're not able to get over the course of the season, because you need the first-and second-string guys to get reps. We hadn't been able to do that for a couple of years.

JAMES FRANKLIN: The extra reps in practice are very, very important.

CHANCE SORRELL: I think those were the hardest practices we had that year. If you weren't a starter or a direct backup, you were in full gear, going one hundred percent, full tackle.

During the season, we're in full gear maybe once a week, but to be fair—and we always joked about this on the offensive line—when we're in uppers [as in, shoulder pads and helmets], it's essentially a full-go practice. The only thing you're not doing is cutting guys.

So, for us, those practices were not any easier. All the skill players got to run around in shorts and we were going full-gallop in the trenches.

I think you get fifteen practices spread out over a few weeks. It definitely helped the team.

JAMES FRANKLIN: We didn't spend the entire time working on BC. The first half of our bowl practices were devoted to program development. Think of it like spring ball. We'd have the players go against each other, work the third-string players in, guys who weren't getting reps in-season.

As we got closer to the game, we got into our normal game week routine.

CHANCE SORRELL: It was cool to be in New York City around Christmastime, to see the tree and all that crazy stuff, the Freedom Tower and other sites around the city.

SAM FICKEN: I got to ring the bell on the Stock Exchange. I'm a finance major, so that was awesome.

CHANCE SORRELL: And then, of course, walking around the stadium before the game. You're in the locker room, and, *Oh, there's Derek Jeter's locker.*

I mean, Yankee Stadium is such a historic place.

SAM FICKEN: We did our walkthrough the day before the game, and one of the equipment guys comes up to me and says, "Hey, you know whose locker that is?"

I'm like, "Yeah."

He's like, "Yes, *you* got Jeter's locker."

I'm like, "Whoa, that's pretty sweet."

GENO LEWIS: It was nice on the day of the game—we didn't even have to wear sleeves. It was late December and like fifty or fifty-five degrees.

SAM FICKEN: Leading up to the game, the weather was horrific. Every day we practiced, it felt like it had rained three inches. It was forty-five degrees. The practices sucked. But the night of the game it was like fifty-five degrees. I think I warmed up in a T-shirt.

It was unbelievable.

And New York City has so many Penn Staters, honest to God, it felt like a home game.

MIKE HULL: It definitely felt like a home game.

CHANCE SORRELL: It was cool to see how many fans turned up. I mean, we were 6–6 at that point and the fans just rallied around the team.

JACK DAVIS: I was literally sitting in the last row in Yankee Stadium. Just snuck in there. That was my last game as a student before becoming the Nittany Lion.

CHRISTIAN HACKENBERG: As an offense, we put up some good numbers that game, won against a top-five defense. It gave me a lot of confidence.

We showed the coaching staff we could do it consistently. And we won a game against a really good opponent. A bowl game. Big lights, big city.

In a way, it was the culmination of everything I went through.

JAMES FRANKLIN: The offense played well early and then late. Early on, we kept getting into what we call the strike zone, the first area where you can score, the high red zone area, and we'd have a penalty or a turnover that killed us.

The press had predicted a defensive showdown, citing the looming battle between BC's bruising rushing attack and Penn State's fierce front seven. In mid-September, the Eagles—led by dual-threat quarterback Tyler Murphy and freshman running back Jon Hillman—had torched ninth-ranked USC for 452 yards on the ground. Meanwhile, the Lion defense, anchored by fifth-year senior linebacker Mike Hull, had yielded just 84.8 rushing yards per game, the lowest in the nation.

JAMES FRANKLIN: The defense had been great at stopping the run all year long.

Boston College had a veteran O-line, a bunch of tight ends, big bodies. They did a great job shifting tight ends, going from heavy sets to regular sets, from regular sets to heavy sets. Not only were they trading the tight ends, but they were trading the offensive tackles from one side to the other. So early on, they had us thinking and not playing as fast as we normally played.

ANTHONY ZETTEL: We were really struggling to stop the run, which is unusual for our defense, and I give their O-line all the credit. They were really big guys who came out and hit you.

MIKE GROSS: It was a fierce battle in the trenches. Anthony Zettel had a tremendous game for Penn State at defensive end, but Boston College ran for a ton of yards—almost three hundred.

JAMES FRANKLIN: As the game went on, we said, Look, we don't need to make some of our more elaborate calls. Let's call base defense and allow our kids to play. I think that was helpful.

Midway through the first quarter, BC's talented freshman Jon Hillman slashed through Penn State's line for a spirited forty-four-yard run, but the Eagle drive ended with a fourth-down stop on the Penn State thirty-yard line. Three plays later, Christian Hackenberg lofted a beautiful pass into the outstretched arms of true freshman Chris Godwin, who high-stepped from the grasp of a would-be tackler and raced down the sideline for a 7–0 Nittany Lion lead.

MATT MILLEN: Hackenberg had time and he dropped it in perfectly.

He had one-on-one coverage on the outside. Saw it right from the start.

Godwin beat the tackle, and seventy-two yards later it's six points.

Soon thereafter, James Franklin tried to surprise the Eagles with an onside kick that was cleanly recovered by Nittany Lion safety Troy Apke, but the officials ruled he was out of bounds when he caught the ball. And so, the Eagles started the next drive on their own forty-eight-yard line and ended it two plays later with yet another long run by Hillman.

This time he reached the end zone.

In a span of four plays, both teams had scored touchdowns.

As the first quarter drew to a close, Hackenberg had Penn State on the move again, hitting Godwin with a short pass for a first down on the BC twenty-one. But when the players switched sides to begin the second quarter, they were missing veteran guard Miles Dieffenbach, who was carted off the field with a leg injury—just five games after returning from an ACL tear.

On the next snap, Hackenberg fumbled the football and the Eagles recovered it. With Dieffenbach on the sideline, the offense gained just sixteen yards in three drives.

JAMES FRANKLIN: That affected us emotionally, physically, strategically. It's the one position where we couldn't afford to lose a guy—on the offensive line. But Derek Dowrey came in and battled. Brian Gaia was struggling a bit early and he battled through it. I was proud of those guys.

At halftime, the Lions and the Eagles were still tied at seven. And when they emerged from the locker room, Penn State's players had not yet worked out the miscues.

Boston College scored on its first two drives of the second half to take a 21–7 lead.

Penn State put together a twelve-play drive, but it was halted by another sack and fumble.

JAMES FRANKLIN: We knew they were going to bring a lot of overload blitzes and we needed to be able to sort those things out. If we were able to do that, their DBs weren't used to covering for very long. They were used to getting to the quarterback and the quarterback getting the ball out of his hands. That's how their defense was devised. And as the game went on, we were able to slide and pick those guys up and give Christian time.

MIKE GROSS: The linemen pass blocked better than they had—well enough to give the quarterback some time. It gave Penn State fans a tantalizing notion of what Christian Hackenberg could do with a better offense around him.

JAMES FRANKLIN: More times than not, we were able to protect him. I'd been saying since day one, if we could give him time, give our receivers a little time to work their routes, we could be pretty good on offense.

CHRISTIAN HACKENBERG: After the season had ended, we had a few weeks to get ready for that game. So Coach Rahne, Coach Donovan, and I got together. We got to really talk. Without school. Just football.

I think the coaches listened to my pain points more. They heard me out.

They weren't going to give me the freedom Bill O'Brien had given me, but if you go back and watch that game, we did a ton of check-with-me's on the sidelines. That was their compromise. To say, Okay, we'll just run a lot of freeze cadence, just see what defense they're in, and then, based on what Ricky sees in the box, we'll get you something to run. Put us in good situations.

So even though we started off a little slow, we were more confident in that game. At least I was individually, but I think as a unit, we were, too.

That was cool. There's a little compromise and it starts working. You start producing.

AKEEL LYNCH: He commanded the huddle and showed his ability. There's a reason he was our captain and our starting quarterback.

DAESEAN HAMILTON: He was poised. When we got in the huddle, we knew what we had to do. He knew what we had to do. He had that killer instinct, basically put us on his shoulders and brought us back and we made plays for him.

ANGELO MANGIRO: We went up-tempo. That was part of our game plan. To get them in a personnel grouping we liked and up-tempo them and it worked. We were down 21–7, we had a miscue with the snap, and we came back and scored on nearly every single drive, I believe.

Late in the third quarter, Von Walker returned a BC punt twenty-six yards to get things rolling. On third-and-nine, Hackenberg found Geno Lewis for a thirty-two-yard strike. A facemask penalty against Boston College moved the ball to the Eagles' fifteen.

On third-and-two at the seven, Hackenberg looked Lewis's way once again, sending the ball toward the goal line.

A BC defender got a hand on the pass before it reached its target.

GENO LEWIS: I ran a slant, won the route, but the ball got tipped. Tipped towards the back of the end zone.

It took the right bounce.

I caught it.

Boom!

Touchdown!

Midway through the fourth quarter, Hackenberg hit Godwin, Lewis, and then DaeSean Hamilton for his third touchdown pass of the day.

CHRISTIAN HACKENBERG: They were running man coverage and I saw him separate a bit from the first defender. Knew there was going to be a tight window but if we could get it in there, DaeSean could make a play. He made a very strong play, catching the ball.

DAESEAN HAMILTON: It was a great throw. I don't know how you even squeeze it into that hole. But that's the type of quarterback he was.

AKEEL LYNCH: We knew that if we just continued to play our game—our receivers continued to make plays and our O-line continued to block—we were going to win the game.

Boston College kicked a field goal with two minutes and ten seconds left to retake the lead 24–21. Hackenberg returned to the field and completed six straight passes. One play later, he tucked the ball and ran for six yards. Akeel Lynch added one more.

And then Sam Ficken—playing in the final game of his Penn State career—strutted onto the field to attempt a game-tying field goal. With hard work and precision, he had turned himself into one of the program's most reliable kickers, piling up 267 collegiate points, including a school-record fifteen straight field goals without a miss between October 27, 2012, and September 14, 2013.

No boot would be more clutch than this one.

SAM FICKEN: There were twenty seconds left when I kicked it. It was fourth down, a forty-five-yarder, obviously a bit longer than most. It's fifty degrees, a little wind—you've got to hit it pretty good.

It's probably the best ball I hit in college.

When it cleared the crossbar, Penn State and Boston College were headed for overtime.

It took all of three plays for BC to reach the end zone. Tyler Murphy found a receiver from twenty-one yards out to give the Eagles their third lead of the night. But the celebration was short-lived as Mike Knoll missed the point-after attempt.

Boston College 30, Penn State 24.

KYLE CARTER: When he missed the extra point, we were like, Oh, man, all we've got to do is score a touchdown and we win this thing. We all knew Ficken was going to make the extra point.

By this point, Hackenberg had completed thirty-one passes for more than three hundred yards. What's a couple more?

Penn State opened with a false-start penalty, pushing the ball back five yards.

On first and fifteen, Hackenberg's pass to Geno Lewis fell incomplete.

GENO LEWIS: Hackenberg threw me a pass in the end zone and it was about to get picked. I ended up punching it out of the DB's hands, man. Saved it.

On second-and-fifteen, Hackenberg missed Lewis again.

On third-and-fifteen, he hit tight end Jesse James, who charged ahead for a first down.

Akeel Lynch took a handoff and lost two yards.

Geno Lynch made a catch at the ten.

GENO LEWIS: And then Kyle Carter ended up scoring the game-winning touchdown.

JAMES FRANKLIN: That was a huge catch.

CHRISTIAN HACKENBERG: That was something we had prepared for. Really hadn't practiced it a ton. But it was in the game plan. Kyle went out and executed it. He's a big, tall guy matched up against a smaller guy. He was able to go up and make the play.

KYLE CARTER: That's a play I'll never forget. Throughout the game, Franklin was calling these little flip screens. The inside receiver would just break out, cut block the outside corner, and Hack would throw the ball to that outside receiver. We ran that play maybe three or four times and set it up to run a fake off it.

Now I'm in OT. To the right side.

We do that flip screen.

I chopped down the guy, Geno caught the ball, and gained about five yards. On the next play, Coach called the same thing to the other side, but with one adjustment: We fake the block and go upfield for the deep ball. As I was jogging over to the line, I knew I was the one option on the play.

I had to sell the fake and, if I did, I'd have the opportunity to be the star of the show.

It was one of those things where you envision the play in your mind before it happens. It was third down, so it was a play that needed to happen, too. Boston College had already scored a touchdown and missed the extra point. All we had to do was score a touchdown, get the extra point, and we'd win.

I ran the route, faked that screen, and the defense bit on it. All it really takes is that DB getting just a half-step behind. Hack already had the ball in the air, nice and high, just how I needed it.

CHRISTIAN HACKENBERG: It was a strong play—with Kyle going through the defender, catching the ball, and maintaining possession throughout the catch.

Great protection, as well.

MATT MILLEN: Carter's in the slot, it looks like he's going to go for the pick, and instead he just runs upfield. The coverage is there. He goes and grabs the ball out of the air.

KYLE CARTER: After that, it was just ecstasy. Everybody jumping around.

At the end of the day, though, Ficken had to come in and finish the game.

We had scored and we were all excited, but now everybody had to calm down. No penalties. Let Fick finish this game off.

Everybody returned to focus.

Snap, hold, kick.

Ficken hits the ball and everybody goes wild.

SAM FICKEN: With so much rain earlier in the week, the field was pretty torn up. On both ends, the spot where they place the ball for the extra point was torn to hell. It was like a sandbox.

Obviously, you pay attention to things like that during the game.

I actually talked to the special teams coach. I said, "We need to either shift the line over or we need to move the tackle over, because I'm not planting in that yard-by-yard box where I'd normally kick. I'll get no traction."

272 | MEN IN WHITE

And, you know, Boston College got the ball first. They scored a touch-down and their kicker missed. I know exactly why he missed: Instead of planting on that firm surface, he planted on that sandbox.

Fortunately, we'd made the decision earlier in the day to go off the A gap to the left on extra points so I could plant on firm ground.

I feel bad for the BC kid, but ultimately it helped us win the game.

MATT MILLEN: The difference in the game is a plant foot from the kicker. Ficken's plant foot sticks and Knoll's slides and it's a one-point win for Penn State.

DAESEAN HAMILTON: When Kyle Carter made that catch, I knew Ficken was going to come in and put it right on the money.

AKEEL LYNCH: Ficken's been money. He defined Penn State through his whole career.

SAM FICKEN: It's a storybook ending. I couldn't have written a better way for it to go.

The team worked so hard, fought through so much. To say we made it to a bowl first off and we won the bowl, it's incredible.

AKEEL LYNCH: We were just tired of being so close. We said this time we have to win the game. Our defense has held us up all year and I think that mindset switched. We realized we've got to start scoring points and win this for our team.

MIKE HULL: It was just fitting that we won in Yankee Stadium in overtime after the roller-coaster ride of a career we had.

MIKE GROSS: A lot of kids made a lot of plays, and the memory I took from that is the Penn State players doing the Lambeau Leap onto the New York Yankees dugout.

GENO LEWIS: Man, that was unbelievable, because we were in New York again. Like, in Yankee Stadium, know what I mean?

In 2013, we opened with a win in MetLife and then we do it again in Yankee Stadium. And now we get bowl rings. It showed me why people go so hard to get to the national championship game. I was like, If this is the Pinstripe Bowl, I can just imagine what the national championship game is like. We were grateful just to have the opportunity to play in a bowl game again.

CHANCE SORRELL: Just having the ability to say, Yes, we had a winning season, and Hey, we're Pinstripe Bowl champions and getting a bowl ring that says champion on the side and not just participant was a big deal. It was like, Wow, there's the sport, there's the stadium, Oh look, there's my name literally engraved on this big, gaudy ring. Looking at the bowl ring I have now, I see that that one was actually pretty small.

KYLE CARTER: My first year at Penn State, we went to the TicketCity Bowl and lost to Houston. It was a bad game, but the experience of playing in a bowl game with your teammates is amazing. Sweet. You get to be out of town for a little while and experience something new. It was the first time since the scandal that we were allowed to play in a bowl game, so we made the most of it.

TIM SWEENEY: In 2012, '13, and '14, the majority of the guys on that team were still Joe Paterno–recruited kids. Not that OB did anything differently. Both recruited high-character guys. And, you know, if it sounds arrogant, I don't mean it to sound arrogant, but that's what the expectations are from the lettermen. We expect you to keep going, keep pushing. That's what Penn State football is about.

JOE JULIUS: In my mind, the guys they said were like . . . I guess, they weren't the highest-level recruits . . . they were all amazing. That team I was on that first year was awesome. Those guys were all studs. And you just can't match the character those guys had, because they all had the chance to leave, they all chose to stay, and they did a really good job of instilling that ethos in my class. A lot of that rubbed off on guys like Trace McSorley, who became such a leader on the team.

In a way, we reaped the benefits of how they handled things. I was fortunate. Like, when I got there, we went to Ireland and then to a bowl game. I didn't have any bowl game ban, because they had lifted it for us.

So the guys before us, the ones that knew they weren't going to go to a bowl game, they were the real heroes. I mean, a lot of guys look towards those bowl games, look towards that kind of stuff, because it's like what else do you play for, you know? You don't just play for a good record, you play to win some hardware at the end.

We saw the ripple effect of all the good things they did and all the things they did right.

It's like a one-in-a-billion chance that you have that many high-character individuals in one place. I mean, that's like the kind of stuff you see when the Constitution gets written, you know what I mean? It's like how do you get so many like-minded individuals to make a humongous decision that will impact the program for the next hundred years? It's amazing, the luckiest thing that could have happened under the circumstances.

THIRTY-TWO

SAY SAY

To a college football coach, recruiting is a high-stakes guessing game. For every amazing success story, you'll find an equally startling five-star bust. Between physical development, emotional intelligence, injuries, classwork, and the frightening assortment of temptations that awaits the typical student on a college campus, there are just too many variables to consider.

But in the class of 2015, James Franklin managed to sign a rare gem—an immensely gifted but equally humble running back with a punishing work ethic and a thousand-watt smile.

As a sophomore, the kid was not even the best running back in his Pennsylvania high school. Now, three years later, he was poised to become the best running back in the nation.

In just a few months, he would blossom into a household name throughout the state, literally leaping his way into the hearts of Penn State faithful with his incomparable acumen for shedding tacklers. Once the game was decided, he'd shed his helmet and circle the field for an hour, shaking hands with those in the stands and signing autographs for anyone who asked.

It's hard to imagine a greater find for a program as embattled as Penn State. Strong and fast, thoughtful and driven, polite to a T, he was the perfect face for the school in its hour of need.

Friends and family members called him Say Say. To everyone else, he was Saquon.

BRIAN GILBERT, HEAD COACH, WHITEHALL HIGH SCHOOL, 2010–17: I have a son two years younger than him, so I had a chance to watch him play all through the youth ranks. And, you know, he was just an average player early on, much like every other kid at the eighty-five-pound level. But one thing that stood out even back then was his infectious smile. How polite he was to the other kids and the adults. That personality we all know—he had that as a kid.

Believe it or not, we had a running back at Whitehall who was better than him but wasn't as disciplined.

BOB HARTMAN, ATHLETIC DIRECTOR, WHITEHALL-COPLAY SCHOOL DISTRICT: We were aware of Saquon through middle school and his freshman year of high school, but quite honestly, we had another really talented running back here at that time. He was in the same class as Say and he was the starter. That kid eventually left our school.

BRIAN GILBERT: There was a big leap in development in the summer between Saquon's freshman and sophomore years. I think it was because of this other running back and because Saquon did not have the confidence he needed. Going into sophomore year, he was actually thinking of not playing. I remember bringing him into the office and telling him he was so talented we saw a future in football if he wanted it. He just didn't have that confidence.

But he did agree to hit the weight room and join our workouts that off-season.

SAQUON BARKLEY: I was real small. Like five-seven, one-fifty-five, going into my sophomore year. Everyone started growing and I was staying the same size. Couldn't just rely on natural talent anymore.

BRIAN GILBERT: When he couldn't lift or do the things some of his peers could, he'd get frustrated. And his way of handling it was to maybe step away from it. As I explained to him, you need to have confidence in yourself, get in the weight room, work a little harder.

SAQUON BARKLEY: I had doubts. I wanted to give up on football. And my father gave me some advice: Once you quit on one thing, you're a quitter for the rest of your life. You'll quit on your family, your job, your career, whatever you decide to do. It made me stick with it. That's when my life really changed.

BRIAN GILBERT: You know, kids develop at different times. Some are early bloomers with full beards in eighth grade and some take a while. He was kind of a late bloomer. So he worked really hard in the weight room.

SAQUON BARKLEY: Every year, I got stronger. Faster in training. More flexibility. Just became a better athlete off the field and a better athlete on the field.

BRIAN GILBERT: At the start of his sophomore season, he was playing JV ball. We had a senior running back on varsity. And throughout the year, Saquon developed more and more.

In the playoffs, he got his chance, and that is where it all jump-started.

BOB HARTMAN: He could do things that other kids could not. As a seventh, eighth, ninth grader, you didn't see it as much, but as a sophomore, you realized this kid has abilities his peers do not. In our last playoff game that year at Delaware Valley High School, he had a touchdown run. It was a special play.

BRIAN GILBERT: The starting running back got hurt, so Saquon got his first touch—one of his first varsity runs—in a playoff game. He broke it for eighty yards right up the middle. Those of us on the coaching staff kind of looked at each other.

"Maybe he should be playing more."

BOB HARTMAN: He was a multi-sport athlete, so he didn't get to spend a ton of time in the weight room. But I remember our coaches saying things like, "Saquon came in the weight room before track and bench-pressed four hundred pounds or squatted four hundred pounds." Some crazy number. A lot of that stuff was natural for him. But he definitely worked hard as a high school athlete.

BRIAN GILBERT: Things he did are still being done today. We'd work out Monday, Tuesday, Thursday, Friday, and he'd get a group of guys in there on Saturday, Sunday, or Wednesday. There were times, weeks and months, when I was like, "Saquon, you need to give your body a break."

My wife laughs about it. We could be sitting down for Sunday dinner and I'd get a text.

She's like, "What, Saquon wants to get in the weight room?"

I'm like, "Yep."

It was contagious. For his teammates and players on future teams, it just became one of those things: "On Saturday afternoons, we meet at the turf to do footwork. On Sundays, we go out and drive the sled."

He was such a great role model that there are kids at Whitehall today who go out on Wednesday, Saturday, or Sunday—days the team's not officially working—and don't know why. They don't know how it started.

Eventually, someone will tell them that Saquon Barkley did that. For him, it just wasn't good enough to work out only on the days Coach said you needed to be there.

BOB HARTMAN: Again, he played multiple sports, so it wasn't like he had the opportunity to really buckle down in the weight room. That's not to say he didn't do anything extra, but he had to make those opportunities for himself. Go at odd times.

SOPAN SHAH, FOOTBALL RECRUITING ASSISTANT, RUTGERS UNIVERSITY, 2012–15: After his sophomore season, the summer before his junior year, Saquon came to a couple of our camps.

He's a Pennsylvania kid, but he's from the Lehigh Valley, so campus-wise, Rutgers is significantly closer to where he's from than Penn State.

Our running backs coach Norries Wilson had a very high opinion of him after seeing him work out, despite the fact that he wasn't even a full-time varsity player. He fit the archetype of the running backs we'd been successful with, going back to Ray Rice and a guy by the name of Jawan Jamison. Kind of a short, stocky, great balance, really-strong-lower-body type. He was really impressive during the summer camp, so we took a chance and offered him.

We had no idea he'd be *this* good.

BOB HARTMAN: He went to a camp at Rutgers and got offered a scholarship. And later that year, Coach O'Brien called. And so, we called OB from my office and Saquon got his offer from Penn State. Even then, Saquon said the right things. He's like, "Coach, you know I'm committed to Rutgers and I'm gonna honor that commitment."

OB was great about it. He knew, of course, that Rutgers was the first offer Say got. He was like, "Wow, you got an offer already. That's pretty good. Take advantage of it."

Then the floodgates opened.

SOPAN SHAH: He ended up committing during a preseason practice in August and he was just . . . so happy. I'd been around the program as a student and a graduate for a total of, I want to say, eight seasons and I can't think of a player who was more happy to receive an offer from Rutgers.

He was ecstatic—through the roof.

We were lucky, we got to him early, and we tried to keep that commitment quiet, but once his junior year started, he blew up. He was putting up ridiculous numbers every single Friday night. I'd check the box scores from Whitehall and it was just eye-popping numbers.

BRIAN GILBERT: He never thought he was going to get a Division I offer, no less one from Rutgers. So he was so excited. At that point, that was the one and only offer. He jumped on it. And then, he made the Nike Combine and the Nike Open in Oregon and offers started coming. Before you know it, he got invited to a Penn State game, a White Out. And, you know, I could tell when he came back . . . There's nothing like a White Out game.

BOB FLOUNDERS: O'Brien invited him up to the Michigan game in 2013. The one Penn State won in four overtimes. Michigan was undefeated at the time and Penn State was down the whole game. They tied it up literally on the last play of regulation. It was just an incredible atmosphere.

SAQUON BARKLEY: The vibe, energy, atmosphere were just amazing. It was the best game I'd ever seen.

JASON CABINDA: I went for that game, too. It was unreal. Like nothing I'd ever imagined. The excitement, the craziness of it all—it was like, "Whoa, this is where I need to be."

Future Penn State standouts Mike Gesicki, Marcus Allen, John Reid, and DeAndre Thompkins were also at that game as recruits.

SAQUON BARKLEY: I don't think you get any better than that. The tradition and the history, being there and seeing the game, that just sold me.

SOPAN SHAH: From a recruiting standpoint, that game was pivotal. It influenced a lot of kids over the next couple of years—kind of changed the perception of Penn State. Kids saw what could be and with high school recruits a lot of it has to do with the vibe they feel in an environment like that. It's hard to compete with that.

BOB HARTMAN: On Monday morning, Saquon was like, "I don't know what to do."

I said, "What are you talking about?"

"That was unbelievable. Penn State was unbelievable. I committed to Rutgers and I don't know what to do."

"Well, just so you know, it's not like that every week," I told him. "Keep your eyes open."

The Rutgers guys got wind of the visit. Midweek, head coach Kyle Flood drove in here to try to put out that fire. It was a practice day and he drove in just to keep Saquon committed.

Then Coach Franklin came along.

SOPAN SHAH: We were aware of the threat from Penn State. We had already seen it with Bill O'Brien. We lost a couple kids to him.

Saeed Blacknall, a great wide receiver, was a year ahead of Saquon Barkley. The gem of our class. He'd committed to us right before the 2013 season started, but that was not a good year for Rutgers. On the field and off the field. There were a lot of off-the-field things with our athletic director and we accepted a rash of decommitments. It was just left and right. Like, we had Cleveland Browns tight end David Njoku and Justin Herron, now an offensive lineman with the Patriots. Saeed was one of the major decommitments. We lost him to Penn State.

Once Franklin took over, though, everything got turned up a notch. Being an NFL guy, O'Brien knew the importance of recruiting, but nowhere near the level that Franklin did.

BRIAN GILBERT: Coach Franklin is a very innovative recruiter. When most coaches come in, they talk to the player's coaches, the athletic director, maybe the guidance counselor. James Franklin went to the cafeteria and asked the cafeteria ladies, "Do you know Saquon Barkley?"

"Oh, yes, he's the nicest kid. He picks up all his trash every time."

He walked down the hall and talked to the custodian, "Hey, there's a football player here, Saquon Barkley, do you know him?"

"Yeah, I know, Saquon. Great kid. He says hello to me every time he passes by."

He would go to those odd places, people you wouldn't expect a Division I football coach to go to, and ask them about Saquon. All of it was to check on his character.

JAMES FRANKLIN: His parents have done a great job. I love his family, his upbringing. And to be honest with you, they have never made football a thing that defines Saquon or their family.

SOPAN SHAH: Great kid, great family. He didn't come from much. His parents were great, but he definitely didn't come from a family of means. He was just very grateful to be there in that position.

I can't recall any other kid being as happy as he was after we told him he had an offer from Rutgers.

SAQUON BARKLEY: I was born in New York, born in the Bronx. Lived there till I was five years old. My mother and father thought it would be a better decision to move out of New York to a more suburban area. To Pennsylvania—where I grew up. That was the sacrifice my parents made.

Saquon's mother, Tonya Johnson, worked two jobs—in retail and a tax office—to help provide for the couple's five children. His father, Alibay, the nephew of three-time world boxing champ Iran Barkley, worked as a cook in a food service company.

Alibay had had a promising career as a fighter, too, but it got derailed by a bum shoulder. Outside the ring, he struggled, serving a year in prison at Rikers Island on a gun charge.

SAQUON BARKLEY: My dad at one point was a functioning drug addict. Making a lot of poor decisions. My mom gave him two choices: You're coming with me or you're not. So moving to Pennsylvania, getting away from that bad environment, helped save him.

The man was there for every step of Saquon's football career—walking his son to practice, cheering him on, talking him through the various hardships. The wisdom he imparted stayed with the child.

BOB HARTMAN: Coach Franklin was here like week four or five of Say's senior year. At that point, Say was really firmly committed to Penn State. And I said to Coach Franklin, You don't have to blow smoke up my ass anymore. Like, This kid's a lock—so how good is he?

We were on the sidelines for the Nazareth game. Coach Franklin was here with Sean Spencer, his defensive line coach.

And Coach Franklin said, "Well, his highlight tape for the first four weeks is as good as that of anybody in the country, and that's no lie."

And then, things really started ramping up. Ohio State, Notre Dame, Missouri offered. Say was torn. He was like, I really want to take those visits. My parents haven't been anywhere. I'd like to get them on a plane and see some of those places.

He was really just entertaining it for his parents. I was like, "Okay, do you want to risk Penn State being angry for some weekend vacations?"

I get it. It wasn't really about him. He was being generous.

Ultimately, he decided not to take any of those visits.

BRIAN GILBERT: Franklin's whole staff was exactly what Saquon was looking for. Down-to-earth, family-oriented. They just did a great job recruiting him.

SAQUON BARKLEY: Coach Franklin didn't talk about football at first. He talked about education. His thing was, "Dominate, educate, graduate." My parents just loved that.

BRIAN GILBERT: For Saquon, it was a no-brainer in the end. The problem was he had to call the Rutgers coach and decommit. And that was very hard for him. He's a pleaser. Hates letting people down.

In high school, he could have a tremendous game, but if we lost, he felt responsible. So the whole decommitment thing had him feeling bad for the Rutgers coaches and the Rutgers team, feeling like he was going against his word. It's not what he's about.

BOB HARTMAN: Yeah, that's a tough thing for a kid to do. Those guys were good people. He liked them. They gave him his first opportunity. And he appreciated all of that.

Saquon ultimately made the call and survived the ordeal. In August of 2015, he reported to Penn State's campus and, of course, got right to work. It didn't take long to make his presence known.

BRIAN GILBERT: If you watch his high school highlight tape, it's one of the most unbelievable films you'll ever see. The only thing that sort of took me by surprise, I guess, was how fast he got to that point in college, too.

It usually takes more time to develop.

THIRTY-THREE

BURY THE TAPE

EARLY SEPTEMBER IN *Happy Valley generally brings with it the prom-ise of a new season, a chance to demonstrate for the world the fruits of the players' stalwart training. In 2015, they had the added benefit of a full year of instruction under James Franklin's staff, ample time in which to master the intricacies of the coach's playbook.*

To address concerns with the offensive line, the team had enlisted two transfer students. One was a six-foot-seven, three-hundred-pound mountain of a man named Paris Palmer. He arrived on campus from Lackawanna Com-munity College soon after Donovan Smith, the Lions' stellar left tackle, had announced he was forgoing his final year of eligibility to turn pro, where he would eventually win a Super Bowl ring protecting Tom Brady for the Tampa Bay Buccaneers.

On paper, all of that sounded encouraging (especially after people got a look at Palmer's admirable talent and work ethic), but football has a funny way of grounding expectations. On September 5, the first Saturday of the school year, the Nittany Lions stepped onto the turf at Lincoln Financial Field in Philadelphia eager to face in-state rival Temple. In years past, the matchup tended to serve as a light early-season spar. This one was more like a gut punch.

Penn State jumped out to a quick 10–0 lead, then absorbed a series of unchecked blows that left the squad staggering. Hackenberg received the largest share of the abuse, spending much of the afternoon scrambling for his life. Temple tied the game midway through the third quarter and moved ahead by a touchdown after a wayward Hackenberg pass ended up in the hands of defensive lineman Sharif Finch, who returned it to the two-yard line.

In one jaw-dropping moment, the Owl defense stormed Penn State's line and toppled the shell-shocked quarterback with a meager two-man rush.

Temple added a twenty-four-yard touchdown run and a field goal in the fourth quarter to seal the victory.

It was Penn State's first loss to the Owls in seventy-four years.

GENO LEWIS: That one hurt.

Temple's supposed to be our little brother. We're not supposed to lose to them no matter what.

BRANDON BELL: It hurt to lose, because, you know, the pride of PA, bragging rights and things of that nature.

Everyone comes for Penn State, that's how it is. I mean, we were down numbers and everybody was gunning for Penn State.

DAESEAN HAMILTON: We went into the season with big expectations and, by the time the game was over, we knew we had a long way to go.

We were a lot better than we were the year before, but there was still a lot of work to do.

BOB FLOUNDERS: Temple had a really good team, but no one knew that. Penn State was a huge favorite and just got dusted 27–10.

RYAN JONES: The players got manhandled. It really drove things home.

Like, *Wow, we've got no depth on the offensive line and don't have much depth anywhere else. How long is it going to take to work through all this?*

BOB FLOUNDERS: Christian Hackenberg took a beating.

GENO LEWIS: Hack got sacked ten times. Something crazy like that. He just kept getting hit, man, and that takes a toll on you.

DAVID JONES: Temple had free rushers coming in all over the place.

CHRISTIAN HACKENBERG: We had some young guys in there and they had a hard time figuring things out.

Paris Palmer, the player tasked with protecting Hackenberg's blind side, was a prime example. Despite efforts to prepare for the role, he simply wasn't ready to step in for Donovan Smith.

HERB HAND: He had the length, he had the size, he was athletic, he could run—he did all the things you want. But he was still learning to play at this level, still learning the offense.

JAMES FRANKLIN: It was obvious to me that he was going to come in here and work. He knew he had a great opportunity—that's one of the reasons he came here—but a lot of guys have great opportunities and they can't figure it out. He figured out how to work, how to eat, how to train, how to prepare, but obviously it was all going to come down to Saturday and how he played.

DUSTIN HOCKENSMITH, SPORTS REPORTER, *PENNLIVE*: Any experience was welcome experience for that offensive line. If Paris Palmer managed to stick at left tackle, play good quality football there, it let Andrew Nelson stay on the right side, gave you options on the inside. Ultimately, the effectiveness of the unit would come down to this: Can Paris Palmer stick at left tackle?

Let's just say, the early results from Palmer and his linemates were dismaying. And the video evidence was replayed time and again on sports highlight shows.

CHANCE SORRELL: That was a very rough game—it accentuated the need for us to work together and understand that, hey, at the end of the day, we have to have each other's backs.

It's not a glorious position. The only time your name gets called is when you give up a sack or you get a penalty. So, you never want to hear your name as an offensive lineman.

The ongoing struggles raised larger concerns about the direction of the program and its marquee player.

NEIL RUDEL, MANAGING EDITOR, *ALTOONA MIRROR*: You had to question the coaching staff's performance—with a quarterback everybody's thinking has a chance to go high in the draft. It just didn't appear that the linemen were comfortable with the schemes.

MARK BRENNAN: It's like the staff had no Plan B, coming out of an off-season when you knew everybody was going to try to test the O-line, knew everybody was going to try to test Paris Palmer. You can't let one guy get exploited over and over and over again and not have a different plan to go to—if nothing more than to save your quarterback and his confidence.

TYLER MATAKEVICH, TEMPLE LINEBACKER: We started to disguise our blitzes. We could tell Hackenberg was really uncomfortable. He started making checks right away. Once we figured that out, we kept disguising. Their line couldn't pick it up.

CHARLIE FISHER: When you get hit, it's going to take a toll on you, no question about it. When you want to affect the quarterback—his eye level, his confidence, everything about him—you hit him and keep hitting him. It takes its toll.

That was the intent of the NCAA sanctions—to basically put the program in a slow, steady decline, right? That's what Mark Emmert wanted to do. So, taking the scholarships away took away talent—guys who could protect Christian. And I don't believe there's any doubt that it affected Christian, not only for those two years, but maybe for his pro career, too.

PAT ZERBE: He was like the most sacked quarterback in college football.

I don't care who you are, that's gonna mess you up. Your internal clock's gonna be off. You're not going to want to step into your throws, because you don't want your front leg taken out.

I'd almost compare it to what happened to Carson Wentz in Philly. He was having an MVP year for the Eagles when he got injured in 2017. After that, you'd see glimpses of his former self for like a quarter, thinking, *Holy cow, this guy is unbelievable.* Then he'd make some bad throws and you're like, *What's going on? Where is the guy we had as quarterback?*

That's what happened to Hackenberg. When you get hit that many times, it stays in the back of your head. We just didn't have the depth on the offensive line for him.

MICHAEL NASH: A friend of mine, a star in high school, played briefly for Florida State. And one of the things Bobby Bowden would get condemned for, but one of the reasons he also had such tough quarterbacks, is he'd never put a red jersey on a quarterback. They were open game in practice. And my buddy, who had people talking about him becoming the starter as, like, a sophomore, got hit so hard he started crying, went back to the sidelines, and could never stand in the pocket again. It ruined him. He was not on the team seven months later.

Hackenberg? I mean, he took that week after week after week.

MARK BRENNAN: Penn State had a junior college transfer named Paris Palmer playing left tackle and they gave that guy no help throughout the game. They didn't adjust. Didn't do anything.

Hackenberg just got beaten down. And to this day, I have no idea what John Donovan, the offensive coordinator, was thinking. You're looking at this guy as your franchise quarterback and he's just getting the living *you know what* beaten out of him.

It was tough to watch.

AUDREY SNYDER: It was like, Oh, this is bad. At some point, you've got to pull this kid or he's going to get hurt.

They never did.

BOB FLOUNDERS: Former players were lighting up social media about the performance.

Bill Belton, one year removed from the program, posted a photo of Kanye West, looking clearly exasperated, with a hand on his head. Lineman Adam

Gress tweeted "offensive coordinator sucks." Donovan Smith declared that this was "exactly" why he had left.

"Can't just dominate the state in recruiting," added Stephon Morris. "How about dominating the state on the field as well?"

Hackenberg's younger brother Brandon, who would join Penn State's soccer team a year later and help lead the squad to a Big Ten Championship in 2021, tweeted: "You have a Ferrari, yet drive 30 miles under the speed limit."

JAMES FRANKLIN: Our best five were playing. The guys backing them up were redshirt freshmen.

CHANCE SORRELL: We understood the frustration there—it may have been voiced a bit, but rightfully so. If I was quarterback and I was getting hit—not just hit but sacked ten times in a game—that needs to be addressed. We had some conversations on the sideline during that game, a mutual understanding that we had to work harder and get better.

JAMES FRANKLIN: We came in at halftime and discussed what we needed to do, but it came down to protection and running the ball. We were not able to do that.

Akeel Lynch, who had replaced Belton at tailback, ran untouched for forty-two yards to secure Penn State's lone touchdown. He logged just thirty-six yards in his other nine carries.

That was not enough to draw attention away from Hackenberg—or, truth be told, the supremely skilled freshman running back waiting in the wings.

MARK BRENNAN: You have Saquon Barkley and you're letting Christian Hackenberg get sacked ten times. *Oh, my goodness.*

And the thing was everybody knew how good Barkley was, because we were at a couple of open practices and he popped a couple of long runs. It was like, *Oh, my god, this guy's unbelievable.* And then . . . was it Akeel Lynch who started? I forget. Yeah, that didn't last long.

BOB FLOUNDERS: Barkley had one carry. They gave the rest to Lynch, based on what he had done the year before. But Barkley's talent was so noticeable in practice that they were like, "Hey, look, we got to find out what we got with this guy." So, yeah, Barkley carried one time for one yard in that game. The next week, he went off.

AUDREY SNYDER: People ask why didn't Saquon Barkley play more? And that's a fascinating question, because they knew he was good. But nobody knew he was *that* good.

SAQUON BARKLEY: It was my first game. When I did get on the field, I was nervous—nervous as heck. Like literally mind-blown. Wow, it's here. I'm actually playing college football.

Temple did a great job. The blitzes they were bringing, we just weren't used to. I remember standing on the sideline, feeling there wasn't much I could do.

DAESEAN HAMILTON: We needed more leadership on the offensive side of the ball, especially when things were going sour in the midst of the game. You want someone to step up and not just talk about it, but actually go out there and make the play for us.

Unfortunately, we didn't have anyone who was able to do that.

In years past, the team could count on the defense to keep opponents in check while the offense worked through its manpower issues, but Bob Shoop's squad was beginning to feel the pinch of the scholarship reductions, too. When Mike Hull moved on to play for the Miami Dolphins, Pry tapped junior Nyeem Wartman-White to replace him at middle linebacker, positioning Jason Cabinda and Brandon Bell on either side of him.

Like Hull, Wartman-White had a nose for making tackles (eleven in the Pinstripe Bowl alone). He had spent the off-season working on the transition from outside linebacker to middle linebacker, studying film to perfect the new tackling angles and learning to project his voice when calling plays for the defense. Along the way, he had also revised his name, shifting from Wartman to Wartman-White to honor the single mother who had raised him. "I want her to feel appreciated every time the announcers say my name," he explained.

BRENT PRY, LINEBACKERS COACH: He was excited about the position change. He saw it as a great challenge, filling in for Mike Hull, taking that spot by the reins. He really worked at it.

BOB SHOOP, DEFENSIVE COORDINATOR: If Mike Hull was an A-plus student as far as football IQ, Nyeem was right there with him. He really relished it. Wanted to be the leader of the defense.

BRENT PRY: He had a great fall camp, physically. Mentally, he learned the position.

And then, after making two tackles in the Temple game, in front of a hometown Philly crowd, with friends and family members lining the stands, Wartman-White's breakout season came to an abrupt halt, leaving the defense without its new leader.

Before long, Bell was sidelined, too, with a high ankle strain.

NYEEM WARTMAN-WHITE: I was on the punt team and this dude was holding me. I had to get him off. I'm trying to swing him left and right and I heard a pop and went straight to the ground.

On the sideline, they told me, you tore your ACL.

JACK HAM, LINEBACKER, 1968–70, SPORTS ANALYST, PENN STATE RADIO NETWORK: The injury was huge, especially the timing.

MIKE IRWIN, DEFENSIVE BACK, RUNNING BACK, TEAM CAPTAIN, 1966: He was the quarterback of that defense—the one everyone was looking to for leadership and play calling.

Now they have to burn a couple of redshirts for true freshmen Jake Cooper and Manny Bowen.

BOB SHOOP: Manny Bowen and Jake Cooper were playing on the scout team on Thursday and, because of a series of unfortunate things in the second quarter, both found themselves in the game during the second half, maybe not fully comprehending the game plan.

JAMES FRANKLIN: We had communication issues. I looked out on the field at one point, and we had Troy Reeder, a redshirt freshman, Cooper, a true freshman, and Bowen, a true freshman, at linebacker.

Manny and Cooper didn't take any reps the week before. They were on the scout team.

We weren't expecting to play them.

TERRY SMITH, ASSOCIATE HEAD COACH, DEFENSIVE RECRUITING COORDINATOR: When you play in big stadiums, you can't verbally communicate. You have to use signals. That's where we had a couple breakdowns.

MARK BRENNAN: Now you have some tough decisions to make at that position.

JACK HAM: The coaches were scrambling around, trying to find any combination that worked.

NYEEM WARTMAN-WHITE: I was so excited for the game and I got off to a quick start in the first quarter. I think I had like three tackles. I go to the sideline and I'm talking to people, joking around. I'm like, "Yo, I like Mike linebacker, because you get a lot of tackles."

A series later, I got hurt. When I got to the locker room, I laughed, because I'm back in Philly, so excited for this game and I literally just said on the sideline, "Yo, I'm going to have a big year."

It was a painful laugh, but still funny, because what are the chances of all that happening?

JAMES FRANKLIN: The momentum started to swing.

DAVID JONES: Temple put together a thirteen-play, ninety-three-yard drive, going the length of the field to score.

JASON CABINDA: We lost a critical piece to our unit and now everyone has to step up, everyone's got to play better.

JAMES FRANKLIN: It was hard to come out after that game and talk about positive things.

AUDREY SNYDER: That was a low point. It was like, Yeah, this is what the sanctions look like.

One of the players later told the press: "It was so bad, we actually buried the game tape."

And we were like, Oh, ha, ha.

The kid said, "No, no, we really buried it!"

CHRISTIAN HACKENBERG: We just grabbed a shovel and went out there. Buried the tape right on the edge of the practice field. Dug a ditch, tossed the tape in, covered it up, and kept moving.

It was like, "All right, we're not gonna talk about this one."

DAESEAN HAMILTON: It was a DVD-ROM-type thing in a little case and the guys made a hole and buried it. A few guys stepped on it.

JORDAN LUCAS: There were too many players for everybody to get a piece of the dirt, but guys like Brian Gaia and Saeed Blacknall stomped on it a couple times. We tried to make it fun, create positive energy around it.

BRANDON BELL: Temple was a good team, so we can't belittle that, but, yeah, that wasn't us. We were fighting to get over that hump, be more than an average team, and we were confident in our ability to do that. But that tape didn't show that. We just wanted to get past it, move on.

JORDAN LUCAS: Let the guys know we're not going to dwell on the past. We lost the game, it's our fault, but we're going to bury this. It's not the end of our season.

CHRISTIAN HACKENBERG: We had so many expectations coming off that Boston College win in 2014. We were very motivated and knew that that Temple team was good. Head coach Matt Rhule had them rolling in the right direction. But we felt we had the pieces to turn the page, make a run, with the way the schedule was set up.

And when you have a loss like that on week one, it's hard. We could have talked about it till we were blue in the face, but I was like, "Dude, let's go bury this thing and keep moving."

CHANCE SORRELL: The last thing you want to do is be depressed for the entire week and lose another game. You learn from the bumps and bruises and just try to get better.

THIRTY-FOUR

SIGNS OF HOPE

THICK GRAY STORM clouds pooled above the campus, pelting the players with rain as they exited the blue team buses and filed through the gate to the locker room. The dousing continued as they took the field for warmups. And later when they donned their helmets, exited the tunnel, and sprinted for the bench. But the student section was out in force, armed with face paint, pom-poms, and cheap plastic slickers, as young Nick Scott waited to receive the opening kickoff.

Despite the ugly weather, moments of magic surfaced in the September 12 home opener against Buffalo, flashes of what could be. "We started to create an identity for this football team," said James Franklin.

Scott, a redshirt freshman running back, cradled that first kick in his arms and raced through the chaos to the Buffalo forty-two-yard line. Redshirt freshman DeAndre Thompkins returned a second-quarter punt fifty-eight yards to set up the team's first score—a well-executed sweep by speedy true freshman receiver Brandon Polk.

The defensive line—anchored by Carl Nassib, Anthony Zettel, Austin Johnson, and Garrett Sickels—gave the Bulls' offense fits, disrupting play after play. Nassib alone logged three sacks, an interception, and two forced fumbles.

Better yet, Penn State's refreshed offensive line kept the Bulls' pass rush away from Christian Hackenberg, despite losing left tackle Andrew Nelson to *a knee injury late in the first half. Paris Palmer—one week wiser—replaced him without a misstep.*

For all the signs of improvement, though, the one that beamed brightest, slicing through the grim ozone like a brilliant bolt of lightning, was the emergence of Saquon Barkley, who opened the fourth quarter with back-to-back bursts for fifty yards. He punctuated the first with a nifty spin move. On the next, he hurdled a Buffalo defender in mid-stride and rumbled for ten more yards. He capped the Penn State scoring with a bruising, nine-yard touchdown run.

In all, sixteen freshmen contributed to the 27–14 victory. Barkley, the backup to junior running back Akeel Lynch, was the one who left everyone buzzing.

BRANDON BELL: It was Akeel Lynch's time to be the starter, but as Saquon flourished, got more comfortable, you couldn't ignore it.

AKEEL LYNCH: When he jumped over the dude from Buffalo, I was like, Yeah, my time is done.

BOB FLOUNDERS: It was only a matter of time before he took the starting job away.

JAMES FRANKLIN: He was making people miss, but also breaking tackles, and you don't get that combination in a freshman. It's usually one or the other.

When you have a guy making plays like that, guys block better.

ANDREW NELSON: As an offensive lineman, it gives you that little extra fire on game day, thinking, If I hold my block for one more second, who knows what Saquon can do?

ZACH LADONIS: Freshmen come in and, you know, a lot of them are cocky.

I was not the most athletic person—I was a long snapper for a reason, let's put it that way—but I'd consistently beat the freshmen in drills, no matter how talented they were, because they hadn't been through college football training.

It's different than it is in high school. Different speed, different pace, you need time to get used to it.

So we were running this one drill in our indoor facility. And one of our strength coaches mispronounced Saquon's name. Saquon finishes the drill, looks at the coach, and goes, "It's Saquon—you're going to know my name by the end of the year."

We were like, "Shut up, freshman. We've heard this before."

Months later, he wins Big Ten Network Freshman of the Year.

CHRIS GODWIN: I kind of knew, just by looking at him, that he was going to be special. He was about two hundred twenty pounds, five-foot-ten, a well-built kid. And then, in the first workout, I saw him start running—a 4.4 forty-yard dash. Then you throw him the ball and he can catch.

CHRISTIAN HACKENBERG: I remember throwing him a toss in practice once. I just wanted to watch him. So I threw the toss and carried out a half-assed fake. He made a jump cut, outran the second level and all of our DBs for like an eighty-yard touchdown.

I looked at Coach Haslett, who was serving as our coaching advisor that 2015 season, right after he made the first cut. It was just a cut, acceleration, and up to full speed within two steps. Haslett just got big-eyed. He looked at me, like, Whoa.

I was like, *Yep.*

TRACE MCSORLEY: It was hard not to just sit back and watch him do incredible things. You know, Coach Moorhead and Coach Franklin, they always talked about how important it is for the quarterback to hand off and carry out a fake. And I would always get negative plays, because I wouldn't carry out my fake. I'd hand the ball off and just watch Saquon work.

BRIAN GILBERT: His balance and his lower body leg strength are exceptional. You gotta wrap him up to get him down. You can't just give him a shot, because he'll bounce off you and keep his balance. What we're seeing in the NFL now is teams trying to bottle him up. They know that if he gets in open space, he can do some amazing things.

MALIK GOLDEN: I had to tackle him twice. It was during practice. I got help on one of them. The other . . . I'll just say that I'm pretty fast and I took a good angle and he left my ass hanging. Like, when I say I thought I had him . . . if it was any other person, I would have tagged him, but he is . . . Saquon is, woo . . . yeah. I'm always amazed when people tackle him alone.

JAMES FRANKLIN: If you were building a Frankenstein running back, you'd find guys that are really fast, really strong, or really explosive, but they'd have deficiencies. I know it sounds crazy, but Saquon really doesn't.

BOB FLOUNDERS: There was another four-star recruit in that 2015 class, a running back from Bishop McDevitt High School in Harrisburg. His name was Andre Robinson, and Andre had an unbelievable career at Bishop McDevitt.

No one knew which of those two guys was going to get Penn State's attention first, because Saquon did not enroll at the university early that year. He had to hit the ground running in August.

A lot of people thought Robinson might be as good as Barkley, but that notion was quickly dispelled.

GREGG GARRITY: Robinson was a higher-recruited running back, but Saquon was hungry. He wanted to learn. He was like a sponge, asking all the older guys what to do. He'd always be in the weight room, getting extra reps. It took countless hours of extra work, practice, and film study to get to where he is now.

CHARLES HUFF: If Akeel was doing something, Saquon was watching him. If redshirt freshman Mark Allen was doing something, he was watching him. He was asking questions. He did a very good job picking up the system. He was always checking in with people.

"Hey, this is what I'm supposed to be doing, right?"

ANDRE ROBINSON: He's the best football player I've ever seen.

JACK DAVIS: I remember going to a practice and seeing Saquon in shorts, the size of his legs, as he sprinted by, faster than the receivers. It helped me appreciate what an outlier he was. That whole season, you'd see guys who thought they had an angle on him and he'd just blow by them.

BRANDON BELL: We all were amazed by what he did in games, but we weren't too surprised, because we'd seen some crazy things at practice.

AUDREY SNYDER: I remember talking to twenty-six people for a big story on Saquon, who wore number twenty-six. They told me that heading into his freshman year, he was making guys in camp look silly. Everybody was like, Whoa, who's this freshman hanging out with the older guys in the weight room? He's so strong.

VON WALKER: He was squatting and bench-pressing, jumping and leaping, and you're like, Wow, what's going on here? Then he starts doing these things on the football field.

Talk about a guy that worked for it.

He doesn't just go to practice and back to his room. The guy works hard. Freakishly hard.

TRACE MCSORLEY: He does things that make you just sit back and go whoa. But with the work ethic that he brings every day to practice, you see where it all comes from. All the success he has on Saturdays, those high-flying plays, you see where it all comes from.

SAQUON BARKLEY: Coming into my freshman year, I looked at the running back board in the weight room and said, Before I leave this place, I want to be tops in every single category at running back. I was able to do that in a couple of months.

KOA FARMER: He's so freaking competitive, man. It's ridiculous. I'm like, Dude, we can just play, we don't have to freaking compete. But he's always competing. That's why he's so successful. He competes in everything he does.

CHRIS GODWIN: Even when he does something right, he's always looking to get better.

ANDRE ROBINSON: He's just a freak. We came in as freshmen and looked pretty much the same. The next winter, he was going thirty, forty, fifty pounds over me in everything.

CHRISTIAN HACKENBERG: Most kids never came over to me after practice. I had to go grab them.

For a year and a half with Gesicki, I had to be like, "Hey, man, you're my roommate" and pull him out to throw.

Saquon? After the first seven-on-seven during summer workouts, he's like, "Hey, I don't think I really have a feel for this route. Can you tell me about it? And I really want to get honed in on my protections. Can we go watch film?"

He was just *sooo* advanced, compared to most kids that age—in his approach and how he carried himself. That's what impressed me the most: his attention to detail.

JAMES FRANKLIN: He was constantly harassing Hack about watching film, throwing the football with him, those types of things. Not only did he want to play, but he was going to make it happen.

AUDREY SNYDER: He had what I always think of as his breakout game against Ohio State. You had Ezekiel Elliott on the other sideline, and you're like, Whoa, this freshman, I think he just one-upped Zeke.

KIRK HERBSTREIT, ESPN ANALYST AND COLOR COMMENTATOR: He went for two hundred yards. I walked out of the stadium thinking this guy—twenty-six—this freshman, he's pretty special.

KOA FARMER: I've never seen someone so explosive, so strong. We call him Hercules, because he's just a beast.

TRACE MCSORLEY: He made everyone around him better. With the way he carried himself, how competitive he was, everyone could see the standard he held himself to.

If he didn't stay and do extra sprints or stay and run routes with the quarterbacks, no one would have said anything. Because, quite honestly, he didn't need to. But because he did those things, because he made sure to bring the running backs with him, the linebackers saw that and Jason Cabinda would do extra work and get all the linebackers to join him. And then, it kind of trickled down. DaeSean Hamilton would do the same with the receivers. I'd do the same thing with the quarterbacks. We all started doing extra work in groups. And then, we all started doing extra work together. And now we're getting together and throwing routes, working on one-on-one goes against the defense or seven-on-seven drills. All on our own time.

Having a guy like that on our team pushed everyone to be better.

ZACH LADONIS: I remember one drill—I think you'll find the video online—but it's basically Saquon and three down linemen against three defensive linemen and a linebacker. He takes the ball, runs a bit to the left. The two linemen in front of him get beat off the ball and he just does what Saquon does. Gets himself in a little ball in the corner, does a spin move, jukes another guy out, and scores.

We were like, What just happened? From that moment on, it was like, all right, we have something really special here. We need to get him the ball, like every play.

GREGG GARRITY: I mean, you can see the clips. Ones-versus-ones, the best on the best. And he put the two linemen and the safety in a blender. He was just . . . I mean, you saw it from afar, even if you weren't on the offensive side of things. Every single day, he'd do something that opened your eyes. From day one, even when he was on the scout team, you'd hand him the ball going against the first defense and he'd split the two tacklers and take it for fifty yards.

The coaches kind of looked at each other and said, "Hey, we might have something here."

JAMES FRANKLIN: Before he got to Penn State, he used to hurdle people all the time in high school and then he said, "I'm not going to do that in college."

I said, "That doesn't make sense, because in high school it's illegal to hurdle people. In college, it's legal."

I'm glad he brought that back.

SAQUON BARKLEY: It kind of started my junior year in high school. I remember one play against a team called Central Catholic. I was watching a cornerback who was pretty good, seeing how he attacked running backs one-on-one. He kept going low.

I said, I'm going to go over top of him. The opportunity presented itself, and I was able to do that.

I started doing it in college, and people loved it. I didn't do it to entertain them. Just to make a play, try to make a guy miss and get in the end zone.

In the years that followed, Barkley would dazzle TV commentators time and again with his bold leaps against defenders from Illinois, Iowa (twice), Maryland, Michigan State, Ohio State, and Rutgers. And yet, as his legend soared, the kid somehow managed to remain grounded.

JAMES FRANKLIN: Since that hurdle in the Buffalo game, there's been a buzz about him. He's handled it well. Better than I would have at that age.

VON WALKER: It's funny to think about that. It's like, Oh, okay, you've got a kid who just literally got recruited, right? He comes onto campus, hurdles one guy in a game, and everyone's like, *What the hell? Who's this guy?* And then, in a couple months, a kid who's eighteen or nineteen years old has a team relying on him for wins, a community relying on him for massive plays.

I can't imagine what that pressure must have felt like.

RICK MCSORLEY, FATHER OF TRACE MCSORLEY: For all the otherworldly talents he has, he couldn't be a nicer kid.

JAMES FRANKLIN: It's amazing all the requests I was getting after the Buffalo game from people who wanted to come to games, excited about him. He was telling me about the people texting him, calling him, sending him messages. His response was, "It's only one game, it's only one game."

MATTY FRESH, PENN STATE STUDENT: He's humble, that will always be the narrative. If you're his teammate, you're thinking this guy's the whole package. Not only is he an all-world athlete, but the way he carries himself . . . I mean, how many all-world athletes over the years were Me guys? We still celebrate them. But to be the whole package? Yeah, if I was in that locker room, I'd aspire to be very similar to him.

JAMES FRANKLIN: I don't want this to come off the wrong way, but he's almost naive to how people see and react to him. It's like he's unaware of it. Even when we'd do our annual poster give-out downtown and he was getting assaulted on the street, it didn't faze him. He had great interactions with every person he came in contact with and then got on the bus and the players gave him a hard time. He just stays true to who he is.

Akeel Lynch accepted Barkley's rise to fame with grace, too. He wasn't replaced overnight. He remained the starter for a few more games, then took the field when called on to give Barkley a break or provide third-down pass protection.

To his credit, Lynch didn't gripe or resist, offering veteran leadership each step of the way. He knew all too well that he had been eclipsed by a rare talent—a once-in-a-generation player.

THIRTY-FIVE

1–0, 1–0, 1–0!!!

COACHES LOVE CATCHPHRASES. *For Notre Dame's Lou Holtz, it was Play Like a Champion Today. For Clemson's Dabo Swinney: All In. When you're trying to lead a team of headstrong young men through the odyssey of a college football season, it helps to have a rallying cry, a go-to sentiment to keep everyone focused on the business at hand. For the social-media-savvy James Franklin, it was 1–0!*

At the start of each week, he posted a tweet that read 1–0! 1–0! 1–0! No matter how the previous game had ended, the team would open with a clean slate and the ambition to go 1–0. It kept the players focused, prevented them from looking ahead to Ohio State when they should be preparing for Illinois. But it also rescued them from dwelling too long on the losses.

With a fresh start each week, the trek was more manageable—a series of bite-sized tasks, sort of like Bill O'Brien's Do Your Job and Joe Paterno's Take Care of the Small Things.

In 2015, a season of incremental change, it was just the sort of outlook the players needed, especially as the team worked to replace veteran stars like Mike Hull and Allen Robinson. There were signs of hope beyond the rising star at running back; you just had to look closely to spot them.

JORDAN LUCAS: We treated each week like we were 0–0 at the start. Saturday determined if we went 1–0 or 0–1. We liked to take that approach.

DAESEAN HAMILTON: Coach Franklin and the staff, they'd always tell us to take one game at a time. Win this week, win this day, win this practice—every rep.

Don't look forward, don't look behind. Treat it like any other game.

JAMES FRANKLIN: We tried our best to be 1–0 come Saturday.

Our guys didn't just say it, they believed in it. They knew if we spent time on preparation, that led to confidence, and confidence led to us being able to go out and execute at a higher level than our opponent. That's all it's about: preparation leading to confidence and confidence leading to execution. The team that executes more on Saturday wins. It's that simple.

CHRISTIAN HACKENBERG: One week at a time, that was our mentality: Build off everything we'd been doing in the prior five or six weeks—improve on our weaknesses, build on our strengths, take it to the next week.

HERB HAND: Some people think you can just roll your helmets out on the field and win. It doesn't work that way.

Winning is difficult.

I don't care if you are on the road or at home, playing an in-conference game or out-of-conference game. It is a week-to-week deal.

On paper, it may look like one team is better than the other. But you still have to go out each week and do the work, execute when the lights are on and the stadium is full.

JAMES FRANKLIN: If you focus all your energy on the task at hand, you're going to be successful more often than not. A lot of the other things are outside your control. Why waste energy on things that don't help? The world is complex enough.

We want to make things as clean and efficient as can be and this is a very useful tool in doing that.

The life of a player is rooted in routine. Wake before dawn, eat breakfast, work out, go to class, eat lunch, practice, eat dinner, go to study hall, and it's lights out. There's little time to think of much beyond homework and Xs and

Os, and that's the point. After the game on Saturday, you're free to enjoy a few hours of student life, then it's back to the grind.

JAMES FRANKLIN: We're pretty focused and strict on our routine. I believe routine is very important for any team or organization. Guys know what to expect.

You don't talk about one game being a big game and not emphasize another game the same way, because guys pick up on that. I want the message to be consistent.

CHARLES HUFF: Consistency doesn't come on game day. Consistency comes with how you work in the off-season, how you work on your own, how much film you watch. Are you taking care of your body? Lifting weights? Doing all those things to put yourself in the best situation?

As great as your last game was, you've got to be consistent and do it all over again.

DAESEAN HAMILTON: Once you get eleven guys out there doing their jobs, everything falls into place. You start playing better football.

BRANDON BELL: We put in the work, confident that we could beat the best teams in the Big Ten and be a contender nationwide. We were just falling short. So, it was tough. But we all continued to work, continued to fight, and never lost hope in getting over that hump, breaking through to nine-, ten-, eleven-win seasons.

As the 2015 campaign unfolded, the growing pains were evident, especially on offense, where the team struggled to find a rhythm. Saquon Barkley rushed for 195 yards and two touchdowns in a 28–3 win versus Rutgers, then got sidelined for weeks with an ankle injury. Christian Hackenberg stepped in with a three-touchdown, three-hundred-yard passing day to beat San Diego State. A week later, fans booed as the squad stumbled to a 20–14 win against error-prone Army. (The Knights fumbled seven times, recovering all but three.) Still, the Nittany Lions pressed onward, reaching 5–1 before a midseason showdown with number-one Ohio State.

If there was cause for admiration, it was on the defense, where sopho-more Jason Cabinda quietly assumed the leadership role vacated by Nyeem Wartman-White at middle linebacker. The transition might have been far more difficult if not for the outstanding play on the defensive line. In one of the year's biggest storylines, senior Carl Nassib emerged as a breakout star.

Franklin loved the guy, held him up time and again as a role model for the younger players—and with good reason. Nassib was like a modern-day Rudy, except that Notre Dame's big-hearted walk-on never blossomed into a consensus All-American, much less a third-round draft pick.

That sweet kid who stayed late to play cards with the campers at Nit-tanyville? He was a demon in pads, storming across enemy lines to rack up sacks, tackles for loss, and forced fumbles. What made his tale all the more remarkable is that the guy had not logged a single start prior to the Temple game—for Penn State or his high school, Malvern Prep, where Nassib had toiled for three years in near obscurity.

If not for Penn State linebacker coach Ron Vanderlinden, who watched Nassib's highlight tape and decided to take a chance on him, the lanky defensive end might have remained in the shadows forever. Instead he got invited to walk on to Joe Paterno's 2011 team, months before Jerry Sandusky uprooted everything.

CARL NASSIB: I didn't have many offers. At that point in my life, I was maybe focusing more on med school. And then I was presented with the opportunity to come to Penn State. I was like, *Oh, this is a dream for me.*

JAMES FRANKLIN: We're talking about a guy who showed up here as a six-foot-five, two-hundred-eighteen-pound walk-on.

ZACH LADONIS: I mean, Coach O'Brien basically told him he'd never play. He said, Yeah, you can join the team—we need people—but you're never going to see the field.

To Carl's face.

And Carl was like, "Well, I'll prove you wrong."

CARL NASSIB: I told him I wanted to play in the NFL and he said, Get the eff out of my office.

BILL O'BRIEN: I questioned how important football was to him.

He said, "Football is really important to me. I'm going to play pro football."

I said, "Are you kidding me? You need to be concerned about playing at Penn State. Forget about pro football."

He proved me wrong.

CARL NASSIB: Towards the end of my sophomore year, I was very close to being cut from the team. One of my coaches came up to me and said I had just made the cut. I was lucky to be here. That's when I realized I needed to be more tenacious, more active in my work ethic.

He took the message to heart. A few months later, he earned a scholarship from O'Brien.

CARL NASSIB: I didn't really hit my stride until later in life. Growing up, I had a very successful older brother, who played football in the league, so I always had to live up to that.

But it shaped me. I always wanted to be the best, always wanted to get better.

BOB SHOOP: He came to me numerous times and said, "Coach, invest in me. I'm a good investment."

This time around, it was Franklin who reaped the rewards. Nassib had added five pounds of muscle one year, fourteen pounds the next, and fourteen more the year after that. Through sheer force of will, he built the body of his dreams and became the player he had hoped to be.

ANTHONY ZETTEL: He had always made plays, but that year he added twenty-five pounds of muscle. He also got a little faster. So he could just bully people around.

AUSTIN JOHNSON: It's rare to see a guy six-foot-seven, two hundred and seventy pounds, move that fast.

JAMES FRANKLIN: Talk about a guy that kept pounding away with a sledge-hammer on a stone with very little success—and yet he kept pounding and pounding and pounding.

SEAN SPENCER, DEFENSIVE LINE COACH: The guy is one of the most intense human beings on the planet. You're in a walkthrough and he's foaming at the mouth, talking about making plays.

CARL NASSIB: I had to control that energy and let it boil up at the right moment. Sometimes it got out and my teammates thought I was crazy, but I just loved playing football.

He set a school record with fifteen and a half sacks in 2015, adding six forced fumbles for good measure. He was just the sort of role model Franklin needed, a tireless warrior adept at keeping his eyes on the prize no matter how rough the journey.

While the coach now had a much deeper roster to work with on the practice field, he was still short on game day talent, routinely pressing new recruits into action before they were fully seasoned. If you turned the clock back a year, they would be playing under the lights in sleepy high school stadiums. Now they were opening at Lincoln Financial Field in Philadelphia with seventy thousand people in attendance and millions more watching from home.

The stakes were so much higher.

KOA FARMER: Temple was my first game. I was a kick returner and they zoomed in on my face in the Eagles' stadium. I'm looking at the kicker and I see my face on the Jumbotron. I'm thinking, *Don't drop the ball—my first play in college football can't be me dropping the ball.*

SAQUON BARKLEY: The first time I scored, I felt like a little kid who just got candy. I wanted my mom, to be honest. I wanted to hug my mom. I didn't know what to do.

GRANT HALEY: A play that I didn't make at Northwestern ended up costing us the game. That stuck in my mind forever. We lost a couple of games after that.

MIKE GESICKI: I got bigger, stronger, and faster, kind of understood the college game more, because of playing in 2014. Going into sophomore year, I had a good spring. Everything was setting up for me to have a successful year. And then, I dropped two balls in the rain game against Buffalo and that was it, mentally. It took me over.

The ball's in the air and I'm thinking, *Oh, man, I got to catch it, I got to catch it. Don't drop it, don't drop it.*

And before you know it one turns into two, two turns into three. I think I ended up having five or six drops. I mean, you would have thought it was a hundred with the way people were reacting.

ADAM BRENEMAN: There's that old saying, the minute you start thinking about catching the ball, you start dropping the ball. It's so true. I've dealt with it before. All receivers have.

MIKE GESICKI: In the night game at Ohio State, I'm wide open. The ball bounces off my chest.

That was the killer.

For a couple of weeks, I knew we were going to run that play. We call it and I'm like, *I'm going to be wide open. This is going to be a big play. Try and get this thing rolling.*

For me, catching the football was never an issue before. It was like, I'm going to go out here, the ball's going to be thrown my way, I just got to go up and get it. And, if you know me, you know I have a lot of confidence in myself. But in 2015, I didn't play with confidence.

All those hours in the gym, the myriad practice reps you could expect to get in years past before setting foot on a game day field, were a luxury. In 2014 and 2015, Franklin's recruits often earned their stripes with real-world experience.

CHARLES HUFF: Nick Scott, Koa Farmer, John Reid, Troy Apke—those guys had success on special teams. And it allowed them to build confidence, reach a comfort level playing college football.

A lot of our special teams guys weren't even playing a year earlier; they were on the sideline redshirting. So to get out there on the field, have some success, play fast, and fly around, let them build confidence, gave them a role and let them have ownership of that role.

If you looked carefully, you could see that confidence sprouting in the offense, too. As Saquon lifted the running game, glimmers of hope emerged in the passing attack, traces of the explosiveness that would characterize the team in 2016. The fledgling receiving corps, blamed for much of the Lions' difficulties in 2014, now had six solid options, with highly regarded freshmen Juwan Johnson and Irvin Charles waiting in the wings.

CHRISTIAN HACKENBERG: The receivers were stronger and faster. They understood things a little more, too.

At times in 2014, we were just going through the motions. Going into 2015, you could see more focus on the details. They understood how to read and defeat coverages with certain routes, really dove into the intricacies of the position.

JAMES FRANKLIN: We worked hard to develop guys, to come up with ways to get them touches and space so they could make plays. And they started coming through. When opponents game-planned for us, they now saw multiple players that could hurt you.

JOSH GATTIS, WIDE RECEIVERS COACH: They continued to grow each and every week. They missed fewer mental assignments in 2015, which was a huge stride. They were unselfish. The numbers declined for a lot of guys, but they accepted their roles and remained active.

You had all these personalities, but they were a tight-knit group.

CHRISTIAN HACKENBERG: They worked together better than almost any other unit on our team. They jelled and pushed each other.

JOSH GATTIS: I thought we were really immature at times the year before and we grew up. Saeed Blacknall, Chris Godwin, DaeSean Hamilton—all those guys got thrown in the deep end and no one had taught them how to swim.

CHRIS GODWIN: I improved in a lot of areas, mainly in my route running and my ability to make plays. My chemistry with my quarterback and my confidence also got better.

DEANDRE THOMPKINS: I learned a lot from those guys—Ham, Chris, and Saeed—just watching them day in and day out, in practice, games, and film. With competitive catches, essentially jump balls with a defensive back, I had trouble at first. But Chris pulled me aside one practice.

"It's not hard," he said. "You just have to focus. Don't freak out when the ball's in the air, don't get nervous—just focus."

From that day on, I worked to be the best guy on the team at that skill. It's kind of hard to top Chris, but you've got to set high goals for yourself.

DAESEAN HAMILTON: It all starts with the work in the summer. We would go out and throw with Hack, get the timing down, and then, when practice came around, Coach Gattis would harp on details, making sure we were perfect in every aspect of our games.

SAEED BLACKNALL: I didn't have the numbers like everyone else. I just stayed focused. That was probably the hardest part—staying with it, staying locked in.

DAESEAN HAMILTON: Every day in practice, we'd do the little things over and over again. Make sure we get it right.

BRANDON POLK: At first, it's hard, because you'll be thinking about certain things and other things start to slack—your route running or your speed. But it gets easier.

DAESEAN HAMILTON: Halfway through the season, we were still making strides, playing a lot better than we were in week one. As long as you do the details right, the ball will find you.

SAEED BLACKNALL: The defense would do some funky stuff in the back end and you'd get your opportunity. Hack looked at you, checked it, and then you'd make the play.

JOSH GATTIS: To be an elite receiver takes confidence—confidence in your ability, confidence that you're going to make each and every play on the field. That's something that Jordan Matthews and Jordan White, the two All-Americans I had coached at other schools, shared: They truly believed they were the best receivers in college football.

It takes reps. Game reps. You get more comfortable as you get on the field.

It's something that can be developed fast, but each guy is different. As a group, we had to continue to show up each and every day, work hard, and push each other.

Much like once unheralded defensive end Carl Nassib.

CARL NASSIB: It's difficult to work hard every day and not see the fruits of your labor till later in life, but those are the lucky people—the ones who strive to be the best they can be and one day look in the mirror and they've achieved that goal. I want to be one of those people.

The challenge, especially in today's dopamine-driven, instant-gratification world, is to find the patience to see the process through, even at Penn State, a program famous for embracing the old-school.

JAMES FRANKLIN: Is this place different? Yeah, because there are really high expectations; there's tradition, and there's history, and although we'd been through some challenges, people didn't want to talk about that. They wanted to talk about the 1982 and 1986 national championships.

We embraced those things.

We woke up every morning and put in a great day's work to build this program to the level where everybody wants it to be.

That's why this place is so special—people want it all.

I don't mean it's a win-at-all-costs place. It's a place that truly values guys getting a real education, guys making a positive impact in the community, guys being successful on the field. The people here don't want to give up one for the other, they want it all.

But to build that takes time.

CHRISTIAN HACKENBERG: One player is not going to turn the tide. You need eleven guys to execute at the same time for a play to be successful.

ANDREW NELSON: It all comes down to execution. If we executed, didn't beat ourselves, people were not going to stop us.

1–0, 1–0, 1–0!!!

THIRTY-SIX

TAXSLAYER BOWL

IN THE END, *there were no signature wins for the 2015 team. No big moral victories, no overtime thrillers. After the crushing loss to Temple, the Nittany Lions won the games they were supposed to win and made little headway against their chief conference rivals. In late October, with a few clutch plays from the young receiving corps, they slipped past Maryland to secure a winning record and the right to play in a bowl game. They added a win against Illinois a week later, then lost three straight—to Northwestern, Michigan, and Michigan State.*

The last defeat was ugly, a 55–16 drubbing from a team headed for a Big Ten Championship. Before calling it a day, Spartan coach Mark Dantonio let his senior center Jack Allen—all 296 pounds of him—line up in the backfield, take a handoff, and rumble through the Penn State defense for a touchdown. Carl Nassib and Garrett Sickels were both sidelined with injuries that afternoon, leaving the Lions' front four much less fearsome.

A day later, James Franklin announced that offensive coordinator John Donovan had been relieved of his duties. The team had struggled all year long to finish drives. In forty-two trips to the red zone, Penn State had scored just twenty-three touchdowns. In a statement to the press, Franklin said, "I have tremendous respect for John and the work he has put in over the last five years. I wish him and his family nothing but the best in the future."

Despite the tough haul, the players welcomed the invitation to play 9–3 Georgia in the TaxSlayer Bowl. It would be the first meeting between the two schools since Penn State had defeated the Bulldogs in the 1983 Sugar Bowl. This time around, there was no national championship ring riding on the outcome. Quarterbacks coach Ricky Rahne would be running the offense, calling the plays from the press box against the top-ranked pass defense in the country.

GREGG GARRITY: I remember those practices for the TaxSlayer Bowl. For some reason, we just started clicking. Our practices got a lot more competitive. Instead of focusing on individual drills, just the offense, it was like, Hey, we'll do some individual drills, but then we're going ones-versus-ones. Loser has to do pushups, up downs, or gassers.

That carried into spring ball in 2016. The energy in the locker room was a lot more upbeat, a lot more competitive, which made us better. I mean, when you have guys like Chris Godwin and Marcus Allen going against each other in practice, guys like Saquon Barkley, Brandon Bell, and Jason Cabinda going against each other, you get better every single day.

JAMES FRANKLIN: Our last practice was as good as any we'd had since camp. The energy, the enthusiasm. We made it competitive—offense versus defense for five pushups, which isn't a big deal, but players didn't want to be the ones to lose, to have to do pushups while the offense or defense was watching. It got really spirited.

BOB SHOOP: It sparked something. I can't really put a finger on it, but the defense was practicing at an exceptionally high level.

RICKY RAHNE: I wanted us to go out there and play fast, play aggressive, and play with a swagger on offense. Everything was not going to be perfect—it never is—but I wanted us to play with a lot of confidence. Whatever Georgia threw at us, we were going to respond.

GENO LEWIS: I was excited, man, because I wanted to play an SEC school. You know, you always hear the talk about the SEC. *Blah, blah, blah.* I wanted to see what all the talk was about.

I was also trying to figure out what I was going to do after the season: if I was staying or moving on. Either way, I needed to have a good game.

GREGG GARRITY: That's when we started to shift the offense a bit, because Joe Moorhead was coming from Fordham to replace John Donovan. It gave us more time to prepare, try different things, and come together as a team.

Those practices were fun.

JOE JULIUS: The TaxSlayer Bowl, that's when you realized how good Trace was going to be. You know, you had Hack who did whatever he could to put a good season together, won a ton of ball games, and then he got hurt in that second quarter.

When Trace came in, it was like a different dynamic.

That's when I knew. It was like, Oh my gosh, this kid's ridiculous.

KOA FARMER: That's when T9 was introduced to college football.

You know, I'm close to Trace. I was roommates with him. Trace, Nick Scott, Manny Bowen, Mike Gesicki, Saeed Blacknall, Jason Cabinda, that whole recruiting class, we're really close to this day, so when we saw one of us out there doing what he was doing, we all got excited.

We were Franklin's first class. And now one of us was going to be the leader of the team. He'd help us build that chemistry with the rest of the roster.

Shifting from Hackenberg to McSorley was not part of the plan, of course—not that early in the game, anyway. But, as Rahne notes, things in football don't always unfold as scripted.

Hackenberg had absorbed hundreds of hits in his three years at quarterback. With a game on the line, he had always returned to the huddle. After thirty-eight starts, he was Penn State's career leader in attempts, completions, passing yards, passing touchdowns, and total offense. In a sport like football, though, you rarely get to exit the stage on your own terms, no matter how hard you work for that privilege.

Hackenberg's heroic run came to a close on the first play of the team's fifth drive. Trailing 3–0, deep in Penn State territory, he took the snap from center Angelo Mangiro, rolled to his left, tucked the ball, and sprinted for a few yards. Linebacker Roquan Smith snared him by the ankles.

TRACE MCSORLEY: Hack rolled out and got tripped up. Someone landed on his shoulder. From the sideline, I could see him, like, rolling it around, trying to loosen up. You could tell something wasn't right.

CHRISTIAN HACKENBERG: It was one of the least violent hits I'd taken in my career. I kind of stepped up and someone tripped me up and then one of the D-tackles landed on me.

I felt my shoulder pop, my right shoulder. I was like, *Damn!*

I got up and it was just hanging.

TRACE MCSORLEY: I think it was Coach Franklin or maybe Coach Rahne who said, "Hey, grab your helmet. Be ready. Just in case." So I grabbed my helmet, put it on, and started doing some light throwing.

Hackenberg tried to gut things out, completing a nineteen-yard pass to Chris Godwin for a first down and then another for five yards. But he was clearly debilitated.

CHRISTIAN HACKENBERG: I threw the next ball and it felt like my arm was attached to that football. Chris Godwin caught it and ripped off like a fifty-yard play.

And I just couldn't . . . like, I just . . .

JAMES FRANKLIN: When he came down on his shoulder, he had sprained his shoulder joint. And when you do that, it's painful. You lose strength. He made some plays there. He was going to try to finish that drive. But once he went inside the locker room, the doctors and the trainers felt he couldn't play. He just wouldn't have the strength in that arm.

TRACE MCSORLEY: I remember seeing Hack run off the field, kind of waving me on.

Coach Franklin grabbed me, pulled me up.

"All right, you're up! Go!"

It was like, *All right, this is it.*

RICK MCSORLEY: We were in a local restaurant in Virginia, watching the game with my in-laws and my mom. We didn't miss many games, even when Trace wasn't starting, but we had decided to skip that one. It was on January 2, so we opted to stay home with our daughter.

My buddy Troy, who used to run the youth football league here, was there in the stands. He gave me the heads-up. "Hey, Trace is warming up. I think he's going in."

It was a neighborhood restaurant slash bar. A bunch of neighbors started coming up, because Trace was playing. It was surreal and nerve-wracking. You're like, *Hey, is he ready for this? Coming in cold?* It's Georgia. And, I know, Georgia had a middling year *for Georgia*, but they still had some dudes on that team.

TRACE MCSORLEY: Hack went into the locker room and I finished the half.

I go in there and see him standing in a towel. Clearly done for the game. It was one of those things. You never know when you'll need to be the guy—until it's your time.

CHRISTIAN HACKENBERG: Trainer Tim Bream took me into the locker room and they ran X-rays.

I had separated my shoulder.

I looked at Tim and Tim looked at me and I was like, "Can we do something about this?"

He goes, "Nah."

And I'm like, "All right [clearly disappointed]."

That was probably the most emotional I've ever gotten. That just sucked.

I knew I wasn't coming back for another season. So that just . . . hurt. A lot.

TRACE MCSORLEY: In my first year in the program, Coach Rahne had explained to me, "We're going to do everything we can to redshirt you, but, you know, if Christian gets rolled up, he needs to come get his ankle retaped, you need to be ready."

So that whole first year, I was preparing, making sure to be ready, in case anything happened. Even something as simple as, like, his cleat comes off and he needs to come to the sideline and get it retied. The game has to go on, so I have to be ready. It's just one of those things.

CHRISTIAN HACKENBERG: I was frustrated that I couldn't go out there. I wasn't able to finish—for the seniors, for myself, for my teammates. That was tough.

When I was in the locker room, I told them that. I had a little breakdown, but it was good.

With the fifty-one-yard pass to Godwin, Hackenberg had moved the team into field goal range. McSorley came on for one play, a two-yard keeper right up the middle, to close out the drive.

Kicker Tyler Davis put Penn State on the board with a thirty-four-yard boot.

But Georgia scored touchdowns on two of the next three drives to open a 17–3 lead. The Bulldogs scored again late in the third to make it 24–3.

Meanwhile Penn State's coaches scrambled to bring McSorley up to speed. Six of his first nine passes fell incomplete. Some were high, some low, and others just plain off the mark. But little by little, he found his rhythm.

TRACE MCSORLEY: It's the same game I'd been playing for years. There's no difference in the field size—length, width, whatever. That's what the guys kept telling me. "Hey, it's the same game you've played since you were nine years old. Just go out, execute, play for the love of the game."

AUDREY SNYDER: Going into that game, I knew Hackenberg was likely to declare for the NFL draft, so I started compiling quotes about Trace McSorley. What's the deal with this guy?

Everybody just raved about him. *He's a winner. He's got the "it" factor. He's going to be great.*

It was like, *How much of this can you really believe?*

And then, he comes into that game and damn near leads the team to a come-from-behind win.

GENO LEWIS: To be honest, I think that offense was designed more for Trace, more for a mobile quarterback. That's why he ended up doing so well, man. That's the difference.

When he was in high school, he lost only one game—ever. He went to like four state championships. But they kept saying, he's not that big.

Y'all might not think he's a quarterback, but he wins. That's all he do is win.

When I saw him go out there, saw how he responded to all that pressure, you could tell. Like, you could tell the people who brought him up, developed him, put him in uncomfortable situations, so he'd learn to be comfortable. That's what he ended up doing.

MALIK GOLDEN: Trace a baller. Trace gonna ball wherever.

JAMES FRANKLIN: It took him a little time to get going. A couple of guys made plays for him to build his confidence and he was able to go from there.

CHRIS GODWIN: In the huddle, he was the same guy we knew in practice, really confident in himself. So we weren't worried at all.

DAESEAN HAMILTON: He was getting the play calls right, making the right reads, doing everything he could to put us in a position to win the game.

GENO LEWIS: He made a couple of completions and his confidence went up. He just went out there and took advantage of his opportunities.

JAMES FRANKLIN: I noticed the shift in him as well, once he started making plays. Coming to the sideline, he was fiery. Up till then, he was doing his job, but at that quarterback position, you need leadership. And after he made a few plays, he came to the sideline with a lot of confidence, a lot of emotion, talking to the guys, encouraging the guys. That's the next step.

JOE JULIUS: It was a coming-out party for sure.

Like, *Hey, you're going to be okay next year. I'm going to step up and do a really good job.*

TRACE MCSORLEY: We were down big and, I mean, basically, I've got nothing to lose.

We had a half to try and come back. It was, you know, all or nothing. Let's go win this game.

At halftime, I started talking to the guys on the offense, got everyone together, and was, like, "Hey, man, we got nothing to lose. Let's just go play our game. Because right now, everyone's counting us out.

We can't get it all back in one play, but let's try and do what we can to get back in this game."

RICK MCSORLEY: It was great when he started to get his mojo back, that hop in his step, and just get hit for the first time in a live setting.

I used to joke with Koa Farmer, one of Trace's roommates, because, you know, quarterbacks never get hit in practice. They're pretty much off limits. I'd say, "Hey, when he's walking down the hall, just nail him one time, so he knows what it feels like."

That Georgia game was the first time he'd taken any real hit in two years.

How is he gonna react?

Late in the third quarter, right after Georgia stretched its lead to 24–3, things started to click. McSorley hit Godwin with a twenty-one-yard pass. Barkley followed with a twenty-nine-yard run to the Georgia nineteen, and two plays later—just seven seconds into the fourth quarter—McSorley found Geno Lewis with a beautiful touch pass in the back corner of the end zone.

CHRIS GODWIN: When he threw that first touchdown to Geno, that really kicked up his confidence. He came to the sideline and, like coach was saying, he was fiery. Showing a lot of emotion.

TRACE MCSORLEY: It was my first touchdown pass. Got me on a roll.

JAMES FRANKLIN: He extended the play with his feet and Geno goes up and makes a play for him.

As a quarterback, that's what you want to do—put the ball in a position where guys have a chance to make plays.

TRACE MCSORLEY: Geno made a *great* play to get a little toe-tap inbounds there.

And then, DaeSean made a great catch over the middle, our defense started playing well, and, as a team, we kind of rallied.

It was pretty cool, that feeling you get when you're able to lead a team.

That's precisely what had brought McSorley to Penn State with the new coaching staff in 2014.

TRACE MCSORLEY: When I flipped from Vanderbilt, it was because of Coach Franklin, his belief in me as a quarterback.

JAMES FRANKLIN: He's got those things you can't add up. He's not going to blow you away with the eyeball test, but he has a unique combination of attributes that allows him to be successful.

With six minutes to go, McSorley got his second touchdown strike, this one a beauty to DaeSean Hamilton, splitting two defenders with a pass from twenty yards out.

TRACE MCSORLEY: We had repped that play in practice. The Georgia defense gave us a slightly different look. But the coaches told me right before we went out on the field, if they give us this look, be ready to throw the ball to DaeSean.

DAESEAN HAMILTON: When I first saw it, it looked like it was going to be long. That's why I dove for it. But it was a great ball, right where it's supposed to be. The only place where I could get it.

And just like that, Penn State was back in the ballgame, trailing by seven points with 6:14 to go. It was now up to the defense to get the ball back in McSorley's hands.

The Bulldogs had already demonstrated their big-play potential, scoring on a deep pass from wide receiver Terry Godwin to Malcolm Mitchell in the second quarter and a bullish third-quarter run by running back Sony Michel, but the team resorted to grind-it-out football, moving fifty yards in ten plays with handoffs to Michel and senior Keith Marshall.

With just under two minutes remaining, the ball sat on the Penn State twenty-three. Bryan McClendon, serving as interim coach for Georgia's recently dismissed Mark Richt, elected to run a play on fourth down instead of attempting a field goal. He had lost his starting kicker to an ankle injury earlier in the game and his backup had missed a try from forty-eight yards out.

JASON CABINDA: Right there, we just kind of buckled up. I think it was a fourth-and-two and we were able to make the stop. Give our offense another chance.

It was a very emotional drive.

McSorley took over at the twenty-five for one last go at a statement win. He started chipping away at the defense with short passes to Barkley and Hamilton, then tucked the ball and scrambled to the Bulldog thirty-nine. Eleven seconds remained on the clock.

Time for an incomplete toss and then a Hail Mary.

TRACE MCSORLEY: We ended up not winning, but we got a chance at a Hail Mary. It was, I think, just a good moment for me and my career—having the opportunity to get out there and lead the team in an actual game. Live action. Bullets flying. Things like that.

ANGELO MANGIRO: We adjusted and started to put some things together. We just ran out of time.

JAMES FRANKLIN: Christian was really good on the sideline. He was right there next to me with a headset on. Coach Rahne was in the booth and he sent messages down that we wanted to communicate to Trace, and Christian was able to help with those things. I saw him supporting him. I saw him encouraging him. Telling him things he was seeing in coverage.

TRACE MCSORLEY: He talked to me after every drive. He was giving me coverages, giving me everything. He was very instrumental to the team's success.

CHRISTIAN HACKENBERG: When I played, the one thing I always did was gather information, go back to the sideline, and share it with whoever was calling plays. "Listen, this is what I see, this is how they're playing this . . ."

I had a whole run of information I didn't get to relay right away, because I was in the locker room. So, when I got back out there, I just got on the headset and started talking to Coach Rahne.

Trace had backed me up for two years. I love that kid. He was a little baller. Has a lot of it-factor in him. So it was cool to see him succeed. And keep it running for the next few years.

That was cool for me. Letting him finish the mission. And he ultimately took it to the next level.

That's what you want to see when you're climbing out of a crisis like the one we had.

BRANDON BELL: People called it a down year for Georgia, but it was still an SEC team. Going up against those guys, flying around, making some plays—it was a good battle.

Trace came in and gave us a shot to win and, even though we fell a little short, it helped our confidence.

JAMES FRANKLIN: Good things were coming. We'd shown it in flashes, but when we played the top-tier teams in the conference, we just weren't able to get it done. We improved on our conference record, but still needed to close the gap on the upper-tier teams in the Big Ten.

THIRTY-SEVEN

EXIT HACKENBERG

CHRISTIAN HACKENBERG HAD demonstrated his commitment to Penn State time and again. He could easily have walked away after the NCAA levied the sanctions, after hearing what Nick Saban had to offer at Alabama, after his mentor Bill O'Brien left to coach in the NFL, and after any number of frustrations tripped him up in 2014. He did not. But as the curtain closed on the TaxSlayer Bowl, he greeted the press outside the locker room and addressed the one question on everyone's mind. He would not be returning for a senior season.

The talk about him being the first pick in the NFL draft had ended, but he was barely two years removed from that splendid freshman campaign. He still had the arm, the build, and the brains to entice league scouts. And he had never once wavered in his willingness to put in the extra work required to advance his game. As he explained to QB guru Jon Gruden on ESPN, "For me to climb that ladder, reach my full potential, this is the best step."

The decision to leave was no surprise. Many in the media had sensed the quarterback was ready to move on. It's the timing that caught everyone off guard. Penn State had a formal announcement for the team's would-be draft picks planned for the following day. But, after years of adhering to the game plan, Hackenberg ignored the play call.

AUDREY SNYDER: We'd probably been asking Hackenberg for like a month what he was going to do after the season and we're standing there in the hallway outside the locker room after the game, interviewing him, and of course, the first question he gets is about the draft.

He brushes it off.

So I shift to another player in the scrum next to Hackenberg and, like ten minutes into the interview session, I hear Hackenberg say, "Yeah, this is it for me—I'm declaring for the NFL."

Everybody's head turned. It was like, *Wait, what?!!*

He just decided mid-interview that he didn't want to wait till the next day to announce it.

So half the reporters go back to the press box to work and Penn State's sports information director is gathering up other players who plan to declare and all these kids are declaring in the hallway, because Hackenberg went off script.

The guy had clearly reached the end. He's just like, *Screw it, I'm going to do what I want.*

DAVID JONES: He was ready to get out. In the post-game, he made it clear that that was it. He was going to try to go pro.

He thanked all sorts of people—everyone but James Franklin.

JACK DAVIS: There was a lot of speculation about Hackenberg's relationship with the coaching staff. He wasn't recruited by Franklin's staff, so that was understandable. And ending the season with four straight losses didn't inspire much confidence that things would be different the next year.

CHRISTIAN HACKENBERG: I didn't write anything down. I didn't script anything. Everything came off the top of my head. You can go back and watch. It was in the tunnel at the stadium. I didn't have a phone. I didn't send anything out. That's not who I am.

But I had a conversation with Coach Franklin in the training room right before I went out there. I thanked him, told him I appreciated everything.

I was twenty years old. I wanted to finish my career on a high note and instead I was taken out of the game in the second quarter with a separated shoulder. So I had a lot going through my mind. It was one of those things that got blown way out of proportion.

DAVID JONES: I remember coming out of that game thinking, The kid they got coming in is what they need. Not because Christian Hackenberg couldn't do the job. It's just that they needed someone who could scramble—run for his life.

It was a matter of style.

CHRISTIAN HACKENBERG: It was a tough decision, because you've invested so much in a place, invested so much in fixing things and making sure the program's where it needs to be. But at the end of the day . . . for once . . . I've got to look out for myself.

For a young man eager to please, it was a momentous decision, one that didn't exactly pan out as he had hoped. Hackenberg would never again reach the same heights on a football field, but it's hard to dismiss what he achieved by bravely stepping forward to lead Penn State's program.

Those seniors who questioned the bravado of the boyish recruit? They learned to admire his conviction. Without it, everything they held dear might easily have crumbled.

CHRISTIAN HACKENBERG: I was put into an extremely unique situation with Bill. I don't think people anywhere else in college football were doing what Coach O'Brien was asking his quarterbacks to do in 2013. Like I said, you literally were an extension of the guy. He trusted you wholeheartedly to get things done. And I did it at a really high level.

And then, you have a new guy come in, a new philosophy, and it was like, "No, don't do that. Just do this; even if it isn't working, just keep doing it, because it will work eventually."

My brain was like, Why? It was the definition of insanity. Doing the same thing over and over again and expecting a different result.

DAVID JONES: It was not a pro-style system, not a system that would benefit him. So everything was working against Hackenberg.

PAT ZERBE: O'Brien's offense fit him much better than Coach Franklin's.

JOHN URSCHEL: I was so sad for Christian when O'Brien left.

I know Franklin. I love Franklin. He's done a great job for Penn State football and we're so lucky to have him, but Bill O'Brien clearly was the coach Christian needed. The two of them got along so well, and Christian was just so confident, so successful, under O'Brien.

I don't think anyone would argue that things would not have turned out better for him personally had he had three more years with O'Brien.

CHRISTIAN HACKENBERG: That's the only time I allow myself to say what if? Right after Bill left. Ultimately, I came here for the guy, and I'll never forget this, I almost had a throwdown with my dad over it. He's like, "Dude, you got to get out of there." But I was in too deep.

Too deep on principle.

I'd had success, but we had some issues and there were so many changes going on—not even from an Xs and Os standpoint, but from a philosophy standpoint. How Coach Franklin saw the program and what he emphasized versus what Coach O'Brien had emphasized.

There was so much change I never really got a chance to focus on myself.

We'd go back and watch film after games and, even though there were things I definitely could have done better, we had so many things to fix that my stuff was almost put on the back burner. I just never took the time to address those issues, because at the end of the day I was still getting it done, still putting us in a position to win games.

I never took time to focus on myself. That's the price I paid for staying and fighting for a bigger purpose, if that makes sense.

DAVID JONES: I don't know if it would have been a whole lot better if OB had coached him those next few years, because Christian wasn't gonna have protection. You can only have so many scholarship players. You can only spread them around so well. And they did not have a viable left tackle after Donovan Smith left.

JACK DAVIS: Christian Hackenberg stayed committed to the program—as a recruit, through the sanctions, through the change in coaching staff. He goes underappreciated not only for what he did on the field, but for keeping other recruits committed to the program.

When you see a five-star player sticking it out, speaking very highly of the experience, that does a lot for the program. He deserves a big thank-you for the success they were able to maintain during those years.

JAMES FRANKLIN: If you think about the impact Christian had on our program, where this program would be without him, it's pretty significant. Everybody looks at the win-loss record, the recruiting class ranking, the touchdown-to-interception ratio, the completion percentage, and there's so much more to the story.

CHRISTIAN HACKENBERG: That freshman year, the expectations got set so high.

When you took a step back and said, Okay, look at what's on paper here, what's on the film, it's clear I was never going to be able to attain all that. The expectations were so unrealistically high it just wasn't ever going to be like that.

It's almost like it was set up for a letdown.

I don't define it as a letdown. A letdown would have been going friggin' two-and-nine.

But, you know, we were able to ride it out. And, like I said, being able to lean on guys in the locker room, guys who were going through it with you, that was bigger than anything.

TRACE McSORLEY: Learning the football side of things from him was a big help. He was really good at watching film and talking through things: how to read a defense, see coverage, figure out where the rush is coming from. That's stuff he had to do a lot in O'Brien's offense.

It helped me immensely to learn from a guy with that football knowledge.

MARK BRENNAN: When you look back, all these years later, it didn't work out for any of those guys in the 2013 group football-wise. So putting that emphasis on education back then, how important was that? Everybody was expecting Hackenberg and Breneman to be big-time NFL players and that obviously didn't work out.

ADAM BRENEMAN: I got hurt and didn't play for two years and Christian took more sacks than anyone's taken, I think, literally in all time. I never saw someone on the ground more than him in those two years. It was just a really tough time for both of us. That's part of our bond.

MARK BRENNAN: Any news on Christian Hackenberg—during his career, after his career, today—people are going to read. Maybe that speaks to the fact he was so unique. They complain about the way his career panned out, but he is beloved. When they see him in person, they always have big smiles on their faces. Everybody comes up to ask for an autograph.

I do think most people, with the benefit of hindsight, understand what he meant to the program. They realize what that moment meant, the day he committed to Penn State.

AUDREY SNYDER: He could've gone anywhere else.

In my mind, Christian will always be paired with Adam Breneman. Both came here despite everything that was laid out on the table. They knew what they were getting into and they stayed.

That to me is Hackenberg's legacy, maybe more than anything he did on the field. He came here when he didn't have to and people respect the hell out of him for that.

MICHAEL NASH: He took so many brutal hits that it cost him a wonderful pro career. I really believe that.

CHARLIE FISHER: It doesn't have anything to do with him being unable to handle it. He's a big, strong guy, as tough as they come.

It's the residual effect of getting hit time and time again. It can create a little more edginess in the pocket, prompt you to move a little quicker than normal, and get you to drop your eye level. You see ghosts, feel pressure that isn't there.

It's happened before. David Carr of the Houston Texans is a great example.

I still believe Christian was a special talent. In the eyes of some, he didn't have the same success at quarterback those last two years. There's a lot to unpack there. But the thing you have to respect is that the kid never complained. He did his job. He showed up.

GARRETT SICKELS: I kind of hate quarterbacks, but, of course, he's my best friend, the best man at my wedding. I lived with him all three years he was there at Penn State, and even after the toughest of games, he was the guy everyone looked up to.

He never once brought up a lack of scholarship numbers, never once blamed a position group. If we lost, he said, "I gotta play better."

That's why so many guys respected him.

CHARLIE FISHER: It wasn't always easy, I'm sure. He had to adapt to a new system, got the hell beat out of him, but the expectations never changed. He was always the savior, the guy who would lead Penn State to the Promised Land, right?

When all is said and done, it's easy to point fingers at James Franklin for Hackenberg's downfall, but that doesn't capture the whole truth, either—the absurdity, the reality, of playing Division I football on a team with half the scholarship athletes of Ohio State and Michigan.

There may have been some tension between the coach and the quarterback at times, but, Hackenberg says, he holds no ill will toward Franklin. He points instead to the extraordinary circumstances that brought the two men together.

CHRISTIAN HACKENBERG: It's tough. He's very different from Coach O'Brien, and I had just turned nineteen when he got the job. The situation never allowed us to get on the same page. And some animosity afterwards kept us from clearing the air. That's something I still hope to do one of these days—clear the air with him.

I'm happy with what he's done with the program, happy for him.

After graduating from Penn State in 2016, Hackenberg's pal Garrett Sickels played on the practice squads for the Colts, Browns, Rams, and Redskins. Brendan Mahon logged two games for the Carolina Panthers. Adam Breneman lost nearly two full seasons to knee injuries after that sixty-eight-yard touchdown catch against Wisconsin his freshman year. He retired from the sport briefly, then transferred to the University of Massachusetts, where he closed out his career.

Christian Hackenberg was selected in the second round of the 2016 draft by the New York Jets. He was on the roster for two seasons, but never once took a snap in an official game.

ADAM BRENEMAN: There's this tradition at Penn State: In the last practice of the season, players all swap jerseys. So a lineman might wear number one and a wide receiver number sixty-seven. And I remember, this was at the TaxSlayer Bowl, Christian knew he was going to leave early for the NFL. I knew I was going to retire from football. No one else knew about any of that yet. And we decided we were going to trade jerseys at our last practice together. It was kind of a symbolic moment. Him wearing eighty-one, me wearing number fourteen.

CHRISTIAN HACKENBERG: The whole thing was so much bigger than us. The deeper and deeper we got into it, the more we realized it. And, as weird as it sounds, that moment would maybe never have happened if things had played out differently. That was a sign of our maturity throughout the whole process. Like Adam said, it was very symbolic. For me, it was like, "Dude, we did this thing together, we stuck it out. We might as well go out together."

THIRTY-EIGHT

DINNER WITH FRANKLIN

JAMES FRANKLIN HAD worked tirelessly for two years to bring his vision for Penn State football to life, giving speeches, hobnobbing with members of the media, posing for pictures, shaking hands, visiting homes across the state—all to generate support for his plan. He had huddled with recruits, students, alums, administrators, lettermen, parents, high school coaches, high school custodians, and, yes, even the ladies in the lunchroom. The man had peerless people skills, and yet one crucial constituency had stubbornly resisted his charm. And so, in the spring of 2016, Franklin set out to convert the nonbelievers inside his own locker room.

It was no easy task. For the players who had pledged their allegiance to the program in the early days of the scandal, rallied around Joe Paterno and then Bill O'Brien, the shift to another coach had been difficult. And before he could meet them, fully get to know them, Franklin was off courting new prospects for the team. More to the point, the veterans on his roster had come to see themselves as more than just student-athletes. They were keepers of the Penn State flame.

When the school's administrators had quietly retreated from the heat of the Sandusky scandal, it was those student-athletes who stood tall, openly declaring their support for the institution and its record.

Continue the mission.

Success with honor.

They now had as much stake as anyone in the future of the program.

James Franklin knew this. For his plan to succeed, he had to have their support. So he came up with an enticing way to get it. "I'd say it took roughly thirty-six hamburger dinners," he explained in a personal essay for the Players' Tribune.

First, he identified a few dozen key players on the roster—guys like Von Walker, Brandon Bell, and Malik Golden—and then three nights a week, over burgers, wings, and buckets of fries, he worked to recruit them, essentially selling them on his Penn State.

Before all was said and done, he had earned himself a signature dish on the menu at the Toftrees Golf Resort pub where most of the outings took place. If you visit The Field Burger and Tap today, you'll find the "Coach Franklin" priced at $15. It's a turkey burger served on a whole grain roll with arugula, tomato, olive tapenade, and goat cheese.

MALIK GOLDEN: Team leaders had a conversation with James after the 2015 season, and that's what really helped us, the internal conversations James was willing to have with us.

He started having dinners with a lot of the older guys.

We told him, it's okay to give the keys to us sometimes, let us help run the program.

He'd been very on top of stuff and kind of took a step back.

That's when we were able to really unleash.

PARIS PALMER: The summer of that year, we had a leadership council meeting and in the meeting we were talking about the season, projections and stuff, and Nyeem Wartman-White asked for the floor.

So James Franklin gives him the floor.

And Nyeem says, You know, I understand wanting to take everything one game at a time, working to be one and oh, but we don't talk about Big Ten Championships enough.

There was a dead silence in the room.

Everyone started thinking, *He's right.*

He was a thousand percent right.

CHRIS GODWIN: It's something we wanted to start talking about. I mean, obviously, we don't like looking too far into the future, but we had to set goals, so that was a goal—to get to Indianapolis for the championship game. We understood it was going to take focus week to week to get to that point.

BRANDON BELL: We focused on one game at a time, but me and Nyeem, back at Big Ten Media Day, started talking about a Big Ten Championship. That was not our main focus. We knew we had to take care of it one week at a time.

PARIS PALMER: From that point on, we carried ourselves as if we were in that conversation.

NYEEM WARTMAN-WHITE: I felt we had the pieces. If we just went into the season thinking *Big Ten Championship*, we'd put it all together.

In my time at Penn State, I'd never heard us say "My goal is to win the Big Ten Championship" out loud, and you should do that. If you believe, you've got to talk about it. Remind yourself every day. Work like a Big Ten champion today, and then tomorrow, and the day after that.

JOE JULIUS: That was the year it all came together. All the pieces kind of fit.

BILLY FESSLER, QUARTERBACK, 2014–17: When you're running a program that's had three different head coaches in five years, trying to get everyone to buy in and do things the way a team needs them to be done, create that chemistry that's so critical to winning football games, it's not easy.

ALEX BUTTERWORTH: In 2012, when Bill O'Brien came to the program, we had been beaten up by the media for months and months. It was easy to develop a mutual hate for the press.

I think O'Brien saw that and said, "Listen, I'm not going to be a friend of the media." He understood what we had just gone through.

When Franklin came in, he immediately embraced the media—social media, too—and it was tough to watch. Because, you know, Joe Paterno was never a big media guy, either.

VON WALKER: Some guys got a little carried away. Like, "Hey, OB was our guy. We just don't trust you, because we don't know you. Your plan doesn't sound like his plan. Your plays don't look like his plays. And your coaching style isn't like his coaching style."

MATT ZANELLATO, RECEIVER, 2011–15: Joe Paterno was a legendary coach, he'd been there forever. Bill O'Brien? NFL mastermind, extremely smart on offense. So it was weird for us to see Coach Franklin act more like a CEO.

He didn't focus squarely on the football decisions. He thought big-picture, weighing in on the uniform design, facilities upgrades, messaging, every facet of the program.

MATT ZANELLATO: It's not like he isn't super smart. But, like, Bill O'Brien was calling the plays.

BILLY FESSLER: I give a lot of credit to the older guys on the team, the ones who showed us how to do things the right way. For me, they set the tone. But, to be honest, there were other guys that our class looked at and said, "Hey, we're not going to be like them, because they don't do it the right way."

VON WALKER: Guys were divided. They didn't see eye-to-eye. And, you know, for some of them, seasons ended. Their careers went on. But, honestly, if we all bought in right away, we could have done something special in 2015. We had some serious talent. Guys from Paterno's last recruiting class. I mean, legit NFL Pro Bowl–type guys.

We could have had a really awesome season. But, at the end of the day, it is what it is. The people who felt that way kind of weaned themselves out.

ZACH LADONIS: I'm not saying we didn't try to buy in. It was just a natural . . . I don't want to say rejection. We were just hesitant to one hundred percent buy in.

It was really hard, because we'd had success with O'Brien and, with the new system, it seemed like we were trying to fit a round peg into a square hole. It didn't really work those first couple of years. The personnel we had didn't fit the structure.

MATT ZANELLATO: No matter what James Franklin did, there would always be a certain stepchild syndrome for us. We were recruited by Joe Paterno, and then Bill O'Brien came in and we had to earn his respect and keep the team together through the sanctions, and finally, after two years, things had settled and we were thinking, *Okay, there's some sense of normalcy.*

And then Bill O'Brien leaves and a whole new staff comes in.

And it's not like Bill O'Brien was fired. He willfully left.

I don't hold that against him, but as a nineteen-, twenty-, twenty-one-year-old kid, it felt like you'd been lied to.

ZACH LADONIS: It was a bit disheartening—because of the way he left and because he'd made some promises he wasn't able to uphold, especially to the scholarship guys.

MATT ZANELLATO: I think a lot of the dissension has to do with how the program Coach Franklin had adopted at Vanderbilt compared to the program he adopted at Penn State.

At Vanderbilt, he was recruiting against SEC powerhouses.

In the South.

At an academic school.

It's a completely different pitch. And, when he got to Penn State, it seemed like he was trying to sell our school as if it were Vanderbilt.

It rubbed some of those older guys the wrong way. We were like, Yes, you should chase the kids you're chasing, but they should *want* to be here. This is a program that has earned the respect—the success with honor—and they should want to be a part of that.

CHRISTIAN HACKENBERG: For us, at that age, it's a big shift. When all you know is a certain thought process, a certain way things are run, and then it flips to the opposite end of the spectrum, that's hard—trying to figure out how to navigate relationships, things like that, amidst all the issues we had.

JAMES FRANKLIN: We had a group of guys who were committed to Penn State, and I showed up and knew them for three weeks before Signing Day. That's not really *knowing* those guys.

That's why those first couple of years were so important—to get to know those guys, build relationships and trust.

ZACH LADONIS: That's kind of what we were lacking—the full, one hundred percent buy-in.

Trust in the coaches and the coaches' trust in us.

They were trying to mold to us, and we were trying to mold to them.

It was just a tug-of-war.

MATT ZANELLATO: There's one moment that really illustrates the disconnect. We were sitting in a team meeting, before the walkthrough on Friday, and we're about to play . . . Wisconsin? And we had some big-time recruits coming to the game. I don't know whose idea it was, but they put this slide up on the projector showing the guys that were coming. And I'm like, *This information seems like it should be for a staff meeting, not a players meeting.*

It was like, "Hey, these guys are coming on a visit this weekend—if you see 'em, make sure you say what's up?"

We're about to play a game in twenty-four hours and you're telling us about some eighteen-year-old kid coming to visit?

I vividly remember Bill Belton running through the locker room, shouting "The recruits are coming! The recruits are coming!" Kind of making a joke of the situation.

ZACH LADONIS: I keep coming back to the circular peg in the square hole reference. That's really what we were experiencing. The offensive system Coach Franklin brought in with Coach Donovan, it didn't really fit into what we were running in the pro-style offense, so it was kind of eye-opening to the players.

Like, *We had this working,* and they came in and were like, *Well, we had this work somewhere else, and we could definitely coach you guys up to do it.* Just that tension.

MATT ZANELLATO: I'm not saying James Franklin was wrong. By no means am I saying that. The man is a recruiting machine. There's a reason Penn

State has had such success in recruiting in recent years. That doesn't just happen. But at the same time . . .

ZACH LADONIS: I don't mean this to be a diss on Franklin or O'Brien, but that year was kind of the tipping point, the time when the older guys—the ones who were there under O'Brien—were dwindling in number because of graduation and there were more of Franklin's guys—for lack a better term—players he'd recruited and brought up through the system.

It was an inflection point: If you didn't buy in, you were on the outside, looking in on something that could be really special.

To smooth the transition, Franklin served up a heaping helping of The Field's famous fries.

JAMES FRANKLIN: I've always been big on hosting players for meals at my home, but before the 2016 season started I wanted to try something more personal. I identified roughly forty guys on the team who were at a tipping point in their careers—players I knew would one way or the other determine the fate of our season—and I invited each out for a one-on-one dinner.

I even let them pick the spot.

CHRISTIAN HACKENBERG: Yeah, I don't know if I ever got one of those invites. [laughter]

VON WALKER: At first, it kind of felt like a job interview, so I was a bit nervous.

He doesn't know me. I'm a run-on. Like, I need to make some kind of impression.

But if you're having a casual conversation with him, he lets you know it's okay to open up. He's just another guy who loves the game of football and wants to help you become the man you want to be. So, yeah, it was pretty nerve-wracking at first, but in the end it was all right.

JAMES FRANKLIN: We got to discuss their biggest questions surrounding the program, as well as what they were excited about and what they were afraid of. We talked about their lives away from football and their long-term goals.

VON WALKER: He kind of laid all his cards on the table. He's an emotional guy. Some men don't feel comfortable being emotional, especially on a football field. But Coach Franklin is the first to start tearing up. Over something special. During practice or a game. The guy lives, breathes, and dies college football. He really does care for his players.

Those meals were him genuinely trying to reach out and say, "Listen, man, I'm on your team. I have your back. But I need you to buy into my vision of what a great football team looks like. Just trust me."

JAMES FRANKLIN: I'm a people person. I've always been a people person. Always been a guy that appreciates getting to know people. I think that's why I was attracted to psychology in college.

VON WALKER: One of my best friends ever, Johnny Wise, was at The Field with his mom on the night I had dinner with Coach Franklin. He came up to say hello.

I introduced him to Coach Franklin. And, you know, Coach Franklin, being the guy he is, literally bought their meal for them.

BILLY FESSLER: I wasn't involved in those dinners, but I do know that it felt different after that. When your best players are all driving in the same direction, all want the same thing, and there's no one holding you back, you have a chance to be pretty good, and that's what it felt like.

NYEEM WARTMAN-WHITE: If everyone was not on the same page, rowing the boat in the same direction, then someone was going to address it.

BRENDAN MAHON: We all took ownership of our responsibilities, put the work in to take that next step to the Big Ten Championship. We implemented our own practices in the summer—a player run, we'd go out for an hour and a half and do half-line stuff, full-team stuff. Not full speed, but we were getting the reps we needed.

CHANCE SORRELL: I was able to play in a few games here and there in 2015, but I started having knee issues. Coach Franklin and the training staff sat me down and said it was more than likely to keep happening. Even though I was getting taped from mid-thigh to my ankle to keep that knee in place, it just wasn't in the cards for me to keep playing long-term.

So 2016 was a transition year for me. I got the opportunity to intern with the strength and conditioning staff, help the guys in the weight room and be out there at every practice, every game. It made me appreciate all the hard work the coaches put in, getting there between 5 and 6 a.m. each day and not leaving until 10 p.m., even though some have families.

That's just the way it is. It was eye-opening to see the things they sacrifice to put the program in a position for success. It made me respect the profession. I mean, a week off for the coaches is essentially unheard of. There's just so much going on, so much to keep an eye on.

I don't know how those guys do that for years and years. You've got to have a passion for it.

MATT ZANELLATO: As a player, I definitely had my own opinions. But now that I'm a coach and I've seen the other side of things, I have a much different viewpoint.

I talked to Trace McSorley after the team won the Big Ten Championship and I was like, "All right, shoot it to me straight. What the hell changed?"

And he said, "We all bought in. Like, everyone wholeheartedly bought in."

As an older guy on the 2015 team, a guy who had been around the Mike Mautis, the Gerald Hodgeses, and the Jordan Hills, that cut deep. I was like, *Damn, did I do everything I could to be a good leader?*

Some of it was a result of groupthink. It was hard to be an outlier in the midst of some of that stuff. But hearing Trace, someone I respect, say that?

It was like, *Damn, that hurts.*

THIRTY-NINE

JOEMO

JAMES FRANKLIN MADE *another wise move that off-season, hiring a former sportswriter to replace John Donovan as offensive coordinator. To be clear, Joe Moorhead's flirt with journalism was brief—mostly just a way to pay the bills while he explored his options as a pro football player—but his route to Penn State was unconventional, nonetheless. Accepting a job on Franklin's staff meant leaving behind a head coaching position at Fordham University, where Moorhead had majored in English and played quarterback in the early '90s.*

Before taking the helm at Fordham, he had coached at Georgetown, Akron, and the University of Connecticut. Not exactly what one would call a show-stopping résumé. But Moorhead clearly had a gift for scoring points. In 2010, he had propelled the Huskies to a Big East Championship and a date with Oklahoma in the Fiesta Bowl. And, in 2012, he had inherited a 1–10 team at Fordham and steered it three years later to an 11–3 record and a Patriot League title.

And, as luck would have it, James Franklin's Nittany Lions had practiced on the field at Fordham in the days leading up to the 2014 Pinstripe Bowl, giving Franklin and Moorhead ample time to discuss their mutual affinity for the West Coast offense. And so, when Franklin decided to part ways with longtime pal John Donovan—who had coached alongside him at Maryland, Vanderbilt, and Penn State—he dialed Moorhead. Not long after that, Moorhead was on his way to Penn State. For many players, that meant learning a third playbook in four years. But this time around they would come to celebrate the change.

MALIK GOLDEN: That was the best decision James Franklin ever made. That dude, like this story about the Penn State resurgence, Joe Moorhead sits atop the list of reasons for that.

He flipped Penn State upside down with his offensive mindset. He was like, "We're not here to be conservative, we're trying to score at the snap of the ball." That ignited a lot of people.

One game Chris Godwin would go crazy, another game DaeSean, then Saquon, Saeed Blacknall, Mike Gesicki. I was like, *What the hell?* DeAndre Thompkins, Irv Charles against Minnesota. He just gave players confidence.

"We don't care who's in the game. If you're in the slot and you've got a post, we're going to hit you on the post and it will be open."

Not many people think like that.

AUDREY SNYDER: You had that buy-in, just like you got with Bill O'Brien.

I mean, the players loved Joe.

TOM PANCOAST: Even the defensive players loved him.

GREGG GARRITY: From an Xs and Os standpoint, he was unbelievable. We'd be in the hotel the night before a game, going through our script, the first ten plays, and he'd say, "Hey, the first play after we cross the fifty-yard line, on the right hash, we're gonna run this play and score a touchdown." And sure enough, after we crossed the fifty-yard line on the right hash and ran the play, it was a touchdown. I mean, the guy was a genius.

MIKE GESICKI: He called it in the Purdue game. First play of the drive, he said we're handing it to Saquon, we're blocking it here, and he's taking it in for a touchdown. And it happened. It was an eighty-yard touchdown. I mean, he'd go out and say, "This is a touchdown."

TOM PANCOAST: It wasn't even a *pass*. It was a run play.

We handed the ball to Saquon and it all happened exactly as JoeMo said it would.

He saw stuff that no other coach sees.

GREGG GARRITY: Talk about second-half adjustments, he was able to see the in-game tendencies of a defense, how the defensive backs and line-backers played, the motions and shifts, how they played cover two, cover three, man-to-man. He would see it all and say, "If they're in cover two, we're going to do this. If they're in man, we're going to do this." That's why we were so successful in the second half that season.

He was the perfect fit for the personnel we had: Trace, an athletic quarterback, not a huge arm. Saquon, who could be a power back or more of a scat back. Big receivers like Chris Godwin, Mike Gesicki, DaeSean Hamilton, guys that could go up and get it, make the big catch when we needed it. That was an awesome group, but I don't think any of that happens without Joe Moorhead.

He was *the* guy. More important than Trace McSorley, Saquon Barkley, or Jason Cabinda. Without him, I don't think we become Big Ten champions. He put you in a position to win.

TRACE MCSORLEY: He just pushed life into our offense.

In the first team meeting, he put the top scoring offenses in the country on the board and he was straight up: These are the top five, Penn State ranks way down low—a hundred-something. In the Big Ten, it was the same. He was saying, This is where we are and that's not acceptable. This is where I expect us to be and what we need to do to get there.

DAESEAN HAMILTON: He said, We're going to have the best offense in the Big Ten. We're going to go out and win a Big Ten Championship. We're going to be one of the top five offenses in the country.

TRACE MCSORLEY: That enthusiasm, that standard of excellence—it's something we hadn't been exposed to before.

MIKE GESICKI: We'd let go of Coach Donovan, who I've got a ton of respect for, and brought in Coach Moorhead. So I go introduce myself. I want to make an impression on the guy, because it's a new year. Time to go out and make a name for myself.

I put every ounce of energy I had into being successful. I was catching at least two hundred balls a day on the JUGS machine. DaeSean Hamilton and I. Sometimes it would be me, DaeSean, and Chris Godwin. Me and Saeed Blacknall. Me and Juwan Johnson. Sometimes I'd grab Tommy Stevens, who was vying with Trace for the starting quarterback spot, and have him throw to me, just so I could get more confidence.

I mean, this is going all the way back to January. We don't have a game for another nine months. I'm working harder in the weight room, all that stuff.

Spring ball comes around. I'm feeling better, making plays, but I've made plays in spring ball before. It's all about making those plays on Saturdays when it *allllll* counts. So, I put in a ton of work.

JOE MOORHEAD: There's a saying that no one rises to low expectations, so we talked about some things we wanted to accomplish during the season and did a little research.

SAQUON BARKLEY: He put up on the board all the successful teams in Penn State history, the bowl games they went to and the points they averaged. Aside from one fluke year, it was all thirty points or up.

AUDREY SNYDER: He had this offense, but people were skeptical about it, because it's from Fordham. How do you make that work at Penn State? There was this whole leap of faith James Franklin had to take with the guy and trust that it was not going to blow up in his face.

DAESEAN HAMILTON: It was exciting to play in that offense—a deep play could happen at any moment. So, you always had to be prepared for your number to be called.

RICK MCSORLEY: I remember being at the first practice that spring when Moorhead started talking about championship standards, having a championship attitude on every play. He knew every position, knew exactly what went right and wrong on every play. Great guy, right guy for the situation. He just took things to another level. He instilled not only the offensive scheme, which was a little more attacking and took advantage of the mismatches we could create with the players we had, but also his confidence in that offense, what it could deliver.

MIKE GESICKI: His confidence is contagious. Week after week, we improved. He came up with a bunch of ways to attack defenses and get certain guys the ball. He was able to spread it out all season long, give us a bunch of weapons that could produce.

SAQUON BARKLEY: When I first met with him, we sat in the office for like an hour. If he didn't have to go to a dinner with his family, we probably would have been there much longer. He was just breaking down the system. The thing he kept focusing on was the playmakers and space. That's all you want as an offensive guy, to get space, be able to make a play and use your talents.

RICK MCSORLEY: Trace told me this story about a touchdown they scored in practice. Coach Moorhead pulled the players aside afterwards and he was *pissed*. Not because they had scored. Because they didn't celebrate.

TRACE MCSORLEY: Once we got through the winter workouts and into spring ball, we started making plays in practice. One time, we hit a big play for a touchdown. And, you know, we kind of gave a few high fives, but we were in practice, so we got ready to run the next play. Moorhead ran all the way down the field to, I think it was Chris Godwin, who had scored the touchdown. He was super pumped up, giving Chris a high five, but he was the only guy down there. That pissed him off.

He came back to the huddle and said, "Hey, guys, if we don't want to get excited about touchdowns, I'll just stop calling these awesome plays. We can run the ball and be super blah."

RICK MCSORLEY: "Look," he said, "we've got to be enthusiastic out here, got to enjoy this game. When we make a play, let's celebrate that play, celebrate that player. Have fun with it."

That's where Trace's home-run swing came from.

Coach Moorhead said, "Hey, get out there, have fun, make something up."

MATTY FRESH: The home-run celebration, that's so iconic. Trace used to do that with Billy Fessler.

RICK MCSORLEY: Trace's roommate Billy Fessler, who was a backup quarterback, would mime tossing him the ball and Trace would take a swing at it.

TRACE MCSORLEY: That started with me and Billy saying, "Hey, if JoeMo wants us to have fun, let's come up with something."

The celebrations, jumping up, fun that you saw those next three years—that's what started it all.

You could see it on the tape of the guys at Fordham. They'd throw a big touchdown and then throw a ball in the air, start chest bumping, going crazy. That's what he wanted—a celebration.

He didn't want us to get penalized for it, but he wanted us to have fun.

BILLY FESSLER: You play this game to have fun, right? That's all it was. You work so hard for those moments. When they finally come, that's a lifetime's worth of work tossed into four seconds. That's how long that play lasts. So, try to enjoy it.

TRACE MCSORLEY: After that meeting, we talked about it. Billy was one of my roommates and he was doing most of the signaling for the plays. He was always on the sideline. So we figured we'd do some kind of celebration while I was heading back to the sideline. Nothing disrespectful to the other team.

I forget exactly how it happened, but someone came up with the idea of a baseball swing, like hitting a home run. We had talked so much about wanting to throw deep passes and we were saying, "Oh, everyone loves long balls, big plays, stuff like that."

BILLY FESSLER: "Wouldn't it be cool to do something that little kids mimic, something that makes them think, *Hey, I'm going to do that, because that's what those guys do.*" So we just started thinking about it. And, you know that saying chicks dig the deep ball? Well, obviously, they dig the long ball as well. So, we talked a lot about, you know, hitting dingers. It just came up that way. "Hey, let's hit dingers."

TRACE MCSORLEY: We go into the weight room one morning and Billy was like, "What if I act like I'm tossing a ball in the air and you swing a bat?"

We did it one or two times in practice and nobody said much. We did it a few times in the spring game and nobody said much. And so, you know, we didn't think it was going to be a big thing. The next thing you know, we get to the season and it becomes a signature thing.

Obviously, Penn State had that immense tradition Coach Paterno had established. We didn't want to take away from that. But, at the same time, we wanted to do something fresh and exciting. And, like I said, it ended up being a signature thing, one the fans enjoyed.

MIKE GESICKI: By the time fall camp came around, we had bought into everything Coach Moorhead was telling us. We all understood our jobs and our roles.

Moorhead's offense was rooted in the West Coast playbook developed by Walt Harris at Pitt, where Moorhead had served as a graduate assistant in the late '90s. It favored shifts in tempo, no huddle, using the running game to draw the defense in close, then striking deep.

JOE MOORHEAD: We wanted to dictate the tempo. Be aggressive, physical in the run game and explosive in the passing game.

ANDREW NELSON: The tempo, spreading guys out and all that, was unconventional, but it really worked.

JOE MOORHEAD: To me, it was about getting into the right play, not running the wrong play quickly. That's one of the benefits of a no-huddle offense, having the coaches control for the most part what play we ran.

ANDREW NELSON: After our first couple of practices, we were bent over, breathing heavy, like, *Cheese and crackers, how are we going to do this?*

Coach Moorhead said, "Listen, this is going to be hard now, but I promise you, when it comes game time, you guys are going to be the ones running to the sidelines, saying go faster, go faster, because the D-line won't be able to take it."

I'm not sure I believed him during practice, because you don't normally put drives together there, but in the spring game I specifically remember jogging off and saying, "Let's keep up the pace. These guys can't take it."

CHRIS GODWIN: Every day we were pushing the tempo faster and faster, so when the games came, they were a little easier than practice. We were dictating the tempo, going as fast as we wanted to go.

BILLY FESSLER: Even young guys like Juwan and Irv stepped up and made big plays. I think that goes back to how competitive we were in practice, guys making those plays over and over again and then having the confidence to go out and make them when their number was called.

That chemistry and that trust, that enjoyment of being in college, playing together every day, went a long way. We looked forward to competing and then going out and having a blast. That's what was special about our group, and it probably helped us win some games. Maybe we weren't quite as talented as the team across from us, but we had each other's back.

JOE MOORHEAD: The thing I told the kids is I'm not here to harp on our past, I'm here to create our future. So whatever occurred in the past, good or bad, we're going to write our own book.

We just put our heads down and went to work.

And it didn't take long for that work—all that JoeMo energy—to produce results on the field.

DAVID JONES: Moorhead's a hell of an offensive mind, man. He taught guys a lot in a short period of time—none more than Trace McSorley.

BILLY FESSLER: Before he got there, I think we were averaging like eighteen or nineteen points a game. In 2016, we averaged thirty-seven.

TRACE MCSORLEY: Every time we stepped on the field our goal was to score touchdowns, put points on the board.

BILLY FESSLER: Coach Moorhead made sure that, one, we were in position to be successful and, two, we trusted what we were doing—that we knew how to loosen up and have fun. And that's something you saw a lot of guys do—play without fear. A lot of the credit for that goes to him.

FORTY

DYNAMIC DUO

IN THE FALL of 2016, Trace McSorley put any lingering reservations about Penn State's offense to rest, nimbly stepping from Christian Hackenberg's shadow to transform the team with his youthful energy. In the blink of an eye, it seemed, JoeMo had two legit superstars at his disposal, leaving the Big Ten Conference's defensive coordinators scrambling to contain them.

Week after week, the TV networks showed up to broadcast the fireworks, delighting fans with the duo's wild improvisation, the beauty of two overgrown kids, McSorley and Barkley, teaming up to take on each would-be challenger, then beaming for the cameras.

By some awesome stroke of luck, the players managed to strike the perfect balance between humility and swagger, promoting Penn State and the NCAA in a fashion so wholesome it would be impossible to imagine just a few years earlier. It made for a truly special locker room culture, one that celebrated not only raw talent, but the contribution from each and every teammate, backup quarterback to long snapper. By virtually all accounts, the unity on the roster was exceptional.

And it radiated from two telegenic folk heroes, a supremely gifted running back and a quarterback forever underestimated because of his height—as if those missing inches somehow eclipsed the four straight trips he made to the Virginia state championship in high school.

AUDREY SNYDER: You look at all these benchmarks for quarterbacks—size and arm strength and all that—and, you know, you just had a five-star quarterback leave the program. Well, now, you get the mobile quarterback, the guy who keeps winning against all odds.

I mean, it's crazy how productive he was.

ANDREW NELSON: The guy's a baller. He might not have the intangibles people look for in a quarterback, but the kid balls out all the time.

BRIAN GAIA: He has great pocket awareness, knows where the pressure is coming and where to run.

JOE MOORHEAD: The phrase Trace and I always used was *Feel the rush, see the coverage.* He had this innate ability to stay calm and keep his eyes downfield when things were breaking down around him. That's something you can teach a bit, but the quarterback has to have it in his DNA.

DAVID JONES: He was *so* elusive. I mean, you could not have had two people better than Saquon Barkley and Trace McSorley to deal with those crappy offensive lines.

McSorley learned how to duck inside, bust the pocket, then throw downfield. And the one thing Penn State did have in abundance is wideouts who could go up and get the ball.

Hackenberg couldn't have made that work. But in 2016 Penn State had the perfect guy to come in and make do. When Hackenberg got dinged up in the bowl game, you could see right away that McSorley was going to have a better chance of *surviving.*

He was so quick. He could duck under people and find a gap in the pocket. And he didn't just run, he kept his eyes downfield.

He was a magician. He really was.

Never took a hit.

Looking back, it's easy to assume that Trace McSorley was a shoo-in for Hackenberg's job, especially after his performance in the TaxSlayer Bowl, but the truth is he needed nearly eight full months to outduel redshirt freshman Tommy Stevens for the starting role.

At six-foot-four, one hundred ninety-three pounds, Stevens was a legit rival—a bit raw as a passer, because he primarily ran the option in high school, but a finalist for Gatorade Player of the Year in his home state of Indiana. He also loved to scrap, owing in part to his roots as a defensive back.

TOM PANCOAST: A lot of people don't know this, but going into that 2016 season, it was probably fifty-fifty on who was going to get the starting job—Tommy or Trace. Tommy was a better athlete, Trace was a smarter football player.

The job ended up going to Trace for good reason—he's now the winningest quarterback in Penn State history—but it was a pretty even race throughout training camp.

JAMES FRANKLIN: That battle was a lot closer than people realize.

TRACE MCSORLEY: We were going back and forth, splitting the first team reps.

Tommy was playing well.

RICK MCSORLEY: Trace had shown he could be a leader on the team and play in that Georgia game, but there was still a healthy competition between him and Tommy coming out of spring camp. In the summer, they were still going at it.

It wasn't until right before the season started that Trace was named the starting quarterback.

TRACE MCSORLEY: I was confident, but I'd be lying if I said I didn't think there was a chance Tommy would be named the starter. Like I said, he played well in camp, brought out the best in me.

TOMMY STEVENS: We were constantly trying to make each other better. Just working, working, working. I think I was able to push Trace. Obviously, I'm not going to take credit for the things he did, but I think pushing him every day helped.

BILLY FESSLER: When Trace was named the starter, Tommy didn't blink an eye. I mean, I know it crushed him. It had to, but he just kept pushing, working, getting better. I'm not sure what Trace's feelings are on that, but that would push *me* to get better every single day, having a damn good football player right behind me, just waiting for his number to be called.

But, credit Trace, he never stopped playing good football. He was Mr. Consistent.

JAMES FRANKLIN: He'd been the backup quarterback for two years but didn't approach it that way. He prepared as if he was the starter.

The mobility both players brought to the position represented a break with the past, a clear step beyond the conservative passing attacks of the Paterno era. It took a few games to fully harness it, but once that happened McSorley merged with Barkley into a formidable one-two punch.

TRACE MCSORLEY: We were able to use the athletic ability at the quarterback position—between me and Tommy, really—to open up our run game. Get a couple more single blocks for the guys on the offensive line. It made one man on the defense hold back, kept him from rushing in on runs.

JAMES FRANKLIN: It was one more thing to defend. It's frustrating for a defense when you stop the run and do a great job in pass coverage and then the quarterback takes off for twelve to fifteen yards—even six yards. It's just one more thing you have to deal with.

It helped Saquon, and I do think it helped our offensive line.

SAQUON BARKLEY: If you loaded the box, you had to account for Trace. And if you accounted for Trace, you had to play man-on-man on the perimeter, and we had the best wide receiver corps in the Big Ten. I'll take those odds any day.

As McSorley's star rose, it spotlit Barkley's humbleness, the team player beneath the brilliant back. When opponents flooded the line of scrimmage, making it nearly impossible for him to run, Barkley would simply step back and block for the quarterback or hover in wait for an outlet pass, performing the humdrum chores required for team success.

TRACE MCSORLEY: He had his explosive games, days when he was unstoppable, rushing for over two hundred yards. But he also had games where he was nearly invisible. When teams were stuffing the box, we'd shift to the pass game and his ability to still be a leader, still have that drive to give everything he had on every snap—that's the most impressive thing he did.

JAMES FRANKLIN: When he had games without the production people expected, it never affected him. It was about the team, doing his job. There was no bad body language.

And when you have an attitude like that, it influences others in a positive way.

BRUCE FELDMAN: He's a great character kid. Great worker. If you spend time around him, you become a believer. He's way bigger than he looks. He works his butt off. It's fitting that on the game-winning play versus Iowa in 2017, he didn't catch the ball. He did something you won't see in the box score. He stoned the linebacker in protection.

Between Barkley and McSorley, Penn State could not have asked for better role models.

ANDREW NELSON: Coach Franklin talked about identity as something all great teams have. In 2015, we were struggling to find an identity. It wasn't until 2016 that Saquon decided he was going to become a leader of the team, give us an identity.

BOB HARTMAN: There was always some level of charisma, likability, that drew people to Saquon, but he has gotten better in the spotlight.

That comes with confidence.

He used to spend a lot of time in my office, making sure he was doing things right. I'd call him down to meet a coach or something, and the first thing he'd say is, "What am I doing wrong?"

Ninety-eight percent of the time, I didn't have an answer for him. He wasn't doing anything wrong. But the fact that that was his response says something about him, the way he saw himself.

AUDREY SNYDER: He's this super nice person with an ungodly amount of talent. When he was a recruit, he'd DM me highlights of his high school teammates. "Hey, take a look at this guy."

Like, *Dude, Penn State's not going to recruit that guy.*

He just wanted to help his teammates.

That was always the thing with him. As good as he was, he . . . I don't want to say he wasn't comfortable with the attention, because he certainly grew into it, embraced it, but there was a genuine part of him that wanted to talk about everybody else.

SAQUON BARKLEY: I just tried to smile, be nice, be kind. Because you don't know—a picture, a smile could change someone's day.

BRIAN GILBERT: Saquon's a product of being undersized when he was young, of having better talent around him, of lacking confidence. He overcame that with hard work. And once he realized what he could do, he worked even harder.

That's a big thing.

You see these kids who get recruited by one school and their attitude changes. They're the man now. The more offers Saquon got, the more he felt like he better not let anybody down.

AUDREY SNYDER: We were at Kinnick Stadium in Iowa once and there's this fan talking trash, like the whole game, right behind the bench. When Juwan Johnson scores the winning touchdown and the game ends, I'm standing there taking video. Saquon starts running towards his teammates, then stops, turns around, and high fives this Iowa fan.

"Hey, thanks, man," he says. "You made it fun."

I asked him about it after the game. "Yeah," he said, "the guy was talking trash the whole game, but it was in a good, friendly way and I thrive off that."

After one Ohio State game, people stormed the field, and these Buckeye fans wanted to get a photo with Saquon. I'm standing there watching and I hear, "Hey, Saquon, can I get a picture?"

I mean, the stuff he was able to do.

He became the face of the program. And it totally helped that he was a Pennsylvania guy. After he declared for the draft, there was this parade in his hometown. Saquon Barkley Day. They had a parade for him before he even got drafted.

What you see is what you get with him—and that was very much true when he was eighteen.

JAMES FRANKLIN: That's probably the thing our team respected the most about Saquon—how he had handled the success from day one.

Even after a second gifted athlete stepped forward to steal some of the spotlight.

MATTY FRESH: Those guys, I mean, they're one and two in my heart. They mean so much to this place. At that time, Barkley and McSorley *were* Penn State. Like Jordan and Pippen in Chicago.

RICK MCSORLEY: I don't know where Trace picked up the pocket awareness or the rapid decision-making. The confidence to trust your eyes and rip it. But even as a young high school player, he just had this suddenness about getting rid of the ball, the football IQ to live to play another down. *Hey, if I can't get a couple yards, I'm going to throw the ball away. I'm not gonna lose yards.*

He has all that stuff. What he doesn't have is the genetics from a height background.

I'm five-ten on a good day. My wife is five-five. We didn't help him in that way. But other than that, he's pretty gifted, well put together.

BILLY FESSLER: He just made great decisions all year long and put us in a position to be successful.

RICK MCSORLEY: I mean, Trace had this belief that every season ended in a championship game. That had literally happened to him throughout his high school career, so he thought that's what would happen in college.

BILLY FESSLER: That's the confidence he had, you know, the swagger he played with. It was, *Hey, I'm going to go out there and let this thing fly. Play with a shit-ton of confidence,* excuse my language. *Let it all loose and play without fear.*

RYAN BATES, OFFENSIVE LINEMAN, 2015–18: Coach talked all the time about having that next-play mentality, and Trace did that perfectly. He might mess up on the previous play, but he didn't let that affect him. He moved on to the next play. Lived in the present.

JAMES FRANKLIN: That's how he was as a teammate, how he supported the guys. It's how he was when they made mistakes, how he was when they made big plays. He always gave credit to the O-line, the receivers, and the running backs. The guy is a model in terms of how you conduct yourself at the most critical position in sports.

MATTY FRESH: You never saw the negative, right? He'd get nailed. I mean, how many hits did Trace McSorley take? He was running around like crazy his whole career. And he never complained to his offensive line about a block missed. It was just, *Let's move on to the next play.*

Same with Barkley. *Let's pop up and move on.* Even today. When Tiki Barber came out and said Saquon Barkley was the wrong pick for the New York Giants, Saquon handled it so well. He said, "You know, I respect Tiki Barber, I love Tiki Barber, but I don't comment on things former players say. I have to do my job."

Are you kidding me? What other player in the league would have said that about someone who called them out?

It just shows you how effectively Barkley and McSorley led that locker room. They were like, *Don't let them get to you, just move on. We'll celebrate when it's our time.*

FORTY-ONE

READY OR NOT

WHEN THE 2016 season began, the players were brimming with confidence. For the first time in years, they had a roster laden with talent, the manpower to compete not only in games but also on the practice field, where heated position battles tempered each athlete with a warrior-like mindset. They had an offense flush with playmakers and a coordinator masterful at deploying them, getting the ball in just the right hands for a quick seven points. And they had unwavering faith in their close-knit community, a bedrock belief in each teammate's ability to step forward and make a catch, a block, or a sack—whatever the team needed.

What they did not have was proof of their progress, the evidence to show they were truly capable of tangling with the nation's top teams. To be honest, they still had some growing to do. That's just the nature of being a college student. You absorb the lectures, try to ingest the salient details, and when the time comes, do your level best to apply those lessons to real life.

As a college football player, however, there's precious little room for error. Even in the best of years, you find yourself facing unexpected challenges with an audience of millions watching to see how you fare. To make matters worse, the 2016 schedule was distinctly unforgiving, pitting the Nittany Lions against in-state rival Pittsburgh in week two and conference rival Michigan, ranked fourth in the nation by the Associated Press, in week four.

Despite all the signs of promise, the players had a few more tough lessons to complete before they advanced.

DAESEAN HAMILTON: We were excited when we installed the new offense. We didn't know exactly what it was going to be like in Big Ten play, but we knew we could make plays against our defense, and it was one of the better defenses in the country.

With all the weapons we had, we knew we could make something happen.

It all comes down to making it happen during the season.

KOA FARMER: It's a game of inches, man. It's crazy how often you look back and you just needed *a half-yard* or a certain tackle or the right angle on this play. So many things ride on those details.

We just had to be more attentive to things—putting your hands up when rushing the passer, throwing the ball a little deeper, so the receiver can react to it. Maybe get an interception here, a TD there. Little things like that.

DAESEAN HAMILTON: You're not going to have instant success. You've got to stay the course, come ready to work every single day. It all comes down to the individual. If you're strong-minded, you bounce back.

TRACE MCSORLEY: The chemistry we had was special. It definitely contributed to what we did on the field. How competitive we were, the work ethic we had—that was just infectious. Seeing one guy do it, you know? It pushed everyone up a level.

GARRETT SICKELS: At camp, everyone was so much closer. That had a lot to do with the strides we made.

CHRIS GODWIN: We believed in the coaches, and the coaches believed in us.

RICK MCSORLEY: And then the season started. We played Kent State and that was okay. Trace did all right there. But we lost to Pitt in a heartbreaker.

BILLY FESSLER: That one was tough.

It was close in the end. Oh, so close. But the players couldn't help but notice the missed opportunities: dropped passes, untimely penalties, an eighty-four-yard kickoff return by Panther receiver Quadree Henderson. Trace McSorley, under pressure from the start, fumbled four times.

The sloppy play was reflected on the scoreboard.

"The Nittany Lions appeared to be coming apart late in the second quarter," wrote David Jones. "They weren't merely trailing 28–7. They were being fooled and blown off the ball and getting whipped at scrimmage on both sides [of the line]."

But they didn't give in. They scored eighteen points in the fourth quarter to make it a thriller. With just over a minute to go, trailing 42–39, they were closing in on the red zone, driving for the win.

BOB FLOUNDERS: Penn State was down three points, at the Pitt thirty-one, on a second-and-nine call. James Franklin said afterwards that somebody ran the wrong route.

GREG PICKEL, PENN STATE BEAT WRITER, HARRISBURG *PATRIOT-NEWS*: I think Irv Charles was supposed to run to the corner, towards the back pylon. Instead, he ran more of a center route, right on top of the safeties. He ran a defender right to where the ball was supposed to land for Mike Gesicki.

TRACE MCSORLEY: I saw Mike, our big athletic tight end, in the end zone and tried to give him a chance to make a play. I just threw the ball too far.

It ended up in the hands of Pitt cornerback Ryan Lewis, giving him the first interception of his five-year career. No one pinned the loss on McSorley's throw, though. In the post-game press conference, a number of Penn State players stepped forward to accept the blame.

SAQUON BARKLEY: We came out a little flat all around. They punched us in the mouth first. We responded, but just had to be ready to play earlier in the game.

JAMES FRANKLIN: Pitt did a really good job with trading, shifting, and motions and we didn't handle that as well as we should. The wave of emotion in the stadium affected our communication early on.

We were going on clap cadence on offense and they were clapping on defense—the officials told us that that was legal—and that hurt us. We jumped offsides a couple times.

TRACE MCSORLEY: Yeah, we had to adjust. We changed our cadence a bit after we got to the sideline and talked to offensive line coach Matt Limegrover.

SAQUON BARKLEY: We were down at one point by twenty-one points and we kept fighting.

JAMES FRANKLIN: The fact that it was that close at the end of the game speaks volumes for us.

TRACE MCSORLEY: We moved the ball in the first few drives, had a few mistakes, but at that point the only thing that had stopped us was us. We just kept shooting ourselves in the foot.

Barkley finished the day with five touchdowns, four on the ground and one through the air. His forty-yard sprint following a short toss from McSorley trimmed Pitt's lead to 28–21.

In all, McSorley hit eight different receivers that afternoon for 332 yards.

SAQUON BARKLEY: Like Coach said after the game, it all depended on how we took the loss. We could be upset, cry about it, let it affect us the rest of the season, or we could grow from it. We could have quit, but we didn't. We just kept fighting.

RICK MCSORLEY: We beat Temple 34–27 a week later, then Michigan came in.

JACK DAVIS: That one against the Wolverines was ugly. I remember seeing Mike Gesicki walking up the tunnel as we were exiting the field, heading towards the locker room. This is quite a few years ago, so it could be revisionist history, but I recall him putting his arm around Saquon. The two of them supporting each other, trying to keep their heads up, after a demoralizing loss.

TRACE MCSORLEY: We got boat-raced. It was bad. From the start to the finish, we got run out the door.

JACK DAVIS: They had lost a bunch of games to end 2015 and now they were two-and-two to start 2016.

I remember talking to people who said, "Franklin's lost this program. These guys aren't bought into what he's selling."

From the outside looking in, it was easy to make that leap. How much was there to build on?

The Wolverines had scored touchdowns on seven of ten drives en route to a 49–10 whipping. They had dominated the Nittany Lions in every measure of the game, piling up more than five hundred yards in total offense, including a whopping 326 on the ground. They had sacked McSorley six times and, aside from one solid run and a couple of catches, they had stopped Barkley dead in his tracks.

To their credit, though, Penn State's players didn't point fingers. They didn't make excuses. They simply took it upon themselves to improve, find the things that didn't work and fix them.

RICK MCSORLEY: That was a tough one. But that's when I realized Trace could be the face of the program, seeing the way he handled himself after the loss. He said something to the effect of "This isn't Penn State football, this isn't what we came here to do. We're going to do better."

In fact, in the post-game press conference, Trace came right out and apologized to the fans.

TRACE MCSORLEY: That's not the Penn State we want to be. Not the Penn State we need to be. Not the Penn State we are . . . That's not us. We don't accept that. We never will.

RICK MCSORLEY: You know, he had started out two-and-two as a high school freshman and that team won the state championship. In 2016, he showed that composure once again—on a much bigger stage.

TRACE MCSORLEY: Everyone was embarrassed. We came back to the locker room and said, "We can't ever let something like that happen again." We came together and started doing these film sessions, started being super honest with each other. If we had to call someone out, we did it.

RICK MCSORLEY: People were down. Obviously, there were a lot of doubters. Brian Gaia, our center, and Trace started arranging these Monday film sessions—Mondays are usually off days for the players—just to get closer as a team. I don't know if they were doing anything real strategic about Xs and Os, but they were getting together as a team. That paid off.

CHANCE SORRELL: The loss to Michigan kind of set the tone for that year. I remember getting a lot of questions from people, hearing, "Man, we really thought this was going to be the year for Penn State." And, similar to the Temple game the year before, that one set us up, showed us we had to move forward, put our heads down and really get after it.

JOHN REID, CORNERBACK, 2015–19: Coach Franklin didn't have to say much, because we were all on the same page. We knew we needed to keep grinding, keep improving every day.

JAMES FRANKLIN: That's what it is—correcting, learning, and growing—but it's magnified with young players.

Franklin's depth chart was stacked with young talent, and due to an unprecedented run of injuries on the defense, those players were playing a bigger role than expected.

MALIK GOLDEN: In the first three games, we lost Jason Cabinda, we lost Brandon Bell, we lost Nyeem Wartman-White. We were down to like no linebackers.

I was about to play linebacker.

JAMES FRANKLIN: In my twenty-two years of coaching, I'd never been part of a team that lost all three of its starting linebackers.

MALIK GOLDEN: The way Coach Pry, our defensive coordinator, handled stuff, what he put in behind the scenes, was amazing.

We had guys who were very talented, they were just young. So we'd make things simple, just fly around. We were getting our asses handed to us against Pitt and at halftime—I don't know why he did this, I don't know if he even remembers it—but he was like, "What do we need to do?"

I said, "Make things simple. Make it four plays and let's go out there and bust their asses."

We ended up coming back. Lost by just three points. That was a stepping-stone.

JASON CABINDA: As we came off the 49–10 loss to Michigan, I remember being with Marcus Allen, watching the film and thinking, *This will not be us again, this will never happen again.*

KOA FARMER: You have to have team chemistry to win games. Have to work towards a common goal. Everyone has to buy in. And we got to a certain point that season where we just said, *Look, we're way too good to be doing this stuff.*

We started working after practice, before practice, watching more film as a team.

Guys who didn't necessarily speak up, spoke up. You could just tell that we cared a lot more.

I'm not saying we didn't care before, but we had to be more proactive with each other.

JASON CABINDA: When you're playing football, you try to drown out the noise, whether it's positive or negative. And we did a good job with that, especially on that 2016 team. We were all about recognizing, at the end of the day, that none of those people saying shit are in this building. None of them are witnessing the work. None of them know.

But *we* know.

JAMES FRANKLIN: Everybody says they want to be successful. Very few people are willing to do the things necessary to be successful.

It's not one moment. It's making the right decision day after day after day.

VON WALKER: When you talk about how we got to a Big Ten Championship, it was a lot of guys with the same goal in mind, working as hard as they could. That sounds like what every team does. But that's not always the case.

That was the first time in my life I was part of a team that was not only close off the field, but also knew how to connect the dots on the field—just make things happen.

FORTY-TWO

MINNESOTA

THE FALLOUT FROM the 49–10 loss to Michigan hung heavy in the air for days, raising deep doubts in the fan base. Hour after hour, members of the media picked through the debris: the stark gap in the quality of the talent at the two programs, Penn State's failure to respond in any meaningful way to the Wolverine onslaught, James Franklin's 0–7 record against ranked teams. Columnists and talk show hosts questioned the coach's preparedness, his clock management skills, his ability to lock down the premier in-state talent, as he had promised to do in his very first press conference.

The growing unease prompted athletic director Sandy Barbour to give the guy a vote of confidence at a midweek banquet in Altoona, assuring a reporter from the local paper that Franklin was not on the hot seat.

The discord was apparent when the team suited up to play 3–0 Minnesota the following Saturday. In many ways, the game was a microcosm of the whole season, a stunning response to everything the players had been through since the Sandusky scandal had engulfed them. They started slow, fell behind, then backs to the wall summoned the means to silence the doubters.

Only this time around, they themselves felt transformed, too. Everything changed in the flash of a single play, one of just three catches redshirt freshman Irv Charles would make in his Penn State career.

RICK MCSORLEY: The game started out ugly. It was a rainy, misty, kind of day. We moved the ball okay in the first half; we just didn't score.

TRACE MCSORLEY: At halftime, we were down 13–3. Running off the field, we were getting booed—*in our own stadium.* We got into the locker room and we were like, "Did that really just happen? Did we just get booed off our own field?"

MATTY FRESH: You wouldn't believe how loud the Fire Franklin chants were.

GRANT HALEY: There were people in the stands with body paint saying Fire Franklin.

ADAM BRENEMAN: The heat was as high as it's ever been. There were rumors that if Penn State lost to Minnesota, James Franklin was going to get fired.

TOM PANCOAST: A lot of people were talking about Franklin losing his job. We were two-and-two. We'd just gotten blown out by Michigan. We hadn't had a good year since he had arrived.

MALIK GOLDEN: We were hearing things whenever we walked off-campus. It was like, If we don't win this Minnesota game, James Franklin's going to get fired. I remember having conversations like that. Like, Damn, who's going to be the coach? Pry? Moorhead? What's about to happen?

Two ho-hum quarters into the game, the question lingered in the air. Penn State's bottled-up offense had produced all of three points and the injury-riddled defense, under first-year coordinator Brent Pry, was in no position to keep things close.

The Gophers had a savvy fifth-year quarterback, two talented running backs, and a receiver who had already logged close to sixty yards in catches drawing a key pass interference penalty on the game's lone touchdown drive.

Wary of Saquon Barkley, Minnesota's defenders were crowding the line of scrimmage, daring the Lions to beat them deep with a pass. But Franklin's squad, unable to adjust, had yet to convert on third down.

RICK MCSORLEY: Trace went into halftime thinking, *There's a chance we need to change up at quarterback.* He didn't know how many series he was going to get in the second half—if Tommy Stevens would come on in relief, to see if he could create something.

And then Irv caught that pass.

Trace stepped up in the pocket, Irv Charles caught that pass, and it was game on.

MALIK GOLDEN: That's all you need in football—one play. It was that one play.

GRANT HALEY: At halftime, team leaders had stepped up and said, "We're fighting for each other, everyone in this locker room. Nobody else matters."

People outside were questioning what was going on. The only people we could count on were each other.

JOE MOORHEAD: We were moving the ball. We just weren't able to turn the yards into points.

TRACE MCSORLEY: We went out for the second half with the mentality that we were gonna win this game. And then we had that big play on third down.

Irv Charles was running down the middle of the field, not really looking back, and I threw the ball. And, as I threw it, I was like, *Shit, he's not looking. He's not gonna see it.*

And then, he kind of hears the crowd erupt. His head turns back and the ball hits him in the chest.

He catches it, throws off the defender, and sprints for a touchdown.

That play turned us around. We started hitting a groove.

Just like that, the tenor of the season changed.

RICK MCSORLEY: The defense came out big in that next series, Trace hit a post, a low post, to Chris Godwin. We scored another touchdown. From that point on, the light was on.

I don't think it was a coaching change. It was a change in the kids.

Hey, give me the ball, we're going to score.

Hand the ball to Saquon, he's going all the way.

Trace hit the go route, hit the skinny post, do something.

Throw it downfield—if they want to play close to the line of scrimmage, we'll show them.

The dynamic changed.

TOM PANCOAST: That was the true turning point of our season. If we lose that game, the program goes in a different direction.

Instead, Trace McSorley, the quarterback overlooked by so many programs in and around his home state of Virginia, stepped forward to lift the team from its inertia. What he lacked in height, he made up for with heart, vision, his feet, and his masterful improvisation.

FRANK BODANI, PENN STATE BEAT WRITER, *YORK DAILY RECORD*: Everything turns around in the third quarter. Trace McSorley, Penn State's sophomore quarterback, starts making plays, using his legs to get free, finding his receivers downfield. One big play to Irv Charles. Second big play to Chris Godwin. Third big play to Mike Gesicki. All of a sudden the stadium's rocking. New ballgame.

DAVID JONES: The first half was as flat as could be and the second half was electric.

I can't remember anything like it, ever.

TRACE MCSORLEY: We'd seen it in spots. In big games, we'd go down early, then have a good second half, firing on all cylinders. So we knew it was in us as a team. We could score points in rapid chunks. We had the talent on defense to wreak havoc. But, like I said, we could never put it together.

We knew we had a chance to be really good. It was just a matter of putting it all together.

JOE MOORHEAD: We were trying to figure out our identity, who we were on offense. And if you look at Trace's body of work, his time at Penn State, the guy just makes plays, whether by design or improvisation.

When you add the element of quarterback run to your repertoire, it forces the defense to defend every blade of grass. You pick up an edge in the run game. It helps the offensive line, the tailbacks, and the pass game, too.

JAMES FRANKLIN: Trace did a great job stepping up in the pocket. A few times when he was waiting to throw, they were close to getting strip sacks, but he avoided that. He can run, but he's not one of those guys that just takes off. He keeps his eyes downfield.

TRACE MCSORLEY: So, yeah, we were getting booed. There were, you know, Fire Franklin chants inside the stadium. And, as a team, we were like, Damn, if we don't win this, our coach will get fired. That was the situation.

Both teams opened the second half with unimpressive drives. And then, five minutes into the third quarter, on a third-and-ten from the Penn State twenty, bodies flying all around him, McSorley slipped away from the pass rush, soft-shoed right up to the line of scrimmage, and in the split second before he crossed the plane zipped a thirty-yard dart to Irv Charles. The young receiver caught the ball at midfield, shook off a would-be tackler, and sprinted fifty yards to the end zone.

The fans were on their feet, and the offense had jettisoned its demons.

On the first play of the next drive, McSorley faked a handoff to Barkley and launched a thirty-six-yard strike to Chris Godwin. That one led to a Tyler Davis field goal.

Penn State 13, Minnesota 13.

One drive later, McSorley stepped up in the pocket and launched a fifty-three-yard strike to a wide-open Mike Gesicki, who rumbled to the Minnesota six-yard line. The resourceful quarterback ran the ball into the end zone from there.

In the span of fourteen plays, he put seventeen points on the board, guiding Penn State to a 20–13 lead. It wasn't just McSorley, though. His teammates had found their mojo, too.

MARK BRENNAN: The receivers had something to prove: They didn't play well at all against Michigan. But they bounced back. I mean, you had an eighty-yard catch, a fifty-three-yard catch, a thirty-six-yard catch. People looked at Barkley and said he was bottled up. Well, yeah, there was a reason he was bottled up, but Penn State was exploiting that and getting those long gains.

In between, the Lions' makeshift defense held the Gophers in check. Junior safety Marcus Allen would finish the day with a career-high twenty-two tackles.

MANNY BOWEN: He was all over the place. Every time his name was called, he contributed.

GRANT HALEY: He played a tremendous game.

MARCUS ALLEN: We stepped up in the second half. We were wrapping up Minnesota's runners and receivers but weren't really bringing that umph in our tackles. Coach was telling us that during halftime and we put that into our game.

KOA FARMER: We just had to dig deep. We were pretty banged up on defense. I think Manny Bowen was playing Mike linebacker, I was playing Will, and true freshman Cam Brown was playing Sam. I don't remember exactly, but we were all basically playing positions we had never played before. It was like, *That stuff doesn't matter, man. We just have to win the game.*

JAMES FRANKLIN: We were on, I think, our sixth middle linebacker. We'd lost another Mike that day, then we'd lost his backup. Manny Bowen had never played Mike linebacker at Penn State, and he played Mike at the end of that game.

BRENT PRY: Brandon Smith and Jake Cooper go down with injuries, and Manny Bowen, who had never played a snap of Mike in his life, has to line up at the end of regulation and play Mike linebacker. He got a quick lesson on the sideline in three of the calls you have to make at Mike and went out there and played well.

JASON CABINDA: When you move to the middle, there's a lot more to see, a lot more you have to feel. You have to be able to see the formation fully. Be able to make not just verbal calls, but also the hand gestures that make sure everybody is on the same page.

Go to the D-line, get them set. Then check with the secondary. You have to be very vocal. It takes a lot of assertiveness.

TOM PANCOAST: Pretty much every scholarship linebacker we had that year got hurt at some point. If one more had gone down against Minnesota, we would've had to send a freshman walk-on in to play Mike linebacker, if I remember correctly.

MANNY BOWEN: Earlier in the week, guys had asked me what we were going to do about the lack of depth at linebacker, and I said if I have to learn Mike, I'm going to learn Mike, and that's what happened. Everyone had to step up and take advantage of the situation. We went out there and played fast and aggressive.

KOA FARMER: We were such a close-knit group. From walk-on to non-walk-on, we had something special in that locker room. We'd lift each other up. Tell each other what we had to do to win this game. And, when that second-half-team mentality caught fire, it was preached in the locker room. Like, *We got to finish this game, man. We got to finish, finish, finish. Let's finish this game.*

BRENT PRY: We didn't play great, but we played well enough in spots to take away the things we needed to take away.

BOB FLOUNDERS: Minnesota had two hundred-yard rushers, a hundred-yard receiver, and somehow lost.

RODNEY SMITH, RUNNING BACK, MINNESOTA: I don't think we scored in the third quarter. They kept us out of the end zone. That's the quarter we lost. We couldn't get points on the board.

MITCH LEIDNER, QUARTERBACK, MINNESOTA: We struggled to get the offense rolling, and they made some plays on offense. I don't know, it just wasn't all there for us.

Early in the fourth quarter, the Gophers tied the score at twenty. And then they launched a nine-play drive to the Penn State twelve-yard line, but senior sub Jordan Smith, filling in for injured cornerback Christian Campbell, intercepted a Leidner pass in the end zone to end the threat.

With just under five minutes to go, the Gophers marched fifty-eight yards in eleven plays to kick a field goal, hoping to escape with a 23–20 win. That left less than a minute for McSorley's reply.

TRACE MCSORLEY: It wasn't looking good. We were down on our own twenty-five-yard line. No timeouts. The first two plays didn't go well and, you know, we had a third down where Chris Godwin made a zig-zaggy catch over the middle to get the ball rolling.

JAMES FRANKLIN: Trace kept his cool. Pressured, throwing off his back foot, he lays it out where Chris could go make a play for him.

CHRIS GODWIN: I think it was designed to go to me. The release on my route was delayed, and Trace realized that. The offensive line gave him enough time to throw the ball up in the air, which allowed me to go make that catch.

McSorley completed a second pass to DeAndre Thompkins to put the ball on the Minnesota forty-eight with thirty-five seconds left. That's when the young quarterback demonstrated what he could do with his feet, tucking the ball and racing into the void that had opened before him.

As he crossed the forty-yard line, the thirty-five, the thirty, and the twenty-five, the seconds ticked away. He ran out of bounds at the twenty-two.

AUDREY SNYDER: The play I always point to in that Minnesota game is the long McSorley scramble to the far sideline. That gets them into field goal range.

You see that and you're like the team's going to come back. They're going to win this game.

RYAN BATES: We were in the two-minute drill and the defensive linemen were twisting, opening a huge hole in the front. Trace saw his opportunity and took it for twenty-five yards.

TRACE MCSORLEY: As I was going through the reads, I saw green grass and I just took off. I was angling towards the sideline, trying to get as much yardage as I could.

JAMES FRANKLIN: I said, "Look, we're going to take one shot at the end zone. Don't do anything that's going to take points off the board and don't take a sack."

We didn't have a timeout.

TYLER DAVIS: I was kicking into the net, making sure I was ready for the field goal attempt, hitting the ball clean.

TRACE MCSORLEY: Fifteen seconds left. We had enough time for one shot at the end zone and we missed on it. And then, Tyler came out.

It was a long field goal, not one of those gimmes. We'd seen him make it before, but it wasn't an easy kick by any stretch. So, yeah, he came out and hit that long field goal to send it to overtime.

For the record, it was Davis's record-setting seventeenth field goal in a row, a true measure of his consistency since edging ahead of Joe Julius in a heated race for the starting role in 2015.

TYLER DAVIS: I didn't even know I was close to the record until Sam Ficken texted me a day earlier. He was like, "Yo, don't even think about breaking my record."

We're good friends, so it was funny. He texted me after the game, too.

MIKE GESICKI: Trace McSorley gets us into field goal range and then Tyler Davis ties the game to send us into overtime.

The Gophers got the ball first, lining up twenty-five yards from the goal line. They tried to run on first down but squeaked out just one yard. They tried to pass on second down, and Mitch Leidner was sacked for a loss. Under heavy pressure, he skipped the next pass off the turf, so Minnesota kicked a field goal to go up by three.

That put the ball back in McSorley's hands—or, more precisely, Saquon Barkley's hands. The running back had been stonewalled all game long, but true to form he waited patiently for his moment in the spotlight. McSorley would finish the day as the team's leading rusher. Barkley didn't mind one bit.

TRACE MCSORLEY: We won it on that first play in overtime. Handed the ball to Saquon and, you know, we always said two-six does two-six things. I mean, he made like four or five guys miss.

KOA FARMER: Two-six came to the rescue and won the game for us.

SAQUON BARKLEY: When we called the play, I looked at the defensive front and thought, *If you get the chance, you've got to make it happen. This is what you live for.* And when I tell you the O-line picked up the run blitz so well, got so much movement, the defense parted like the Red Sea. And when I got to the safety, running to the left, I was like, *I've got to make him miss.*

RYAN BATES: We ran an inside zone and I got up to the linebacker and cut him off, so Saquon cut off me and scored the touchdown.

FRANK BODANI: Saquon Barkley saves the day.

MATTY FRESH: He just electrifies the place and, from there, it was *on.* If I look back at my life, I don't know that I could come up with another momentum shift that size. I mean, you felt it.

At halftime, everybody's down in the dumps. Everyone wants Franklin fired. There's no faith. And then, the players come out and win that game.

You have that big eighty-yard touchdown by Irvin Charles and the team never turned back. It was just incredible.

JACK DAVIS: I was always terrified I was gonna draw an excessive celebration penalty on the team if I joined in the festivities as the Lion, but that time I figured the game was over. I remember running into the scrum with all the linemen. I couldn't see anything, because I'm about five-foot-seven, jumping in there with a bunch of offensive linemen and Saquon Barkley. But that was incredible.

Like, we still had something to play for. We could still make the season mean something.

AUDREY SNYDER: I remember getting a video on the field at the end of the game. I just happened to catch Moorhead and Barkley together. Barkley goes up to Moorhead and he says something like, "Way to go, coach. Thanks for believing in me."

TRACE MCSORLEY: Saquon might not have put up big numbers in regulation, but they were keying on him so hard, sending two, three guys to him. I said, "Keep plugging, just keep plugging, you're going to get one." And, at the end, he was able to pop through. When you get him one-on-one with a safety, good things usually happen.

AUDREY SNYDER: From that moment forward, the team caught lightning in a bottle. Off they went.

MIKE GESICKI: You don't try to put that feeling into words. You watch the celebration. That speaks volumes for what that win meant to everyone in the program. Coaches, training staff, players, starters, backups, red-shirts—it didn't matter. That was a team celebration, a team win.

BRANDON BELL: The leadership kicked in. The young players—stars like Saquon and Trace—kicked in when we needed it. Things just started to align.

After that, we just went to town, man. We were not going to be stopped.

FORTY-THREE

REDEMPTION

SOME MOMENTS IN *sports transcend all others. You don't see them coming, but once you watch them unfold, you feel forever changed, moved beyond the mortal by the majesty of a mind-blowing touchdown catch or a do-or-die home run. For Penn State people, the 2016 Ohio State game provided just such a moment, a special teams play that will linger in memory for decades.*

It binds two young players, both defensive backs, but involves subtle contributions from a host of others. Together, in a span of eleven seconds, they restored Penn State's program to prominence, releasing it from the manacles of the Sandusky scandal with a hard-fought victory against the nation's number-two team.

Fittingly, it all occurred at Beaver Stadium, to the thrill of a prime-time White Out crowd.

MALIK GOLDEN: That house was rockin', man. I get goosebumps just thinking about it.

JASON CABINDA: It was absolutely insane, one of those moments when you're like, This is exactly why I came here.

TRACE MCSORLEY: You see everyone out there dressed in white.

SAEED BLACKNALL: Nothing but white. And everybody's going crazy.

TRACE MCSORLEY: It's the best sight in college football.

To this day, I can't think of anything better than running out of the tunnel into a White Out.

GREGG GARRITY: That was the first time we used fireworks in Beaver Stadium, too. We ran out of the tunnel and, we're used to the fans going ballistic, but those fireworks go off, and, you know, I'm getting goosebumps now just thinking about it.

We had a lot going for us that game.

We got the White Out.

We got the number-two team in the nation on the other side of the field.

TRACE MCSORLEY: The last time we'd played one of the top teams in the country, we got boat-raced in our store. So, it was like a redemption game for us. We needed to go out and show the nation we were for real.

JAMES FRANKLIN: We prepared all week long to go out and play confident.

JASON CABINDA: I still remember how crisp practice was that week, how locked in everybody was.

TRACE MCSORLEY: I had one of my worst practices ever.

I don't know what it was, but I was just . . . I made the wrong reads, I was missing throws.

But we get into that game and it just had a different feeling. I remember on the bus ride over to the stadium, I felt like something special was about to happen.

I didn't know what. I just had that feeling.

After the overtime win against Minnesota, the Nittany Lions had taken another step forward on offense, stretching a slim three-point lead against Maryland into an emphatic 38–14 win. They did it with explosive plays:

a forty-five-yard bolt by Saquon Barkley, a seventy-yard pass to DeAndre Thompkins, and a twenty-five-yard run by true freshman Miles Sanders.

So here they were—fresh off a bye-week—eager to prove themselves against one of the nation's premier programs, a conference rival that had beaten them in four straight tries.

Penn State won the coin toss and elected to receive the ball first.

TRACE MCSORLEY: Coach Franklin wanted to be aggressive, try to get a drive going. Get the ball in Saquon's hands early. Let him get the ball rolling.

The drive started on the twenty-five-yard line. On the first play, McSorley faked a handoff to Barkley and ran for five yards. On the next play, he faked the handoff, added a quick pump-fake, and tucked the ball in Barkley's grip. The back zipped through the line and into the secondary, rumbling to midfield. Next came a Barkley run for no gain. And then McSorley faked another handoff and hit a wide-open Mike Gesicki.

In four plays, the Lions had reached the Ohio State twenty-five-yard line.

But they stalled in the red zone and the sure-footed Tyler Davis trotted out to attempt a thirty-nine-yard field goal. At that point in the season, he had made eighteen consecutive kicks without a miss—the most successful start of any kicker in Penn State history.

This next one left his right foot on a low trajectory and, with a good push at the line, an Ohio State defender reached up and got a hand on the ball, spiking it to the turf.

It was a sign of things to come.

While the two teams pressed on, working to find a rhythm, the score remained deadlocked at zero. And then, with thirty-eight seconds to go in the quarter, an Ohio State punt dropped from the misty nighttime sky through the outstretched hands of sophomore John Reid, giving the Buckeyes possession at the Penn State thirty-eight. The miscue led to a Buckeye field goal.

And yet, the early score left the Lions feeling oddly self-assured. In shades of what would become the signature play of the night, safety Marcus Allen had vaulted the Ohio State line unblocked. Just a touch more to the left and he would have met the kick head-on.

TOM PANCOAST: Our special teams coach, Charles Huff, prided himself on turning us into one of the best special teams units in the country. He placed a huge emphasis on it, hyped up that side of things, and people really embraced it.

GRANT HALEY: Marcus had run through the line pretty clean. I remember him going to Coach Huff, saying, "I can get through! I can get through!"

MARCUS ALLEN: I had jumped over the line clean. Nobody touched me.

But I missed the ball. It was a little to the left.

So I went back to the sideline to talk to Coach Huff.

"Where am I supposed to be to block the kick?"

"If they are on the right hash," he said, "they're going to try to kick it over the left guard."

I knew that opportunity was going to come again.

GREG PICKEL: Penn State had seen something on film. Marcus Allen said after the game that they knew Ohio State wanted to go over that guard, because almost every kick Tyler Durbin makes goes over that guard.

EVAN SCHWAN, DEFENSIVE END, 2012–16: We knew that, if that situation came up again, we'd be able to block the field goal.

For it to matter, though, the Lion defense would have to keep the score tight. The Buckeyes had a young receiving corps, but, with three-year starter J.T. Barrett—a favorite to win the Heisman Trophy—and running back Curtis Samuel in the backfield, the team was putting up close to fifty points a game.

The Lions' front four, meanwhile, was missing Garrett Sickels, who had rounded into a fearsome, All–Big Ten defensive end. After flying to Los Angeles during the bye-week to visit his girlfriend, he had gotten waylaid by a flight delay that made him late to a team meeting.

Franklin had suspended him for the first half.

Any concern that may have caused was offset by the return of two star linebackers.

BRANDON BELL: Jason Cabinda and I were both coming off injuries. We were supposed to play limited snaps but weren't going to be denied.

JASON CABINDA: I had missed five games with a broken thumb. Had to have surgery and it ended up getting infected. My lord, I was mad. I wanted them to just cast me up and let me play.

They're like, "This isn't something you can risk. Trust me, you don't want to live the rest of your life without a thumb."

But I wanted to play so bad.

By the time he was cleared to return, he was raring to go.

BRENT PRY: In a big game like that, your big dogs want to be out there.

They were so mature, so smart, they knew what was going on as soon as the ball was snapped.

JASON CABINDA: Brandon Bell made huge plays. He was all over the field.

BRENT PRY: Against Minnesota, against Maryland, we couldn't make certain adjustments. When a coach identified pressure, we just had to ride it out. With experienced guys back on the field, you could change a call, make an adjustment, from the sideline. That was big for us.

Bell would finish the night with eighteen tackles, Cabinda with thirteen. Each had one sack.

With their teammates, they held the Buckeyes in check for much of the half. In fact, Penn State did not surrender a touchdown until late in the second quarter, and even then a bobbled snap cost Ohio State the extra point. On the next drive, J.T. Barrett narrowly escaped an all-out blitz at midfield and scrambled for nineteen yards. A Buckeye field goal made it 12–0.

On offense, things were less promising. On the first play of the second drive, Mike Gesicki twisted an ankle trying to make a diving catch, and, with the star tight end hobbled, McSorley missed on his next nine pass attempts. That put Barkley in a tough spot, too. Aside from one small burst, he was held to a few yards here and there for five drives.

With time winding down in the half, Penn State was still struggling to move the ball.

TRACE MCSORLEY: If I remember correctly, the Buckeyes were getting the second-half kickoff. If we go into halftime down twelve and they come out and score a touchdown, it's a completely different ballgame.

JASON CABINDA: We had to get something going. A field goal or something.

CHRIS FOWLER, ESPN PLAY-BY-PLAY ANNOUNCER: A passing game that had been in a deep freeze for more than a quarter came alive on that drive.

Miles Sanders fielded the kickoff and returned the ball to the twenty-five. With sixty-four seconds to go, Trace McSorley rolled to his right and saw no one open, so he stepped out of bounds for a one-yard gain. On second down, he handed the ball to Barkley, who ducked two tackles and barely crossed the line of scrimmage. With third-and-eight looming, James Franklin made an unorthodox decision, one that caught Ohio State's staff by surprise.

RICK MCSORLEY: We called a timeout with just under a minute left. You can see it on the video. Urban Meyer saying, "They called timeout?"

He figured we'd let the clock run down and punt, not give them time to score.

My buddy in the stands was like, "What? Are they nuts?"

But it was the right call.

Before the game, Coach Franklin had said, "Look, we're gonna be aggressive, we're playing to win."

They took a chance and it worked.

TRACE MCSORLEY: The first two plays didn't get much, but then we got a first-down throw to Chris Godwin. That got the ball rolling. At that point, we knew we had to push the tempo, try to move the ball downfield. We had one timeout left. We had to get something going quickly.

McSorley tucked the ball and ran on the next play. He got dropped for a one-yard loss. With twenty-nine ticks left, Franklin used his final timeout.

On second and eleven, under heavy pressure, McSorley scrambled to the right and lofted the ball down the sideline to DaeSean Hamilton.

TRACE MCSORLEY: That was a play we had drawn up during the week. We knew they were going to try to get single blocks up front and play man-to-man down the field, so it was a double move down the middle. Great route. The hardest part was Malik Hooker. He was a ball hawk, one of the top defensive backs in the country. I had to know where he was at all times, kind of leave it outside. DaeSean did a great job adjusting to it.

The catch was good for thirty-four yards. Hamilton corralled it with two defenders at his back and stepped out of bounds at the twenty.

TRACE MCSORLEY: There were twenty-one seconds left and we had no timeouts, so we were going to get one or two shots at the end zone and then have to send the field goal team out.

On the next play, McSorley tried to hit Barkley on a wheel route to the end zone, but the Buckeyes had the play well defended and the ball fell harmlessly to the turf.
That left fifteen seconds, time for just one more crack at the end zone.
The Lions stepped to the line with Chris Godwin on the right flank, Saeed Blacknall on the left, and DaeSean Hamilton in the slot.

TRACE MCSORLEY: I knew I had one-on-one with Chris. That's the guy I was going to.

TOM PANCOAST: Mike Gesicki had sprained his ankle in the first quarter, so I ended up playing nearly the whole game at tight end. At that point, I was used to playing maybe thirty-five to forty snaps on offense a year. That night, we had sixty or seventy.

On that play, Raekwon McMillan, a linebacker who eventually got drafted in the second round, ended up in one of the gaps I had to pass-protect on. I had to keep him from blitzing.

Trace ended up throwing a perfect ball and Chris made a great catch.

TRACE MCSORLEY: It gave us life. Got us back in the game.

McSorley underthrew the ball just a touch, giving Godwin a chance to shield it from the defender. Moments before halftime, the Buckeye lead was trimmed to 12–7.

GRANT HALEY: As soon as we got into the locker room, I remember Trace and DaeSean, D. Hammy, just freaking out, screaming "We can do this!"
I don't think anybody's energy was down. We really felt confident.

SAQUON BARKLEY: A lot of people didn't believe in us, didn't give us a chance, but the whole team was just laid back. Even later, when it was 21–7, we had no change of heart. We knew we were going to win the game, no matter what.

JASON CABINDA: It's our home field. We got to take control here. So going into that second half, we knew it was three-and-out on defense, get the ball back, and our offense would score. They get hot in the second half. So, if we could get the ball back to Trace, we'd be in good shape.

TRACE MCSORLEY: Garrett Sickels was coming back in the second half, too, and he was pissed off that he didn't play. He was just sitting there at his locker, fuming. I'm like, *All right, we're going to be able to make a run at these guys.*

JASON CABINDA: Sickels comes out like a madman, a freaking madman.

MALIK GOLDEN: He was a maniac.

BROCK HUARD, COLOR COMMENTATOR, ESPN: He single-handedly took over that game.

DUSTIN HOCKENSMITH: I have never seen Garrett Sickels play like he did in that second half. Three and a half tackles for loss. Two and a half sacks. A year earlier, I think he had three sacks and five tackles for a loss the entire season.

He came out with some serious steam—to the point where Franklin was talking about suspending him for the first half of every game.

DAVID JONES: The defense dominated Ohio State at the line of scrimmage. You could see some issues on Ohio State's young offensive line. They had youth all over the field, but you didn't expect Penn State to just lay waste to right tackle Isaiah Prince, a four-star recruit. I mean, he got his lunch handed to him. Both defensive ends, Garrett Sickels and Evan Schwan, played great.

DUSTIN HOCKENSMITH: Ohio State had given up five sacks in its first six games. Penn State got six, plus eleven tackles for loss.

JASON CABINDA: Everything was set up for this magical finish. It was like a freakin' movie.

And, as with any epic sports film, the team was hit with more challenges before the finale.

Minutes into the third quarter, Ohio State running back Curtis Samuel exploded through a hole in Penn State's line and raced the length of the field for a touchdown. In a heartbeat, the lead was back to twelve points.

GARRETT SICKELS: It was a simple mistake. We came to the sidelines and Coach Pry, Coach Spencer, Coach Banks just said, "Hey, everyone take a deep breath." We knew there was going to be a big play or two in the second half and we were like, *Okay, that's out of the way. Now it's on us to make sure they don't score again.*

TRACE MCSORLEY: We were down most of the game, but it was kind of back and forth. We had spurts where we showed what we could do and then Ohio State would come right back. Curtis Samuel had that long touchdown run. We gave up a safety on a punt. There were a few moments where it seemed like it was getting out of reach for us.

NEIL RUDEL: A blocked field goal, muffed punt.

MARK BRENNAN: Safety on a bad snap.

NEIL RUDEL: That was going to be the storyline of the game.

Instead, Penn State's players found ways to hang tight, summon the grit they had honed in those lean scholarship years. That muffed punt in the third quarter is a prime example. Moments after the Samuel run, Penn State's offense was struggling to respond, leaving true freshman Blake Gillikin in a bind on fourth-and-eleven.

The young punter stepped onto the rain-swept field and settled into position at the fifteen.

MATTY FRESH: The ball was snapped over his head.

KIRK HERBSTREIT: It just sailed.

MATTY FRESH: It rolled into the end zone and one of the Ohio State players comes flying in.

I'm thinking, There's no way Blake Gillikin lands on this ball.

BLAKE GILLIKIN: When I saw it release high, my first instinct was to jump. I thought I was going to get it but didn't.

When I turned around, there were only two options—fall on it or kick it out of the end zone. In high school, I once had the same situation and kicked the ball out of the end zone, but I thought I'd heard somewhere that that isn't allowed in college.

MATTY FRESH: How many times does a punter beat a player who's got a head start on him? He's got to hightail it backwards and fall on that ball. That safety he took keeps it manageable, keeps it twenty-one to seven.

BLAKE GILLIKIN: I heard an Ohio State guy behind me—on the film, he was close—so I was just trying to get back to that ball as fast as possible to save those points. I heard him huffing and puffing.

STEVE JONES: Gillikin's an excellent athlete and his athleticism showed. To get back there and have the awareness to make that play . . . I think it's the single most underrated play of the game.

MATTY FRESH: There were a lot of bounces like that in the game. You were holding your breath the whole time.

DAVID JONES: There were two points when you're thinking, Gosh, they've got no shot. Twelve to nothing with a minute left in the first half, facing third-and-eight deep in their own territory. And twenty-one to seven, after Ohio State had scored twice around a Penn State three-and-out. In both situations, things looked hopeless.

Adding insult to injury, the Lions now had to kick the ball back to Ohio State, and the Buckeyes returned it to the forty-yard line. It was hard not to see the game slipping away.

The Buckeyes sensed it, too. J.T. Barrett was animated on the sideline, coaxing his teammates to deliver the final blow.

If Penn State's players felt anxious, they didn't show it.

On first down, redshirt freshman defensive end Shareef Miller streaked past Buckeye tight end A.J. Alexander and blew up the handoff to Mike Weber. J.T. Barrett answered with a short pass and a scramble for a first down. He ran on the next play, too. And then, on second-and-five, Garrett Sickels fought through a block for a blindside sack. The Buckeyes were soon lined up for a fourth-down play on the Penn State thirty-eight, but an illegal procedure penalty set them back. They punted instead, pinning the Lions deep.

Sickels halted the Buckeyes next drive with a sack, too.

JASON CABINDA: At this point in the game, momentum is shifting. We know you're ranked number two, but we're right here. We started making plays and it was like, "All right, we got 'em. Right where we want 'em. It's Beaver Stadium, baby!"

GARRETT SICKELS: Our defense was rolling. That O-line had only given up like five sacks to that point and we were able to get J.T. Barrett on the ground.

URBAN MEYER: Their D-line was controlling the line of scrimmage.

TRACE MCSORLEY: I don't want to say it was do-or-die time, but we knew we were down fourteen going into the fourth quarter. We had to make something happen.

DAVID JONES: Joe Moorhead called a great game, even considering that a lot of the stuff he did didn't work. I love the fact that he kept taking deep shots. I thought the early deep shots were smart. Doesn't matter if they don't hit. You have to present that threat, particularly to a young defense that fast and that good. You've got to keep them thinking, keep them moving in different directions, so you can misdirect them. And that bore fruit later in the game.

Penn State opened the fourth quarter on its own ten-yard line. With the pocket collapsing around him, McSorley rushed forward and fired a pass to a wide-open Gesicki, who limped back to the line of scrimmage. Barkley broke free on the next play, darting right, finding a hole, and streaking across midfield to the thirty-seven. And then, Saeed Blacknall got open deep and caught a pass at the two.

Just like that, the Lions were in scoring position.

TRACE MCSORLEY: As I came back through the progression, the corner was leaning way inside and Saeed was kind of alone on the sideline, so I just put the ball to the outside. Saeed is a big dude, really good at using his body to shield the defender from it. I put the ball where only he could get it.

On the next snap, Gesicki slipped behind the coverage and stood wide open in the end zone. McSorley saw him and launched the ball. Wide right.

Bum ankle or not, the tight end had no chance to make the play.

RICK MCSORLEY: My gut sank when Trace missed Gesicki.

TRACE MCSORLEY: It was so wide open. I couldn't believe I had missed it.

To this day, my dad still gives me crap for that throw.

"Dude, what were you throwing to? He was *wide* open."

On the next play, Trace rolled to his right, eyeing Gesicki, then tucked the ball and made a beeline for the pylon.

TRACE MCSORLEY: It was that same kind of play. I'm rolling out, looking for Mike, but once I got that edge, I had my sights on the corner. When it got a little tight, I tried to dive down into the sliver of space that I saw.

KIRK HERBSTREIT: Ohio State knew he was going to keep it, and it was a footrace.

CHRIS FOWLER: McSorley makes up for the misfire by taking it in himself.

KIRK HERBSTREIT: Five plays, ninety yards for the touchdown.

STEVE JONES: At this point, the defense is playing really well. I'm thinking if they get a three-and-out, Penn State could tie the game. Get another three-and-out and they can win.

TRACE MCSORLEY: Now the fans really get into the game and we build off that energy.

GARRETT SICKELS: No matter who was in, we were making plays on offense, defense, special teams.

GREGG GARRITY: The momentum *really* started to turn when Cam Brown, a freshman, blocked the punt.

MARK BRENNAN: Here's a guy they were going to redshirt. He ends up working his way into the starting lineup when the linebackers are hurt. Now Bell and Cabinda come back and all of a sudden you have this guy on special teams who's played a lot of football.

JAMES FRANKLIN: It also helps that he's six-five.

The defense had come up big on the ensuing drive, pressuring the Buckeyes into a botched handoff, then a timeout on third-and-ten to talk things over. The Lions ultimately held them to three yards on three plays to force a punt. And then the freshman Cam Brown added more pressure, storming through the line and getting a hand on the kick.

JASON CABINDA: Cam's a big, long guy and he was able to get the arms stretched out.

GREGG GARRITY: I was in the zone, getting ready to receive the punt, and I hear a double thump.

I didn't see the ball get blocked, but I heard it.

JAMES FRANKLIN: I don't even know what happened. I just heard the thud.

JASON CABINDA: The ball lands at the line of scrimmage. A huge flip in field position. That's when the Ohio State players started looking at themselves like, *We got a problem.*

The Penn State sideline is fired up and the crowd is playing into it like crazy. You can't hear anything.

The final twelve minutes were a test of wills. First the Buckeye defense had to step up and preserve the seven-point lead. After a short pass from McSorley to Gesicki, a horse-collar tackle on Barkley gave Penn State the ball first and goal at the ten, but three big stops later Tyler Davis returned to the field to kick a thirty-four-yard field goal. It was now a four-point game.

And then, J.T. Barrett led the Buckeyes on their best drive of the half. With a mix of runs and passes, he moved the team downfield, eating up clock. With 5:30 to go, Ohio State had a first down on the Penn State thirty-one. Barrett's next pass fell incomplete. The one after that, to Samuel, netted three yards. On third down, with the coaching staff frantically trying to change the play call from the sidelines, he floated a pass down the middle of the field. It hit Penn State defensive back John Reid in the hands, but he failed to make an over-the-shoulder catch.

EVAN SCHWAN: If we get a turnover, our offense is playing well enough to go down the field and score. So huge third-and-seven there and John Reid almost intercepts that ball.

Thank god he didn't, because that set up the field goal block.

GRANT HALEY: John should have had the pick, but I guess God had other plans.

JASON CABINDA: J.T. Barrett was hesitating to go to the sideline after that, so we thought they might be scheming, trying to catch us sleeping. At this point in the game, they might go for it.

But the kicker finally comes in. It's like, Yeah, let me get the field goal unit out there.

MALIK GOLDEN: We had an amazing coaching staff that year. We were always prepared, especially on special teams. Huff was a monster on special teams.

We were clicking, just meshed really well, and I think we played very good complementary football. Ha, now I'm speaking like a damn analyst. But during the big moments that season somebody made a play and that's what it comes down to in football.

TOM PANCOAST: We spent a lot of time emphasizing special teams play. We had a fifteen-minute special teams meeting every day, devoted multiple periods in practice to special teams work.

KOA FARMER: We practiced that block countless times that week, Marcus stepping up and hitting that ball down. We basically had a double team to the left of the long snapper. Had to get some push there, so Marcus could sneak a bit closer to the football. If he's an inch backwards, he's not blocking the kick.

GRANT HALEY: That was just a great design by Coach Huff.

SAM WILLIAMS, SPECIAL TEAMS ASSISTANT: That was the exact situation we were looking for.

From snap to kick, it's 1.5 seconds. There's three and a half rotations from the snapper to the holder. You can't see that with the naked eye, right? You've got to slow it down. We coached the hell out of 1.5 seconds, man.

There was a serious weakness on the O-line for Ohio State. Urban was throwing a lot of the redshirts on the O-line and he would put them on the field goal team. And going into that game, there were red flags at that position. We found that weakness.

JAMES FRANKLIN: You play hard six seconds at a time. When opportunity comes, you take advantage of it.

EVAN SCHWAN: As you can see, they're on that same right hash as earlier in the game. So right now, me, Parker Cothren, Grant, and Marcus are all together saying, "Hey man, we got this. We got to do it."

MALIK GOLDEN: The tackles got a good push, the guys on the edge bent the corner well, Grant picked a good angle in case the ball did bounce. Everyone played a role.

JAMES FRANKLIN: Marcus Allen timed his leap perfectly, jumping at just the right moment to get a hand on the kick and deflect it to Grant Haley.

SAM WILLIAMS: When the ball is snapped, Marcus doesn't start running until the holder catches it. It's all about timing. And you can't just jump. If you're not in the flight of the ball, you can't intersect the trajectory. So, you've got to know the angle of flight, where it will meet your hands.

GRANT HALEY: It just hit his hand and bounced. I don't know how many times it bounced. Two times? And then it popped right up into my hands.

TRACE MCSORLEY: Sometimes, with special things, you've got to get a bit lucky. You could roll a football a million times and it won't roll perfectly once. That time, it just happened to bounce right into Grant's arms.

JAMES FRANKLIN: Just like that, Grant was off to the races, sprinting toward the Buckeyes' end zone. And that's when the noise in Beaver Stadium became truly deafening.

JASON CABINDA: I'm watching this kicker running Grant down and I'm like, How the hell is this kicker keeping up with Grant. But that kicker had some speed on him.

JAMES FRANKLIN: My only thought was: *Holy hell, Ohio State's holder and kicker are hauling ass!*

Like I have no idea where Urban Meyer found those kids, but they were like the two fastest specialists on the planet.

GRANT HALEY: Every time I watch it, it's like, *Don't get caught by the kicker.* That's what goes through my head—*Please, don't get caught by the kicker.*

TRACE MCSORLEY: On the sideline watching, it felt like time stood still.

CHRIS GODWIN: I'm watching Grant run and I'm like, *Ain't no way he's about to score.*

JASON CABINDA: When we see Grant fall into the end zone, the crowd just e-rupted.

BRENDAN MAHON: You could feel it throughout your whole body. The whole stadium kind of just lifted up. You really can't describe the feeling, but that is why you come to Penn State, for nights like that.

VON WALKER: It wasn't just the players. You had literally every single Penn State fan in the world clinging to those opportunities, right? Like, you have a deep-rooted passion for Penn State football not only in the state of PA, but all over the country. And I don't really know how to explain it, but those moments just mean everything to everyone. When they happen, you have a team of 107,000 inside the stadium, especially during a White Out.

JACK DAVIS: You never talk when you're in the Lion suit. But the stadium was so loud during Haley's runback that I was screaming. Only time I ever made any noise in there.

ADAM BRENEMAN: For decades and decades, people will remember that as one of the greatest plays in Penn State history—a program with a lot of history.

GRANT HALEY: I'm sure Penn State people everywhere can say, Oh, this is where I was when I saw the blocked kick.

MATTY FRESH: The next four minutes were the longest of my life. After they blocked the field goal and returned it for a touchdown. Everyone's going crazy. Those of us who had been around the program our whole lives were speechless. Like, We can't believe what we just saw. We're not screaming and jumping around. We're just standing there in complete shock. Thinking, We're going to beat Ohio State. I mean, that hadn't been done in that stadium since 2005. It was incredible. And, like I said, there was 4:27 left on the clock. We still had to hold them off.

TRACE MCSORLEY: Like, This game ain't over.

JASON CABINDA: I think there were four minutes and twenty-seven seconds left when that drive started and I just looked at it as if it was a winter workout and we were at the last station, the go-around. Just give it everything you've got. That's what we did.

DAVID JONES: They still had to survive J.T. Barrett.

TRACE MCSORLEY: Our defense had to go out there and stop 'em. They went out and got two or three sacks in a row. I just had to take a knee.

JASON CABINDA: We came up with a couple of critical sacks and were able to stop their final surge.

MALIK GOLDEN: It was like, Holy crap, we about to do it!

Trace took a knee and before you could go shake hands, the fans started coming.

AUDREY SNYDER: It was one of those pure college football moments.

In the chaos of the field storming, I ended up next to Chris Godwin. I had my phone rolling and I remember asking him a basic question: "Hey, what's going through your head right now?" And he looked at me like he had just seen a ghost. He was so shell-shocked.

The guys didn't know what to say. It's like their minds had just blacked out.

JAMES FRANKLIN: When that kick was blocked, it was like all this bundled-up angst and emotion was released, not just inside that stadium, but all over the world—wherever there are Penn State fans.

GRANT HALEY: It was just a relief—for the players, the coaches, the team. It's all the hard work we had put in throughout the season. The preparation didn't start that week, it had started in January.

JASON CABINDA: B-Bell, Brandon Bell, put it best in the locker room. He said no crying, none of that sad stuff. This wasn't a fluke. This is who we are. Be proud.

JAMES FRANKLIN: A week after that game, Shawn Allen, Marcus's dad, brought me a picture of that blocked kick framed alongside one of the gloves that Marcus had worn during the game and one of the gloves worn by Grant Haley. It's one of the most thoughtful gifts I've ever been given. I have it hanging in my basement at home. Every time I pass it, I can't help but smile.

FORTY-FOUR

COMEBACK KIDS

FANS LOVE THE thrill of a come-from-behind victory. Coaches? They hate suspense. They work hour after hour looking for ways to flush any mystery from their lives. That's what all that film study is for. And the meticulously scripted practice drills. The 6 a.m. workouts in the dead of winter. And those Friday night hotel rooms just off campus. If removing one unknown might grant you an extra sliver of control, why not give it a try?

And so, one lingering concern for the coaches as the 2016 season unfolded was the team's habit of starting slow. "We hate the first half," James Franklin quipped.

In an ideal world, you score on the first drive and never look back. Penn State's players had a custom of falling behind early—against Pitt, Minnesota, and Ohio State—before springing to action. While that made for spellbinding television, it unnerved the coaches. And, as those come-from-behind wins mounted, the kids themselves were puzzled to explain what exactly it was that was holding them back. Pregame jitters? Inexperience? The thing that was truly odd, they agreed, was the otherworldly calm in the locker room. No one panicked, even when the score got ugly. Each simply trusted that someone somewhere on the team would step forward to help them win.

MALIK GOLDEN: I don't know what it was about that team. We started every game horribly and were always coming back. That was the tale of the season.

BRANDON BELL: It's a testament to the teams we were playing. The Big Ten was strong that year, and, like I said, everyone's always gunning for Penn State.

It's also a testament to our leadership: players and coaches coming together, having faith, and continuing to battle. Those second halves, man, were miraculous.

BRIAN GAIA: I don't know if we could put a finger on it. I think it was just some of the younger guys on the offense getting a little more comfortable with the schemes the other team was running. They'd see things here and there that let them play a little faster.

RICK MCSORLEY: When the lights came on, things just started clicking. Either we made great halftime adjustments or somebody made a play and things started rolling.

Against Minnesota, it was the touchdown pass to Irv Charles that sparked the rally. Against Ohio State, it was special teams plays by Cam Brown, Marcus Allen, and Grant Haley. The details shifted, but the storyline remained the same: The team struggled, then found a way to win.

After upsetting the Buckeyes, the Lions earned their first national ranking in five years, cracking the Associated Press poll at number twenty-four. Days later, they found themselves mired in a 17–17 stalemate with 3–4 Purdue. "In the first half, we were playing tense," said Trace McSorley. "We came out in the second half and played loose."

Linebacker Brandon Smith made the first big play, an interception returned to the Boilermaker twenty-four. Then McSorley hit Chris Godwin with a short touchdown pass. And, before you knew it, the offense had exploded for forty-five points. Final score: Penn State 62, Purdue 24.

JACK DAVIS: If you look at Trace's completion rates for the season, we weren't methodically driving the ball downfield. It was a lot of home-run celebrations. The offense was delivering explosive plays, always taking that shot.

DAESEAN HAMILTON: It all starts with opponents thinking about taking away Saquon, one of the best running backs in the nation. That opened up the passing lanes for guys like myself, Mike Gesicki, Chris Godwin, DeAndre Thompkins, Saeed Blacknall. Once that happened, teams were caught off balance. We hit them with a run or a pass for twenty-five yards. Big plays.

JOE MOORHEAD: The offense was predicated on running the ball success-fully, but when you're able to do that, it forces defenses to commit numbers to the box, either with secondary support or pressure. When you do that, you create one-on-one matchups on the outside.

If a team gave us a favorable box to run the ball, we exploited it with Saquon. And if a team was adamant about shutting him down, we threw the ball deep.

GREGG GARRITY: Saquon is the one that sticks out to most people, but top to bottom our roster was filled with guys like Trace McSorley—undersized quarterback, not a huge arm, just a winner; guys like defensive tackle Parker Cothren, who, you know, wouldn't jump out at you on film, but filled his role; Jason Cabinda and Brandon Bell—not overly gifted, just hard workers, great leaders. We could rally around those guys.

JASON CABINDA: There wasn't a game we went into that we didn't feel we were going to win.

It didn't matter what the score was.

We walked into that locker room at halftime and there was not one head down. We knew who we were and we knew we were going to find a way. That's the type of team we were. At the end of the day, we weren't going to stop fighting till that clock hit all zeroes.

BRANDON BELL: It was our mindset. Never got too down, never got too high on ourselves. We tried to stay even-keeled. No matter what happened early on, we knew we were talented enough to counter it.

The coaches harped on us about the slow starts. It didn't matter. It was zero–zero coming out for the second half.

BRIAN GAIA: Whether we were down three touchdowns, two touchdowns, one touchdown, we knew our offense could put points up and our defense could stop the other team.

Occasionally—like, say, against 5-4 Iowa—the Lions jumped to an early lead and pressed on to a decisive win. (Tommy Stevens capped the scoring in that one with a touchdown run on a jet sweep.) But a week later, the players would fall ten points behind 5-5 Indiana, only to respond with a 24-7 fourth-quarter run.

BILLY FESSLER: I do think you have to learn how to win, figure out what it takes to compete at such a high level. It's not easy. But once we figured out how to win, things took off.

TRACE MCSORLEY: That's one of the things about that offense: We had so many weapons outside. We had one of the best running backs in the country. It was almost like, pick your poison.

CHRIS GODWIN: Knowing that I didn't have to make the play, Saquon didn't have to make the play, DaeSean didn't have to make the play—knowing that we had six, seven, eight guys that could make a play—it was big, because you felt confident in everything we were doing.

MIKE GESICKI: It's about opportunity and confidence. If you have the opportunity to make the play and you're confident you can do it, it's almost written in stone.

BILLY FESSLER: There were moments when maybe we should not have won games, when a younger team that didn't have the experience of losing on the road twice would not have been able to fight through the adversity. But in those two losses early in the year we were still figuring out, you know, how to compete. Once we created a little momentum, it all took off.

SAQUON BARKLEY: I give credit to the coaches, JoeMo and his offensive staff, for setting up our playmakers, putting them in a position to make plays. I'd say that's the key to our second-half success.

TRACE MCSORLEY: He did a good job making sure we were in the right play. And he was down on the field, so we could have person-to-person contact on the sidelines between drives. That was big for us.

He'd talk to the quarterbacks, so we were all on the same page, knew what he was looking for and what to go to on certain looks.

AUDREY SNYDER: The way his mind worked, the players loved everything about it. And, once his offense started working, you got this buy-in. The players thought, We can't be stopped.

To me, that's the scary part about that team. Once they got rolling, they believed they could beat anybody.

JOE MOORHEAD: It's about ball placement and understanding coverage, pre-snap and post-snap. Trace had reads, knew where he needed to go with the ball based on safety rotation—one-high, two-high, things like that. Not only was he throwing the deep ball well, he was throwing it to the right person.

When things broke down and he escaped, he was able to keep his eyes downfield and still go through his progressions.

MIKE GESICKI: Week in, week out, it was a bunch of guys making plays.

TRACE MCSORLEY: Big, strong, fast guys who could adjust to a ball. If teams were loading the box, trying to stop the run, it gave us one-on-one match-ups.

If that's what we saw in the first couple drives, we'd attack with those guys. Loosen the other team up and make them take players out of the box, devote them to pass coverage.

VON WALKER: On the football field, I was worried about *my* job, right? If I was not in the game, I was watching, paying attention, worried about what I needed to do to win. But I went out every game expecting to win.

I think a lot of guys felt that way. I still don't understand it to this day. But it was Coach Franklin's coaching staff and our team. We were down in some big games. Usually at halftime, somebody—a coach or a player—is going to speak up and start yelling about mistakes. I don't know how it happened. But they were so methodical in their approach that season. We would come in, the offense would sit on one side, the defense on the other, and we would go through the issues raised during the game, little nip-and-tuck changes we needed to make. There wasn't much yelling. It was very calm, even if we were down by more than one score.

I have this memory of sitting there, and being like, *Man, how is everybody so calm right now?*

TRACE MCSORLEY: There weren't a lot of changes. It was little things here and there. Sometimes we had to execute better. Other times, Joe Moorhead would throw in a new wrinkle—a way to attack a certain look. It depended on how the game was going.

EVAN SCHWAN: That's something we tried to figure out throughout the year. Honestly, I don't have an answer for why we always came out stronger in the second half.

We didn't change our game plan. Guys didn't do anything special. Everyone just kind of realized what was on the line. We came together as a team.

JASON CABINDA: You go out there in the first half and get a feel for how they're trying to attack you and in the second half you make adjustments and execute.

At the same time, I credit our strength coach Dwight Galt for what he did in the off-season. Our D-line and O-Line were able to wear teams down over the course of a game. When we got to the third and fourth quarter, you saw a ton of tackles for loss, a ton of sacks, negative-yardage plays. That's what was slowing teams down, disrupting their rhythm.

BRANDON BELL: We matured fast and knew the circumstances didn't matter. We had to just go out there and make it happen on Saturday.

BRENT PRY: At the start of the year, the plan was to have veteran linebackers and a veteran back-end help bring the young defensive front along. But we got thrown a curveball with the injuries to Brandon Bell, Jason Cabinda, and Nyeem Wartman-White. So, guys had to grow up fast.

EVAN SCHWAN: It's something we dealt with all year, especially early on against Michigan. When Jason and B-Bell were down, the young guys had to make plays. We established depth because of guys that had to step up and play.

BRANDON BELL: Guys were in and out of the rotation all year long.

MARCUS ALLEN: They studied the game, paid attention in meetings.

BRANDON BELL: They matured in their approach to practice and meetings. Taking more notes, more intricate notes, watching more film, individually and collectively.

BRENT PRY: The adversity we faced and the way the kids handled it became a positive. Instead of slipping sideways after a couple of tough losses, the guys set their jaws, worked hard, and kept seeking results.

JAMES FRANKLIN: If we get one percent better in the way we take notes in meetings, that helps. If we're one percent better in how we sleep, our nutrition, hydration, how we take care of our bodies, that's going to help.

It has a more dramatic impact than you think, because everybody else focuses on the Xs and Os, bench presses, and schemes. So, if we do a better job focusing on those other areas—treatment, hydration, nutrition, sleep, note taking, discipline—it can have a big impact. Those one percents add up.

KOA FARMER: Coach Pry and Coach Franklin always said, next-man-up mentality. That was preached throughout the locker room. If you're on that depth chart, prepare to be a starter, because we had a history that season of guys getting hurt.

TRACE MCSORLEY: At linebacker, offensive line, running back, wherever, the next guy had to step up and play. That was our mentality.

KOA FARMER: I was floating back and forth between linebacker and safety. Different positions at linebacker, different positions at safety. That's how I had to think. I was studying every play, every position, because I knew someone could get hurt on any play.

That's what we were going through as a program.

JASON CABINDA: That's another great thing about the guys we had. They were willing to do whatever was best for the team, switching positions or playing on the scout team, whatever the need might be. When you have guys who don't care about the individual recognition, guys who only care about winning, you're going to have success.

BRENT PRY: Sometimes seeing the plays at live speed, getting used to the game speed, was a factor. As we went through the season, guys were able to make adjustments. You could see the experience building. The guys up front, especially, were able to do it.

Robert Windsor, Kevin Givens, Shareef Miller, Ryan Buchholz, you're talking about a bunch of redshirt freshmen. As the year went on, they got more comfortable at their positions and we got comfortable doing more with them. They allowed us to take the handcuffs off.

Sometimes, in the first half, I was somewhat conservative, trying to let guys get their feet wet, see how we were doing before we got to the two-hundred-level skills.

JASON CABINDA: Coach Pry really believed in the talent we had and gave guys confidence. And when you play with confidence, you just play better. You're more productive, faster, all those things.

EVAN SCHWAN: He was always one-hundred-percent honest. When we watched film, he critiqued the performance, not the performer. He didn't make it personal.

JASON CABINDA: He made guys bring it every single day. Inspired us to do better. That's why we were able to have such success on defense, even with the adversity we faced that year.

TRACE MCSORLEY: There were ups and downs throughout the season, tough teams each and every week. We always had to get better, take the next step in our preparation.

Coach Moorhead always said, Just take that next step, continue to climb, climb, climb.

JASON CABINDA: It's all about building on what you did last year, the week before, the day before—all those things.

BRENT PRY: There wasn't one superstar who gobbled up all the accolades. We had a unit of guys that really enjoyed playing together. Malik Golden, Brandon Bell, Evan Schwan, those guys just got it. Some didn't show up on the record boards in our weight room, but, man, they got out there on the field and knew how to play.

That ability to rebound from each setback, turn a game around with one clutch play, led to a certain swagger, a youthful exuberance rarely seen on Penn State teams.

NEIL RUDEL: You could see it on the sideline—the fun they were having, the camaraderie they were building. They were using so many players, building so much depth, you could see the effect on the whole team.

TRACE MCSORLEY: It was a ton of fun. You'd see the guys out there doing celebrations, high-fiving, little dances. Everyone on the offense was having fun putting points on the board. No one was worried about individual statistics, just team success.

That was the best part. We were doing it together, all having this success together. That made it more fun.

MIKE GESICKI: If you're making plays, you're walking to class and people are looking at you differently. Treating you differently. It's like, *Whoa, what's going on here?*

EVAN SCHWAN: People I'd never met in my life would say, "Hey, great game."

And, for the most part, the players didn't let that sudden celebrity go to their heads. They graciously accepted it, ever mindful of the potential pitfalls, even amid their joyous on-field celebrations.

TRACE MCSORLEY: We obviously knew we couldn't go across the line, couldn't do anything to draw attention to ourselves. Coach Franklin's big thing was celebrate with your teammates. Come to the sidelines and have fun. Smack each other, hit each other in the chest. Don't do anything to draw attention to yourself. Don't be disrespectful.

RICK MCSORLEY: He had to come out every once in a while and have a talk with the players. Trace scored one against Temple, his first rushing touchdown, dove and kind of ran around in the end zone near the student section, and Coach Franklin said, "Hey, buddy, tone it down a little. Not everyone at Penn State is ready for that."

When we played Iowa, Saquon scored a long touchdown on a wheel route. And the last five yards, he high-stepped it a little. Coach Franklin pulled him aside on that one, too.

So, celebrate with your team, but don't make anybody feel bad.

As the season progressed, the players let the scoreboard do the talking: 62–24 versus Purdue, 41–14 versus Iowa, 45–31 versus Indiana. After a rough start, they were 9–2.

JAMES FRANKLIN: I think all good teams overachieve. That's what you're trying to do, maximize the opportunities, the talent you have. You do that with great chemistry, relationships, trust and love for one another. You've heard me say those things before. You prepare like crazy, so when the opportunities come, you can take advantage of them.

By mid-November, when the Nittany Lions beat Rutgers 39–0, the pundits were talking about Penn State as a legit contender for the Big Ten title. The one problem? To achieve that goal, the team would first have to leapfrog Michigan in the conference standings.

FORTY-FIVE

DOWN TO THE WIRE

PENN STATE FANS *now found themselves in the odd position of rooting for archrival Ohio State. Hours before James Franklin's players took the field for the final game on their schedule, the Buckeyes were hosting number-three Michigan. With a win, they could knock the Wolverines from the top spot in the Big Ten East, opening the door for the Nittany Lions, who would simply have to beat 3–8 Michigan State to earn a trip to Indianapolis for the conference championship game.*

The Penn State campus was buzzing with anticipation all week.

University officials even contemplated airing the Ohio State–Michigan broadcast on the scoreboard in Beaver Stadium. But the idea of creating such a spectacle made 1-0, 1-0, 1-0 Franklin uneasy. His players were already dealing with a change in routine, due to the team's Thanksgiving celebration on Thursday. Why add another distraction during the pregame warmup?

"I'd prefer to hand out mini TVs to everyone who comes into the stadium," the coach joked in his weekly press conference. "Do you think the athletic director Sandy Barbour will go for that?"

By this point in the journey, though, the players were accustomed to navigating the ups and downs of a college football season. In fact, they almost welcomed the chaos.

They also knew that Michigan State was no pushover. Seven days earlier, the team had almost handed 9–1 Ohio State its second loss of the season, foiled only by an errant pass on a late two-point conversion attempt. The final score: 17–16.

Penn State's players had a score to settle with the Spartans, too, bristling at the 55–16 beating the Lions had received in East Lansing in 2015.

Still, with all the talk of titles and playoff berths, it was hard to maintain the usual focus.

TOM PANCOAST: Late in the year, we were on a plane, flying back from Indiana. We're all sitting together, watching ESPN, or maybe ABC, on the TVs in front of us, and they post something about our chances of going to the playoffs. In all the years we'd played, we had never been mentioned in a conversation like that. Now we're in the conversation, but the graphic says we have less than a one percent chance of making the Big Ten Championship game.

Under the graphic, it says, Penn State needs *chaos.*

That's all it said.

We all looked at each other and laughed.

BILL FESSLER: [laughter] Tommy and I were sitting next to each other on the plane, just, you know, shooting the bull and watching ESPN.

We saw that and got fired up.

We're like, "*Chaos, that's all we need!*"

TOM PANCOAST: With three games left in the season, we needed Michigan to lose twice. The Wolverines had won seven of their first nine games by fourteen points or more. They were blowing everyone out.

Well, that night, Michigan had to go play at Iowa. We landed at Penn State, ended up going out to dinner at Bar Bleu, and watched Michigan lose to unranked Iowa.

Now we're looking at each other like, "Well, *chaos.*"

BILLY FESSLER: We're losing our minds. "Hey, here we go!"

JACK DAVIS: Me and Francis Alvare, the mic man, were sitting at the hotel bar in Indiana that night, and who comes up next to us to watch the Michigan-Iowa game?

Trace's dad.

It was the three of us watching, cheering, very aware that if Iowa pulled off that upset, there was a path.

TOM PANCOAST: Clemson ended up losing that night, too. Bunch of chips end up falling.

So, we kept messing with each other. Every time we saw a team ranked ahead of us lose, we'd be like, "Guys, *chaos!*" And sure enough, *chaos* happened.

In all, five teams ranked ahead of Penn State in the Associated Press poll lost that Saturday: number-two Clemson, number-three Michigan, number-four Washington, number-eight Texas A&M, and number-nine Auburn. That put the Nittany Lions on the cusp of a berth not only in the Big Ten Championship Game, but even the college football playoff.

A week later, Penn State's players followed the come-from-behind win in Indiana with a 39–0 shutout in a driving rain at Rutgers.

And so, on November 26, they were still in the running for a trip to the Big Ten title game. They just needed a little help from Ohio State . . . and the good sense not to get too caught up in the drama unfolding in Columbus, overlooking the threat from Michigan State.

JAMES FRANKLIN: We managed it during the week, urging the guys to stay focused on the things that truly matter—continuing to develop, to support each other. Overall, they tuned things out pretty good.

TRACE MCSORLEY: The Michigan game was on TV before our game. If Michigan won, they were going to the Big Ten Championship Game. If Ohio State won, we'd have to beat Michigan State.

Nothing mattered if we didn't win that game.

That was a down year for Michigan State, but they were a talented team. They had just struggled to win games. Based on records, a lot of people assumed we'd win, but it was not going to be a cakewalk.

We had to try really hard not to focus on the Michigan–Ohio State game. I mean, human nature, it's damn near impossible not to check the scores. You wake up and that game's on and, you know, before you leave the hotel to head to the stadium, it's on in everyone's room. That's what everyone was watching before we left.

MALIK GOLDEN: Franklin was like, We don't care about the game, saying all the things you say as a coach. As a player, you're like, *Screw it, we need to know if we get to play next week.*

JACK DAVIS: I lingered in the cheerleader locker room for as long as I could to watch Ohio State–Michigan. But, you know, the Nittany Lion needs to be on the field for the game. So, I pulled myself away from the TV in time to run to center field and do crowd control.

In the student section, everyone was clearly distracted, looking at their phones, fighting to get cell service to figure out what was happening in that other game.

ALLISON WILLIAMS, SIDELINE REPORTER, ESPN: Everybody had an eye toward the other game into the first quarter. As I was walking behind the Penn State bench, you could see guys looking into the crowd. We had a cart cam behind the bench with the Michigan–Ohio State game on it. People in the crowd were watching it and guys on the sideline would shout out, "What's the score? What's the score?"

MATTY FRESH: Everyone in the tailgate lot was huddled in front of the TV. Some guy's got the cable hooked up and we're watching Ohio State–Michigan and it's, like, time to go into the stadium. We're not going to see the end of the game. And, of course, the strategy inside the stadium was to silence everything. Franklin wanted to keep the noise out—for good reason. And now you've got the *College GameDay* people putting the TV up, you know, twenty feet in the air. One side of the student section is watching the action on this little monitor.

ALLISON WILLIAMS: I had talked to Trace and Brandon Bell before the game and both were like, It doesn't matter. But I don't know how much I believe them. I think they really tried to focus on Michigan State. Because that's the Franklin way. *Michigan State, Michigan State, Michigan State.* The 2015 game against Michigan State, that's the fuel they wanted to tap into. Because it allowed them to maintain control. They can't control what happens in Michigan–Ohio State.

In 2015, the Spartans had laid a beating on the Nittany Lions, closing out the 55–16 win with that nine-yard touchdown run by the team's beefy center, straight through the heart of Penn State's defense. If the PSU players were eager for payback, they didn't show it—not early on, at least.

The offense went three-and-out on the first drive, just as word leaked that Ohio State had kicked a last-second field goal to send the game in Columbus into overtime.

Buckeye quarterback J.T. Barrett crossed the goal line from seven yards out on the first possession to put Ohio State up by seven.

Michigan answered moments later with a five-yard touchdown pass on fourth-and-goal.

In the meantime, Michigan State's unheralded offense had driven seventy-six yards for a field goal in State College.

And now it was Michigan's turn to take the lead in Columbus, opening the second overtime period with a successful field goal attempt to put the Wolverines up by three.

Trace McSorley started Penn State's second drive with a deep pass to Saeed Blacknall. The ball landed five yards out of reach. On the next play, Saquon Barkley was tackled for a loss of two. On third down, McSorley narrowly escaped a blitz and floated the ball downfield toward DeAndre Thompkins. It bounced off his hands. That sent the offense to the sidelines.

TRACE MCSORLEY: We're not even on the field and we hear the crowd start cheering.

BOB FLOUNDERS: A crazy eruption.

MATTY FRESH: This entire section is cheering. And you can't get phone service in Beaver Stadium. It's impossible. It's like, What's going on? And then, like the Wave, the info slowly works its way to our side.

"Ohio State has scored in overtime. You're not gonna believe it. They're gonna beat Michigan!"

ALLISON WILLIAMS: I remember the whole place going nuts, at a very random point in the game. This roar that started kind of small, then got bigger and bigger and bigger.

TRACE MCSORLEY: I was standing next to Mike Gesicki and he goes, "Well, Ohio State just won." We looked at each other like, *All right, we got to kick it into gear. Win* this *game.*

JAMES FRANKLIN: I didn't find out until the crowd had erupted. Trace came to me on the sidelines and asked what's going on? I told him I assumed Ohio State had won. He didn't bat an eye.

BOB WISCHUSEN, PLAY-BY-PLAY ANNOUNCER, ESPN: The Buckeyes scored in double overtime. And now James Franklin and the Nittany Lions know it. If they win today, they're going to the Big Ten Championship Game.

JACK DAVIS: I was worried Penn State might not finish the job. Because at that point, the game was still up in the air.

MALIK GOLDEN: We were losing, playing poorly, and then Michigan lost. It was like, *Hey, we can't lose this game. Turn it up!*

JASON CABINDA: You try not to let that other game influence how you play, but it solidifies what you're playing for—a chance to go win the Big Ten Championship.

AMANI ORUWARIYE: We just need to focus on our jobs, do what we got to do.

JACK DAVIS: The game changed. Whether Joe Moorhead started making adjustments or what, I can't say. I wasn't standing too close to the team, but I can speak for the fans.

The student section was suddenly much more focused on the game in Beaver Stadium.

CHRIS GODWIN: It was in our hands. We just had to take control and put some points on the board.

Michigan State moved forty-nine yards on its second possession to kick a second field goal.

MIKE GESICKI: After that, we got a drive going. Got a few points up on the board.

A Tyler Davis kick trimmed Michigan State's lead to 6–3, but the Spartans rolled out another field goal drive and made it 9–3. Penn State responded with a ten-play touchdown drive. Michigan State kicked a field goal.

At halftime, the Spartans led 12–10. On offense, they had lost starting quarterback Damion Terry to a concussion early in the second quarter but continued to play with heart. On defense, they held Saquon Barkley to just nine yards on nine carries.

If there was a bright spot for the Nittany Lions, it's that they were down by only two points. The defense had yet to force a punt, but somehow managed to halt four Michigan State drives inside the fifteen, holding the Spartans to field goals.

JAMES FRANKLIN: We didn't play the way we wanted to play in the first half. Got behind on the sticks. Michigan State had too much success on first and second down, especially at the beginning of drives. But we did a great job when they got in the red zone, held them to field goals. The defense kept us in the game.

EVAN SCHWAN: In the first half, we kind of struggled getting them off schedule on first and second down. But, as soon as they got into the red zone, it was all or nothing. The fact we kept them out of the end zone was a huge momentum swinger.

BRANDON BELL: We weren't doing anything crazy scheme-wise. We just had to get off our heels, beat blocks, and get to the ball.

GARRETT SICKELS: Keep our poise and do our jobs.

ALLISON WILLIAMS: In the second half, Penn State was like a different team.

MIKE GESICKI: At halftime, the passing game was a point of emphasis. Obviously, Michigan State's goal was to stop the running game.

JAMES FRANKLIN: They were doing a lot of cross-dog blitzing with the two inside linebackers to make it difficult for us to run. They were widening the defensive ends and rushing them up the field to take some of our perimeter run away. As a result, they were playing really soft at defensive back, basically saying, we're going to overload the box and make it difficult for your young offensive line. We're not going to allow you to get chunk plays.

But we had talented wide receivers and our offensive line did a good job of straining and protecting.

TRACE MCSORLEY: We knew we had to take some shots downfield and loosen them up. We hit a couple and they kept doing what they were doing, leaving one-on-one matchups on the outside, so we kept taking advantage of it.

MIKE GESICKI: We came out and tore them apart in the passing game. It didn't matter if it was Chris Godwin, Saeed Blacknall, DaeSean Hamilton, or myself. There were a bunch of plays to be made and we made them.

Four minutes into the third quarter, McSorley found Chris Godwin wide open on the left sideline and hit him with a thirty-four-yard touchdown pass. Four minutes after that, McSorley stepped up in the pocket and tossed a forty-five-yard strike to Mike Gesicki. And then Godwin got loose down the middle and McSorley lofted a pass that hit him in stride from fifty-nine yards out.

By quarter's end, the Lions were leading 31–12.

Right before that third touchdown play, the team had lost Barkley for the day to a twisted ankle. Not even that could slow the attack down, though. Andre Robinson stepped forward to replace him and in the fourth quarter added a touchdown run and a touchdown catch.

Early in the year, Penn State's players had dared to envision making a December trip to Indianapolis, and now with a 45–12 win they were headed to Lucas Oil Stadium for the Big Ten title game.

BOB FLOUNDERS: The Spartans had bottled up Barkley, but Trace McSorley threw some really good balls. He ended up with three hundred and eighty yards.

The team won going away.

MARK DANTONIO, HEAD COACH, MICHIGAN STATE: It was all Penn State in the second half.

MARK BRENNAN: An argument can be made—and I know, because I made it—that that was the single best game by a Penn State quarterback ever.

Against the number-eighteen pass defense in the nation, McSorley averaged twenty-two yards per completion—over sixteen yards per attempt. That's *unbelievable*.

Go back through the record book. We've never seen anything like it.

You talk about what was on the line, about how good that pass defense had been—it held J.T. Barrett and the kid from Michigan in check—and this guy shredded them. Absolutely shredded them.

With just under four minutes to play, McSorley tossed in a little retribution, too. Ahead 38–12 and piloting a squad of backup players, he fielded a snap just inside the fifty-yard line, took a half-step backward to avoid a Spartan blitz, and floated his final pass of the day into the outstretched arms of Andre Robinson. After watching the running back cradle the ball and sprint to the end zone, the Lion signal caller stepped toward the sideline, delivered his iconic home-run swing, then raised his right hand to his forehead in a military salute.

NEIL RUDEL: Obviously, they were trying to roll the score up a bit and send a message to Michigan State.

JASON CABINDA: Anytime you play like that it leaves a sour taste in your mouth. So, there was that feeling leaving Michigan State in 2015 that we had to come back and really give it to them.

I'm glad we were able to do that.

MIKE IRWIN: Everybody wondered how long it would take Penn State to get back to national prominence. They're in a conference with Ohio State, Michigan, and Michigan State, all preseason top-ten teams, and here's lowly Penn State, not even in the top twenty-five at the start of the year.

It's just amazing how quickly they turned that program around. You felt so good for everyone involved—the fans, the coaches, and especially the players.

JASON CABINDA: For us, just knowing how far we'd come and what the program had been through, it was huge.

JOE JULIUS: On the stage afterwards, it was awesome. We got the hats, all the memorabilia.

EVAN SCHWAN: I was standing with some of the guys that had stuck around at Penn State. I put that Big Ten East Championship hat on. We reminisced a bit. But our work was not done.

MALIK GOLDEN: After the last game of the season, we'd usually have the week off, watch the Big Ten Championship Game on TV.

Now we're actually playing in it. That was just absurd.

FORTY-SIX

WHY NOT US?

AT LONG LAST, *the moment of truth had arrived. Five full years after being sanctioned by the NCAA, left for dead by the media, Penn State's players were seated in the locker room at Lucas Oil Stadium in Indianapolis, preparing to play Wisconsin for a conference championship. "Why not us?" DaeSean Hamilton asked the group before taking the field. "Why can't we win this?"*

Why not us?

That was the question of the day.

Despite the eight-game winning streak, the clutch October victory against Ohio State, the Nittany Lions entered the game as underdogs. The oddsmakers in Las Vegas favored Wisconsin by two-and-a-half points. The pundits at ESPN, FOX Sports, even the Big Ten Network were all choosing the 10–2 team from Madison. Big Ten commissioner Jim Delany appeared to be lobbying for Ohio State and Michigan to represent the conference in the playoffs.

For the players, there was so much riding on the outcome: a chance not only to prove they were worthy of respect, but also to redeem the university, demonstrate once and for all that the man-hours they had poured into rescuing the program, that grief they had taken for holding fast to Joe Paterno's Grand Experiment, every last sacrifice they had made for the greater good—all of it was noble. Because the program was well worth saving, the ideals it embraced too precious to lose, despite the awful misdeeds of one vile ex-coach.

To accomplish all that—truly complete the mission—the Nittany Lions would have to dig deeper than ever before, against a team that had an abundance of talent and ambition, an offense that led the nation in time of possession and a defense that allowed just 13.7 points per game. They would have to do it with two redshirt freshmen—Ryan Bates and Steven Gonzalez—starting on the offensive line.

Were they up to the challenge? Who could say?

JACK DAVIS: That game was so ugly early. It seemed like the miracle run had to come to an end.

CHRIS GODWIN: I don't know what happened in the first half, but it felt like we couldn't do anything on offense and *they* were running for, like, seven, eight yards a pop.

JAMES FRANKLIN: Their O-line was having its way with our D-line. Their D-line was giving our O-line fits. Some of the young guys on that O-line were struggling, so we were trying to get them calmed down.

TRACE MCSORLEY: That was one of the most physical games I've ever played in. We tried a handoff on the second play and Wisconsin linebacker T.J. Watt just took me out.

I didn't even have the ball and I just got walloped.

He hit me right in the chest, got me off my feet, and drove me into the ground. I get up and look over to the sideline and my boy Billy Fessler's standing there with our signals.

He's like, *Whoa, are you okay?* Starts giving me that look.

BILLY FESSLER: I thought Trace had gotten his head knocked off.

We were running a zone-read play and hadn't seen Wisconsin do this once on film, but they must have said, "Hey, if you get zone read, mass charge and just smoke the quarterback."

Watt put his helmet right under Trace's chin, Trace's head snapped back and his feet were over his head. It was bad.

But Trace popped up real quick.

TRACE MCSORLEY: I look at Billy like, *Ohhh, did that just happen?*

It was kind of funny. We had one of those moments, like, *Are you good?*

Yeah, I'm good. Let's go!

BILLY FESSLER: He gave me a funny look, then put a big smile on his face.

That's when I knew. *Trace is locked in—we got a shot today.*

To those watching from home, it seemed like more of a long shot.

After a Penn State punt, the Badgers' offense began its relentless assault, pounding away at the Lions' defense with All-Conference rusher Corey Clement. The brawny back carried the ball eight times in thirteen plays, finally serving as a decoy when fullback Austin Ramesh charged across the goal line from a yard out to give Wisconsin a 7–0 lead.

After a second stalled Penn State drive, Clement took a handoff, side-stepped a diving Grant Haley, and burst down the sideline for a seventy-yard touchdown.

Wisconsin 14, Penn State 0.

MALIK GOLDEN: Wisconsin had some dawgs on that offensive line, man. They were just massive. Waaay bigger than us.

BRANDON BELL: The biggest linemen I'd ever played against.

MALIK GOLDEN: They'd just run the ball. Like, *We about to run it and you got to stop it.*

CORY GIGER, SPORTSWRITER, *ALTOONA MIRROR*: That's what Wisconsin does. Line up and try to push you around.

MALIK GOLDEN: They were one of the best running teams in the country, so, yeah, they're going to have their way. Eventually, you have to show some will. Step up.

We had to make them pass. Make them uncomfortable.

BRANDON BELL: They were getting off the ball quicker than we were. That's what they were known for. We just had to get set, get our feet on the ground, and play ball.

Saquon Barkley opened the Lions' next drive with a darting twenty-two-yard rush. McSorley took it from there, launching quick strikes to DaeSean Hamilton and Mike Gesicki for the Lions' first score.

Wisconsin 14, Penn State 7.

But any solace the team took from that effort was short-lived. Minutes later, on a third-and-one call from the Penn State thirty, center Brian Gaia snapped the ball over McSorley's head. When McSorley tried to pounce on it, the ball bounced into the arms of Wisconsin linebacker Ryan Connelly, who secured it and twisted his way into the end zone.

Wisconsin 21, Penn State 7.

As the offense stumbled along, searching for a rhythm, the Badgers widened the gap. With just under ten minutes to go in the half, Wisconsin stopped Penn State on fourth-and-two, then used the short field—and backup running back Dare Ogunbowale—to score a fourth touchdown.

Wisconsin 28, Penn State 7.

JAMES FRANKLIN: I went for it a couple times on fourth down, because we weren't having a lot of success stopping Wisconsin. Short field, long field, it didn't matter. They were just getting ahead on the sticks. It was always second-and-five, second-and-four.

So I tried to be aggressive and go for it on fourth down.

Didn't work either time, but our defense stepped up.

TRACE MCSORLEY: It was like the Pitt game. It might even have been the same score—28–7—at one point.

We were getting beat up. I'm on the sidelines with Mike Gesicki. We look at each other and he's like, "We're not losing this game. It's the same exact score, but we ain't losing this one."

We knew we could come back. It was, *All right, we're just gonna climb that hump again. Come out on top.*

MIKE GESICKI: I said, "It's just like Pitt, but we're going to finish this thing off."

And that's exactly what happened.

With 3:25 to go in the second quarter and the ball near midfield, Franklin took another crack at a fourth-down conversion. T.J. Watt stormed the pocket, jarred the ball from McSorely's grasp, and recovered the fumble inside Penn State territory.

But the defense rose to the challenge, holding Clement to a short gain and breaking up two pass plays to force a punt.

Joe Moorhead's offense took over on the ten-yard line with 2:18 to go and, much as it had since the overtime win against Minnesota, willed its way to a crucial score.

MALIK GOLDEN: Saeed Blacknall, that's the Saeed Blacknall story.

BILLY FESSLER: Saeed went crazy in that game.

TRACE MCSORLEY: He just kept saying, "Trust me, trust me." He's got tremendous speed on the edge and we said let him do what he does, let him work against man coverage.

On first-and-ten, McSorley hit Blacknall for twelve yards. Then he threw a couple of passes to DaeSean Hamilton. Then another twelve-yard strike to Blacknall. On first down at the Wisconsin forty, Blacknall charged right at reserve cornerback Lubern Figaro, who had surrendered the first-quarter touchdown to Gesicki, and did a quick curl.

Before he had even turned, the ball from McSorely was on its way.

Blacknall caught it, spun from Figaro's grasp, and sprinted thirty yards to the end zone.

When the players exited the field, making their way to the locker room at halftime, the task before them seemed less daunting. If anyone lacked the resolve to mount another comeback, he was soon reminded of what was at stake—by a player who had seen his career combust two months earlier with a second, soul-crushing knee injury.

Like Michael Mauti before him, Nyeem Wartman-White refused to quietly concede.

GRANT HALEY: At halftime, the one thing I'll always remember is Nyeem snapping.

TRACE MCSORLEY: We were on the other side of the locker room and I could hear him screaming.

MALIK GOLDEN: He wasn't playing. He was out with a torn ACL, acting more like a coach. There was a lot of swearing, a lot of "You got to man up!"

JORDAN SMITH, CORNERBACK, 2013–16: Everyone's sitting around like, "What is going on? Nah, this can't be it." We'd had games like this before, but it felt different. It was a championship game. And Nyeem is *pissed*. You can feel his energy. Some guys were trying to be vocal, like, "Come on, come on!" But Nyeem's the one that took us there.

NYEEM WARTMAN-WHITE: We down fourteen points! We don't do this!
We don't give up twenty-eight points!

GARRETT SICKELS: "That's not how Penn State plays!"

VON WALKER: By the end, he was literally foaming at the mouth, the most upset I've ever seen him. He was hurt. He couldn't be out there. The guys saw how much it meant to him.

JAMES FRANKLIN: Nyeem was one of the more respected players on our team—for his football IQ, his demeanor, the type of teammate he was. He just had a good way about him.

JORDAN SMITH: He was a three-year starter. We had seen him do his job, do everything right, put his body on the line for us.

MALIK GOLDEN: Football ain't complicated—you got to beat the dude in front of you. So he was like, "It's going to come down to will. We want it more than they do."

I knew in my stomach we were not about to lose that game. There was no panic in anyone's eyes. We had some dawgs in that locker room.

SAQUON BARKLEY: We knew we were fully capable of making plays. At any moment, we could make a play that would turn the game around.

GRANT HALEY: In the first quarter, every team's going to show you something you haven't seen on film. They showed a bit with their runs and their play-action pass. And so, we just adjusted to that by being more aggressive, playing more man coverage, saying to the corners and safeties, do your job. We need more people in the box to stop the run.

That's what really changed the game.

BRANDON BELL: They were not doing anything we didn't expect. They were just out-executing us. We had to lock in—focus.

MIKE GESICKI: I remember Franklin coming in and going, "We got 'em right where we want 'em."

I'm like, We're down *two scores,* but we got 'em right where we want 'em.

JAMES FRANKLIN: In the last eight games of the year, we had averaged twenty-seven points in the second half and only given up six, so I told them that.

TRACE MCSORLEY: We were able to use tempo. Get them on their heels a bit. With us going as fast as we were, they had to stay in base calls, as opposed to dialing up blitzes.

The coach made a point to talk with those freshmen on the offensive line, too.

JAMES FRANKLIN: I said, "Just strain, give us a little more protection. All we need is a little more time and Trace will be able to make plays. So will our wide receivers."

DAVID JONES: The pass that really got things going was the one to Saeed Blacknall on the deep cross.

JOE MOORHEAD: We threw a post route and he caught it in front of the safety and scored.

TRACE MCSORLEY: Wisconsin had just missed a field goal. We're in the TV timeout, getting ready to go back on the field. It's me, Coach Moorhead, Billy, the quarterbacks, and Coach Franklin. Coach Moorhead looked at Franklin. "What do you think? Should I call *the shot*?"

Franklin looked at him. He's like, "What do you think? What do you want to do?"

Moorhead says, "I want to call the shot. I *want* it."

Franklin's like, "All right, if you want it, you got it."

So Moorhead brings the offense together. He's like, "Hey, where we at? What yard line?"

"We're on the thirty."

"This is a seventy-yard touchdown play. We're going to be dancing in the end zone."

And lo and behold, that's what happened.

MIKE GESICKI: He's like, "If we protect here, it's a seventy-yard touchdown."

Next play was a seventy-yard touchdown.

On the very first offensive play of the second half, as JoeMo predicted, Trace McSorley dropped back and put the ball in the air. Saeed Blacknall hauled it in forty-seven yards downfield.

SAEED BLACKNALL: When the ball came, I saw someone pass in front of me and miss the tackle.

DAVID JONES: It looked like safety D'Cota Dixon and the nickelback ran into each other.

SAEED BLACKNALL: Then all I saw was open field. I just ran. Never looked back.

Wisconsin 28, Penn State 21.

GUS JOHNSON, PLAY-BY-PLAY ANNOUNCER, FOX SPORTS: One play, seventy yards. We've got a ballgame in Nap Town.

TRACE MCSORLEY: From that point on, I had that feeling.
We're *winning* this game.
We just felt like we had that control.

With McSorley settling into his rhythm, taking charge in the pocket, you could feel the momentum shifting. First, a pitch to Barkley, good for sixteen yards. Then a toss to Godwin for fourteen more. And six plays later, the Lions' star running back plunged in from the one.
Wisconsin 28, Penn State 28.

SAEED BLACKNALL: Trace was able to lead us, even in our lowest moments that night. No matter how big the gap in score, he kept preaching to us on the sideline, saying "We're going to be all right, we're going to be all right."

MARK BRENNAN: Early on, he was getting hit, didn't look quite right, and, by the end of the game, he was just destroying a very good defense, one that was giving everybody fits that year.

NEIL RUDEL: At one point, he was nine-for-nine for like 250 yards.

Wisconsin's offense, now struggling, leaned once again on Clement and the ground game, muscling its way to the Penn State five, before kicking a field goal to retake the lead.
Wisconsin 31, Penn State 28.

That set the stage for DaeSean Hamilton, who made two clutch catches on the next drive. And then, true to form, McSorley and Barkley teamed up to salt the game away.

JACK DAVIS: Saquon Barkley's wheel route was right in front of me. If you look at that iconic picture of him catching that ball with T.J. Watt chasing him, you can see me looking on, very nervous about whether he's gonna haul that one in. Thankfully, Trace put it right on the money.

Joe Moorhead saw Barkley one-on-one with linebacker T.J. Watt and called the play. Two-six zipped past the outmatched defender to the end zone and McSorley hit him in stride for a 35–31 lead.

TRACE MCSORLEY: JoeMo checked into the perfect play.

SAQUON BARKLEY: We caught them in the look we wanted.
    When I saw it, I was like, *Oh, we got 'em.*
    I just had to trust my speed, trust Trace.
    Trace put the ball right where it needed to be.
    Nobody talks about it, but that was a perfect ball.

TRACE MCSORLEY: Might be my best throw at Penn State.

BOB FLOUNDERS: Some teams were afraid to test Wisconsin's secondary, because of the plays it had made. Penn State didn't see it that way. They went after those guys.
    Saeed Blacknall and DaeSean Hamilton were terrific.

DAVID JONES: They caught everything thrown at them.
    And remember, after the Pitt game, Hamilton had to endure all the questions about that dropped pass at the end. In this one, he goes crazy.

The team added a field goal to go up by seven.
Wisconsin 31, Penn State 38.
Before resting easy, the defense had to take the field one last time.

Wisconsin started its final drive on the twenty-five-yard line and pressed on for ten grueling plays. With sixty-four seconds to go, the Badgers were looking at a fourth-and-one call.

They called timeout to discuss the play.

The ball was sitting on the Penn State twenty-four.

Everyone in the stadium knew what was coming.

MALIK GOLDEN: Cory Clement was a load to tackle. He was a load to tackle, for sure.

TRACE MCSORLEY: We're up seven and they're starting to drive, trying to score a touchdown to tie the game.

MALIK GOLDEN: They were marching down the field. They had three consecutive first downs. They were just marching and marching, and it came down to fourth down. Like fourth and inches.

STEVE JONES: One of those line-in-the-sand moments. If Penn State stops it, it's over.

TRACE MCSORLEY: And, you know, Wisconsin, every third-and-short, it seemed like they were getting it. Just running the ball, getting a half-yard past the first-down line and moving the chains.

I'm on the sideline, trying to keep my composure. I knew it was down to this play.

If we stop them, we win.

MALIK GOLDEN: We knew they weren't about to pass the ball. When you're the best running team in the country, you're not going to pass on fourth-and-inches. So we got a lot of push from the defensive line and guys made a play.

The Badgers pitched it to the boundary. I honestly thought they were going to try to beat us with speed, to the field where I was at. They ran to the boundary and Grant Haley made a hell of a play.

BOB FLOUNDERS: Earlier in the game, on the long touchdown run by Corey Clement, Haley did not make the tackle. He lost contain, let him get to the sideline, and they scored.

On fourth-and-one, they ran right at his side of the field. The kid's a hundred and eighty pounds. He stepped up and hit Clement low.

GRANT HALEY: It was a play we had talked about at halftime. They ran the counter a lot. And we were in a sneak situation. It was fourth-and-one, so we knew they were going to run the ball.

Earlier in the game, they had blocked down, like a crack block, and split outside. This time, they blocked down and I triggered right there. I was able to get him wrapped up by the legs. Marcus came to finish him off.

MARCUS ALLEN: I just went to tackle the ball, to be honest. I was so zoned in on making a play.

COREY CLEMENT: It was all about who wanted it more. One yard—either I get it or I don't.

EVAN SCHWAN: I was on the bottom of the pile and I got up and heard everyone cheering. I looked to my left and Jason Cabinda was on top of the dude and the ball was short.

Before calling it a day, the referees watched the play on video to confirm the call.

STEVE JONES: The Big Ten Championship lies on a measurement.

JACK DAVIS: That review felt like it took forever. I wasn't letting myself celebrate until the call was confirmed.

GUS JOHNSON: Did he get it?
  [pause]
  Nooooo!
  Penn State holds with 1:01 to go. What a stop!

ANDREW NELSON: You're at a loss for words at a moment like that.

JAMES FRANKLIN: They had been running the ball pretty much at will all night. That was the difference in the first half. Their O-line was controlling the game, their D-line was controlling the game. So for us to get a stop like that was huge.

The game was all but over. Penn State just had to find a way to kill the clock.
Three handoffs to Barkley bled fifty-four seconds. And then . . .

TRACE MCSORLEY: Wisconsin still had their timeouts. We needed to do something to ensure we won the game. In the end, it was fourth down, like three seconds left.

EVAN SCHWAN: I was on the sideline and we didn't know if we were going to punt the ball or send Trace back out to run the clock out. There was a lot of back-and-forth between the coaches. Pretty stressful moment. But they made a great decision, putting the offense out there.

TRACE MCSORLEY: They said, Just run backwards and keep your eyes on the clock. Stay in bounds. If we give up a safety, who cares? We're up enough.

Just stay in bounds until you see zeros on the clock.

So, I'm running back, looking at the clock, and it's taking forever to tick down. Finally, I see it hit double zeros and I slide down.

ANDREW NELSON: You almost can't put it into words.

People have no idea about the inside perspective, what we each had been through to get to that point.

MALIK GOLDEN: We were like, "Yo, we just won the Big Ten Championship. Like, that is *crazy.*"

TRACE MCSORLEY: From that point on, it was surreal—being on the field, getting up on the podium, celebrating with teammates, confetti falling. In the locker room, everyone's going nuts.

If you've seen the videos, Penn State likes to do dance parties in there. That's the year all that started. That was the culmination of it. We had reached the goal we had set for ourselves.

JAMES FRANKLIN: When you walk across the field to shake that other coach's hand, that's when it starts to sink in . . . When you stand up there and raise that trophy in front of all the fans and they're going berserk, that's when it hits home.

It's amazing, when you think about where we were when I had arrived three years earlier. With sixty-five scholarships and a lot of challenges. It wasn't always easy to see it from the outside, but steps were being made.

TRACE MCSORLEY: I remember being up on that podium, looking out over the scene, seeing the fans still in the stadium. I locked eyes with my parents and it was just a surreal moment, to sit up there and take it in, having just won the Big Ten Championship Game no one thought we could reach.

JASON CABINDA: It was like Penn State is back. For real. It still gives me chills, man, I swear.

JOE JULIUS: Everybody was like, "Yeah, we're back, we're back."

It wasn't just because of us, though. It was the culmination of all the good decisions that were made, all the things those guys did back in '12 and beyond. If it wasn't us, it would have been the kids the next year. It was just bound to happen, because of the guys who made all the right decisions.

KOA FARMER: I remember walking back to the hotel. The fans were there. We were freaking having a party in the lobby.

MALIK GOLDEN: I didn't sleep on my right shoulder for like a month after that game.

Yeah, I didn't practice the whole bowl week. Not until the day before the game. A lot of guys were banged up. We lost dang near our whole offensive line.

Penn State finished fifth in the final poll, one spot beyond the playoff foursome.

The team closed out the season in the Rose Bowl.

FORTY-SEVEN

IN THE END

THERE ARE A *thousand ways to measure the effort required to restore Penn State's football program. It took one out-of-this-world running back, two determined head coaches, three exceptional quarterbacks, five stellar recruiting classes, and dozens of unheralded walk-ons.*

If you had the patience, you could probably count up the practice sessions they each attended, the hours they poured into meetings and film study, maybe even the calories they consumed at the training table. Toss in the number of clutch catches, tackles, and kicks across those five seasons and you begin to see the magic in what they pulled off, the kismet of a kid named Saquon Barkley and a kid named Trace McSorley popping up on campus in the school's hour of need.

But that still doesn't account for the intangibles: the muscle, sweat, level of faith it took to commit one's body and soul to the rebuilding effort, to accept with humility the long odds, heartbreaking losses, month after month of hardships, all for the sake of an idea, success with honor, a chance to leave behind something larger than yourself.

And that's ultimately what it took to reclaim what Jerry Sandusky nearly destroyed.

CHRISTIAN HACKENBERG: I don't know if you can count on one hand how many programs would have been able to survive what we survived.

Thrive the way we did. To be a part of that is really humbling. As a freshman, I don't think I fully realized how impactful it would be in the Penn State community. I'm proud to be a part of that group of guys. They're special.

GREGG GARRITY: I mean, everybody that joined the program at that time did it for the love of the game, right? It wasn't for a bowl game. It wasn't for national championships. It was because we loved the game. We were all like-minded. And, yeah, we were very close come 2016.

We had some freak athletes on the team, but it's not like we were far better than everybody else. We just had a very, very good team chemistry. We still talk every day, try to get together when we can. At my wedding, they were all there. Special group of guys.

MALIK GOLDEN: I won't go down in history as the best Penn State player ever, but as long as I go down as one of the most loyal players, I'm fine with that. Me and the group of guys that came here in 2012 and stayed through it all.

MICHAEL MAUTI: Looking back, it easily could have gone the other way. When you watch *Saving the Roar,* you're like, This could have gone either way when we were sitting there at oh-and-two in 2012.

But in 2016, I'm standing on the sideline in Pasadena. Penn State's in the Rose Bowl.

The fifth-year seniors on that team were true freshmen in my last season. We were the catalysts. Those guys are the ones who kept it together. It's hard to believe we made it back in that time span, given the rules under which we had to play. That's a credit to O'Brien and Franklin, Saquon and Hackenberg, who bought into everything we were preaching.

A lot of guys deserve credit.

TRACE MCSORLEY: If you ask me, football is one of the greatest sports, because one single player can't take over a game. You know, if LeBron turns it on in any NBA game, his team could win. It's kind of up to him. But in football, the best player's not even on the field half the time.

CHRISTIAN HACKENBERG: That's what makes Penn State so special. There are so many people there who just live it, breathe it, and love it. Like, I still talk to Kirk Diehl once a month. Spider Caldwell? Every time I go back there, I go into Spider's office, sit down and talk.

He's the guy who told me to wear number fourteen.

I wanted to wear six or some shit. He's like, "No, you're wearing fourteen."

I'm like, "Why?"

He's like, "It's a legacy number. The last national championship quarterback wore it, so you're wearing it."

Those are the conversations you have, the people you build relationships with. That's something I value a lot more than the game of football.

That's why I say I was in too deep. Leaving after that freshman year would have been the easy way out. And I hadn't made one decision up to that point that was the easy way out. So why do it now, when it's selfish? That's not in my DNA, not how I'm wired.

For the players on that 2016 team, the journey ended in the Rose Bowl, not the College Football Playoff, as some had hoped. Penn State was matched with 9–3 USC, another talent-laden team that had struggled early in the year, then found its footing alongside a promising young quarterback, dashing off eight straight wins. True to form, the Lions fell behind early, then stormed back to take a two-touchdown lead, but this time their opponent refused to buckle. The 52–49 shootout ended on a field goal, the last play of the game.

Penn State had lost, but not without delivering another electric performance. In one stretch, JoeMo's effervescent offense scored twenty-eight points in four plays. The highlight of the night—one that people still rave about to this day—showcased Saquon Barkley at the peak of his powers, darting left and right through a maze of USC defenders.

DAVID JONES: Best run I ever saw.

RICH SCARCELLA, SPORTSWRITER AND COLUMNIST, *READING EAGLE*: Barkley took a handoff from Trace McSorley, saw no room inside, bounced the play outside, made six defenders miss, and beat All-America cornerback Adoree' Jackson to the left corner of the end zone.

DAVID JONES: I've probably watched that play more than any single play I've covered in person. At one point in the clip, there are four Trojans around him—two right behind him, two in front of him—and they all miss. He makes them *all* miss.

I still get chills watching that.

KIRK HERBSTREIT: That's Saquon Barkley in a nutshell. The play is designed to go up the middle, but he bounces it outside and two defenders have a chance to make a play. He shakes the safety. Another safety comes up. *He* misses him, too. Then Barkley cuts all the way back across the field and shows you the speed to take it to the end zone.

JOE MOORHEAD: It's a procession of missed tackles.

When USC finally claimed the victory on a successful forty-six-yard kick, Penn State's players were deflated. The post-game locker room—so often a tableau of singing and dancing—was suddenly a warren of whispers.

But the disappointment lifted. In time, all the athletes who stayed true to the school came to appreciate what they had accomplished with their dedication to the program. No one loss could take that away.

KOA FARMER: It was always a dream to play in that game. I grew up five minutes from the Rose Bowl. When I was a kid, my parents used to put me in the stroller and jog me around the stadium. I literally went to elementary school down the street.

I never thought I'd end up at Penn State and come back home to play in the Rose Bowl. During the season, I always gave my tickets away, because my parents didn't come to a lot of games. But I always said, If we ever go to the Rose Bowl, I get everyone's freaking tickets. I gave you mine, I'm getting yours when we go to Pasadena.

The moment I knew we were going to the Rose Bowl, I got up and said, "All right, I need everyone's freaking tickets—every one of you."

I think I had literally fifty-eight tickets to that game.

CARLA NEAL-HALEY: As much as I would have loved to see Penn State play in the national championship series, it was kismet for my family that we went to the Rose Bowl instead.

My other son was a football manager for USC. So, both of my boys were on the field. One of my favorite pictures of my children shows Grant and Wesley together—Wesley in his USC manager's gear and Grant in his Penn State football gear.

For us, that was a big moment.

MALIK GOLDEN: Walking out and seeing half the stadium in Penn State colors—oh, man, that was crazy. Penn State fans showed up.

KOA FARMER: We lost, but just to be a part of a game like that, the history of the two programs that played that day . . . we ultimately put on a show, we put on a show.

EVAN SCHWAN: We made it to the Rose Bowl and people still doubted us, calling the season a fluke. Winning eleven games isn't a fluke. Winning the Big Ten Championship—after being down by twenty-one points against a really good Wisconsin team—that's not a fluke. What did we have to prove? That Penn State was back.

CHARLIE FISHER: It's a story bigger than football. We hear that cliché a lot, but it's true. Those kids taught me about overcoming adversity. When things are tough, that's when you find out a lot about the character of a man. And those five seasons tell you everything you need to know about Penn State football.

BOB MORGAN: I like to brag that we went through all that and we've still had more wins than Michigan since that time.

JAMES FRANKLIN: I know it's about wins and losses, but it's also about preparing your guys for life, and I know that our seniors, our guys, were ready to go take on whatever life has.

CHRISTIAN HACKENBERG: I never wanted to be a martyr. At least, I can put my head down at night and say, *Hey, the people who matter respect what I did.* And, as the team keeps growing and the program keeps going in the direction it's going, that's all the validation any of us needed. We could be two or three head-coaching changes removed from Coach Franklin now and we just didn't allow that to happen. And that's ultimately because of those guys in the locker room. That's what I'm most proud of. I feel very fortunate to have been a part of that bunch, to have been a captain for two years, the guy who led that bunch.

SILAS REDD: I never again played football like I played at Penn State. I never got back to that level. I scored more touchdowns, but I didn't do what I needed to do for the Trojans. I had some good games, hundred-yard games, here and there, but I didn't do what I wanted to do. That hurt.

But I met some of my best friends here in California. Met my wife. My life is cool. I don't know what would have happened if I had stayed at Penn State, but I can't say I regret the decision to go, because I have a beautiful wife, a beautiful son. I'm happy.

Before I left for my visit to USC, though, Coach O'Brien and I had a really good meeting. Coach London, the running back coach at the time—he and I had a great relationship. My friends—it was all good. All good, man. My decision to leave didn't have anything to do with those people.

Maybe I never got to express that, but I want to take the time to say now that it was never about the team and it was never about the new coaches, because they made it very worthwhile to stay.

It wasn't them. It wasn't them.

Silas Redd played his final two seasons for USC. He signed with the Washington Commanders as an undrafted free agent, but his NFL career came to a premature halt with a preseason knee injury. He returned with his family to Los Angeles, where he now works as a personal trainer.

Christian Hackenberg was selected by the New York Jets in the second round of the 2016 NFL Draft. He remained on the roster for two seasons, but never got to play in a league game. He now coaches with Bill Belton at Winslow Township High School in New Jersey. In 2021, the two steered the Eagles to the NJSIAA Group 4 Central Championship Game.

Adam Breneman left Penn State in late 2015, with a degree in hand, after suffering through a string of knee injuries. In 2016, he returned to the field at UMass and led the country in receiving by a tight end for two seasons. He continues to showcase his diverse talents as a coach, a political consultant, an entrepreneur, and a social media star. The candid interviews he recorded with old teammates for the Adam Breneman Show *podcast* helped to guide me through this book project.

Michael Mauti rehabbed the knee he injured in 2012 and played five seasons in the NFL, two for the Vikings and three for the Saints—all while battling severe ulcerative colitis. In a 2015 game broadcast on Thursday Night Football, *he blocked a punt and returned it for a touchdown.*

Michael Zordich signed with the Carolina Panthers as an undrafted free agent in 2013, then tore an ACL on the first play of his first preseason game. After a year on the Saints' practice squad, he retired from football and went to work on a twelve-thousand-acre cattle ranch in southeast Ohio. He's now a partner at the Fancy Meats processing plant in Cadiz, Ohio.

John Urschel played three seasons of pro ball for the Baltimore Ravens, then walked away from the game in his prime to pursue a career in mathematics. In 2021, he earned a PhD at the Massachusetts Institute of Technology and later served as a Junior Fellow at Harvard.

Matt McGloin kept proving the doubters wrong, logging four full seasons with the Raiders and brief stretches with the Eagles, Texans, and Chiefs before exiting the game. He has worked as an analyst and sideline reporter for the Big Ten Network and cohosted the weekly Paydirt *podcast with Tom Hannifan.*

Sam Ficken also moved on to the NFL, kicking for two years with the Rams and two years with the Jets. When he isn't on the football field, he makes his way back to Wall Street.

Saquon Barkley played one more season at Penn State, finishing fourth in votes for the Heisman Trophy. He was selected by the New York Giants with the second overall pick in the 2018 NFL draft.

Trace McSorley owns nearly every major quarterback record at Penn State, setting single-season marks for most passing yards, most passing touchdowns, and total touchdowns. He also holds the career mark for most yards on offense. He was drafted by the Baltimore Ravens in the sixth round of the 2019 draft, then crossed the country to play for the Arizona Cardinals. On December 21, 2022, he was named the team's starter for a week sixteen matchup with Tom Brady and the Tampa Bay Buccaneers. The Cardinals lost in overtime 19–16.

In 2020, Matty Fresh's musical tribute to the quarterback spawned four thousand clips on TikTok, creating a viral video movement. The original video, uploaded to YouTube in 2018, has been viewed more than 7.8 million times.

Nick Scott and Grant Haley each won a Super Bowl ring with the L.A. Rams. Chris Godwin and Donovan Smith earned one with the Tampa Bay Buccaneers. Jordan Lucas received his while playing for the Kansas City Chiefs.

Kevin Givens, Jordan Hill, Miles Sanders, Garrett Sickels, and Anthony Zettel have all played in the Super Bowl.

Adrian Amos, Troy Apke, Ryan Bates, Brandon Bell, Cam Brown, Jason Cabinda, Mike Gesicki, Blake Gillikin, DaeSean Hamilton, Mike Hull, Brendan Mahon, Connor McGovern, Carl Nassib, Amani Oruwariye, John Reid, Allen Robinson, and DeAndre Thompkins have all played at least one game in the NFL.

On June 21, 2021, in an Instagram clip shot in the backyard of his childhood home, Nassib became the first active NFL player to acknowledge that he is gay, prompting a run on his jersey at the league partner Fanatics website. He received public support from Penn State, the Las Vegas Raiders (where he played for two seasons), and the NFL. "I was proud of Carl when he led the nation in sacks," James Franklin tweeted. "But I'm even more proud of him now."

Billy Fessler and Nayeem Wartman-White coach alongside Joe Moorhead at the University of Akron.

Bill O'Brien coached seven years for the Houston Texans, then served as the offensive coordinator and quarterbacks coach for the Alabama Crimson Tide, before returning to New England as the Patriots' offensive coordinator once again.

In 2023, James Franklin entered his tenth season as Penn State's head coach, fresh off a return trip to the Rose Bowl where he emerged with a 35–21 win over eighth-ranked Utah.

ACKNOWLEDGMENTS

It all starts with the players from those five seasons.

Without them, there is no book.

They had little reason to talk to me, especially given the way they'd been mistreated by the press, and yet they shared their stories with me. Not just their triumphs, but also their trials.

And they trusted me to treat those stories with the dignity they deserve.

I've done my best to honor that trust, to piece together their observations in a way that accurately reveals what they experienced. I am deeply indebted to the coaches, sportswriters, alumni, lettermen, and other figures quoted in the book, too. I'd like to single out Spider Caldwell, one of the most generous souls I've ever met.

I am forever grateful to Mark Brennan and Mike Poorman, pals from my days of covering Penn State football as an undergrad. Both listened carefully to my idea for the book, offered crucial guidance, and cheerfully responded to every needy text that followed.

My heart brims with gratitude to these terrific people, as well.

To Andy Zipfel, who sat beside me years ago at *ESPN the Magazine* and thought to reach out when he heard I was writing a book. He offered to put me in touch with his friend Rick McSorley.

To Rick McSorley, who read Andy's email and agreed to talk to me, then put me in touch with his son Trace.

To Pete Kowalski, who volunteered to introduce me to folks in PSU's Athletic Department. And to the many generous PSU people who helped along the way, particularly John Affleck, Thomas Berner, Ryan Jones, Kristina Petersen, Steve Sampsell, Brian Shoenfelt, and Scott Sidwell.

To Andrew Destin, who spent a good part of his senior year helping me with research.

To PSU classmates and lifelong friends: Mark Ashenfelter, Carol Rath Gosser, Liz Kahn, Rob King, Chris Lindsley, Chris Loder, Greg Loder, Celeste McCauley, Richard McRae, Dan Oleski, Susan Kearney Rash, and John Severance. To Katie and Liam of Airbnb, York and Mara Ast, Adam Balkin, Rick and Linda Brooks, Danielle Claro, Ryan Eberts, Marissa Feind, Bruce Feldman, Adam Fisher, Larry Frascella, Sandra Garcia, Pat Hanlon, Mike and Marian Hoffman, Brad and Tanya Hunt, CarolLee Kidd, Desmond and Kerry Lyons, J.R. Mangan, Tom Mangan, John McAlley, Tom and Sylvia McLoone, Rob Michel, Graham Miles, Dan Peres, Linda Pierpont, Andy Regal, Alan Richardson, Brian and Keira Smith, Allen St. John, Bill Tonelli, Jason and Anne Valentzas, Michael Weinreb, Jessica Welke, Seth Wickersham, and Jeff Wise for their unwavering support.

To my Consumer Reports colleagues Jerry Beilinson, Wendy Bounds, Glenn Derene, Sara Morrow Harcourt, and Jen Shecter, who rallied to my side as I attempted to report and write a book while holding down a full-time job.

To David Halpern, who shepherded me and my half-baked idea from proposal to manuscript to printed book with boundless grace and enthusiasm. To Marc Resnick, who listened intently to the pitch, said, "yes," then gave me the time, space, and direction to make it soar. To Lily Cronig, who patiently guided me through the final steps, and Nikolaas Eickelbeck, who came up with the awesome cover design.

To the Palazzi family, anchored by my other mother Vivian, for lifting my spirits at every turn; Jerry Raymond and Gail Keating for pushing me to pursue my dream of authoring a book; my brothers, Kevin and Greg Raymond, who offered food, a place to sleep, wise counsel, a laugh, whatever I needed, on my many trips to State College for research (and, yes, maybe a football game); and my mother Pudgy Raymond, who stopped hundreds—if not thousands—of unsuspecting strangers on the streets of Pennsylvania to talk up this project for three years running. If the book becomes a bestseller, it will be because of her.

To my sons, Adam and Will, who inspire me each and every day with their thoughtfulness, passion, and creativity. And, finally, to my radiant wife (and fellow wordsmith), Lynne Palazzi, who shouldered a lion's share of the work at home to free me up to think and write. Trust me when I tell you, without her selflessness and persistent encouragement, there is indeed no book.

AUTHOR INTERVIEWS

Brandon Bell, February 15, 2022.

Mark Brennan, September 3, 2020.

Sara Butcher, September 17, 2020.

Alex Butterworth, January 21, 2022.

Brad "Spider" Caldwell, July 20, 2021.

Karen Caldwell, August 31, 2021.

Kyle Carter, November 18, 2021.

Keith Conlin, March 29, 2021.

Jack Davis, February 25, 2022.

Jesse Della Valle, April 11, 2022.

Koa Farmer, August 9, 2021.

Billy Fessler, June 9, 2022.

Sam Ficken, March 17, 2022.

Charlie Fisher, October 11, 2021.

Craig Fitzgerald, April 8, 2021.

Bob Flounders, September 17, 2020; January 20, 2022.

Matty Fresh, March 18, 2021.

Gregg Garrity, September 9, 2020.

Brian Gilbert, December 14, 2021.

Malik Golden, August 27, 2021.

Christian Hackenberg, October 1, 2021.

Bob Hartman, October 7, 2021.

David Jones, June 19, 2022.

Ryan Jones, May 20, 2021.

Joe Julius, August 26, 2021.

Vadim Kaloshin, January 10, 2022.

Zach Ladonis, July 13, 2021.

Geno Lewis, September 27, 2021.

Lance Lonergan, September 30, 2021.

Rick McSorley, May 7, 2021.

Trace McSorley, May 28, 2021.

Bob Morgan, November 11, 2021.

Stephon Morris, August 6, 2021.

Michael Nash, May 22, 2022.

Carla Neal-Haley, May 26, 2022.

Rob Nellis, February 28, 2022.

Tom Pancoast, January 7, 2022.

Venita Parker, January 6, 2022.

Neil Rudel, September 18, 2020.

Lydell Sargeant, October 15, 2021.

Sopan Shah, January 24, 2022.

Eric Shrive, March 19, 2021.

Garrett Sickels, August 17, 2021.

Rick Slater, February 11, 2022.

Jordan Smith, October 27, 2022.

Audrey Snyder, February 3, 2022.

Darian Somers, April 21, 2021.

Chance Sorrell, October 11, 2021.

Matt Stankiewitch, September 9, 2021.

Tim Sweeney, June 14, 2021.

John Urschel, September 10, 2021.

Von Walker, August 28, 2020.

Michael Weinreb, November 29, 2021.

Troy Weller, February 13, 2022.

Allison Williams, September 1, 2020.

Sam Williams, August 7, 2021.

Michael Yancich, August 12, 2021.

Matt Zanellato, March 21, 2022.

Pat Zerbe, May 28, 2021.

NOTES

THIS STORY COULD not have come to light without the players, coaches, and others who agreed to share their experiences with me. Over the course of two years, I interviewed sixty people for the book. (See "Author Interviews" for a list of names and dates.) In between, I pored through hour after hour of archived material. A few of the quotes in the italic text were pulled from news stories. Everything else comes from those author interviews, podcasts, official transcripts, online video clips (where I could see and hear the person speaking), and first-person stories published in print and online. Here's a list of the additional sources.

Introduction

Michael Mauti: Players' public statement, GoPSUtv, July 25, 2012.

Joe Paterno: Sally Jenkins, "Joe Paterno's First Interview Since the Penn State-Sandusky Scandal," *Washington Post,* January 14, 2012.

Silas Redd: *Adam Breneman Show* podcast, November 21, 2019.]

Michael Zordich: Mike Poorman, "How Zordich, Mauti & Penn State Handled the Ultimate in Negative Recruiting," StateCollege.com, July 28, 2016.

One: All In

Jordan Hill: Interviewed by Matthew Ogden, Matthew Paolizzi, and Samuel Brungo, *Podward State* podcast, November 12, 2020.

Michael Mauti: *Adam Breneman Show* podcast, October 1, 2019.

Matt McGloin: *Adam Breneman Show* podcast, October 8, 2019.

Bill O'Brien: Interviewed by Tim Sweeney and Keith Conlin, *Goon Show* podcast, July 31, 2013; interviewed by Arielle Sargent, GoPSUtv, April 12, 2018.

Two: OB

Michael Mauti: *Adam Breneman Show* podcast, October 1, 2019.

Matt McGloin: *Adam Breneman Show* podcast, October 8, 2019.

Bill O'Brien: Penn State press conference, November 20, 2012.

Brandon Short: "Bill O'Brien to Coach Nittany Lions," ESPN.com News Services, January 5, 2012.

Three: Blindsided

Adrian Amos: *The Journey: Big Ten Football 2014*—Penn State Senior Class Feature, Big Ten Network.

Adam Breneman: *Adam Breneman Show* podcast, October 8, 2019.

Michael Mauti: *Saving the Roar*, 2021; interviewed by Mark Brennan, *Fight On State*, Big Ten Media Day, July 26, 2012; *Adam Breneman Show* podcast, October 1, 2019.

Matt McGloin: *Adam Breneman Show* podcast, October 8, 2019.

Steve Jones: *Saving the Roar*, written and directed by Michael P. Nash, 2021.

Bill O'Brien: Interviewed by Chip Minemyer, *Tribune-Democrat* (Johnstown, PA), August 8, 2021; *Saving the Roar*, 2021; Big Ten Media Day press conference, Big Ten Network, July 26, 2012.

Silas Redd: *Adam Breneman Show* podcast, November 21, 2019.

Michael Zordich: *Saving the Roar*, 2021.

Four: The Ones Who Stayed

John Bacon: *Saving the Roar*, written and directed by Michael P. Nash, 2021.

Mike Hull: *The Journey: Big Ten Football 2014*—Penn State Senior Class Feature, Big Ten Network.

Pete Massaro: Media Day interview, *Blue-White Illustrated*, August 9, 2012.

Michael Mauti: *Adam Breneman Show* podcast, October 1, 2019; interviewed by Matt McGloin and Tom Hannifan, *Paydirt* podcast, November 12, 2021.

Bill O'Brien: Interviewed by Arielle Sargent, GoPSUtv, April 12, 2018; *Tribune-Democrat* (Johnstown, PA), August 8, 2021; Big Ten Media Day press conference, Big Ten Network, July 26, 2012.

Michael Zordich: Interviewed by Matt McGloin and Tom Hannifan, *Paydirt* podcast, November 26, 2021.

Five: Rally Time

Michael Mauti: Interviewed by Matt McGloin and Tom Hannifan, *Paydirt* podcast, November 12, 2021.

Bill O'Brien: Big Ten Media Day press conference, Big Ten Network, July 26, 2012.

Allen Robinson: Interviewed by Mark Brennan, *Fight On State*, July 31, 2012.

Michael Zordich: Interviewed by *Blue-White Illustrated*, July 31, 2012.

Six: Going Public

Steve Jones: *The Journey: Big Ten Football 2014*—Penn State Senior Class Feature, Big Ten Network.

Michael Mauti: Players' public statement, GoPSUtv, July 25, 2012; interviewed by Matt Mc-Gloin and Tom Hannifan, *Paydirt* podcast, November 12, 2021; *Adam Breneman Show* podcast, October 1, 2019.

Matt McGloin: *Paydirt* podcast, November 26, 2021; *Paydirt* podcast, November 12, 2021.

Bill O'Brien: Post-game press conference, November 17, 2012; midweek press conference, October 12, 2012.

Michael Zordich: interviewed by Matt McGloin and Tom Hannifan, *Paydirt* podcast, November 26, 2021; players' public statement, GoPSUtv, July 25, 2012.

Seven: Lost Boys

Adam Breneman: *Adam Breneman Show* podcast, November 21, 2019.

Justin Brown: Oklahoma University press conference, *Tulsa World,* August 7, 2012.

Anthony Fera: Personal statement, *Onward State,* August 3, 2012.

Silas Redd: Personal statement, ESPN, November 29, 2012; *Adam Breneman Show* podcast, November 21, 2019.

Adam Rittenberg: "Don't Blame PSU's Red for Move to USC," ESPN, July 31, 2012.

Eight: Run-ons

"Athletic department official: Audrey Snyder, Nearly one year later, Penn State's work through NCAA sanctions continues to be a learning process," Harrisburg *Patriot-News,* May 31, 2013.

Bill O'Brien: *Goon Show* podcast, July 31, 2013.

Brandon Smith: Post-game press conference, November 18, 2017.

Nine: The Walk-on QB

Matt McGloin: Tony Mancuso, PSU Football profile, September 24, 2012; *Paydirt* podcast, November 12, 2021; *Adam Breneman Show* podcast, October 8, 2019; *Paydirt* podcast, November 26, 2021.

Bill O'Brien: Interview aired on WNEP-TV (Scranton), December 28, 2016; post-game press conference, *Blue-White Illustrated,* November 17, 2012.

Ten: Charlie Mike

Pete Massaro: Interviewed by Mark Brennan, *Fight On State,* August 23, 2012.

Stephon Morris: Interviewed by Mark Brennan, *Fight On State,* August 23, 2012.

Matt Stankiewitch: Interviewed by Mark Brennan, *Fight On State,* August 23, 2012.

Eleven: Names to Remember

John Cappelletti: Heisman Trophy acceptance speech, December 13, 1973.

James Franklin: Jourdan Rodrigue, "Nittany Lines: More uniform reactions, Paris Palmer, and the brother of QB1," *Centre Daily Times,* July 17, 2015.

Garry Gilliam: Media Day interview, GoPSUtv, August 10, 2012.

Matt McGloin: *Paydirt* podcast, November 26, 2021.

Bill O'Brien: *Tribune-Democrat* (Johnstown, PA), August 8, 2021.

Joe Paterno: Richard E. Peck, *Something for Joey*, Laurel Leaf, April 1, 1983.

Twelve: Rough Start

Derek Day: Post-game press conference, September 1, 2012.

Jordan Hill: Post-game press conference, September 1, 2012.

Matt McGloin: Post-game press conference, September 8, 2012.

Stephon Morris: Post-game press conference, September 8, 2012.

Bill O'Brien: Associated Press, "Penn State Pep Rally Opens Historic Football Weekend," *TribLive,* August 31, 2012; post-game press conference, September 8, 2012; midweek press conference, September 11, 2012; interviewed by Piers Morgan, *Piers Morgan Tonight,* December 30, 2012.

Thirteen: Battling in the Big Ten

Adrian Amos: Interviewed by Mark Brennan, *Fight On State,* September 29, 2012.

Kyle Carter: *FTB Throwback: Leap of Faith—Penn State vs. Northwestern 2012,* February 2, 2021.

Donnie Collins: *FTB Throwback: Leap of Faith—Penn State vs. Northwestern 2012,* February 2, 2021.

Pat Fitzgerald: Post-game press conference, October 6, 2012.

Gerald Hodges: Interviewed by Mark Brennan, *Fight On State,* September 29, 2012; post-game press conference, October 6, 2012.

Charles London: Post-game press conference, October 6, 2012.

Venric Mark, Jr.: Post-game press conference, October 6, 2012.

Michael Mauti: Interviewed by Mark Brennan, *Fight On State,* September 29, 2012; post-game press conference, October 6, 2012.

Sean McDonough: ESPN broadcast, November 10, 2012.

Matt McGloin: *Paydirt* podcast, November 12, 2021; *Paydirt* podcast, November 26, 2021; interviewed by Dave Revsine, Gerry DiNardo, and Howard Griffith, Big Ten Network, October 12, 2012; Stephen Pianovich, "Lions Revving Up Offense with NASCAR Look," *Daily Collegian,* October 10, 2012; post-game press conference, October 6, 2012; *FTB Throwback: Leap of Faith—Penn State vs. Northwestern 2012,* February 2, 2021.

Stephon Morris: Interviewed by Mark Brennan, *Fight On State,* September 29, 2012.

Bill O'Brien: Midweek press conference, October 2, 2012; midweek press conference, November 20, 2012; midweek press conference, September 11, 2012; midweek press conference, November 13, 2012; interviewed by GoPSUtv, October 6, 2012; midweek press conference, October 16, 2012; post-game press conference, October 27, 2012; post-game press conference, November 10, 2012.

Allen Robinson: Interviewed by Matt McGloin and Tom Hannifan, *Paydirt* podcast, November 12, 2021; post-game press conference, October 6, 2012.

Chris Spielman: ESPN broadcast, November 10, 2012.

Michael Zordich: Post-game press conference, October 6, 2012.

Fourteen: Losing Mauti

Jordan Hill: Post-game interview, *Blue-White Illustrated,* November 17, 2012.

Gerald Hodges: Post-game interview, *247 Sports,* November 17, 2012; post-game interview, GoPSUtv, November 24, 2012.

Steve Jones: *The Journey: Michael Mauti—Penn State Football,* Big Ten Network, April 29, 2013.

Michael Mauti: *The Journey: Michael Mauti—Penn State Football,* Big Ten Network, April 29, 2013; interviewed by Matt McGloin and Tom Hannifan, *Paydirt* podcast, November 12, 2021; *Adam Breneman Show* podcast, October 1, 2019; post-game interview, GoPSUtv, November 24, 2012.

Matt McGloin: Post-game press conference, November 17, 2012; *Paydirt* podcast, November 12, 2021; *The Journey: Michael Mauti—Penn State Football,* Big Ten Network, April 29, 2013.

Stephon Morris: Post-game press conference, November 17, 2012.

Bill O'Brien: Midweek press conference, November 20, 2012; post-game press conference, *Blue-White Illustrated,* November 17, 2012; post-game press conference, November 24, 2012.

Matt Stankiewitch: Post-game press conference, November 17, 2012.

John Urschel: Post-game press conference, November 17, 2012.

Michael Zordich: Post-game interview, *Blue-White Illustrated,* November 17, 2012; *The Journey: Michael Mauti—Penn State Football,* Big Ten Network, April 29, 2013.

Fifteen: Senior Day

Jake Fagnano: Post-game press conference, November 24, 2012.

Jordan Hill: Post-game press conference, November 24, 2012.

Michael Mauti: Post-game interview, GoPSUtv, November 25, 2012; *Adam Breneman Show* podcast, October 1, 2019.

Matt McGloin: *FTB Throwback: Leap of Faith—Penn State vs. Northwestern 2012,* YouTube, February 2, 2021; interviewed by Tony Mancuso, GoPSUtv, November 20, 2012; *Adam Breneman Show* podcast, October 8, 2019.

Bill O'Brien: Midweek press conference, November 20, 2012; post-game press conference, November 24, 2012; *Tribune-Democrat* (Johnstown, PA), August 8, 2021.

Ted Roof: Post-game press conference, November 24, 2012.

Ron Vanderlinden: Post-game press conference, November 24, 2012.

Michael Zordich: *Saving the Roar,* written and directed by Michael P. Nash, 2021.

Sixteen: The Quarterback of the Future

John Bacon: *Saving the Roar,* written and directed by Michael P. Nash, 2021.

Adam Breneman: Interviewed by Steve McGrath, *Beyond the Helmet* podcast, YouTube, July 8, 2020; *Adam Breneman Show* podcast, August 27, 2019; *Adam Breneman Show* podcast, September 9, 2019; *Beyond the Helmet* podcast, YouTube, July 8, 2020.

Christian Hackenberg: *Adam Breneman Show* podcast, August 27, 2019; interviewed by Andrew Porter, TSP Radio, Philadelphia, 2012; interviewed by Samantha Eisenberg, *Christian Hackenberg Part 1,* YouTube, December 11, 2013.

Steve Jones: *Saving the Roar,* 2021.

Bill O'Brien: Interviewed by Samantha Eisenberg, *Christian Hackenberg Part 1,* YouTube, December 11, 2013; *Saving the Roar,* 2021.

Garrett Sickels: *Adam Breneman Show,* September 9, 2019.

Pete Thamel: "Sanctions Decimate the Nittany Lions Now and for Years to Come," *New York Times,* July 23, 2012.

Seventeen: Enter Hackenberg

Tyler Ferguson: Interviewed by John Zaninovich, *Move My Mass* podcast, December 22, 2020.

Christian Hackenberg: Interviewed by Mike Hall, Big Ten Network, December 3, 2013.

Bill O'Brien: Interviewed by Samantha Eisenberg, *Christian Hackenberg Part 2,* YouTube, December 11, 2013.

Eighteen: Living Up to the Hype

Garry Gilliam: Post-game interview, *Nittany Extra,* August 31, 2013.

Christian Hackenberg: Post-game press conference, *Fight On State,* August 31, 2013; post-game interview by Tony Mancuso, GoPSUtv, August 31, 2013.

Ty Howle: Post-game interview by Tony Mancuso, GoPSUtv, August 31, 2013.

Bill O'Brien: Interviewed by Jeannine Edwards, Syracuse–Penn State broadcast, ESPN, August 31, 2013; midweek press conference, September 3, 2013; post-game press conference, GoPSUtv, August 31, 2013.

Nineteen: Run-ons, Take Two

George Curry: Interviewed by WNEP-TV (Scranton), November 2, 2013.

Bill O'Brien: *Penn State Football 2013—Run-on Program,* GoPSUtv, October 25, 2013.

Twenty: Nittany Nation

Jason Cabinda: Midweek press conference, September 15, 2015.

Tom Hannifan: *Paydirt* podcast, July 22, 2022.

Gerald Hodges: Interviewed by Tony Mancuso, GoPSUtv, October 23, 2012.

Twenty-One: Four-OT Win

Adrian Amos: Interviewed by Tony Mancuso, GoPSUtv, October 12, 2013.

John Bacon: *Penn State Classic, 10/12/13 vs. Michigan,* Big Ten Network.

Saquon Barkley: *The Journey: Saquon Barkley Talks In-State Rivalries & Michigan,* Big Ten Network, September 24, 2016.

Kyle Baublitz: Post-game press conference, October 12, 2013.

Bill Belton: Interviewed by Mike Hall, Howard Griffith, and Glen Mason, Big Ten Network, October 14, 2013; interviewed by Samuel Brungo and Will Pegler, *Podward State* podcast, March 15, 2021.

Glenn Carson: Post-game press conference, October 13, 2013.

Sam Ficken: *Penn State Classic, 10/12/13 vs. Michigan,* Big Ten Network.

Christian Hackenberg: *The Journey: Big Ten Football—Christian Hackenberg Feature,* Big Ten Network, January 27, 2016; post-game press conference, October 12, 2013.

Matt McGloin: *Paydirt* podcast, November 12, 2021.

Matt Millen: Michigan–Penn State broadcast, ESPN, October 12, 2013.

Bill O'Brien: *Tribune-Democrat* (Johnstown, PA), August 8, 2021; *Penn State Classic, 10/12/13 vs. Michigan,* Big Ten Network; midweek press conference, October 15, 2013; NFL Combine press conference, *PennLive,* February 28, 2018.

Allen Robinson: Interviewed by Matt McGloin and Tom Hannifan, *Paydirt* podcast, November 12, 2021; post-game press conference, October 12, 2013; *Penn State Classic, 10/12/13 vs. Michigan,* Big Ten Network.

Joe Tessitore: Michigan–Penn State broadcast, ESPN, October 12, 2013.

John Urschel: *The Journey: Big Ten Football—Christian Hackenberg Feature,* Big Ten Network, January 27, 2016.

Twenty-Two: Hitting the Books

Todd Blackledge: Ohio State Week Q&A, Penn State Football, October 24, 2013.

Grant Haley: Midweek press conference, September 22, 2015.

Brian Irvin: *Rise and Rally* interview recorded by Steve Lin, YouTube, July 31, 2012.

Michael Mauti: *Rise and Rally* interview recorded by Steve Lin, YouTube, July 31, 2012.

Mac McWhorter: Interviewed by GoPSUtv, November 4, 2012.

Andrew Nelson: "Why I Chose PSU," ESPN, February 14, 2013.

Bill O'Brien: Midweek press conference, October 23, 2012; interviewed by Jim Axelrod, *CBS Evening News,* December 2, 2013.

Joe Paterno: Tim Layden, "Joe Paterno 1926–2012," *Sports Illustrated,* January 30, 2012.

Brady Rourke: Interviewed by GoPSUtv, September 23, 2012.

John Urschel: *Black History Month: John Urschel, Mathematician,* Big Ten Network, February 15, 2020.

Twenty-Three: Beating the Odds

Glenn Carson: Post-game interview, Madison.com, November 30, 2013.

Bill O'Brien: *Tribune-Democrat* (Johnstown, PA), August 8, 2021; post-game interview, Tony Mancuso, GoPSUtv, November 30, 2013; post-game press conference, November 30, 2013.

Mike Patrick: Penn State–Wisconsin broadcast, ESPN, November 30, 2013.

Twenty-Four: Exit O'Brien

Adam Breneman: Interviewed by Matt McGloin and Tom Hannifan, *Paydirt* podcast, July 13, 2022.

Mike Gesicki: *Adam Breneman Show* podcast, November 5, 2019.

Larry Johnson: Press conference, January 3, 2014.

Dave Joyner: Press conference, January 2, 2014.

Andrea Kremer: Q&A with David Jones, *PennLive,* May 22, 2013.

Bill O'Brien: *Dan Patrick Show,* January 15, 2014; David Jones, "Bill O'Brien, the Outsider, Arrived at the Perfect Time; Maybe He's Leaving at the Right Time, Too," Harrisburg *Patriot-News,* January 1, 2014.

Twenty-Five: Paterno People

James Franklin: Year-end press conference, January 21, 2017.

Robbie Gould: Chicago Bears locker room interview posted on YouTube by Chris K, November 9, 2011.

Michael Mauti: *Adam Breneman Show* podcast, October 1, 2019.

Stephon Morris: *Saving the Roar*, written and directed by Michael P. Nash, 2021.

Bill O'Brien: Interviewed by Andrea Kremer, *Real Sports with Bryant Gumbel*, May 21, 2013.

Chima Okali: Player interviews posted by Mark Brennan, *Fight On State*, November 9, 2011.

Silas Redd: *Adam Breneman Show* podcast, November 21, 2019; interviewed by Big Ten Network, November 9, 2011.

Michael Robinson: Memorial service remarks aired on WTAE TV (Pittsburgh), January 27, 2012.

Nate Stupar: Player interviews posted by Mark Brennan, *Fight On State*, November 9, 2011.

Michael Zordich: Player interviews posted by Mark Brennan, *Fight On State*, November 9, 2011.

Twenty-Six: Enter Franklin

Adam Breneman: *Adam Breneman Show* podcast, October 22, 2019.

Jason Cabinda: *Adam Breneman Show* podcast, October 22, 2019.

Bruce Feldman: Interviewed by Joe Starkey and Chris Mueller, *Starkey and Mueller Show*, 93.7 the FAN (Pittsburgh), January 7, 2014.

James Franklin: Interviewed at practice facility, *Blue White Illustrated*, November 15, 2017.

Mike Gesicki: *Adam Breneman Show* podcast, November 5, 2019.

Grant Haley: *Adam Breneman Show* podcast, October 15, 2019.

Twenty-Seven: First Impressions

Adrian Amos: Interviewed by Tony Mancuso, GoPSUtv, January 15, 2014.

Adam Breneman: Interviewed by Tony Mancuso, GoPSUtv, January 15, 2014; *Adam Breneman Show* podcast, October 1, 2019.

Jason Cabinda: *Adam Breneman Show* podcast, October 22, 2019.

James Franklin: Press conference, January 11, 2014; press conference, December 31, 2016.

Christian Hackenberg: *The Journey: Big Ten Football—James Franklin Feature*, Big Ten Network; *Adam Breneman Show* podcast, August 27, 2019.

Mike Hull: Interviewed by Tony Mancuso, GoPSUtv, January 15, 2014.

Jordan Lucas: Interviewed by Tony Mancuso, GoPSUtv, January 15, 2014.

Michael Mauti: *Adam Breneman Show* podcast, October 1, 2019.

Cael Sanderson: Interview recorded by Joe Hermitt, *PennLive*, May 16, 2014.

Twenty-Eight: Dublin

Ed Cunningham: Penn State–UCF broadcast, ESPN, August 30, 2014.

Sam Ficken: *Unrivaled: The Penn State Football Story—Travel to Dublin, Ireland*, produced and edited by Shadé Olasimbo, YouTube, July 5, 2018; post-game interview, GoPSUtv, August 30, 2014; post-game press conference, August 30, 2014.

Bob Flounders: Bob Flounders and David Jones recap, *PennLive*, August 30, 2014.

James Franklin: Interviewed at Dublin Airport, GoPSUtv, August 27, 2014; *Penn State Football 2014: James Franklin in Ireland—Day II*, GoPSUtv, August 28, 2014; *Unrivaled: The Penn State Football Story—Extended Game Highlights vs. UCF*, GoPSUtv, September 5, 2014.

Christian Hackenberg: Post-game press conference, August 30, 2014.

Michael Hazel: "Game Week Arrives as Lions Prep for Trip Across the Pond," Penn State Football, August 25, 2014.

David Jones: Bob Flounders and David Jones recap, *PennLive*, August 30, 2014.

Ryan Keiser: Post-game interview by David Jones, *PennLive*, August 30, 2014.

Akeel Lynch: *Unrivaled: The Penn State Football Story—Episode 1—Teaser*, August 27, 2014.

Twenty-Nine: Bye Bye Bowl Ban

Doug Chapman: "Penn State Sanctions—BTN Football and Beyond," Big Ten Network, September 25, 2013.

Mark Emmert: "Former Senator Mitchell Tapped to Monitor Penn State," Reuters, August 1, 2012.

Pat Forde: "Penn State Sanctions—BTN Football and Beyond," Big Ten Network, September 25, 2013.

James Franklin: Press conference, September 9, 2014.

Mike Gross: "Penn State's Bowl Ban and Scholarship Reductions Lifted, Will Reinstatement Wins Come Next?," *LancasterOnline*, September 9, 2014.

Mike Hoover: Interviewed by Lea Eder, *Daily Collegian*, September 8, 2014.

Mike Hull: Press conference, September 9, 2014.

Juwan Johnson: Tyler Donohue, "Penn State Recruits React to NCAA's Repeal of Bowl Ban and Scholarship Reductions," *Bleacher Report*, September 9, 2014.

Geno Lewis: Press conference, September 9, 2014.

Nina Mandell: "NCAA Was Wrong to Reduce NCAA Sanctions," *USA Today*, September 8, 2014.

Angelo Mangiro: Press conference, December 13, 2014; press conference, September 9, 2014.

George Mitchell: "NCAA to Gradually Restore Penn State Scholarships, *USA Today*, September 24, 2013.

Thirty: Losing

Adam Breneman: *Adam Breneman Show* podcast, August 27, 2019; *Adam Breneman Show* podcast, November 5, 2019; *Adam Breneman Show* podcast, December 18, 2019.

Derek Dowrey: Interviewed by Arielle Sargent, GoPSUtv, September 20, 2016.

James Franklin: Post-game press conference, September 27, 2014; midweek press conference, September 1, 2015; midweek press conference, November 24, 2015; midweek press conference, October 7, 2014; practice interview recorded by Elijah Hermitt, *PennLive*, October 29, 2014; midweek press conference, November 17, 2015; midweek press conference, September 2, 2014; post-game press conference, December 27, 2014; midweek press conference, October 21, 2015; Media Day press conference, August 5, 2017.

Brian Gaia: Post-game press conference, October 31, 2015.

Mike Gesicki: *Adam Breneman Show* podcast, November 5, 2019.

Mike Gross: "Penn State's Problems Begin at Offensive Line," *LancasterOnline,* September 30, 2014.

Christian Hackenberg: *Adam Breneman Show* podcast, August 27, 2019.

DaeSean Hamilton: Post-game press conference, November 1, 2014.

David Jones: Q&A with Joe Rexrode, *Detroit Free Press,* November 28, 2014.

Angelo Mangiro: Press conference, December 13, 2014.

Herb Hand: Midweek press conference, October 9, 2014.

Andrew Nelson: Practice interview, *PennLive,* August 17, 2016.

Thirty-One: Pinstripe Bowl

Kyle Carter: Post-game interview recorded by Elijah Hermitt, *PennLive,* December 27, 2014.

James Franklin: Press conference, December 7, 2014; post-game press conference, December 27, 2014.

Sam Ficken: Post-game interview, GoPSUtv, December 27, 2014.

Mike Gross: Game recap with Gordie Jones, *Lancaster Sports,* December 28, 2014.

Christian Hackenberg: Post-game interview, GoPSUtv, December 27, 2014.

DaeSean Hamilton: Post-game interview, *Black Shoe Diaries,* December 27, 2014.

Mark Holtzman: Pinstripe Bowl press conference, December 17, 2014.

Mike Hull: Post-game interview recorded by Elijah Hermitt, *PennLive,* December 27, 2014; post-game interview, GoPSUtv, December 27, 2014.

Akeel Lynch: Post-game interview by Frank Bodani, *York Daily Record,* December 28, 2014; post-game interview, *Black Shoe Diaries,* December 27, 2014.

Angelo Mangiro: Press conference, December 13, 2014; post-game interview, *Black Shoe Diaries,* December 27, 2014.

Matt Millen: Boston College–Penn State broadcast, ESPN, December 27, 2014.

Anthony Zettel: Post-game interview, *Black Shoe Diaries,* December 27, 2014.

Thirty-Two: Say Say

Saquon Barkley: ESPN *College GameDay* feature, GoPSUtv, September 29, 2017; interviewed by Peter King, NBC Sports, September 14, 2018; "Why I Chose Penn State," *Allentown Morning Call,* February 4, 2015; *Dan Patrick Show,* January 29, 2020; interviewed by Russell Wilson, ESPN, April 18, 2018.

Jason Cabinda: *Adam Breneman Show* podcast, October 22, 2019.

James Franklin: Media Day press conference, August 5, 2017.

Brian Gilbert: ESPN *College GameDay* feature, GoPSUtv, September 29, 2017.

Thirty-Three: Bury the Tape

Saquon Barkley: Practice interview recorded by Elijah Hermitt, *PennLive,* September 14, 2016.

Mark Brennan: "The NitWits," *Altoona Mirror,* September 6, 2015.

Jason Cabinda: Post-game interview, GoPSUtv, September 5, 2015.

Bob Flounders: Game recap with David Jones, *PennLive,* September 5, 2015.

James Franklin: Practice interview recorded by Elijah Hermitt, *PennLive,* September 2, 2015; post-game press conference, September 5, 2015; midweek press conference, September 8, 2015.

Adam Gress: Josh Moyer, "Frustration Bubbles Over Among ex–Penn State Players on Twitter," ESPN, September 8, 2015.

Brandon Hackenberg: Josh Moyer, "Frustration Bubbles Over Among ex-Penn State Players on Twitter," ESPN, September 8, 2015.

Christian Hackenberg: Post-game press conference, September 5, 2015.

Herb Hand: Practice interview, *Lancaster Sports,* August 6, 2015.

Jack Ham: Interviewed by Bob Flounders and Dustin Hockensmith, *Keystone Kickoff* podcast, Keystone Sports Network, September 18, 2015.

DaeSean Hamilton: *Unrivaled: The Penn State Football Story—Episode 2,* GoPSUtv, September 12, 2015; midweek press conference, September 8, 2015.

Dustin Hockensmith: Preseason analysis with Greg Pickel, *PennLive,* July 27, 2015.

Mike Irwin: "The NitWits," *Altoona Mirror,* September 6, 2015.

David Jones: Halftime analysis, *PennLive,* September 5, 2015.

Jordan Lucas: Midweek press conference, September 8, 2015.

Tyler Matakevich: Post-game press conference, September 5, 2015.

Stephon Morris: Jason Kirk, "Penn State Lost to Mid-Major Temple, and Former PSU Players Are Furious," *SB Nation,* September 5, 2015.

Brent Pry: Temple Week Q&A, Penn State Football, September 3, 2015.

Neil Rudel: "The NitWits," *Altoona Mirror,* September 6, 2015.

Bob Shoop: Blue-White game press conference, April 18, 2015; midweek press conference, October 29, 2015.

Donovan Smith: Josh Moyer, "Frustration Bubbles Over Among ex–Penn State Players on Twitter," ESPN, September 8, 2015.

Terry Smith: Buffalo Week Q&A, Penn State Football, September 10, 2015.

Nyeem Wartman-White: Donnie Collins, "Penn State's Wartman Changes Name to Honor Mother," *York Dispatch,* May 14, 2015; Carl L, "Penn State Linebacker Nyeem Wartman Road to Recovery," YouTube, December 16, 2015; interviewed by *PennLive,* Big Ten Media Days, August 2, 2016.

Thirty-Four: Signs of Hope

Saquon Barkley: ESPN *College GameDay* feature, GoPSUtv, September 29, 2017; Rose Bowl press conference, December 30, 2016.

James Franklin: Post-game press conference, September 12, 2015; *The Journey: Saquon Barkley's Athleticism,* Big Ten Network, September 29, 2017; midweek press conference, September 15, 2015; Media Day press conference, August 5, 2017.

Chris Godwin: Midweek press conference, September 22, 2015; interviewed by Chris Pizzo, Big Ten Network, October 26, 2015.

Kirk Herbstreit: *Unrivaled: Penn State Football Story* interview, October 21, 2017.

Charles Huff: San Diego State Week Q&A, Penn State Football, September 24, 2015.

Akeel Lynch: Interviewed by Kevin McKee, the Lion 90.7 FM, Penn State Student Radio, April 2, 2016.

Trace McSorley: "Trace McSorley Shares Why Extra Tape Study Has Been So Vital for Penn State," *RoarLionsRoar,* 2016.

Andrew Nelson: Saquon Barkley feature, Big Ten Network, August 31, 2016.

Andre Robinson: ESPN *College GameDay* feature on Saquon Barkley, GoPSUtv, September 29, 2017.

Thirty-Five: 1–0, 1–0, 1–0!!!

Saquon Barkley: Big Ten Network feature, August 31, 2016.

Saeed Blacknall: Post-game press conference, September 26, 2015; practice interview, Go-PSUtv, November 8, 2017.

Adam Breneman: *Adam Breneman Show* podcast, November 5, 2019.

James Franklin: Midweek press conference, November 5, 2019; post-game press conference, November 27, 2016; Blue-White press conference, April 18, 2015; midweek press conference, October 20, 2015; post-game press conference, October 31, 2015; midweek press conference, October 13, 2015.

Josh Gattis: Maryland Week Q&A, Penn State Football, October 22, 2015; interviewed by Tony Mancuso, GoPSUtv, June 10, 2015; Media Day interview, *Times Leader Sports* (Wilkes-Barre), August 4, 2014. **Josh Gattis:** Maryland Week Q&A, Penn State Football, October 22, 2015; interviewed by Tony Mancuso, GoPSUtv, June 10, 2015; Media Day interview, *Times Leader Sports* (Wilkes-Barre), August 4, 2014.

Mike Gesicki: *Adam Breneman Show* podcast, November 5, 2019.

Chris Godwin: Interviewed by Tony Mancuso, GoPSUtv, December 1, 2015.

Christian Hackenberg: Post-game press conference, October 10, 2015; midweek press conference, September 1, 2015.

Grant Haley: *Adam Breneman Show* podcast, October 15, 2019.

DaeSean Hamilton: Interviewed by Tony Mancuso, GoPSUtv, September 16, 2014; post-game press conference, November 1, 2014; midweek press conference, September 16, 2014; post-game interview recorded by *DK Pittsburgh Sports,* October 10, 2015.

Herb Hand: Rutgers Week Q&A, Penn State Football, September 17, 2015.

Charles Huff: San Diego State Week Q&A, Penn State Football, September 24, 2015.

Austin Johnson: Interviewed by Tony Mancuso, GoPSUtv, August 7, 2015.

Jordan Lucas: Post-game press conference, October 10, 2015.

Carl Nassib: Interview recorded by Elijah Hermitt & Greg Pickel, *PennLive,* April 1, 2015; interviewed by Darren Waller and Donny Starkins, *Comeback Stories* podcast, Blue Wire, September 30, 2021; interviewed as Lott Impact Trophy candidate, YouTube, December 4, 2015; post-game press conference, September 12, 2015; midweek press conference, October 20, 2015.

Andrew Nelson: Post-game press conference, October 10, 2015.

Bill O'Brien: Interviewed by FOX 26 Sports (Houston), December 8, 2015.

Brandon Polk: Blue-White press conference, April 25, 2018.

Bob Shoop: Blue-White press conference, April 18, 2015.

Sean Spencer: Army West Point Week Q&A, Penn State Football, October 1, 2015.

DeAndre Thompkins: Interview recorded by Elijah Hermitt, *PennLive,* September 17, 2016.

Anthony Zettel: Post-game press conference, September 12, 2015.

Thirty-Six: TaxSlayer Bowl

Jason Cabinda: Post-game press conference, January 2, 2016.

James Franklin: Athletic Department statement, November 29, 2015; interviewed by Tony Mancuso, GoPSUtv, December 23, 2015; post-game press conference, January 2, 2016; *The Journey: Trace McSorley,* Big Ten Network, December 1, 2016; post-game interview, November 28, 2015.

Chris Godwin: Post-game press conference, January 2, 2016.

Christian Hackenberg: Post-game interview recorded by *Blue-White Illustrated,* January 2, 2016.

DaeSean Hamilton: Post-game interview recorded by GoPSUtv, January 2, 2016.

Geno Lewis: Post-game interview recorded by GoPSUtv, January 2, 2016.

Angelo Mangiro: Post-game press conference, January 2, 2016.

Trace McSorley: Post-game interview recorded by *Penn Live,* January 2, 2016; post-game press conference, January 2, 2016; *The Journey: Trace McSorley,* Big Ten Network, December 1, 2016; post-game interview by Tony Mancuso, GoPSUtv, January 2, 2016.

Ricky Rahne: Practice interview, GoPSUtv, December 31, 2015.

Bob Shoop: Practice interview, GoPSUtv, December 29, 2015.

Thirty-Seven: Exit Hackenberg

Adam Breneman: *Adam Breneman Show* podcast, August 27, 2019.

James Franklin: Midweek press conference, November 17, 2015.

Christian Hackenberg: "Gruden's QB Camp: Christian Hackenberg," ESPN, April 19, 2016; *Adam Breneman Show* podcast, August 27, 2019; post-game interview recorded by Mark Wogenrich, *Allentown Morning Call,* January 2, 2016.

Thirty-Eight: Dinner with Franklin

Brandon Bell: Post-game interview by *Blue-White Illustrated,* December 4, 2016.

James Franklin: "Roaring Back," *Players' Tribune,* September 1, 2017; post-practice interview recorded by *Blue-White Illustrated,* November 15, 2017; "Coaches Caravan" interview recorded by Mark Brennan, *Fight On State,* May 6, 2014.

Chris Godwin: Post-game interview recorded by *Blue-White Illustrated,* November 26, 2016.

Christian Hackenberg: *Adam Breneman Show* podcast, August 27, 2019.

Brendan Mahon: Interviewed by Dave Revsine, Big Ten Network, July 25, 2016.

Paris Palmer: Interviewed by John Black and Paul Clifford, *Football Letter Live,* Penn State Alumni Association, December 4, 2020

Nyeem Wartman-White: Big Ten Media Day interview recorded by *Blue-White Illustrated,* July 25, 2016; interviewed by Dave Revsine, Big Ten Network, July 25, 2016.

Thirty-Nine: JoeMo

Saquon Barkley: Rose Bowl press conference, December 30, 2016.

Mike Gesicki: Rose Bowl press conference, December 30, 2016; *Adam Breneman Show* podcast, November 4, 2019.

Chris Godwin: Post-practice interview recorded by *Blue-White Illustrated,* August 11, 2016.

DaeSean Hamilton: Rose Bowl press conference, December 30, 2016.

Trace McSorley: Rose Bowl press conference, December 30, 2016.

Joe Moorhead: Rose Bowl press conference, December 30, 2016; introductory press conference, December 16, 2015; introductory press conference at Mississippi State, November 30, 2017.

Andrew Nelson: Blue-White press conference, April 16, 2016; post-practice interview by *Blue-White Illustrated,* August 18, 2016.

Forty: Dynamic Duo

Saquon Barkley: Interviewed by Lisa Byington, Big Ten Network, October 9, 2016; "Saquon Barkley: The Making of a Superstar," Penn State on *PennLive,* December 4, 2017.

Ryan Bates: "The Journey: Saquon Barkley Discusses Leadership," Big Ten Network, September 24, 2016.

Bruce Feldman: *Rich Eisen Show,* September 29, 2017.

James Franklin: Post-game press conference, October 8, 2016; Signing Day press conference, February 6, 2019; midweek press conference, October 4, 2016; post-game press conference, October 8, 2016; Media Day press conference, August 5, 2017; *The Journey: Saquon Barkley Discusses Leadership,* Big Ten Network, September 24, 2016.

Brian Gaia: Interviewed by Rick Pizzo, Glen Mason, and Anthony "Spice" Adams, Big Ten Network, January 2, 2017.

Trace McSorley: *Adam Breneman Show* podcast, October 29, 2019; interviewed by Arielle Sargent, GoPSUtv, October 9, 2016; Rose Bowl press conference, December 30, 2016.

Joe Moorhead: Interviewed by David Jones, Penn State on *PennLive,* December 21, 2021.

Andrew Nelson: Blue-White press conference, April 16, 2016; *The Journey: Saquon Barkley Discusses Leadership,* Big Ten Network, September 24, 2016.

Tommy Stevens: Interviewed by Nick Polak, *Roar Lion Roar* podcast, October 19, 2022.

Forty-One: Ready or Not

Saquon Barkley: Post-game interview recorded by HappyValley.com, September 10, 2016; post-game interview recorded by Mark Wogenrich, *Allentown Morning Call,* September 10, 2016.

Jason Cabinda: *Adam Breneman Show* podcast, October 22, 2019; interviewed by Matt McGloin and Tom Hannifan, *Paydirt* podcast, August 24, 2022.

Bob Flounders: Post-game recap with Greg Pickel, *PennLive,* September 10, 2016.

James Franklin: Post-game press conference, September 10, 2016; midweek press conference, September 27, 2016; "Unrivaled: the Penn State Football Story—Training Camp Recap/Kent State Preview," GoPSUtv, September 2, 2016.

Chris Godwin: Post-game interview recorded by *Blue-White Illustrated,* November 27, 2016.

DaeSean Hamilton: Rose Bowl press conference, December 30, 2016.

David Jones: "But for One Bad Pass, Trace McSorley Might've Led a Penn State Comeback Win for the Ages," *PennLive,* September 10, 2016.

Trace McSorley: Post-game interview recorded by *Blue-White Illustrated,* September 10, 2016; midweek press conference, September 13, 2016; post-game interview recorded by Elijah Hermitt, *PennLive,* September 10, 2016; post-game interview recorded by *Blue-White Illustrated,* September 24, 2016.

Greg Pickel: Post-game recap with Bob Flounders, *PennLive,* September 10, 2016.

John Reid: Rose Bowl press conference, December 28, 2016.

Garrett Sickels: Post-game press conference, November 26, 2016.

Forty-Two: Minnesota

Marcus Allen: Post-game press conference, October 1, 2016.

Saquon Barkley: Post-game interview recorded by *Times Leader Sports* (Wilkes-Barre), October 1, 2016.

Ryan Bates: Post-game press conference, October 1, 2016.

Frank Bodani: Post-game recap, *York Daily Record,* October 2, 2016.

Manny Bowen: Post-game press conference, October 1, 2016.

Adam Breneman: *Adam Breneman Show* podcast, October 15, 2019.

Mark Brennan: "NitWits, Penn State vs. Minnesota Recap," *Altoona Mirror,* October 2, 2016.

Jason Cabinda: Midweek press conference, September 15, 2015.

Tyler Davis: Post-game press conference, October 1, 2016.

Bob Flounders: Post-game recap with David Jones, *PennLive,* October 1, 2016.

James Franklin: Post-game press conference, October 1, 2016; interviewed by Brian Tripp, Big Ten Network, October 1, 2016.

Mike Gesicki: Post-game press conference, October 1, 2016.

Chris Godwin: Post-game press conference, October 1, 2016.

Grant Haley: *Adam Breneman Show* podcast, October 15, 2019; post-game press conference, October 1, 2016.

David Jones: Post-game recap with Bob Flounders, *PennLive,* October 1, 2016.

Mitch Leidner: Post-game press conference, October 1, 2016.

Trace McSorley: Post-game press conference, October 1, 2016.

Joe Moorhead: Interviewed by David Jones, Penn State on *PennLive,* December 21, 2021.

Brent Pry: Brent Pry Q&A—Purdue, Penn State Football, October 27, 2016.

Rodney Smith: Post-game press conference, October 1, 2016.

Forty-Three: Redemption

Marcus Allen: Post-game press conference, October 22, 2016.

Saquon Barkley: Post-game press conference, October 22, 2016.

Saeed Blacknall: *Unrivaled: the Penn State Football Story—Episode 7,* GoPSUtv, October 21, 2016.

Adam Breneman: *Adam Breneman Show* podcast, October 15, 2019.

Mark Brennan: "NitWits, Penn State vs. Ohio State Recap," *Altoona Mirror,* October 24, 2016.

Jason Cabinda: 2016 Penn State vs. Ohio State game replay on Facebook Live, April 18, 2020; *Adam Breneman Show* podcast, October 22, 2019; interviewed by Dave Revsine, Big Ten Network, October 25, 2016; post-game interview by Arielle Sargent, GoPSUtv, October 23, 2016.

Chris Fowler: Ohio State–Penn State broadcast, ESPN, October 22, 2016.

James Franklin: Post-game interview by Arielle Sargent, GoPSUtv, October 21, 2016; post-game press conference, October 22, 2016; "Roaring Back," *The Players' Tribune,* September 1, 2017.

Blake Gillikin: Rose Bowl press conference video recorded by Abby Drey, *Centre Daily Times,* 2016.

Chris Godwin: "Penn State Relives 2016 Season," B1G Video Recall, Big Ten Network, May 11, 2020.

Grant Haley: 2016 Penn State vs. Ohio State game replay on Facebook Live, April 18, 2020; *Adam Breneman Show* podcast, October 15, 2019; post-game interview recorded by State-College.com, October 23, 2016.

Kirk Herbstreit: Ohio State–Penn State broadcast, ESPN, October 22, 2016.

Dustin Hockensmith: *Keystone Kickoff Show* podcast, Keystone Sports Network, October 25, 2016.

Brock Huard: Michigan State–Penn State broadcast, ESPN, November 26, 2016.

David Jones: Post-game recap, YouTube, October 2016; post-game recap with Bob Flounders, *PennLive,* October 23, 2016.

Steve Jones: 2016 Penn State vs. Ohio State game replay on Facebook Live, April 18, 2020.

Brendan Mahon: Post-game press conference, October 22, 2016.

Trace McSorley: "Penn State Relives 2016 Season," B1G Video Recall, Big Ten Network, May 11, 2020.

Urban Meyer: Post-game press conference, October 22, 2016.

Greg Pickel: *Keystone Kickoff Show* podcast, Keystone Sports Network, October 25, 2016.

Brent Pry: Brent Pry Q&A—Purdue, Penn State Football, October 27, 2016.

Evan Schwan: 2016 Penn State vs. Ohio State game replay on Facebook Live, April 18, 2020.

Garrett Sickels: Post-game press conference, October 22, 2016.

Neil Rudel: "NitWits, Penn State vs. Ohio State Recap," *Altoona Mirror,* October 24, 2016.

Forty-Four: Comeback Kids

Marcus Allen: Rose Bowl press conference, December 28, 2016.

Saquon Barkley: Rose Bowl press conference, December 30, 2016.

Brandon Bell: Rose Bowl press conference, December 28, 2016; interviewed by Dave Revsine, Big Ten Network, November 15, 2016.

Jason Cabinda: Interviewed by Matt McGloin and Tom Hannifan, *Paydirt* podcast, August 24, 2022; Rose Bowl press conference, December 28, 2016.

James Franklin: Interviewed by Dave Revsine, Gerry DiNardo, and Howard Griffith, Big Ten Network, December 4, 2016; Media Day press conference, August 5, 2017; midweek press conference, November 29, 2016.

Brian Gaia: Interviewed by Rick Pizzo, Glen Mason, and Anthony "Spice" Adams, Big Ten Network, January 2, 2017.

Mike Gesicki: *Adam Breneman Show* podcast, November 5, 2019; Rose Bowl press conference, December 30, 2016.

Chris Godwin: Post-game interview recorded by *Blue-White Illustrated*, September 17, 2016.

DaeSean Hamilton: Rose Bowl press conference, December 30, 2016.

Trace McSorley: "Nittany Lions' Big Second Half Crushes Purdue, 62–24," Associated Press, October 29, 2016; Rose Bowl press conference, December 30, 2016.

Joe Moorhead: Rose Bowl press conference, December 30, 2016.

Brent Pry: Brent Pry Q&A—Purdue, Penn State Football, October 27, 2016; Rose Bowl press conference, December 28, 2016.

Neil Rudel: "NitWits, Penn State vs. Michigan State," *Altoona Mirror*, November 28, 2016.

Evan Schwan: Rose Bowl press conference, December 28, 2016; midweek press conference, November 29, 2016.

Forty-Five: Down to the Wire

Brandon Bell: Post-game press conference, November 26, 2016.

Mark Brennan: "NitWits, Penn State vs. Michigan State," *Altoona Mirror*, November 27, 2016.

Jason Cabinda: Post-game press conference, November 26, 2016; post-game interview recorded by *Blue-White Illustrated*, November 26, 2016.

Mark Dantonio: Post-game press conference, November 26, 2016.

Bob Flounders: Game recap with David Jones, *PennLive*, November 26, 2016.

James Franklin: Derek Levarse, "Penn State Has Huge Opportunity Against Spartans," *Times Leader Sports* (Wilkes-Barre), November 25, 2016; post-game press conference, November 26, 2016.

Mike Gesicki: Post-game press conference, November 26, 2016.

Chris Godwin: Post-game interview recorded by *Blue-White Illustrated*, November 26, 2016.

Mike Irwin: "NitWits, Penn State vs. Michigan State," *Altoona Mirror*, November 27, 2016.

Amani Oruwariye: Post-game press conference, November 26, 2016.

Neil Rudel: "NitWits, Penn State vs. Michigan State," *Altoona Mirror*, November 27, 2016.

Evan Schwan: Post-game press conference, November 26, 2016; midweek press conference, November 29, 2016.

Garrett Sickels: Post-game press conference, November 26, 2016.

Bob Wischusen: Michigan State–Penn State broadcast, ESPN, November 26, 2016.

Forty-Six: Why Not Us?

Marcus Allen: Rose Bowl press conference, December 28, 2016.

Saquon Barkley: Post-game press conference, December 4, 2016.

Saeed Blacknall: Post-game interview recorded by *Times Leader Sports* (Wilkes-Barre), December 4, 2016.

Brandon Bell: "Penn State Relives 2016 Season," B1G Video Recall, Big Ten Network, May 11, 2020; interviewed by Dave Revsine, Gerry DiNardo, and Howard Griffith, Big Ten Network, December 4, 2016.

Mark Brennan: "NitWits, Penn State vs. Wisconsin," *Altoona Mirror*, December 5, 2016.

Jason Cabinda: *Adam Breneman Show* podcast, October 22, 2019.

Corey Clement: Post-game press conference, December 4, 2016.

Bob Flounders: Post-game recap with David Jones, *PennLive*, December 4, 2016.

James Franklin: Post-game press conference, December 4, 2016; post-practice interview recorded by Elijah Hermitt, *PennLive*, September 14, 2016; interviewed by Scott Van Pelt, *SportsCenter Live,* ESPN, December 4, 2016; interviewed by Dave Revsine, Gerry DiNardo, and Howard Griffith, Big Ten Network, December 4, 2016.

Mike Gesicki: Post-game press conference, December 4, 2016; "Penn State Relives 2016 Season," B1G Video Recall, Big Ten Network, May 11, 2020.

Cory Giger: "Big Ten Championship Preview with Neil Rudel," *Altoona Mirror*, December 2, 2016.

Chris Godwin: "Penn State Relives 2016 Season," B1G Video Recall, Big Ten Network, May 11, 2020.

Grant Haley: "Penn State Relives 2016 Season," B1G Video Recall, Big Ten Network, May 11, 2020; interviewed by Dave Revsine, Stanley Jackson, and Howard Griffith, Big Ten Network, December 4, 2016.

DaeSean Hamilton: "The Journey: 2016 Big Ten Football Championship—Wisconsin vs. Penn State (Enhanced Replay)," Big Ten Network, December 6, 2016.

Gus Johnson: Penn State–Wisconsin broadcast, FOX Sports, December 4, 2016.

David Jones: Post-game recap with Bob Flounders, *PennLive*, December 4, 2016.

Steve Jones: "Penn State Unrivaled: Big Ten Championship Recap," GoPSUtv, December 15, 2016.

Trace McSorley: "Penn State Relives 2016 Season," B1G Video Recall, Big Ten Network, May 11, 2020; post-game press conference, December 4, 2016; interviewed by Alex Roux, *Take Ten* podcast, Big Ten Network, July 14, 2020.

Joe Moorhead: Interviewed by David Jones, Penn State on *PennLive*, December 21, 2021.

Andrew Nelson: Post-game interview by *PennLive*, December 4, 2016.

Neil Rudel: "NitWits, Penn State vs. Wisconsin," *Altoona Mirror*, December 5, 2016.

Evan Schwan: Post-game interview by *PennLive*, December 4, 2016.

Garrett Sickels: Post-game interview recorded by *Times Leader Sports* (Wilkes-Barre), December 4, 2016.

Nyeem Wartman-White: "Penn State Unrivaled: Big Ten Championship Recap," GoPSUtv, December 15, 2016.

Forty-Seven: In the End

James Franklin: Interviewed by Rick Pizzo, Glen Mason, and Anthony "Spice" Adams, Big Ten Network, January 2, 2017; Twitter, June 21, 2021.

Malik Golden: Post-game interview recorded by GoPSUtv, January 3, 2017.

Christian Hackenberg: Post-game interview recorded by *Blue-White Illustrated,* January 2, 2016.

Kirk Herbstreit: USC–Penn State Rose Bowl broadcast, ESPN, January 3, 2017.

David Jones: Game recap with Bob Flounders, *PennLive,* January 3, 2017; Penn State on *Penn-Live,* December 21, 2021.

Michael Mauti: Interviewed by Matt McGloin and Tom Hannifan, *Paydirt* podcast, November 19, 2021.

Joe Moorhead: Interviewed by David Jones, Penn State on *PennLive,* December 21, 2021.

Silas Redd: *Adam Breneman Show* podcast, November 21, 2019.

Rich Scarcella: "An Oral History: Saquon Barkley's Unforgettable Rose Bowl Run," *Reading Eagle,* July 9, 2017.

Evan Schwan: Rose Bowl press conference, December 28, 2016.

INDEX